I0753037

COLORFUL JOURNEY

An Artist's Adventure:
Drawing Every Town in New Hampshire

Sue Anne Bottomley

 Published by Piscataqua Press, an imprint of RiverRun Bookstore, Inc.
Printed in the United States.

Book design by Karin Tracy; print preparation by Vicki Brown

Acknowledgements

My project DRAW-NH involved two years of driving throughout New Hampshire, my birth state, with my sketch pad. My husband came with me to about ¾ of the towns. He never complained when we got lost, or when we made endless u-turns (19 in one particular day!) as I settled into the very best view of each town. Some towns spoke to me immediately and I quickly knew what I wanted to capture on paper. Others required at least four passes through town, or maybe six and then a protracted time of walking around. Only very occasionally did I approach a town with a clear idea of something there that needed to be drawn. Mostly it was an expedition of discovery. While I was drawing and painting, my husband and our dog Hank took walks and naps, and the former plotted the route to the next town. I am very grateful for our atlas of every road in the state, although it did beguile us onto a few very narrow, rutted cowpaths.

Once home, and after the drawing was completed, we scanned the drawing and made color adjustments so that it would look perfect online. Bruce, my husband and master printer, kept track of all the images in his computer records and managed their presentation on my blog *www.colorfuljourney.us* as well as the production of cards and prints that we sell at art/craft/farmers markets. This book would remain only a dream in my imagination without my kind, patient, computer guru husband. He was a solid sounding board for many artistic decisions too.

To our first born, Karin Tracy, goes all the credit for the graphic design of the book. It was a pleasure to work with her and wonderful to realize that all this expertise resides in the family. Other family, neighbors, and friends encouraged me as I went along. "How's that project going? How many towns done?" No one called it a crazy project, for which I was and am very grateful.

Scott Campbell, director of the Langdon Public Library in Newington, helped me with his enthusiasm for my drawings, and by sharing his technical knowledge of publishing. He introduced me to Tom Holbrook, publisher of Piscataqua Press and owner of RiverRun Book Stores in Portsmouth and across the river in Kittery, Maine. Tom quickly embraced the opportunity to publish a New Hampshire themed art book and gave great support throughout the project.

Other people have guided me by sharing their love and knowledge of New Hampshire. One such person is Rebecca Rule. She has written many books specializing in the humor of the inhabitants of the Granite State, and she shares her stories in numerous speaking engagements sponsored by the NH Humanities Council. Other NHHC speakers—Dartmouth Professor Emeritus Jere Daniell, retired NH Agriculture Commissioner Steve Taylor, and many more—contributed insights to my understanding and appreciation of New Hampshire. Thanks to them all, and to the Humanities Council for its sponsorship of these enlightening presentations.

Freelance writer Melanie Plenda captured the essence of my project in wonderful articles she wrote for the *NH Union Leader* and NH Public Radio, as did *Kearsarge Magazine* and *Arts Guide* publisher Laura Jean Whitcomb. The *NH Chronicle* team, Mary-Paige Provost and Paul Falco, were wonderful to work with, and produced their own work of film art in my 6 minutes of fame, shown three times so far on WMUR. The Adventures in Learning program at Colby-Sawyer College in New London afforded me wonderful opportunities to share my love of on-location drawing with aspiring and established artists from throughout the local area.

Thank you, all!

May 2014

Dedication

To my wonderful family and to the memory of my art professors at the University of New Hampshire.

A Colorful Journey

Upon moving back to New Hampshire after 40 years away, I started to draw my surroundings, both our town and those nearby. One day I counted the towns in my drawings—nineteen. In a flash, the idea came to me to just keep going…to do a drawing in every town. Research showed that there are 221 towns and 13 cities. For simplicity here, I call them all "towns". So I kept up a pace of ten per month, and every town was down on paper in two years.

With two maps, an atlas, a GPS, and a snack, I set off about twice a week. I drove to each town, often for the first time ever, with almost always no preconceived idea of what would inspire me once there. I paced around to find the best angle. Drawing on site, no matter the weather or season, is my idea of a great time, so I never drew from a photograph. I like the high energy and the immediacy of standing in the middle of the road with my sketchpad! It focuses the mind. Details and patterns jump out at me. To capture the essence of a place, I move objects around a bit, too. My tools were pencil, ink, watercolor, and colored pencil, in various combinations. Sometimes the color was added at home within 24 hours, when my memories were fresh. The website *urbansketchers.org* was a constant inspiration to me—artists from all around the world recording their lives and their surroundings in on-location drawings.

Several recurring themes in the drawings are bell towers, carved eagles, bandstands, town greens, churches, schools, and mills, as well as mountains and lakes. Drawing figures as they fit into a landscape or street scene is fun.

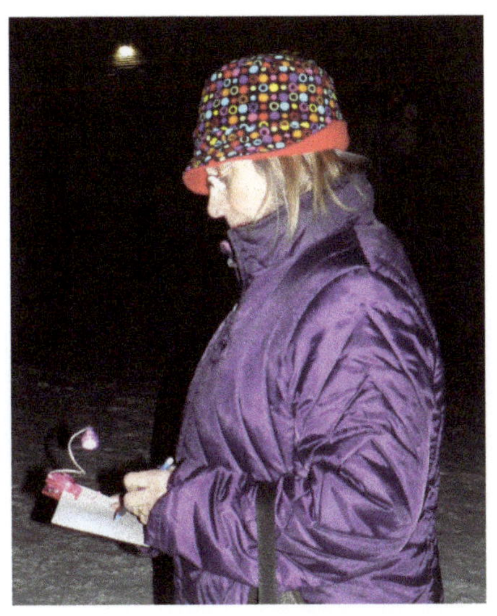

The artist, undeterred by weather or darkness

One thing I learned early in the project is that there are many localities in the state that are not actual towns but villages, which are locally recognized and named areas of a town, many with their own Post Office and Zip Code. Some have achieved a level of name recognition that overtakes that of their town. So, readers looking for well known places such as Woodsville, Groveton, Elkins, and many others won't find them in the index here, although many do feature in the accompanying text.

I am not a historian and did no original research. All the minor historical notes in the text are from online sources which come from local town historical societies, or from helpful advisors. Most of my 'facts' are probably accurate. Various themes show up in the texts, including land grants, names and name changes of towns, border changes, mills, memorable inhabitants, railroads, tourism, architectural styles, and community spirit.

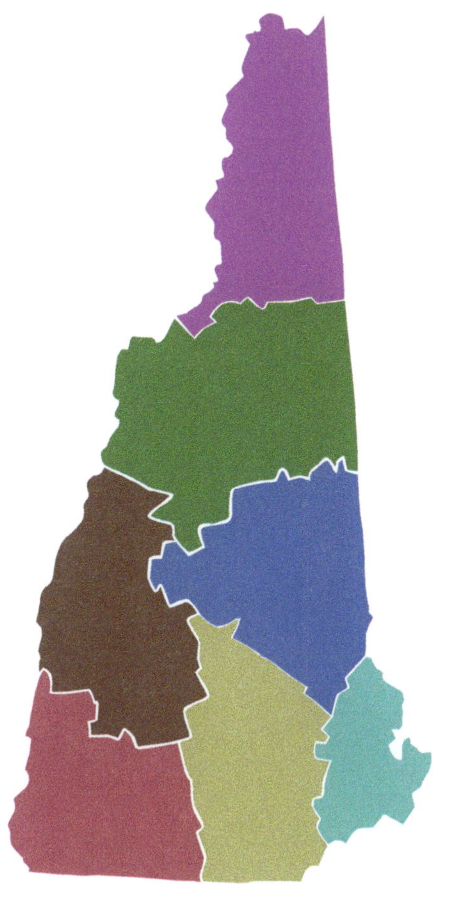

DARTMOUTH-SUNAPEE
LAKES
MERRIMACK VALLEY
MONADNOCK
NORTH COUNTRY
SEACOAST
WHITE MOUNTAINS

New Hampshire Regions

DARTMOUTH-SUNAPEE 5
LAKES 43
MERRIMACK VALLEY 81
MONADNOCK 125
NORTH COUNTRY 169
SEACOAST 187
WHITE MOUNTAINS 223
INDEX OF TOWNS 258

Dartmouth-Sunapee

ANDOVER

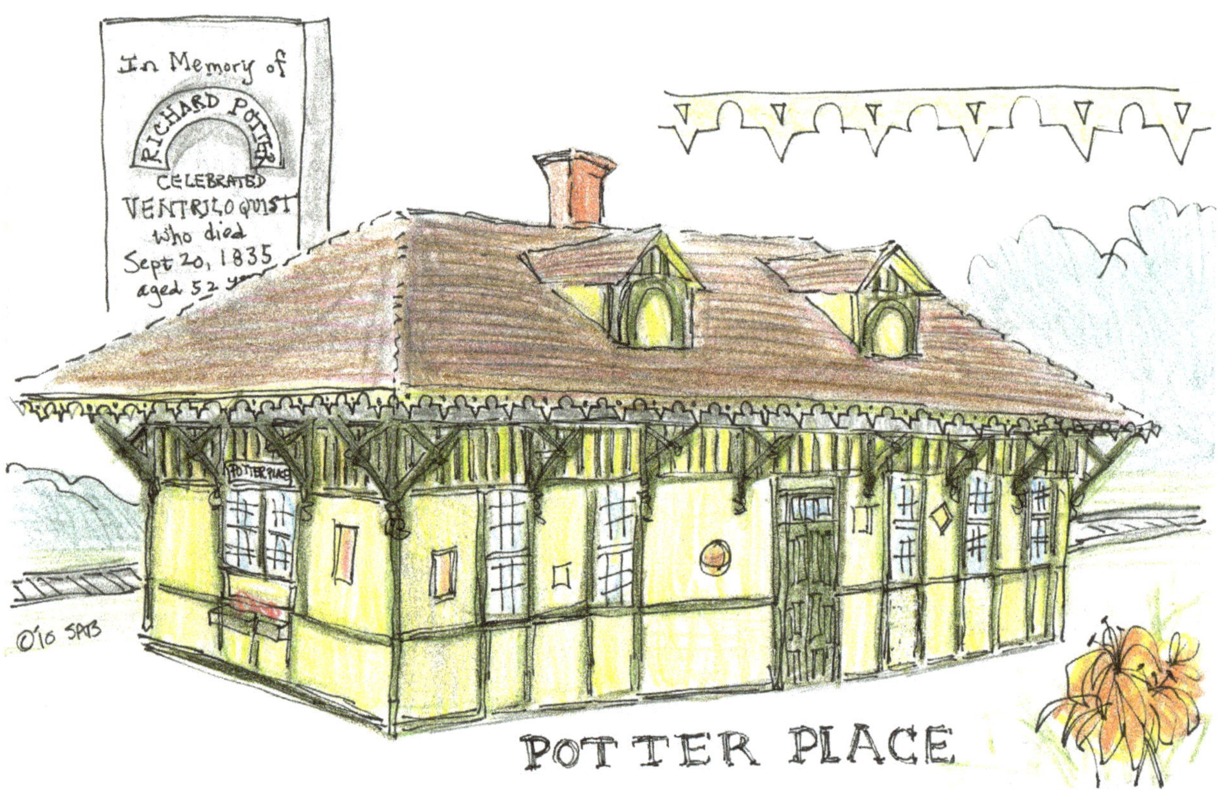

The Potter Place Railroad Station sits on the edge of the town of Andover. In the 1800s, you could get this far by train from Boston in four hours.

Potter Place was the name of the large estate of Richard Potter (1783-1835). Born in Boston, educated in Europe, he became America's first magician, hypnotist, and traveling showman. There are several accounts of his life online, and his illusions are still remembered. I have never seen the word *ventriloquist* on a gravestone before! Proctor Academy takes up most of downtown Andover.

Andover has a wonderful, old-fashioned Fourth of July Parade. And it is always very warm in this sheltered valley.

BRADFORD

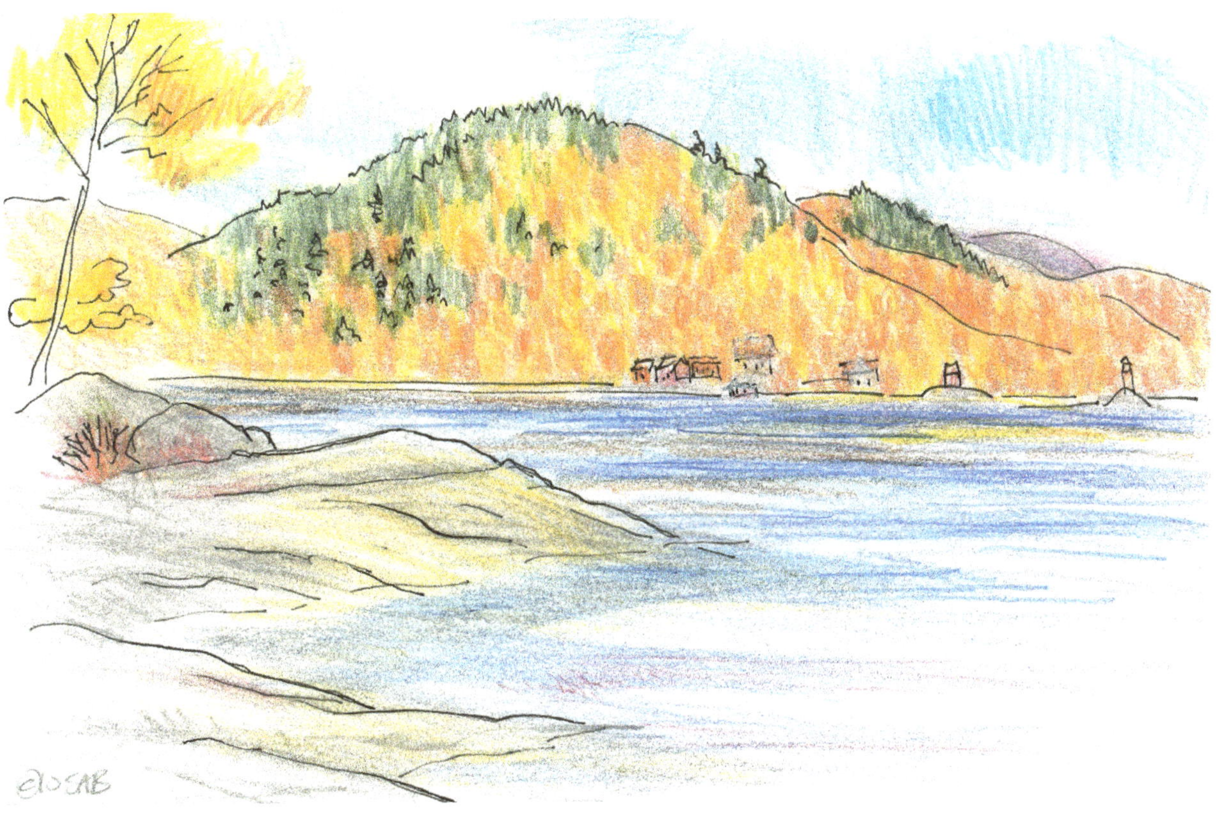

My sister and I always called this round hill Gumdrop Mountain.

French's Beach at Lake Massasecum, Bradford, is a secluded spot. The green pine trees set off the colors of the maple, oak, birch, and beech trees.

In past times, summer people from Boston and New York City came to Bradford to sip the mineral waters and relax on hotel porches. Our family came to stay with our grandmother and visit our aunt, Dr. Anne Wasson, who set up her first practice as a GP on Water Street. We were always in town for Independence Day. My best memories are the butter and lemon barbequed chicken and the fireworks.

CANAAN

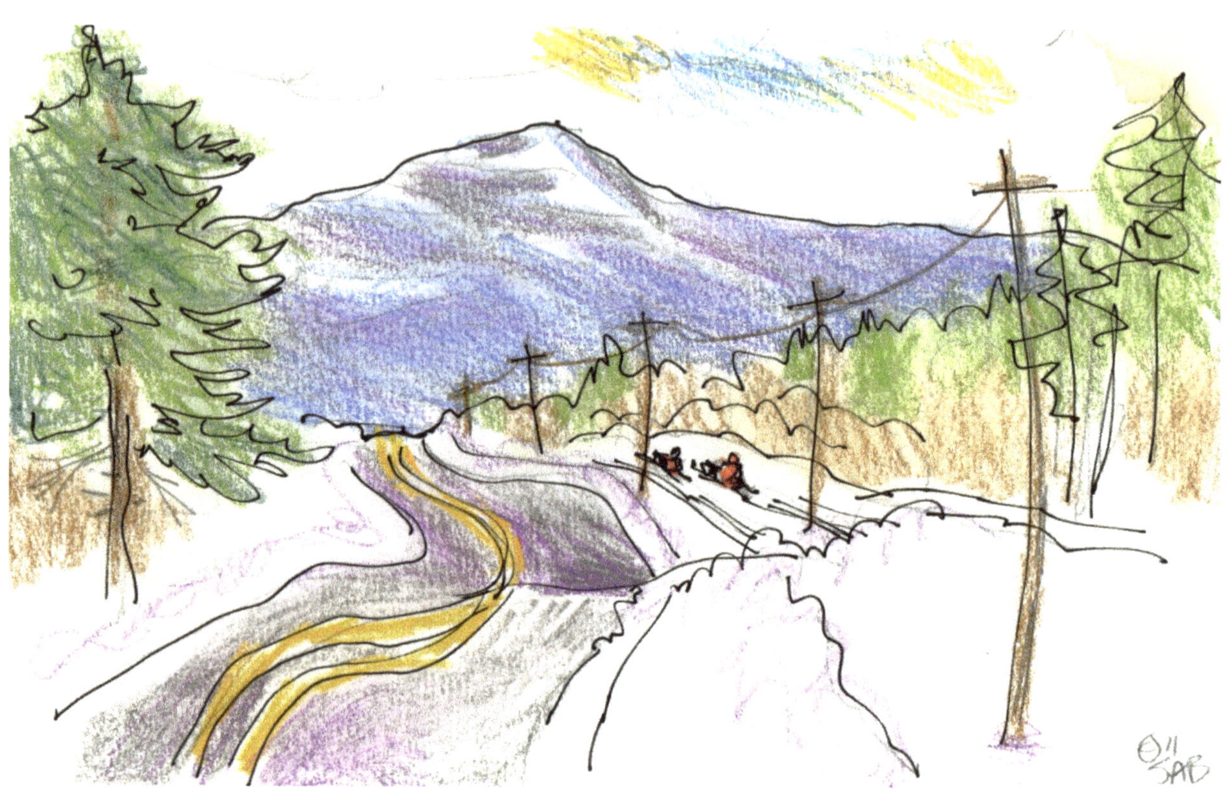

Mount Cardigan is not in Canaan, but this view is from the town. And that counts because I get to make up the rules.

After parking my car off to the side as far as possible, I quickly sketched the peak. It had just snowed, and therefore there wasn't a lot of room on the shoulder. Just when I had finished drawing, the two people on snowmobiles zoomed out of the woods and into my art.

Canaan is home to the Cardigan Mountain School, for boys grades 6–9.

CLAREMONT

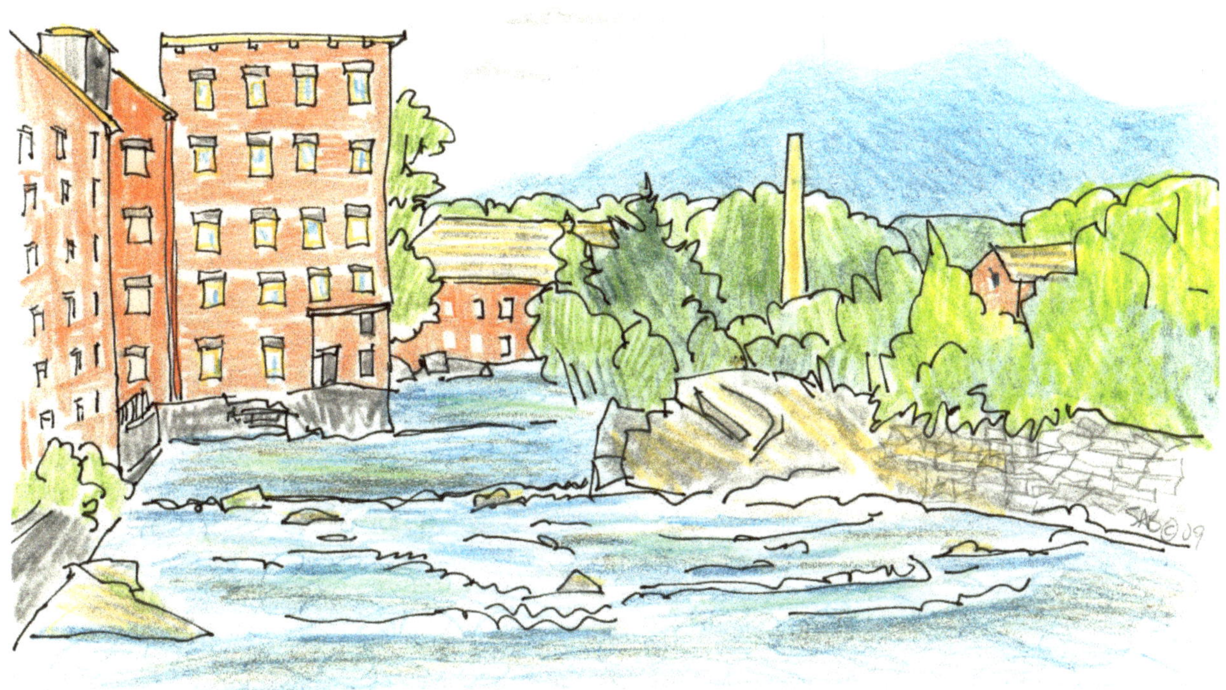

The beautiful Mount Ascutney, across the state border into Vermont, forms the backdrop to the town.

Claremont, with a current population of 14,000, was a town whose prosperity and identity was based on the mills.

The mills' products once included cotton and woolen textiles, lathes and planers, and paper. The Sugar River, rushing into the Connecticut River from Lake Sunapee, generated the waterpower. The sturdy brick buildings are now being renovated and finding new commercial uses. The imposing Claremont Opera House, around the corner from this mill, is in a Renaissance Revival style.

CORNISH

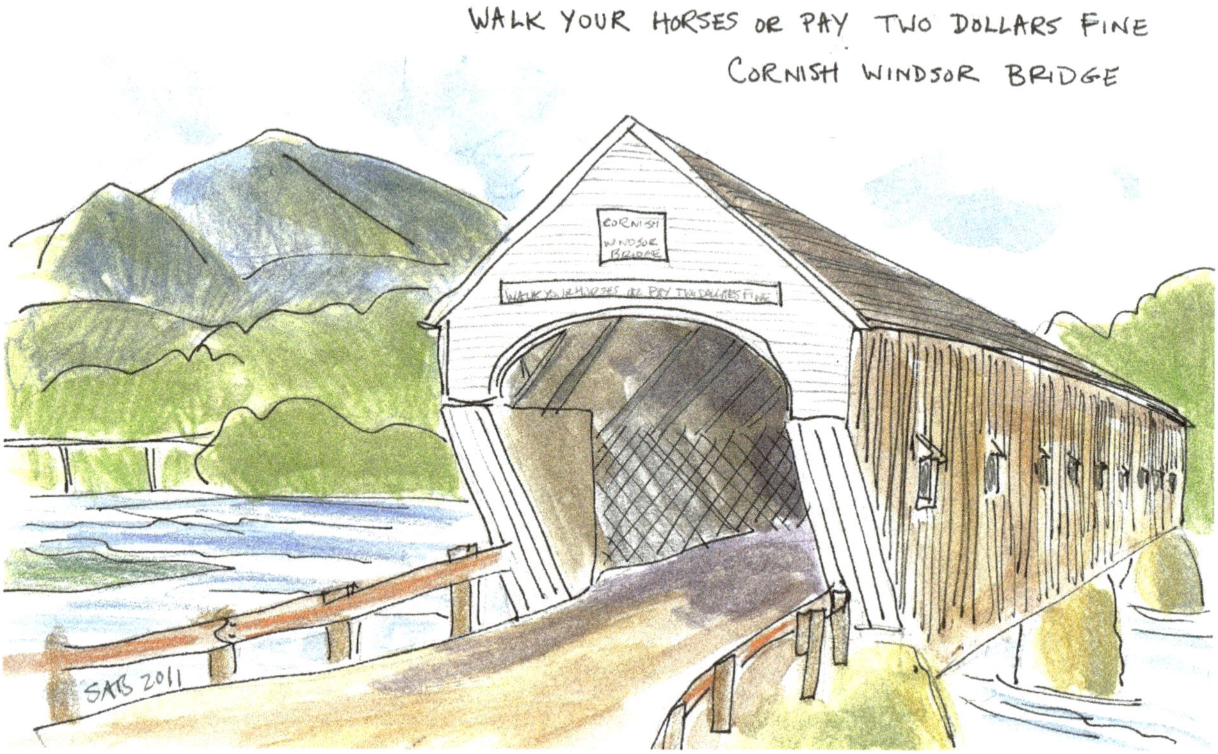

WALK YOUR HORSES OR PAY TWO DOLLARS FINE
CORNISH WINDSOR BRIDGE

The Cornish-Windsor Covered Bridge, with its 450-foot span, crosses the Connecticut River connecting New Hampshire with Vermont.

Even though it is a narrow, old, wooden bridge, it is a very busy one as there are few bridges crossing this wide river. Some of these bridges are one lane wide, and you just take your turn passing through them. This one has two lanes, and the whole bridge has been washed away three times in storms. A toll taker no longer is employed to collect to the two-dollar fine. The sign is just kept for history's sake.

I had to stand in the middle of the road with my pen and paper as I drew this.

CROYDON

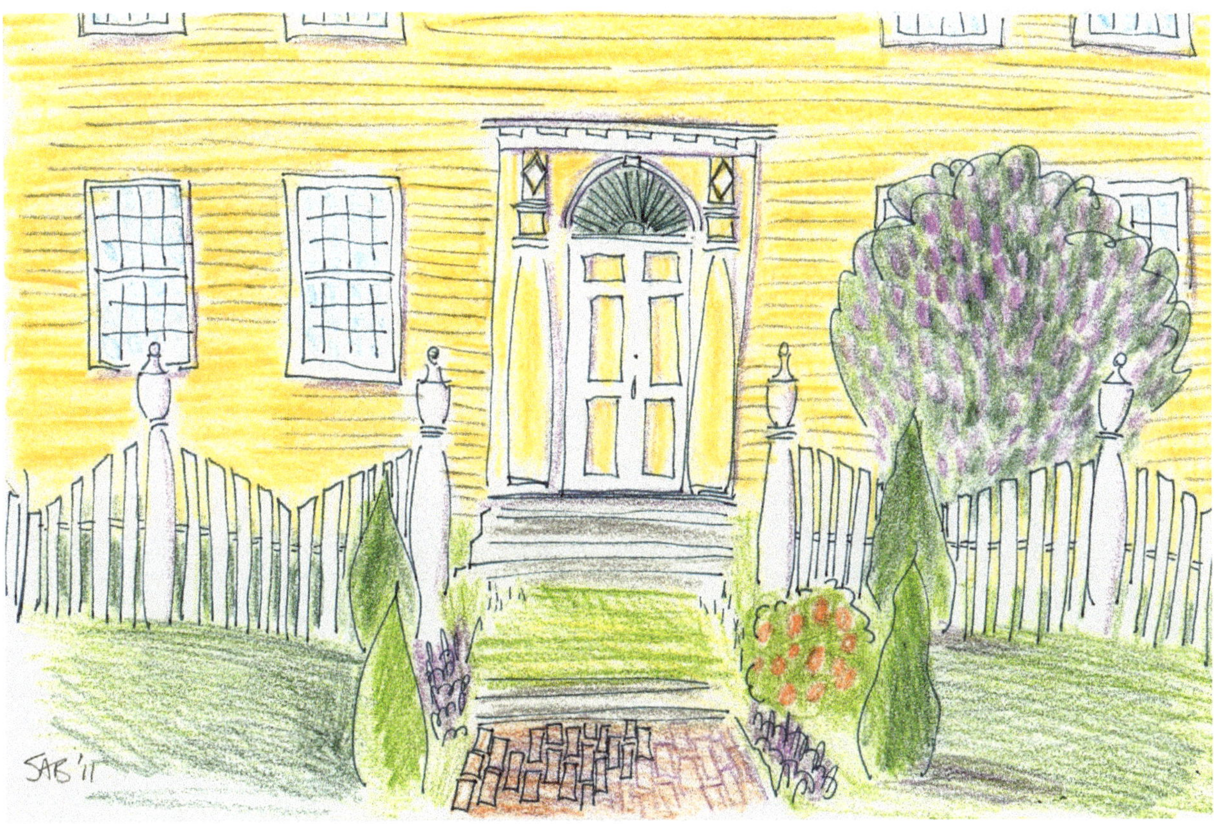

Croydon is proud of its one-room Red Schoolhouse, in use since 1794.

I was attracted to the house of Samuel Morse, Esq. (*not* the inventor of the telegraph) by its frontier grandness, the color, the doorway, and of course the unusual white picket fence.

The house was built in 1815 as the judge's home, law office, and courtroom. Since it was raining hard, I drew this from the car. A few stares came my way because my car was parked at an odd angle, to maximize my drawing viewpoint. As my DRAW-NH project progressed, I learned to better explain what I was doing.

DANBURY

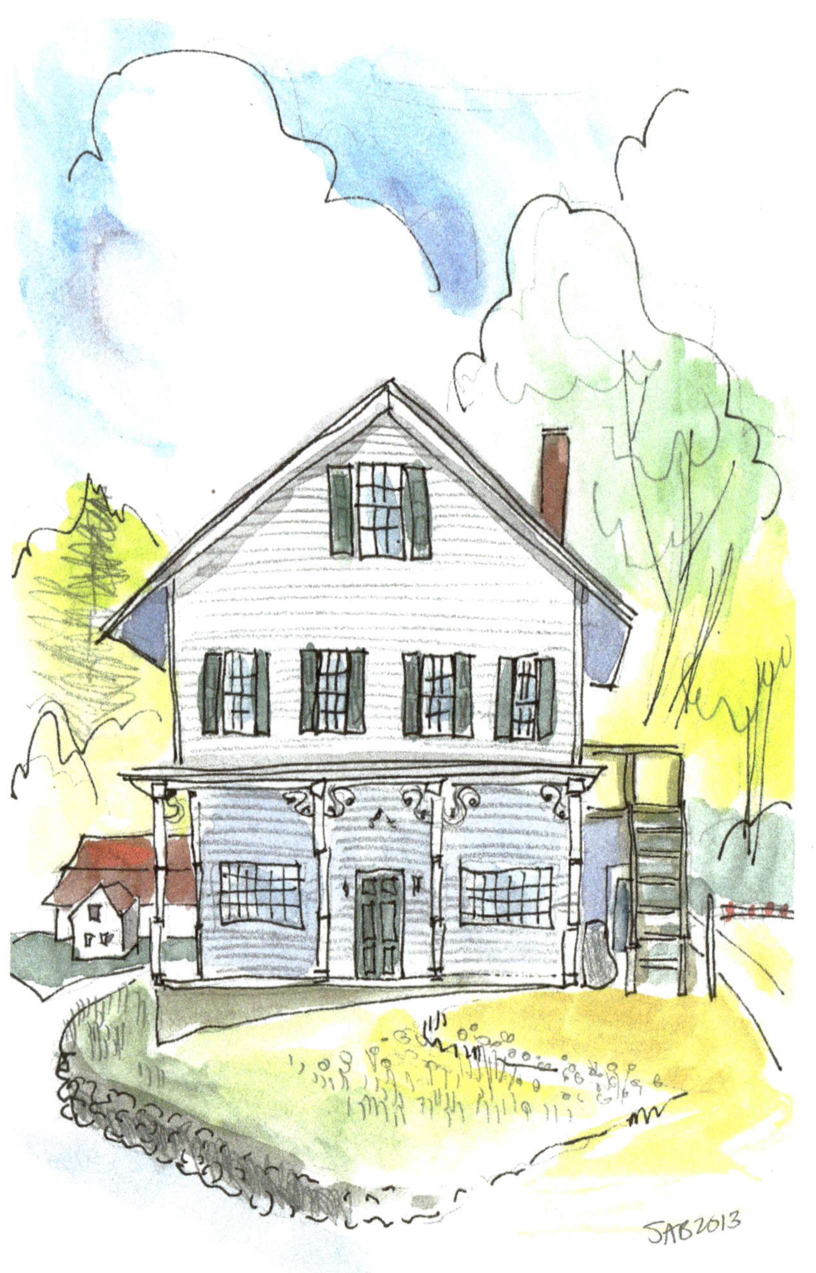

Danbury's town lines have shifted over the years. It was first a part of Alexandria, and then it annexed parts of Wilmot and Hill.

It boasts two general stores on opposing corners, a grange, and a church or two. The solid-looking town library is the George Gamble Library, built in 1912. For recreation, the Ragged Mountain Ski Resort beckons and the Sunapee Ragged Kearsarge Greenway trail goes through town. As well, the 56 mile long Northern Rail Trail passes this white building (subsequently painted yellow) with the attractive wooden porch trim.

I couldn't choose between the two general stores as a subject, but you can see one in the background.

DORCHESTER

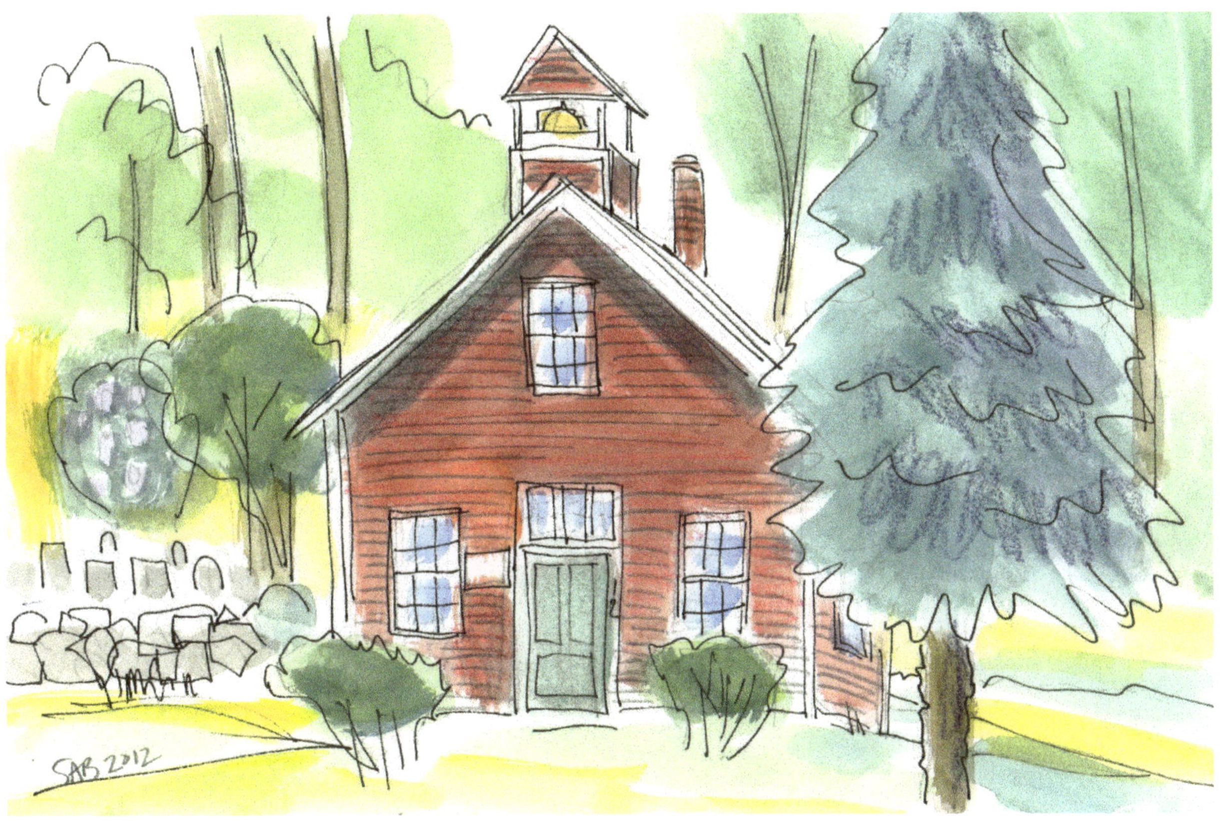

While I was drawing this, a few people were busy tidying up gardens for the approaching Memorial Day weekend. They didn't ask what I was doing.

I liked the classical simple design of the former schoolhouse, constructed with painted red clapboards, and now used as the town historical society. This small town is named for Dorchester, England.

At a population of under 400 people, it is half of what it was at one time. Its former industries were sawmills, shingles and clapboards, and the production of charcoal. Many towns in New England lost half their population in the mid to late 1800s due to westward migration after soldiers returned from the Civil War.

ENFIELD

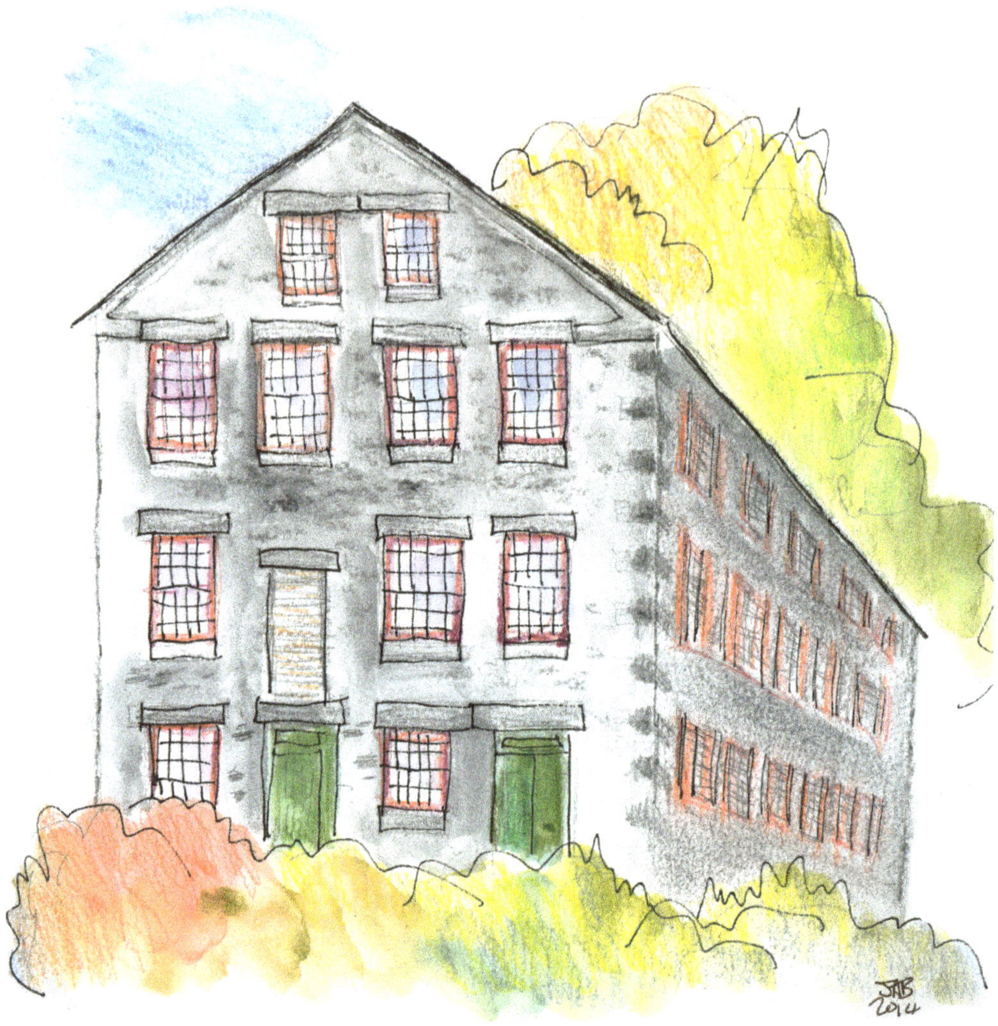

The Stone Mill, dating from 1849, held three stories of water-powered machinery. The red window trim is a cheerful note against the dark gray granite.

Shaker Bridge across Mascoma Lake has just been reconstructed.

The Shaker community in town reached its peak in the mid nineteenth century with 300 residents, one hundred buildings, and 3000 acres to farm. The Enfield Shaker Museum aims to educate and enlighten visitors about this religious sect. The Museum's Harvest Festival features games, music, and demonstrations of old time skills, as well as hands-on opportunities.

GOSHEN

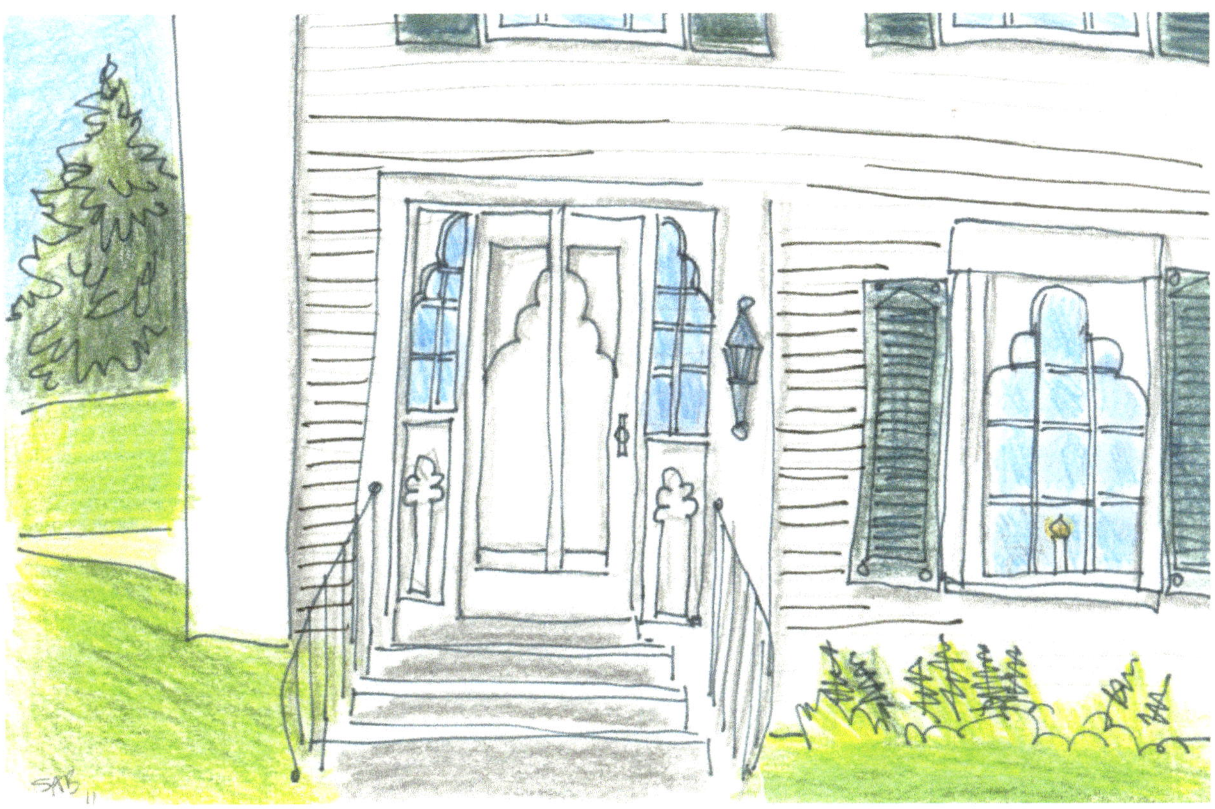

Goshen is the first town I visited after I officially decided to draw every town in New Hampshire. I had already drawn 19 towns.

This town was settled in 1768, as a part of Saville (which is now called Sunapee). Part of the town borders Mount Sunapee State Park. Early settlers came from Goshen, Connecticut. There is of course a Goshen in England, so perhaps this is where the name originated. It is Hebrew for an area in Egypt.

The unusual window treatments on this Community Church caught my attention. Constructed of white painted wood and clear glass, they deserved a close-up study.

GRAFTON

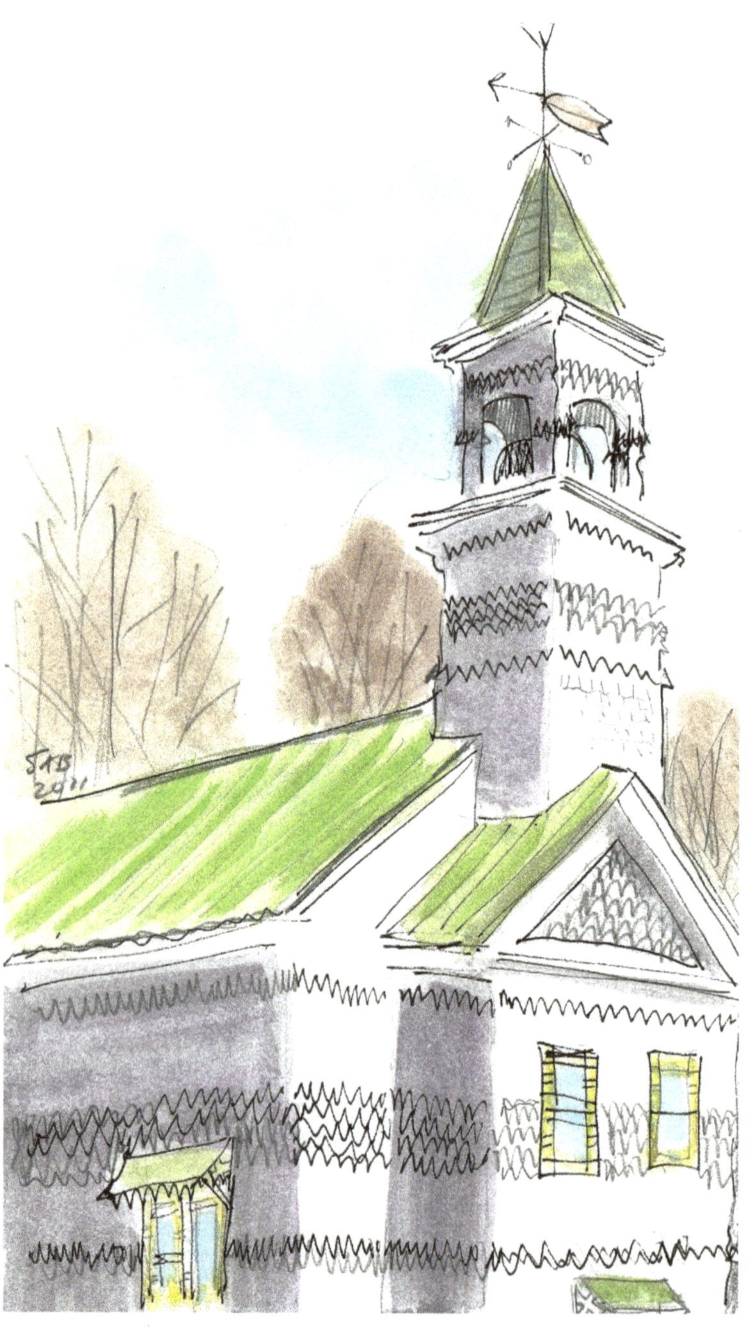

The East Grafton Christian Union Church is covered in white wooden shingles. Where I have drawn the zigzag lines is where the shingles went into a very eye-catching pattern. They caught the late afternoon rays of the sun and had a mesmerizing effect: think of wind-ruffled dove feathers.

When this building was first shingled, it had a fashionable brown stain. Somewhere along the line, it became even more fashionable to have a white painted edifice. Current plans by the Grafton Historical Society call for fundraisers to save the old structure.

The old meetinghouse has been moved twice, and was modified into a Victorian style in 1896.

GRANTHAM

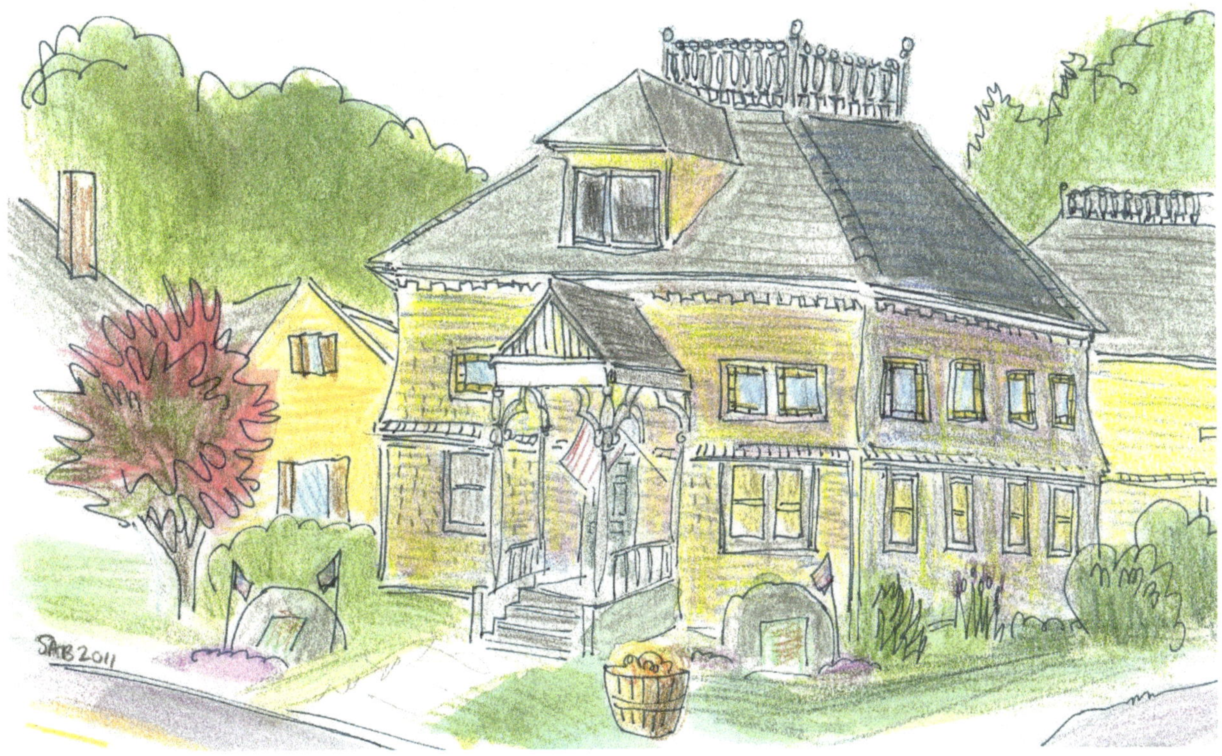

It took me a while to get to know quiet little Grantham. In the fall, decorative scarecrows line Main Street as part of a Fall Festival.

It was raining heavily as I sat in the car and drew the Dunbar Free Library in Grantham.

It is newly painted, and renovated with a new addition in the back. The town is named for a family of original settlers. Local shopping is plentiful in the village, just off of Route 89. And in the woods, to the east of the highway, are the 750 or so homes that make up the development called Eastman. With a golf course, lake, restaurant, and recreation center, it is a well-designed place.

GROTON

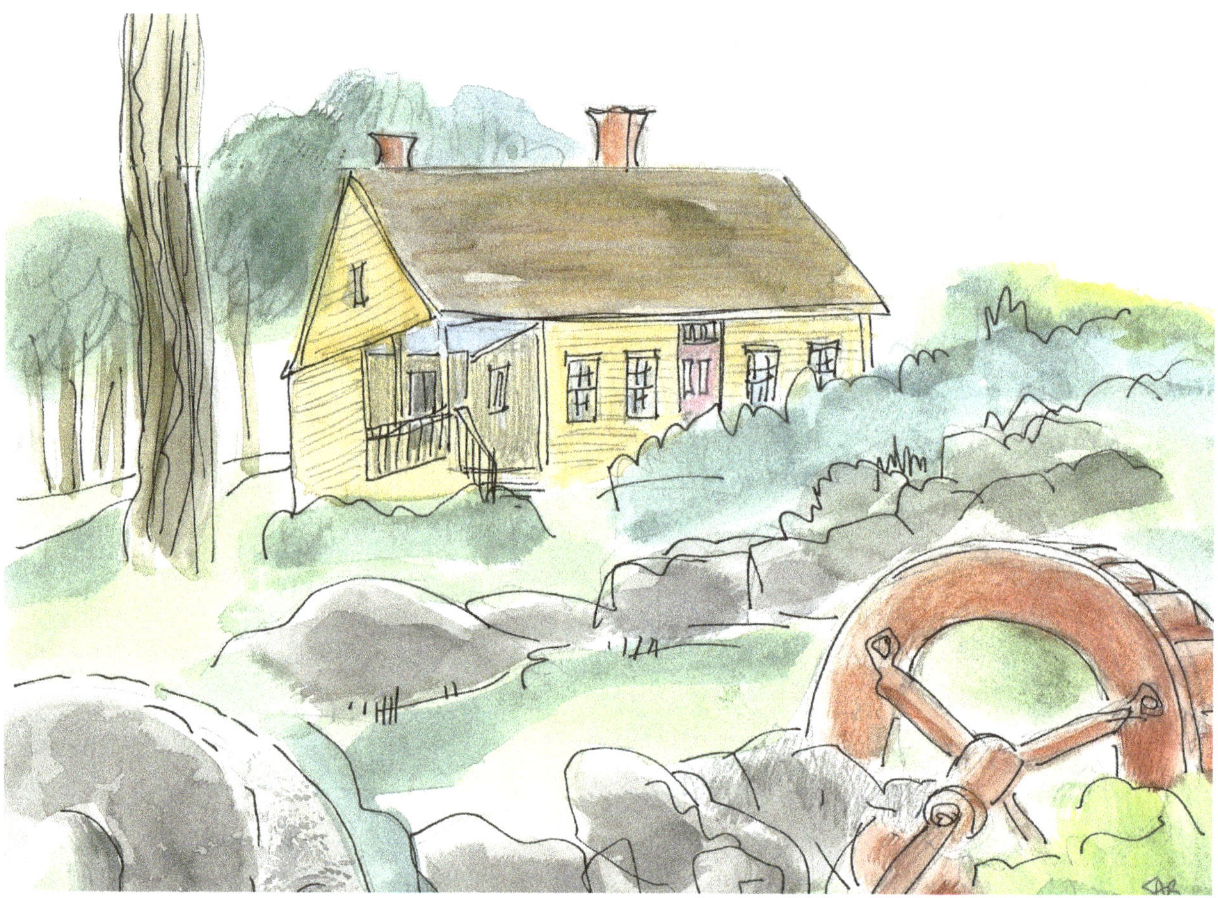

Groton, with a population under 600, is a hilly, rural place.

When a signpost beside this house came into view, we stopped the car to read and investigate. It told that this simple, yellow painted, wooden house is one of the many homes in New England once occupied by writer and religious leader Mary Baker Eddy. Walking around the edge of the grassy area, I found the rusty remains of an old mill.

I met a resident of Groton who sells jellies and jams at craft fairs. He kindly invited me to draw his goat farm.

HANOVER

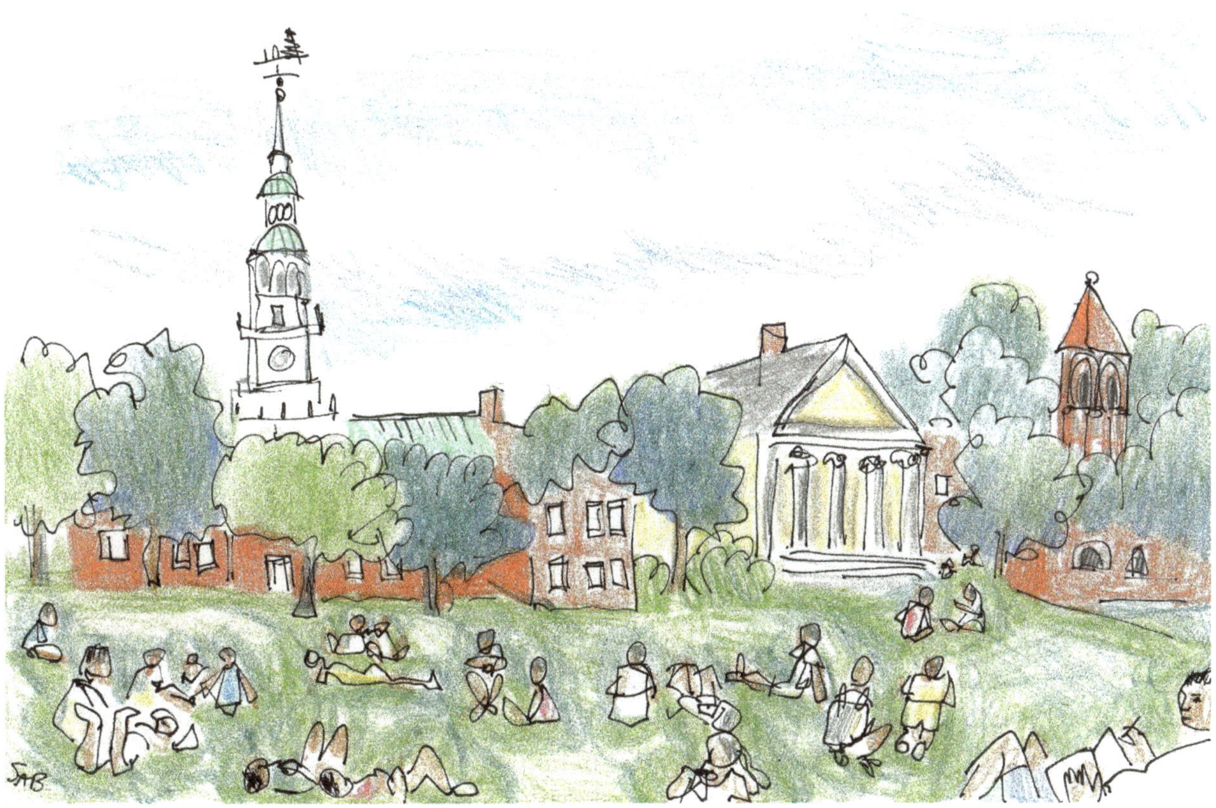

The Hood Museum of Art, on the campus of Dartmouth College, has wonderful, ever changing exhibitions, and a permanent collection dating back to 1772.

It was finals week, and multitudes of students were studying, chatting, and sunning themselves on the green of Dartmouth College in Hanover.

Dartmouth, the smallest of the eight Ivy League institutions, is actually a university, but nobody is in a mood for a name change. Its shift to coeducational came in the early 1970s, about 200 years after the founding. The commercial part of Hanover itself is a charming, mini-urban space of a few blocks. The shop fronts remind me of London, all brick with lots of white painted trim. The town shares a school district with its Vermont neighbor Norwich.

HENNIKER

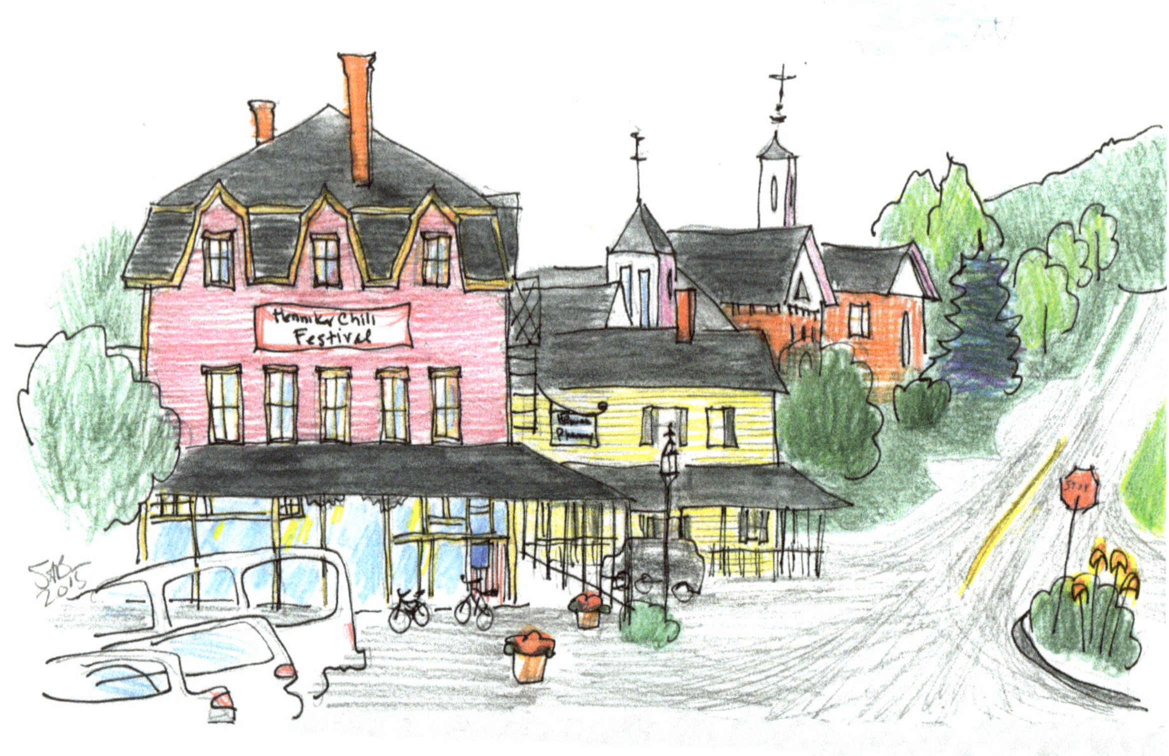

Henniker is named for a London merchant, a dealer of leather and fur. It had three earlier names: Number Six, Todd's Town, and New Marlborough.

I stood in the street to draw the main crossroads on a hot, steamy, summer's day. Mid-day as I recall. When classes are in session for New England College, the streets are quite a bit more bustling. The old pharmacy sports a new coat of pink paint to replace the grey that had faded over decades.

Nearby is the popular ski resort Pat's Peak.

HILL

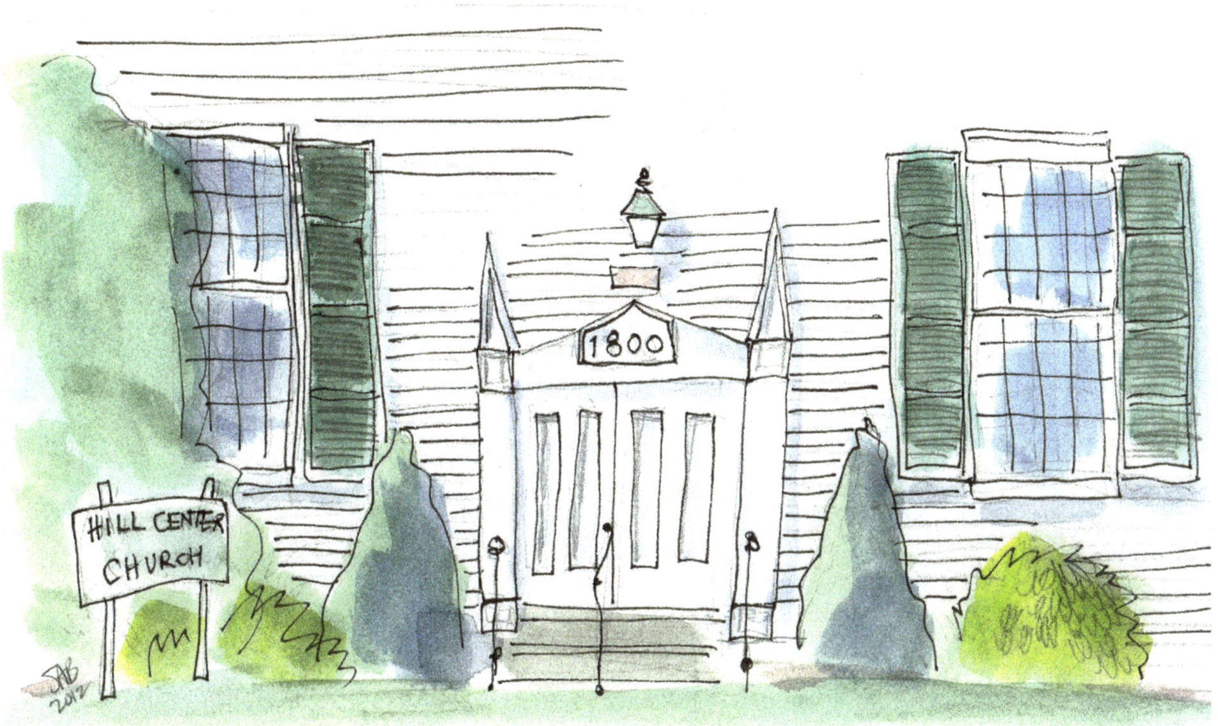

I enjoyed some great vistas of blue misty mountains as I was driving around the hills of Hill.

The town of Hill was once called New Chester, changed to Hill in 1837 and named for Isaac Hill, a governor of the state.

In 1941, the village settlement was moved to higher ground because the Franklin Falls Dam was under construction. I drove all through the back roads of Hill before I found this little church. The doorway appealed to me, next to the shrubbery with matching pointed shapes. I probably wouldn't be able to find it again without help.

HILLSBOROUGH

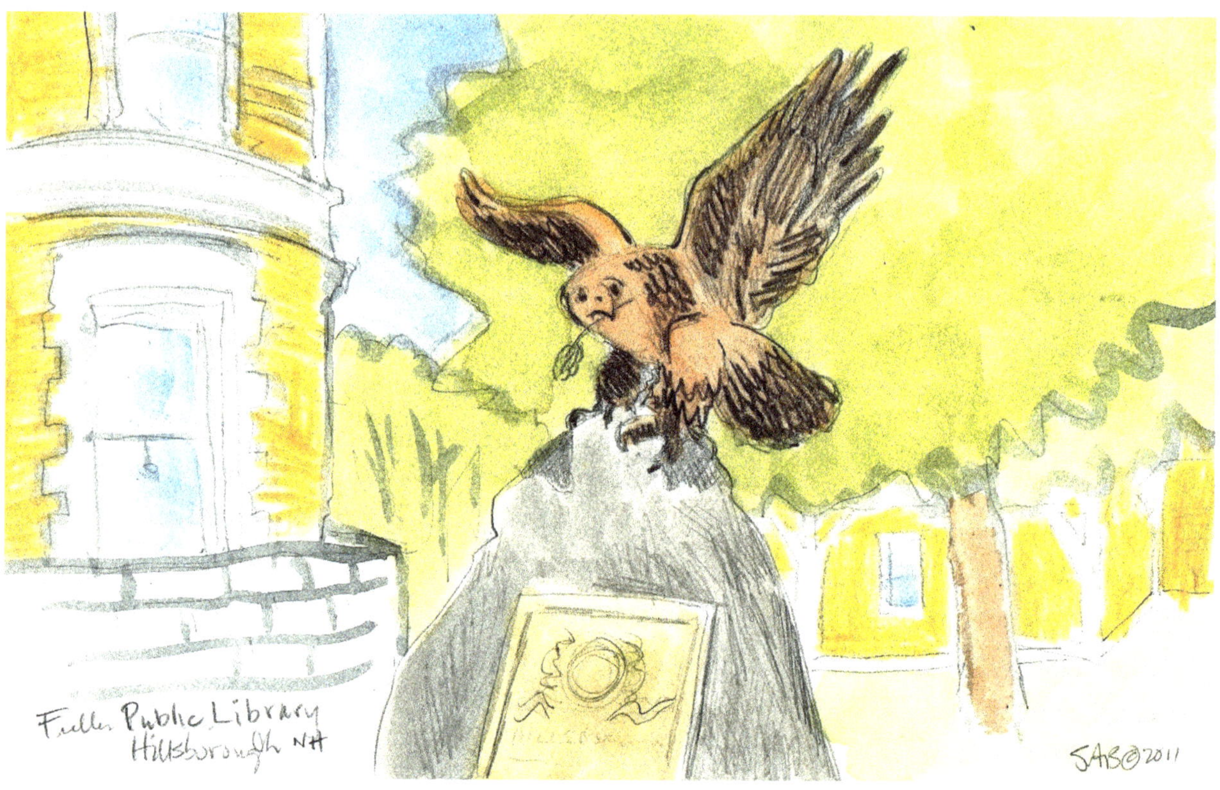

There are certain things I find I must draw. One of them is eagles.

This bronze statue, mounted onto a large granite boulder, sits at eye level. It serves as a war memorial next to the Fuller Public Library in Hillsborough. Someone put a dried plant stalk in his beak. It seemed appropriate and I liked the look. Sculpture appeals to me, and I enjoyed viewing this one from all directions. The library is within the Governor John Butler Smith home, given to the town in 1926.

The 14th President of the United States, Franklin Pierce, came from Hillsborough.

LEBANON

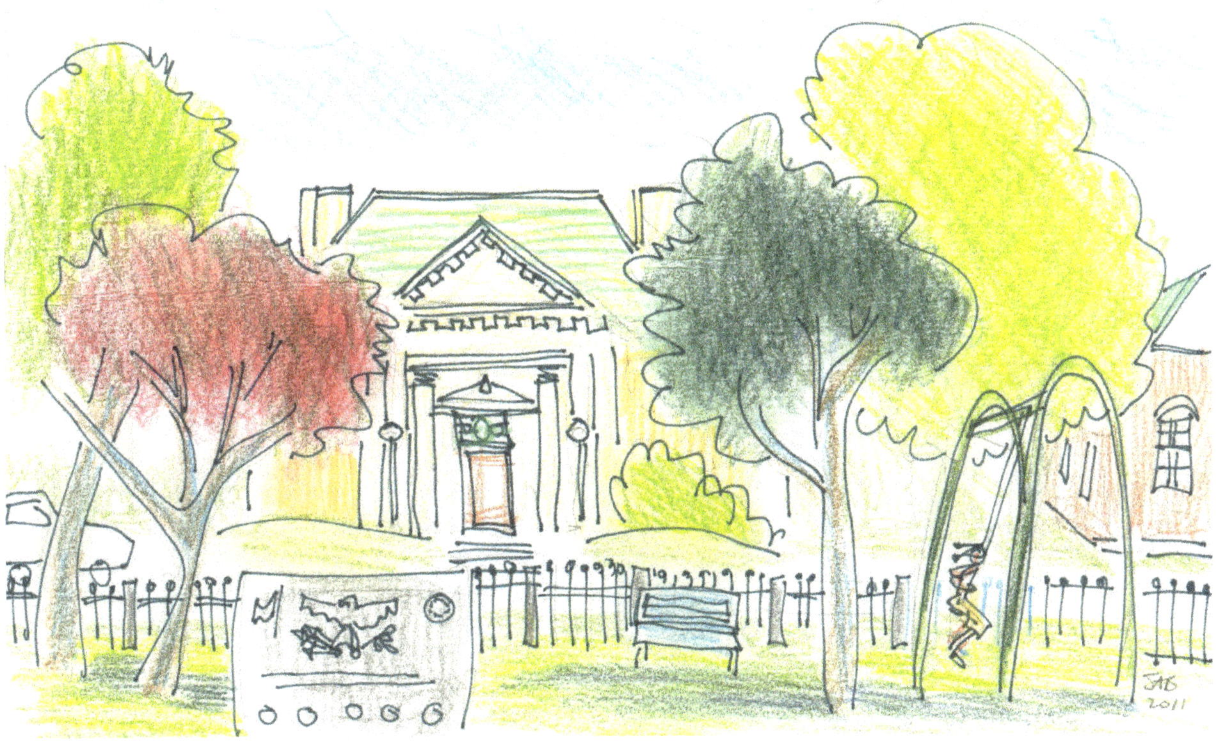

Located in a renovated textile factory nearby is The Alliance for Visual Arts (AVA).

Colburn Park sits in the middle of old Lebanon. I had in mind to draw the town library, the yellow brick building with columns. Not until I got there did I decide to include the trees, the Veterans' Memorial, and the child on the swings.

The city hall, with the opera house in the same building, is around the corner. Urban parks have intrigued me for a long time. This one is square, surrounded by shady streets, and around that are some fine old buildings. The park is used by people of all ages, and it serves a real community need.

LYME

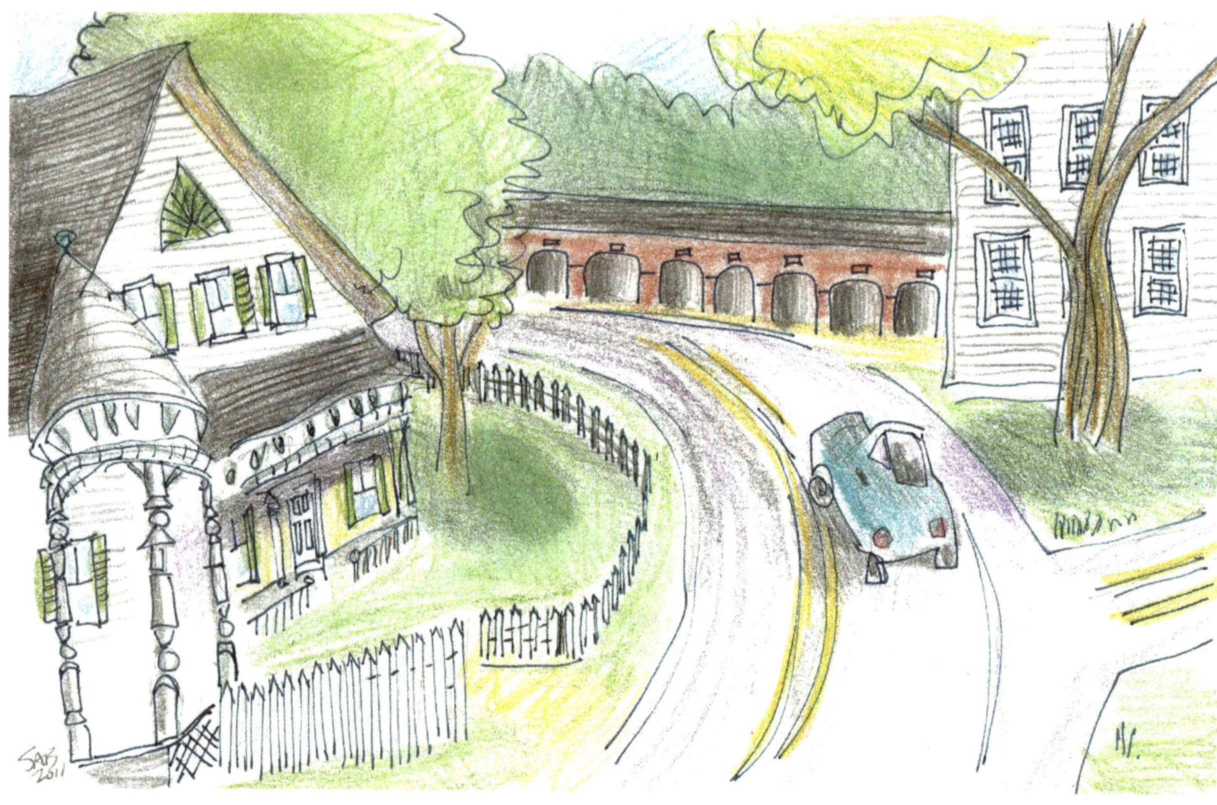

Lyme is a town along the Connecticut River, which forms the border with Vermont. In the background is a partial view of a building of 27 stalls for horses and carriages. It continues on for a long way!

The stalls are no longer used, but a remnant of past times when the churchgoers arrived in this fashion. On the right is the church. On the left of the curve, behind the white picket fence, sits a home built in the late Victorian era. And on the roadway is a car of my own style, indeterminate era.

The attractive, rectangular town green is next to a general store, post office, and art gallery.

NEW LONDON

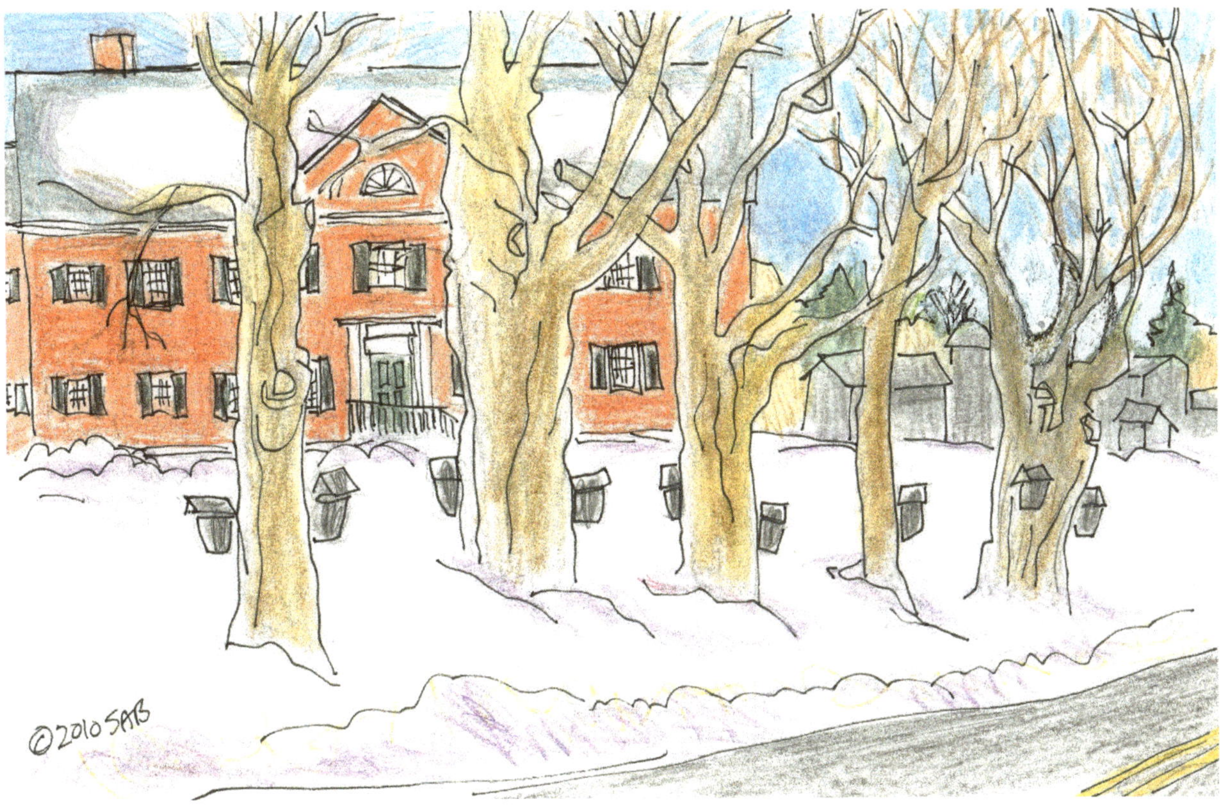

Behind the Tracy Memorial Library is a garden designed by the famed Olmsted brothers.

My hometown, New London, has a population of about 4,400 residents, and an additional 1,000 students at Colby-Sawyer College. On the campus, a row of very old and weather-scarred sugar maple trees are being tapped for spring sap.

Classes in the science of maple syrup production are offered at the college. The town's main street follows along a ridgeline with mountain views in all directions. The summer stock theater, the Barn Playhouse, has been keeping people laughing and crying since 1933. A regional hospital is just off Main Street. The Historical Society is a 12-building village.

NEWBURY

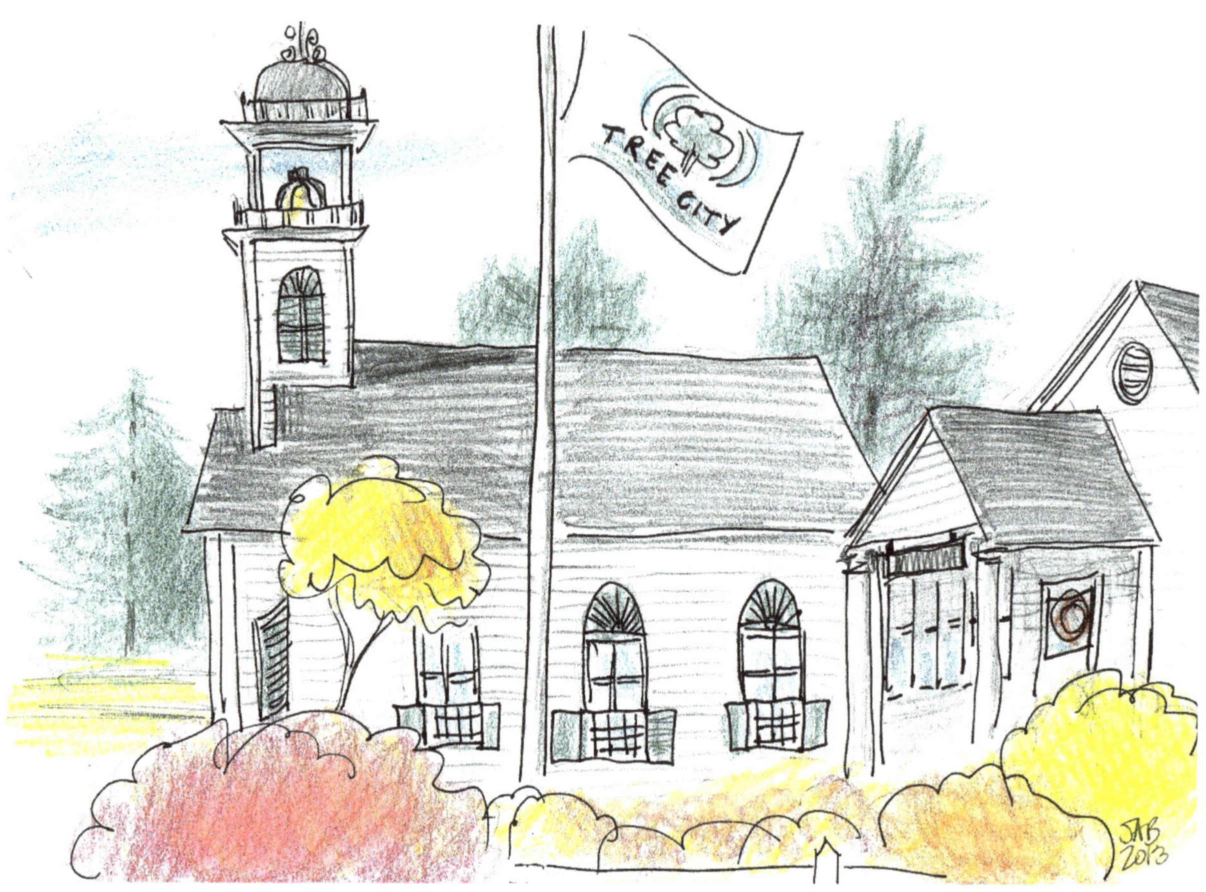

According to historical sources the small town of Newbury, under the shadow of Mount Sunapee, has had several names–Dantzic, Hereford, and Fishersfield. It became Newbury in 1837, five years after the meetinghouse was built.

No one knows for sure why the pulpit is just inside the front doors, but it certainly would have been awkward to be a latecomer to services. This meetinghouse was recently completely renovated. The area was a bustling summer resort in the era of train travel and steamboats. The town, at the southern end of Lake Sunapee, is still a busy place with skiing, boating, and a state beach.

A stiff breeze was blowing off the lake on this day. I was searching for the best angle to include both the school and the meetinghouse.

NEWPORT

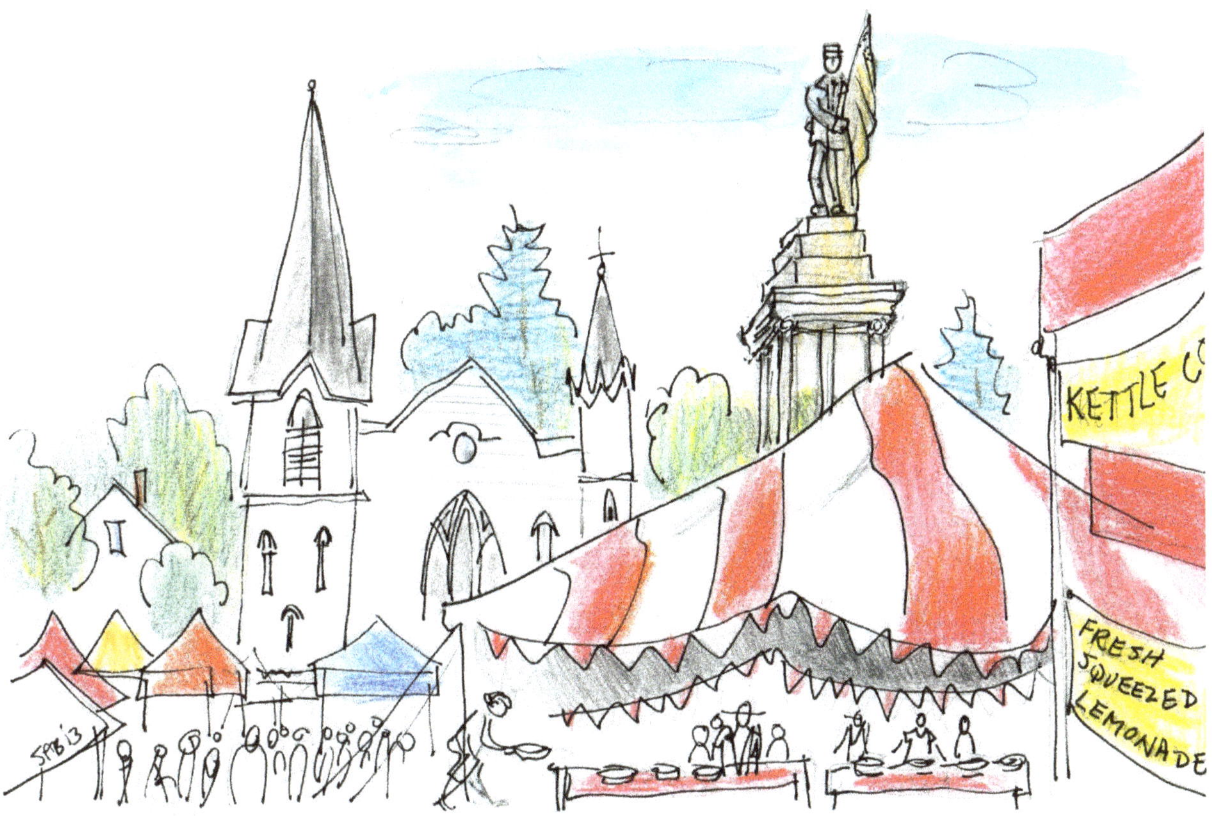

Newport was one of 33 towns along the border that decided to become part of Vermont from 1781 to 1782.

Newport hosts an annual Apple Pie Fair, an early harvest fair of sorts. The red striped tent held the homemade apple pies for sale. They were sold out by the time we got there, although we did manage to get a piece of apple crumble (à la mode) at another tent.

The town green is flat, rectangular, and grassy. There's an art/craft/farmers market there every week in the summer, and it's also a place for wintertime fun on the ice rink. The tall, brick, Newport Opera House continues to be a lively social center in the town.

ORANGE

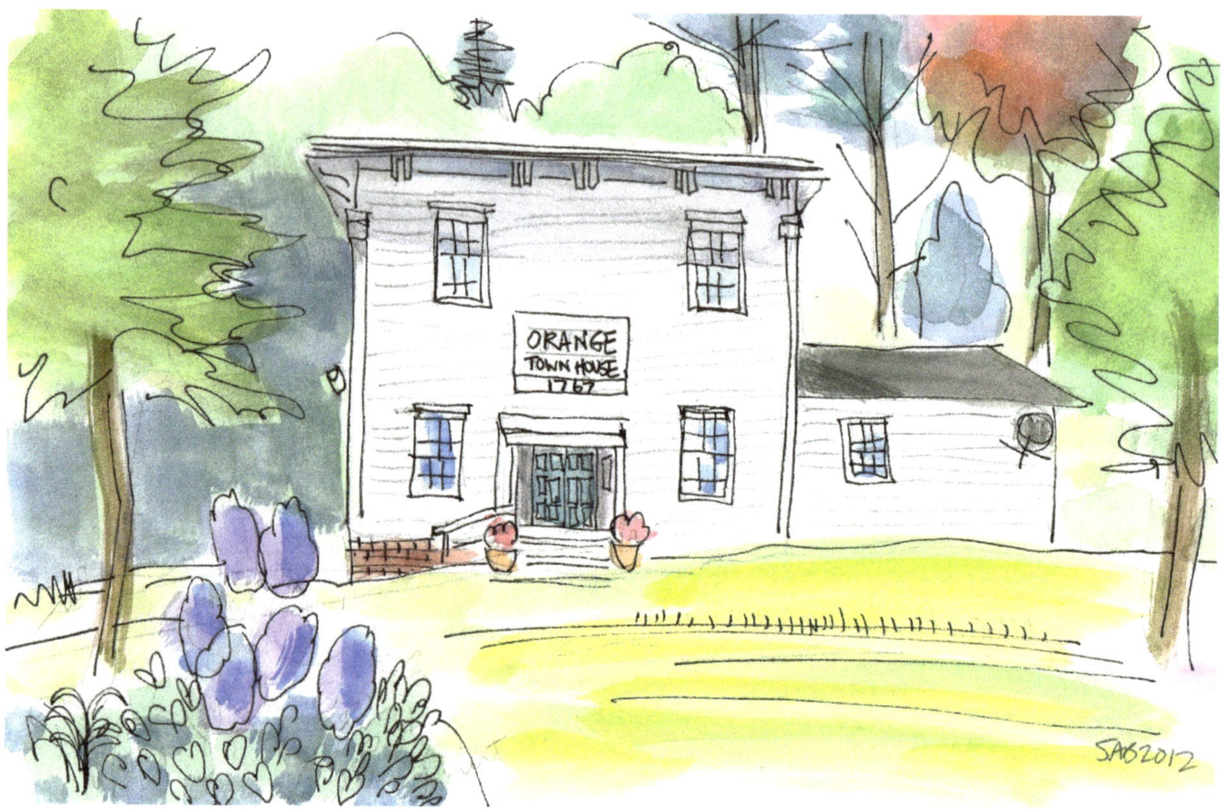

Orange is a rural place. The town, population under 350 people, used to be called Cardigan after George Brudenell, the fourth Earl of Cardigan. Cardigan State Park and Mount Cardigan occupy much of the town's land.

The purity and simplicity of this building's design pleases me. Most towns in New Hampshire would call this sort of building a town hall, rather than a town house. Today they both usually mean town offices. The annual town meeting is held there if a town's population has not outgrown the space. I had to move around a bit here, as a caretaker was mowing the grass.

The shrub in bloom is a lilac bush, the state flower but not a native plant.

ORFORD

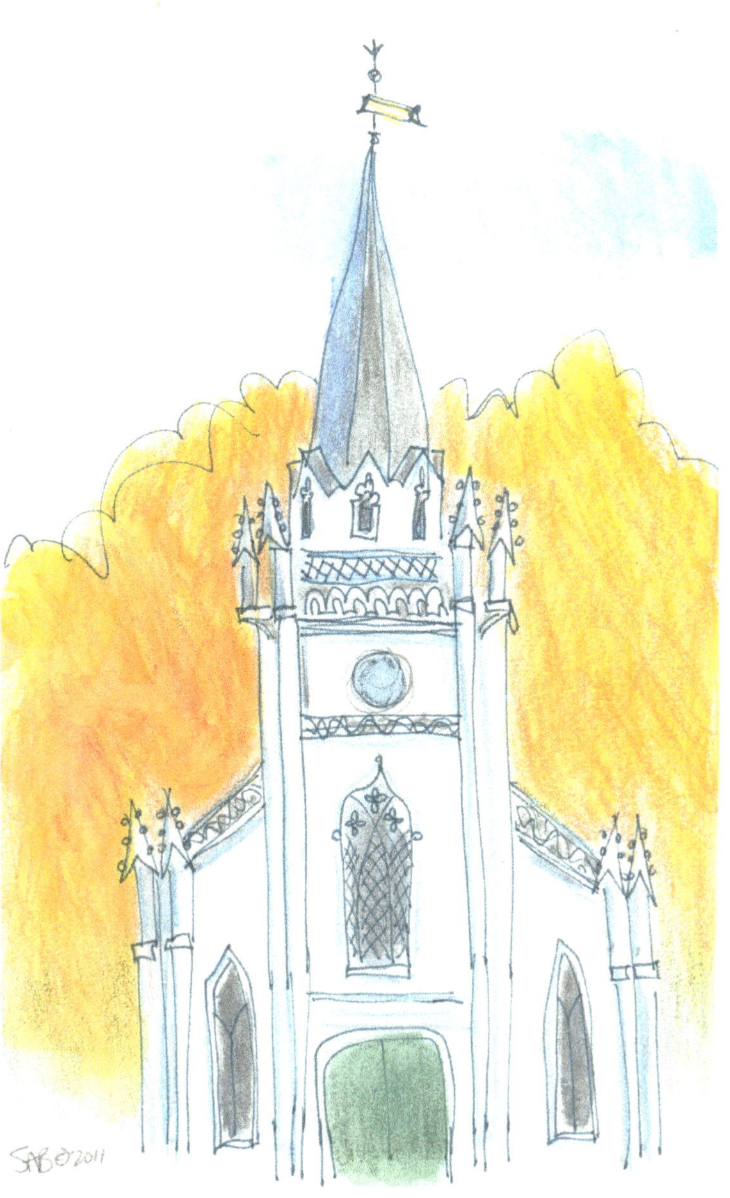

Orford was named for Robert Walpole, the Earl of Orford.

I liked the architecture of this church, the United Congregational Church. It is in the Gothic Revival Style, all in wood. Originally gray, it is now white with gray trim. The architect was Moses Gerrish Wood, and his architectural flourishes are enchanting.

Orford, two towns north of Hanover, is a charming place with homes stretched out beside a long town green, and seven early houses along the ridge. There was once a steam powered paddleboat ferry to Fairlee, Vermont, across the Connecticut River.

The original name of Orford was Number Seven, as it was one of the fort towns along the Connecticut River.

PLAINFIELD

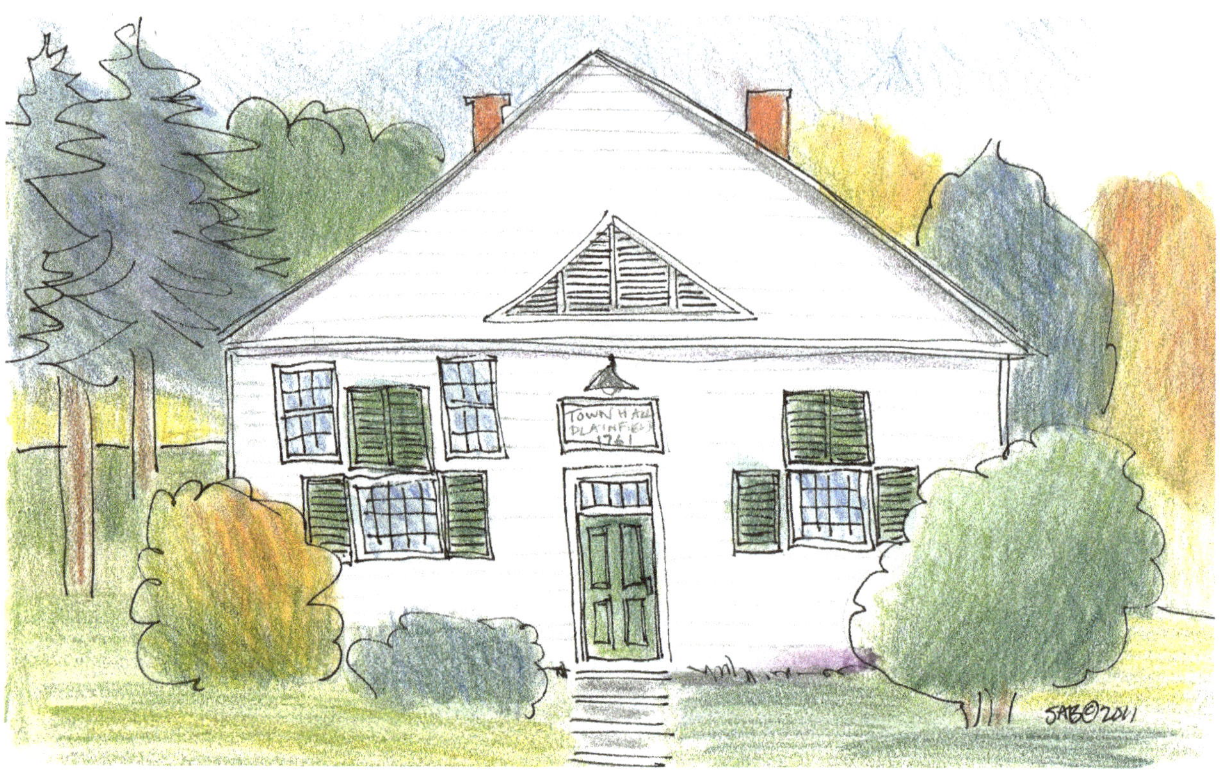

Plainfield has a treasure inside the town hall: a stage set designed by Maxfield Parrish, painted in 1916 and restored in 1993. He was a top ranked American artist and illustrator, and a resident.

His work can be seen on the backdrop, six wings, and three overhead drapes. The original lighting mimics the change in light from dawn to noon and back to dusk. The public is invited to see the light changes on certain Sunday afternoons. The stage is still used by the town for various events, and all the children in town are raised with the admonition of *"Don't touch the curtain"*.

Plainfield is home to Kimball Union Academy.

SALISBURY

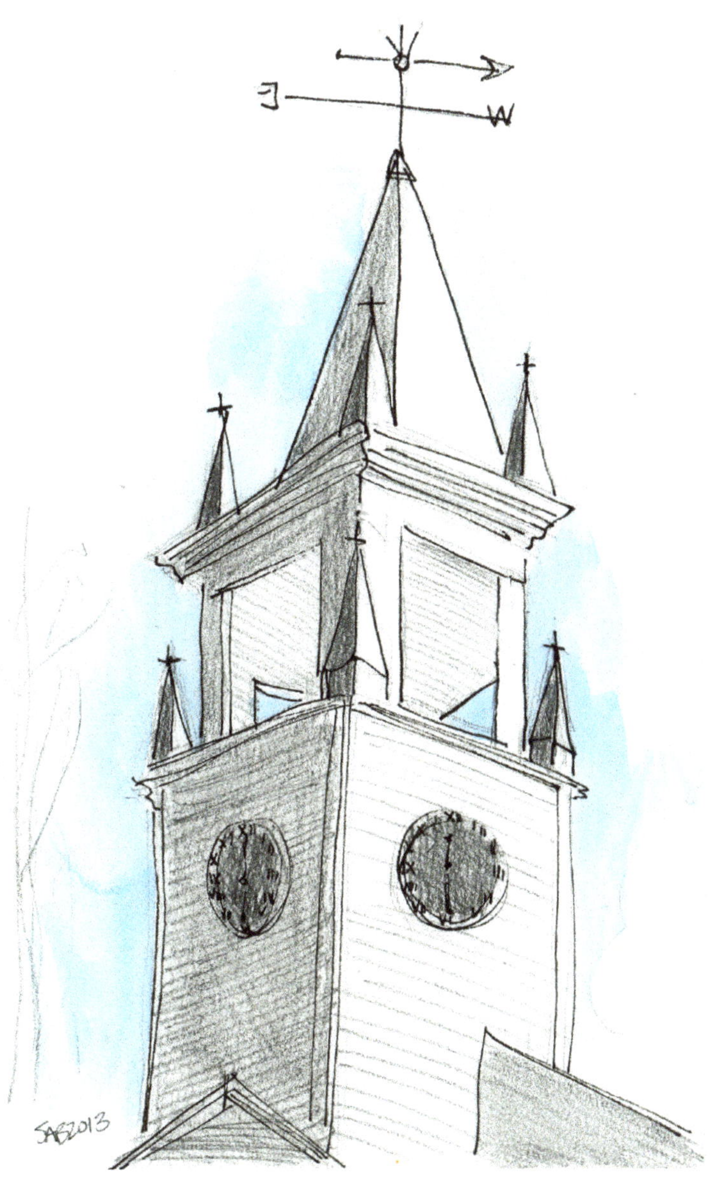

Craning my head back, I drew the fine old wooden steeple of the meetinghouse. The style of the peaked pyramids on the four corners seems familiar to me. It resembles other buildings in neighboring towns.

Salisbury was first called Baker's Town, then Stevenstown, Gerrishtown, New Salisbury, and finally changed to its present name in 1768. Next to this building are the graveyard, a hearse house, the town offices, and a new town library. They are all in a row, with several matching white colonial style houses nearby. I always imagine that brothers built the matching houses.

Persistence was required this day to draw outside, as it was black fly season.

SPRINGFIELD

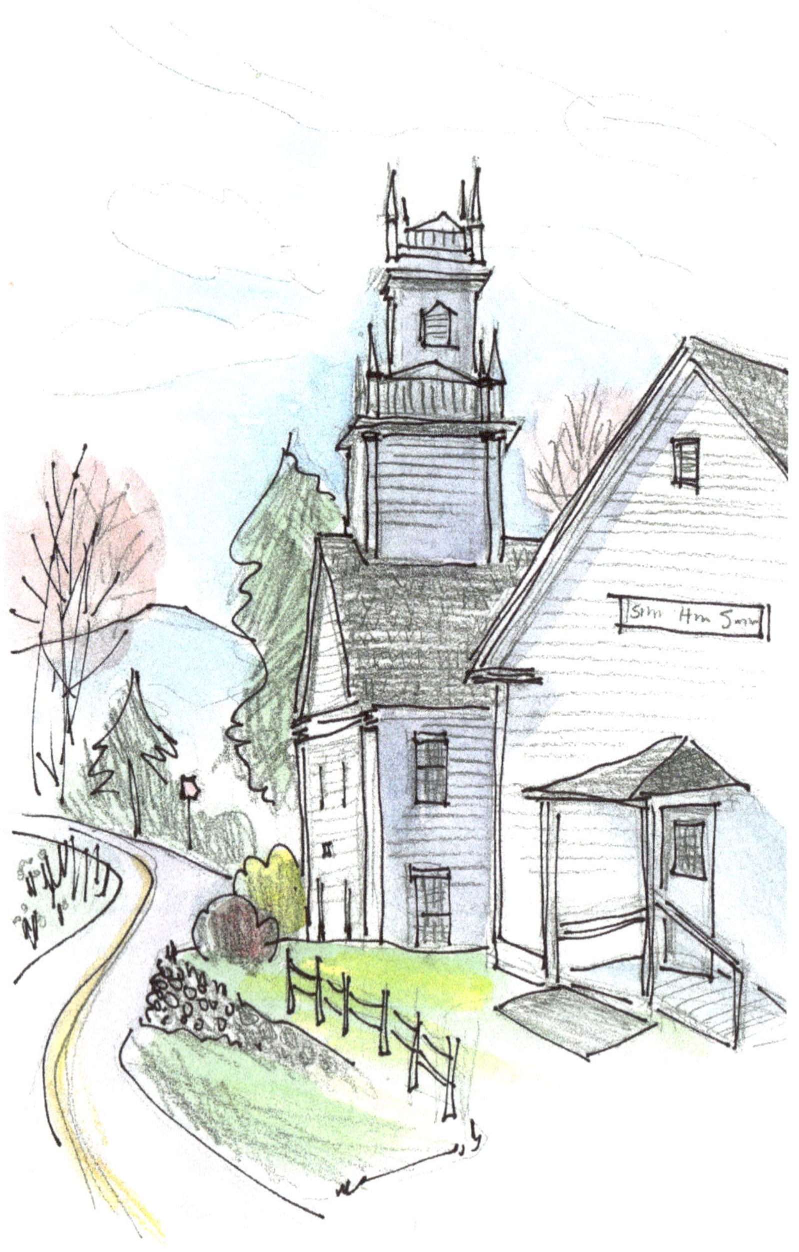

With a small population of under 1,300 people, Springfield nonetheless boasts this fine old meetinghouse (1797) which was recently restored. We once enjoyed a talk there on local flora and fauna.

On the way home, at dusk, we spotted a fine looking moose giving us the once over from a nearby field, its eyes glowing in the dark from our headlights.

On the right sits the Springfield Historical Society in the former Center School. After a more modern school was constructed, it became the town library. Now a new library is attached to the town hall.

Springfield and New London share Little Lake Sunapee, often called Twin Lake due to the peninsula that almost cuts it in half.

SUNAPEE

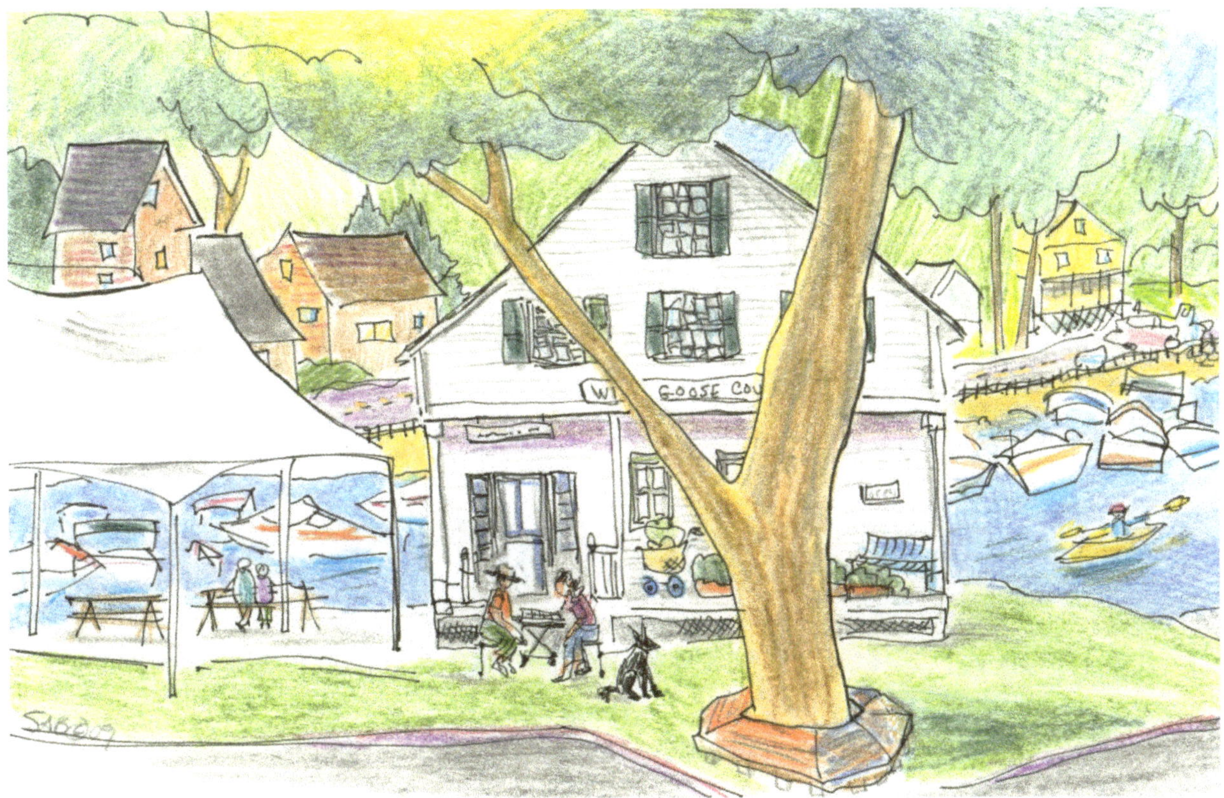

Through the magic of drawing, I reshaped the massive tree to show the store behind it.

Sunapee was an industrial town before it was a resort. Clothespins and hames were manufactured along the Sugar River. Signs at the Hames Park explain that a hame is part of a harness for a pair of horses.

As word of the beauty of Lake Sunapee grew, hotels rose along the shores for visitors who came and stayed all summer. The hotels are gone, but families still arrive. Several boat cruises for tourists chug out into the lake every day. Harbor events keep the town a lively place: 5k runs, chowder challenges, open air concerts, and a rubber ducky race on the Sugar River.

SUTTON

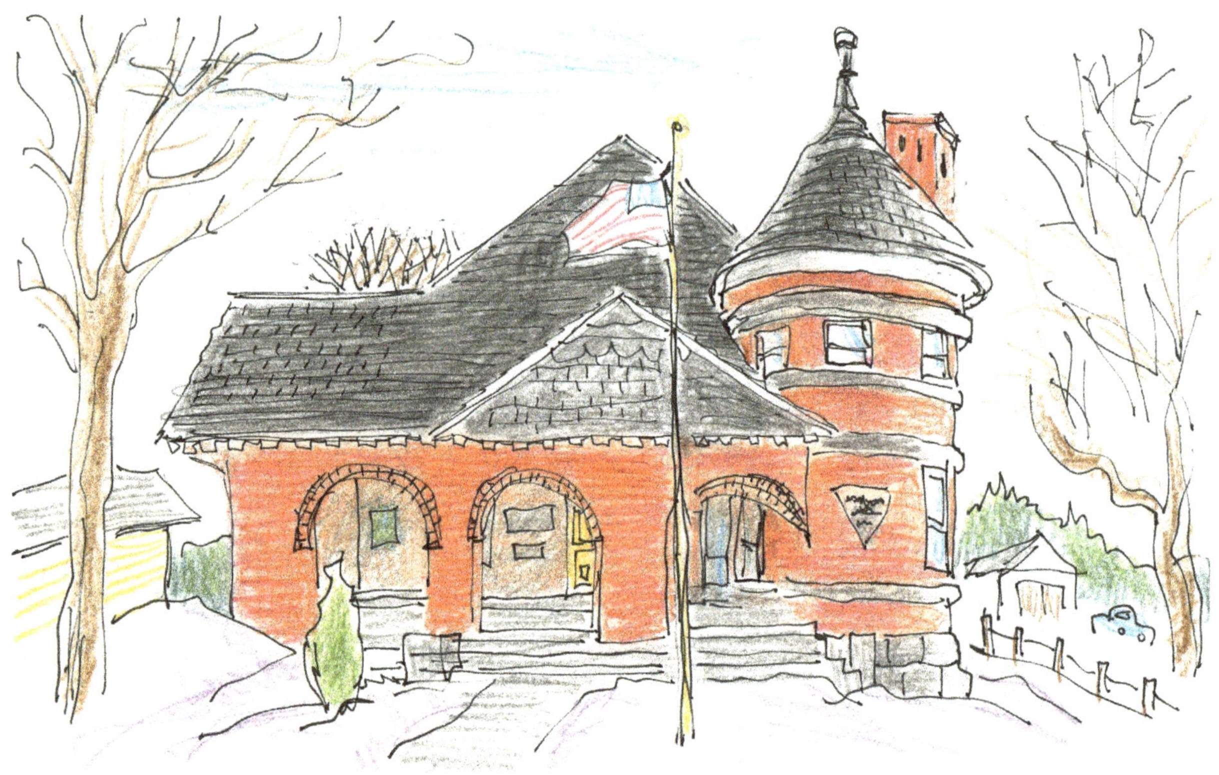

The variety of architecture in New Hampshire is astounding. This brick and granite building, Pillsbury Memorial Hall, was constructed in the village of Sutton Mills in 1891.

The interior is lined with beautiful charcoal portraits of village elders, all in place since the building was new. It serves as local government offices and community space. Note the small scale of the surrounding buildings in comparison. Yes, its name comes from the family that started the flour company in Minneapolis, Minnesota. Originally from New Hampshire, they have been generous contributors throughout this area.

The recently renovated Vernondale Store is on a sharp turn on the road through North Sutton.

UNITY

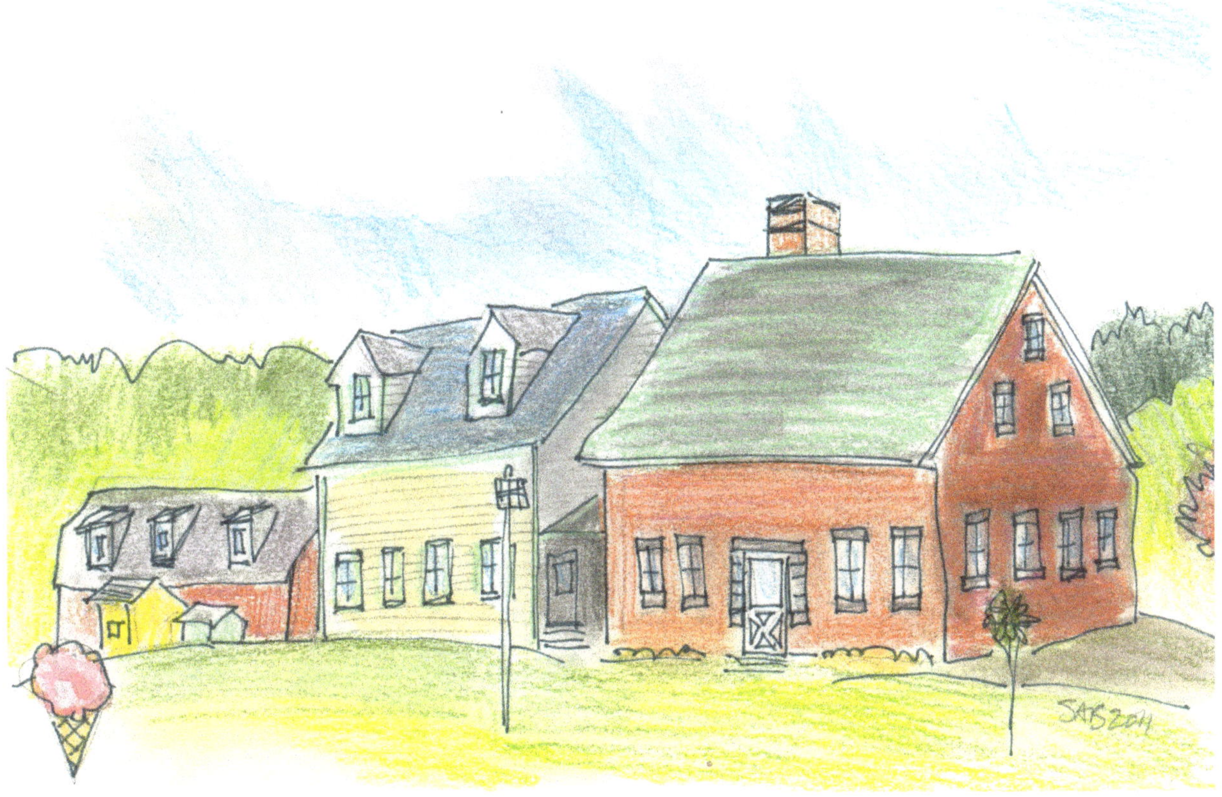

Candidates Obama and Clinton met in town in 2008 to pledge their unity in the fall campaign.

In 1753, this town was known as Buckingham in the Province of New Hampshire. And the Massachusetts government at the time also claimed the area. When they resolved their dispute, the name of Unity was chosen in 1764.

This scene called to me for several reasons. Brick buildings are beautiful, and ice cream signs are fun to draw. It was a blue-sky sunny day and we enjoyed our treat at the Brick Farm.

WARNER

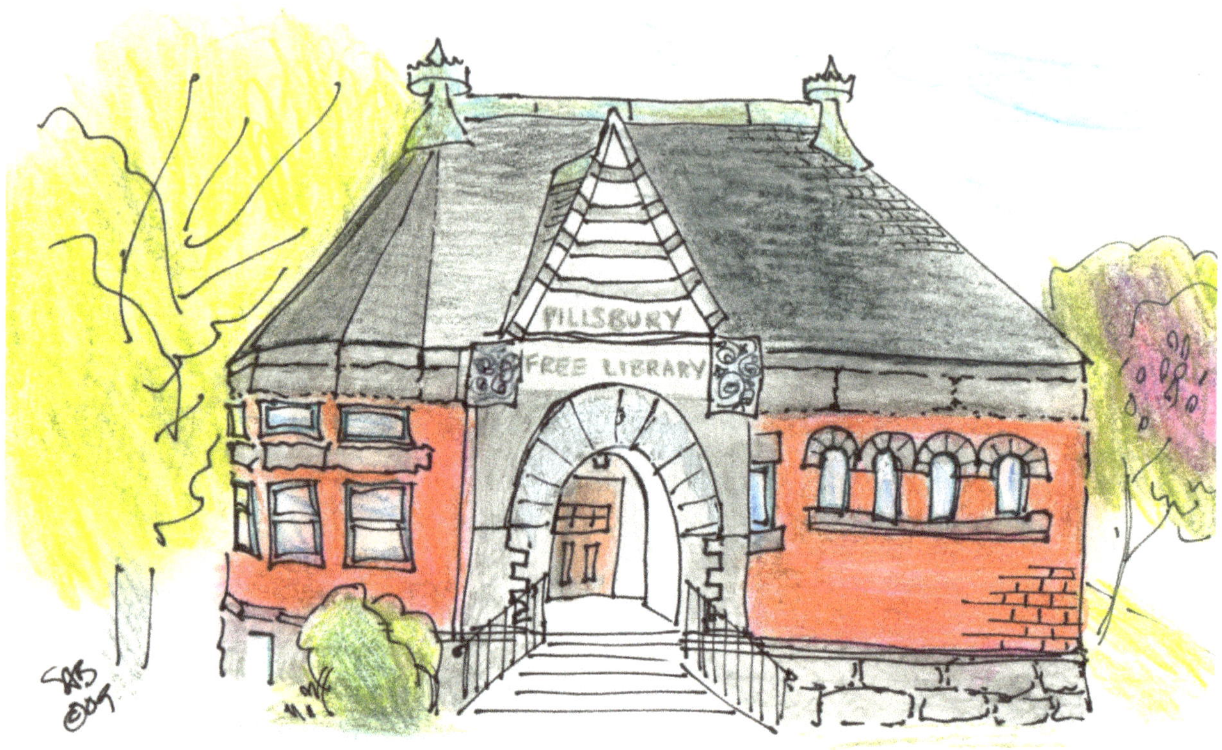

When my grandmother lived in Bradford in the 1950s, she used to take the bus into Warner to shop. I believe it had a fabric and notions shop. It still has many fine shops, as well as the Mt. Kearsarge Indian Museum and the New Hampshire Telephone Museum.

The town's first name was Number One, then Jennesstown, then Amesbury. In 1774, it became Warner. The Pillsbury family funded the Pillsbury Free Library, circa 1905. They moved to Minnesota and founded the Pillsbury Flour mills, but they never forgot their New Hampshire roots.

Warner is home to many writers, artists, and craftspeople. And to MainStreet BookEnds, an independent bookstore.

WASHINGTON

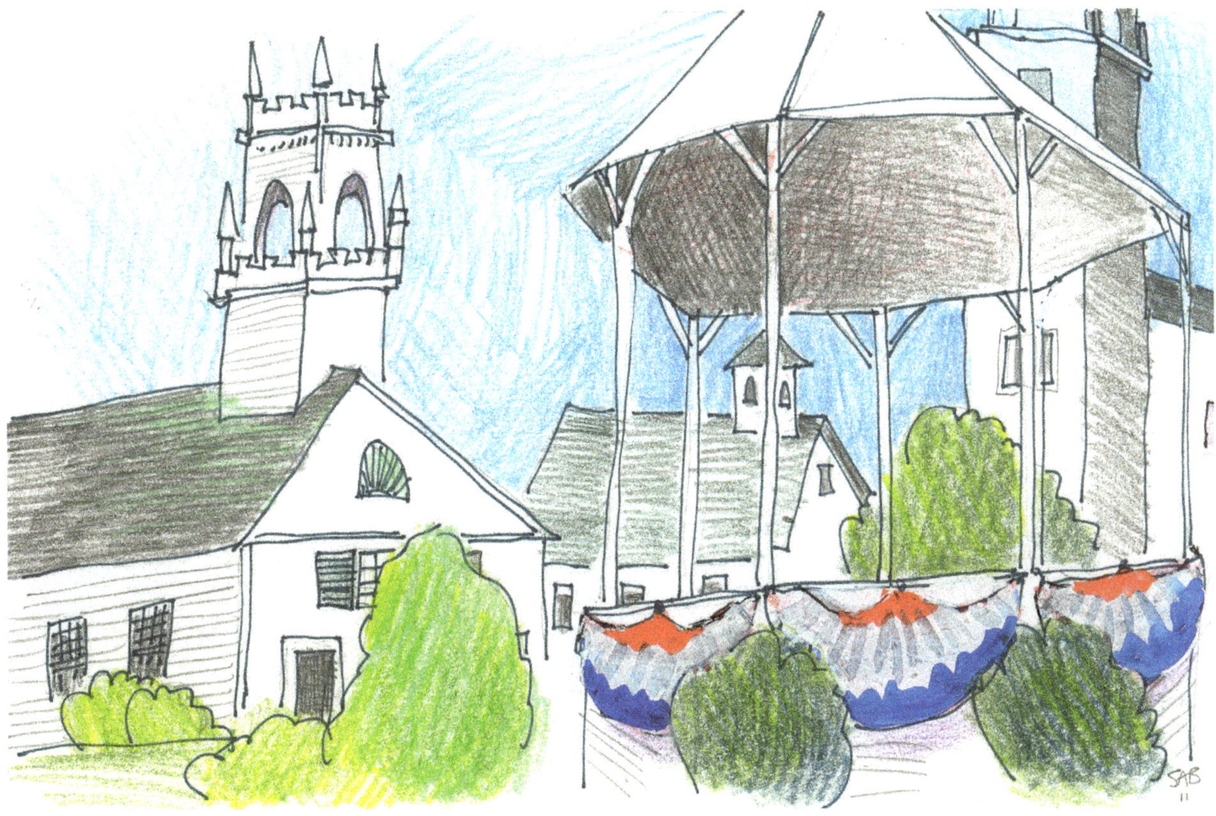

Washington has 26 lakes and ponds and is home to Pillsbury State Park.

Washington was the first town in the U.S. named for George Washington. In the foreground is the bandstand decorated with cloth bunting for Memorial Day.

Most towns keep the decorations up through Independence Day. In the background are the church, a school, and the town hall. They are painted wooden frame buildings. The town halls of New England are where the annual town meetings take place. Every citizen has one vote, on important topics that need to be resolved, mostly having to do with the annual budget.

WEBSTER

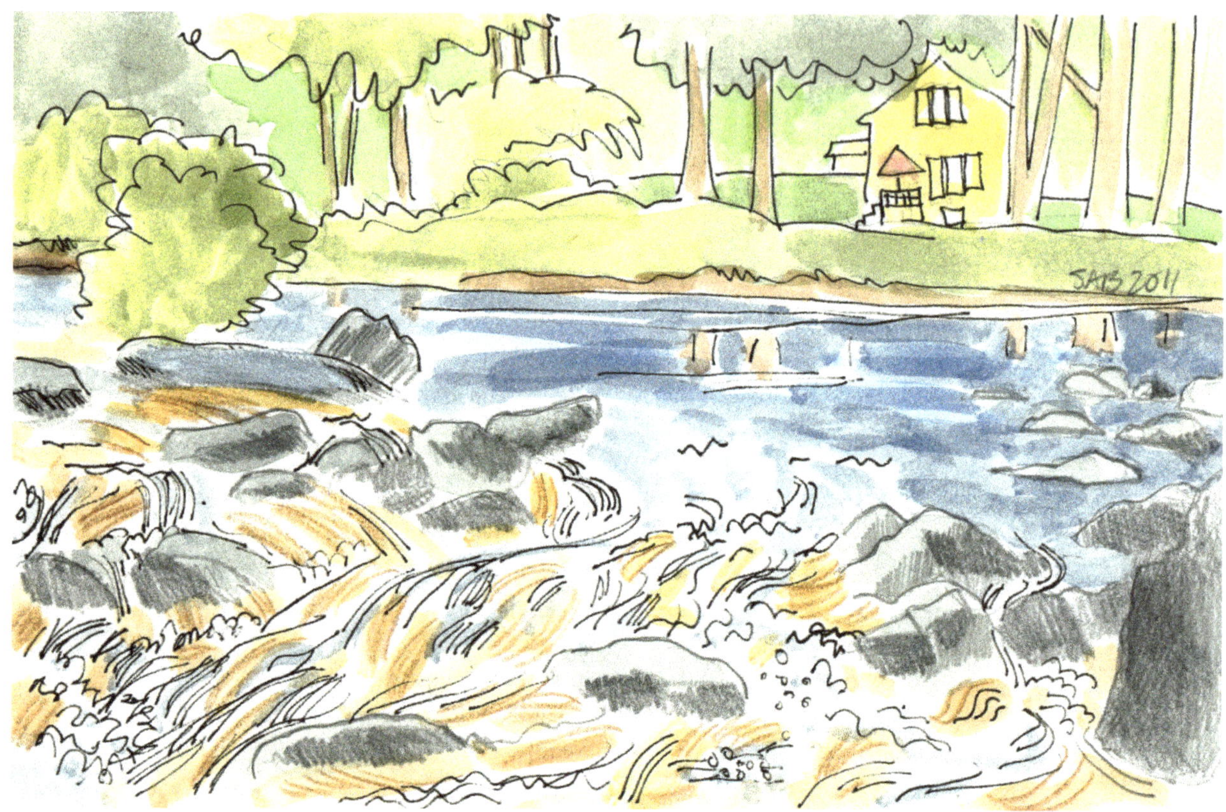

The Blackwater River in Webster starts at Pleasant Lake, where we live in New London. I tried to capture a corner where the quiet dark water meets the drop off, and then flows over the granite rocks.

The water is ale colored from the tannins in the water. It is a challenge to draw moving water, but it was beautiful to look closely at the rocks and shapes of the currents. Originally a part of Boscawen, Webster was formed in 1860 and takes its name from the statesman Daniel Webster.

The road follows along the Blackwater River for quite a while, with many places to pull off.

WENTWORTH

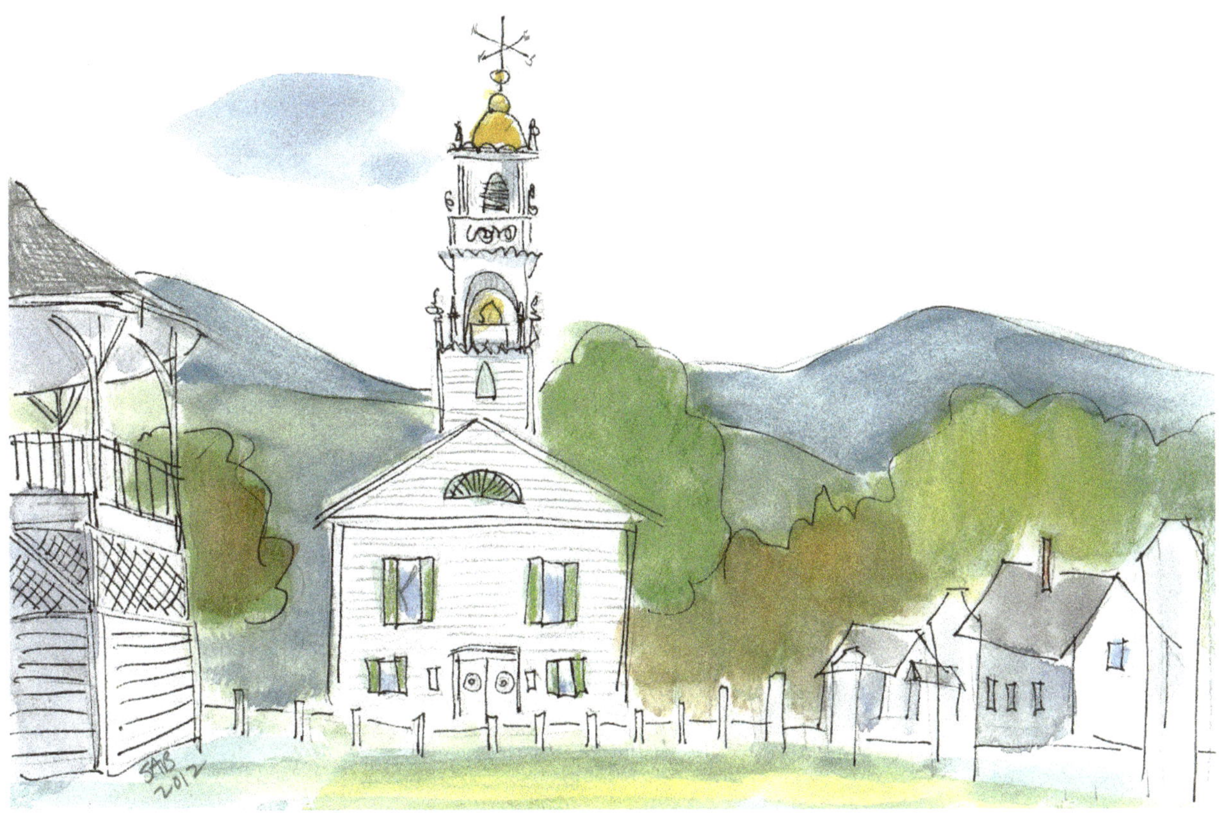

Wentworth is home to Plummer's Ledge Natural Area and part of the White Mountain National Forest.

Wentworth was named for the Governor Benning Wentworth in 1766. The town common, surrounded by an unusual fence, is exceptionally picturesque.

With the Federal style Congregational church at one end, and the town library, post office, and town offices along one side, it presents a compact visual scene. The band-stand is in the middle of the green of course, and many lovely homes sit in the shade on the other side.

WILMOT

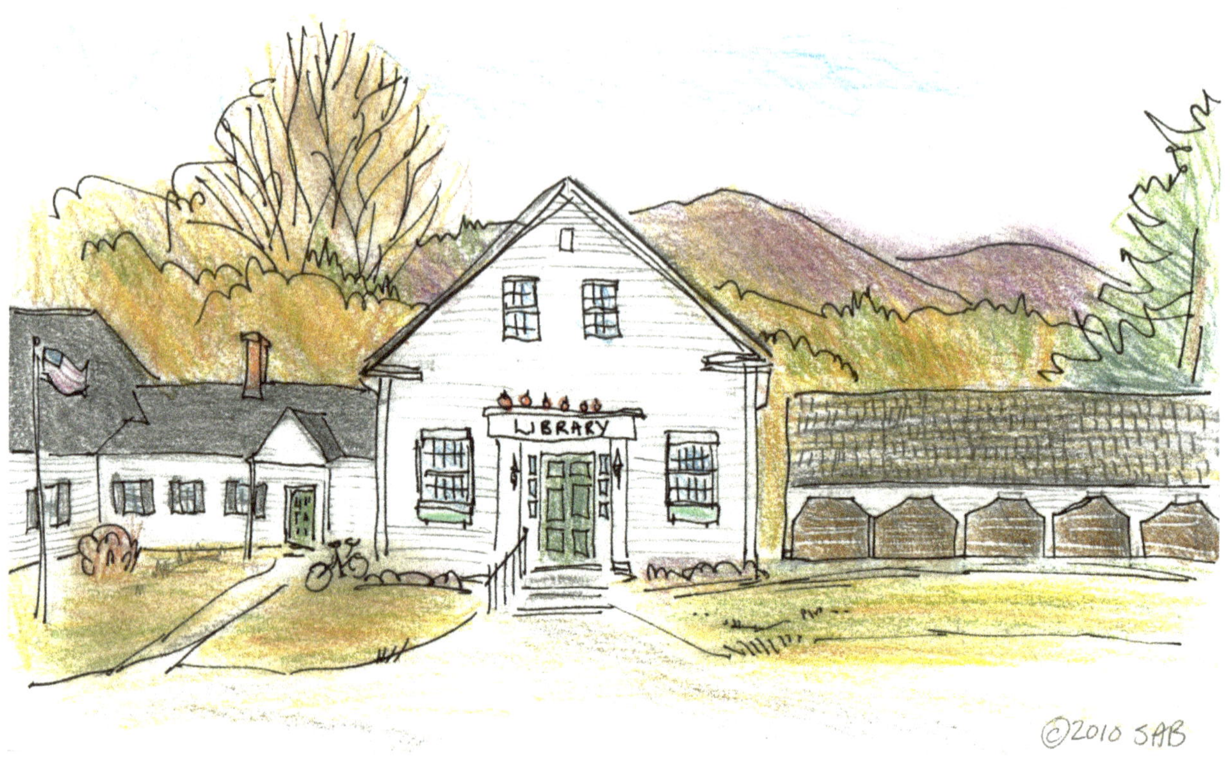

Wilmot was formed in 1807 from parts of New London. Their fine town library with a very active director and programs is attached to the town hall, seen at the far left of the drawing, while Bog Mountain is off in the distance.

The old horse stalls remain from past times. The First Congregational Church, next to the library, was recently lifted off of its original foundation and provided with a brand new one.

Wilmot Flat is another village in the town, where the post office and the community center sit opposite the Wilmot Baptist Church. All the residents have a fine view of majestic Mount Kearsarge.

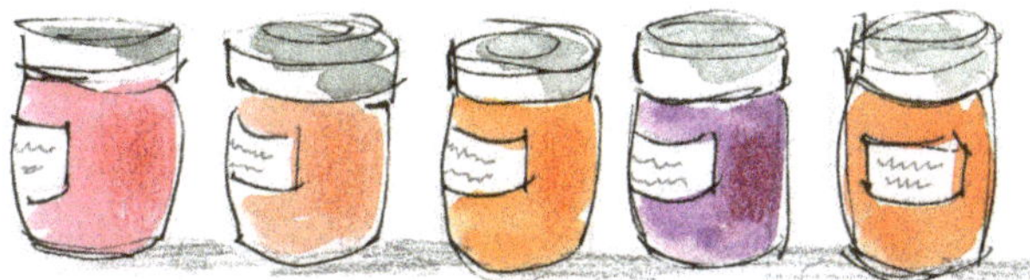
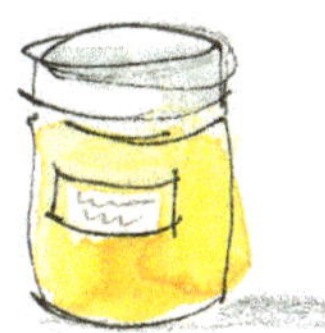

Lakes Region

ALEXANDRIA

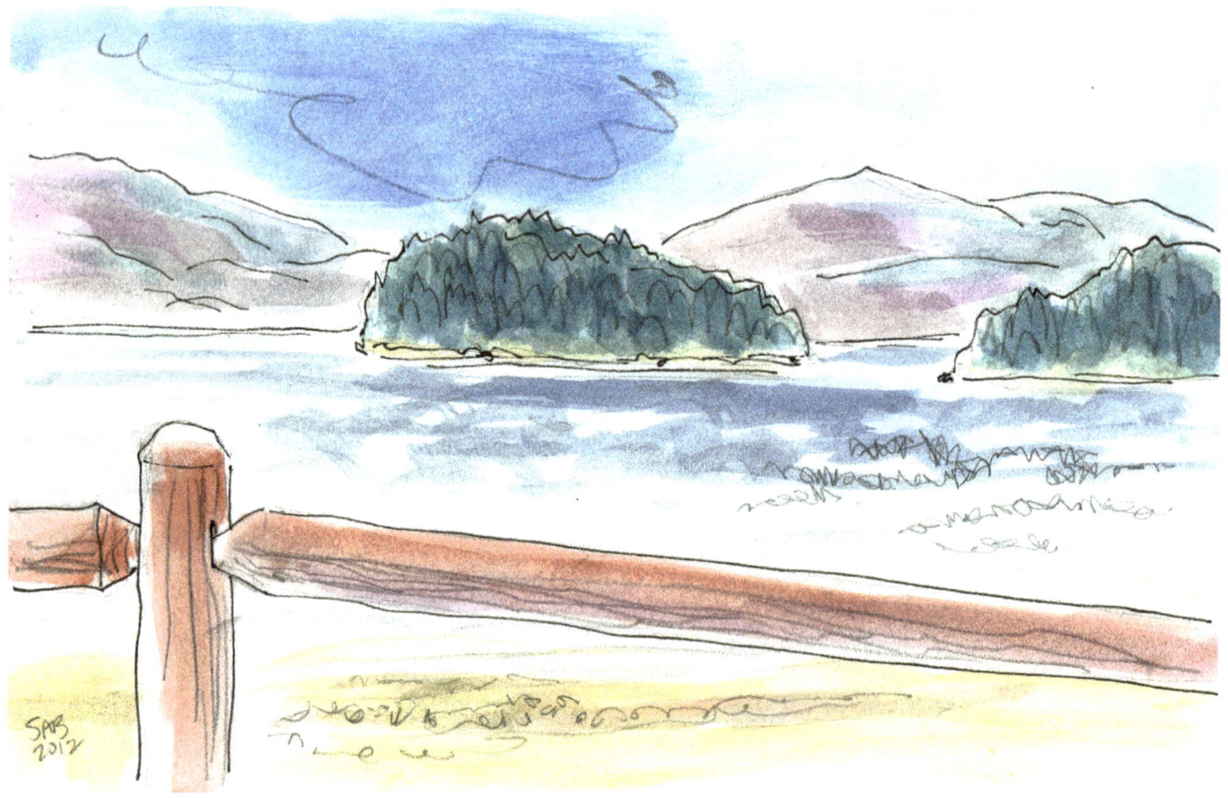

First settled in 1769, the town was named for Alexandria, Virginia.

The northwest edge of the town borders Newfound Lake. The day I drew this, the blue waters were clear of winter's ice except for this eastern end of the lake. The strong wind and wave action had broken up the ice into tiny pieces, all uniform in size, sparkling like diamonds, and floating on the waves like a blanket of jewels.

Alexandria is home to Cardigan Lodge, an Appalachian Mountain Club facility.

ALTON

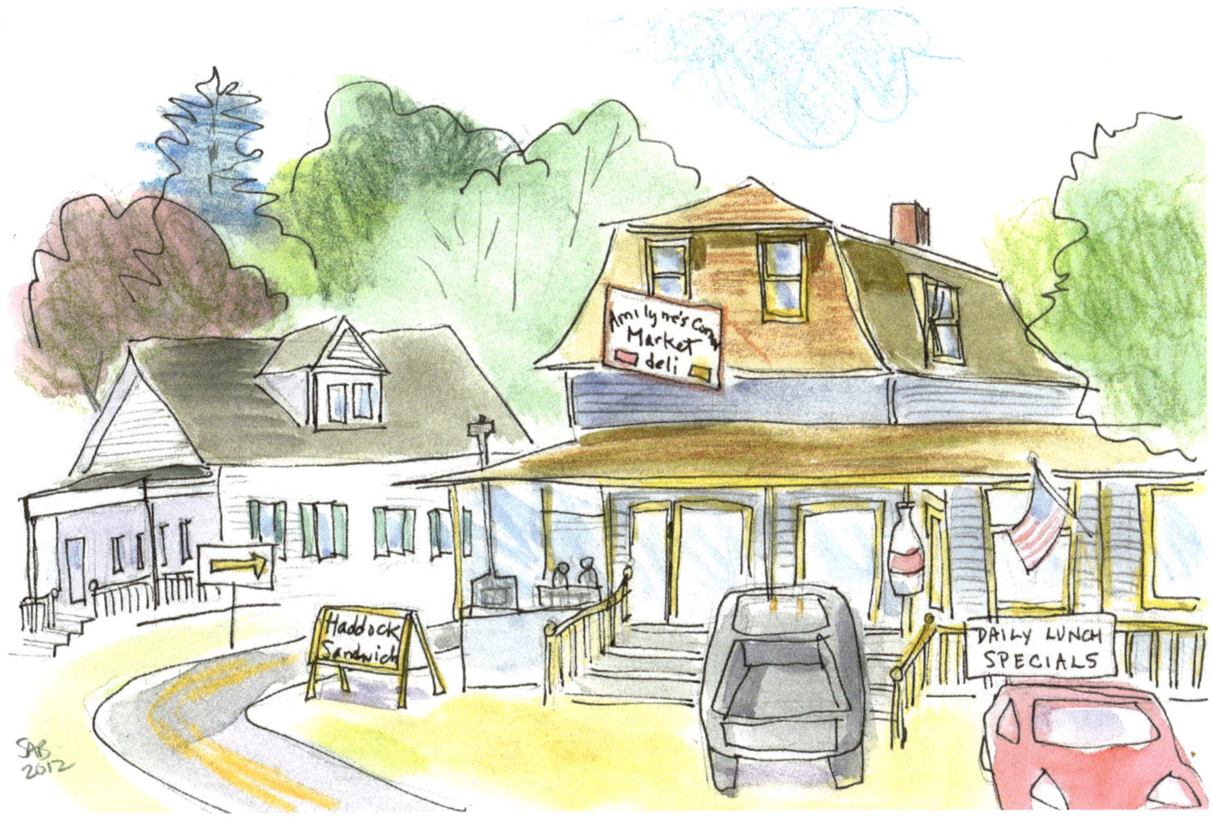

Alton's community center is in the old railroad station.

Alton Bay is at the southernmost end of the large Lake Winnipesaukee. The roads fork here, going up both sides of the lake.

In the bend of the western road is this Victorian era building, Amilyne's Corner Market. Earlier known as Busy Corner Store, it was then owned by my husband's aunt and uncle. Hundreds of motorcyclists were passing in front of me as I drew this. It was Bike Week and a real exercise in concentration. I considered drawing the motorcycles, but it's hard to draw a blur.

ASHLAND

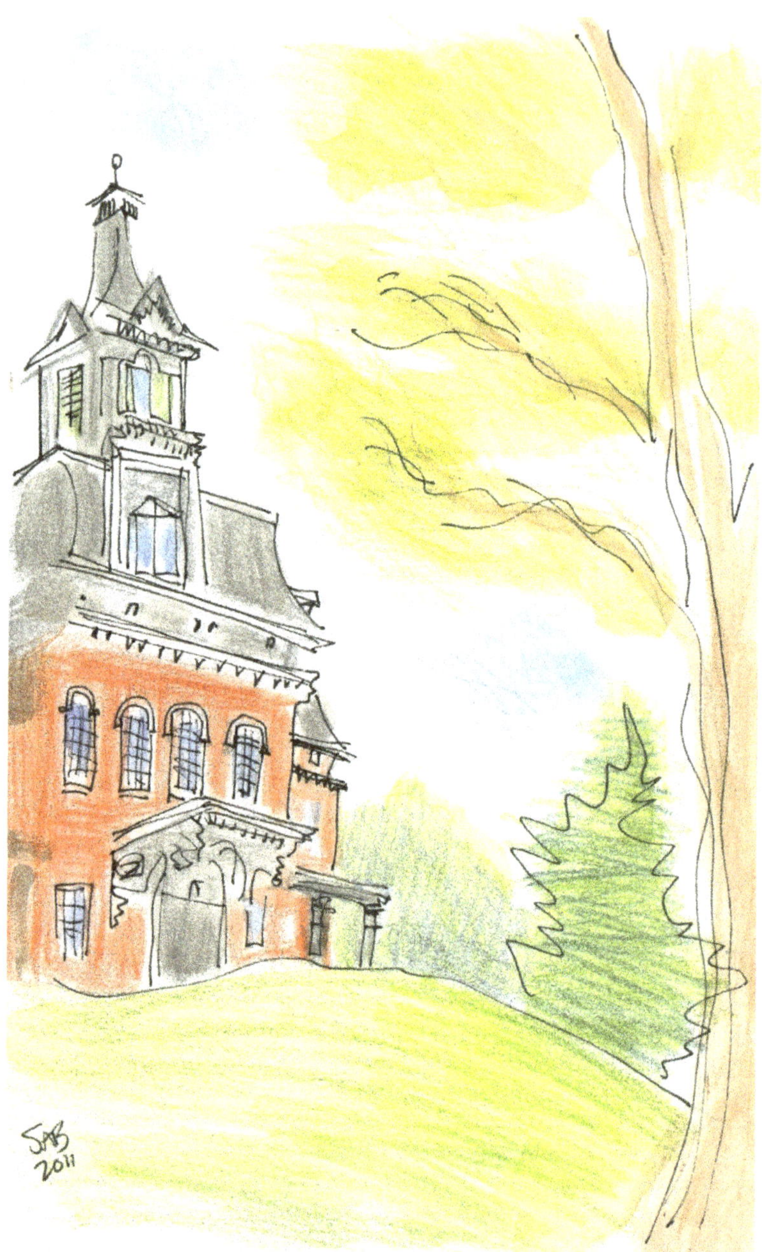

The Squam River drops 112 feet here, and the water power ran the mills to produce hosiery, gloves, wood products, and paper.

The former Grammar School, 1878, sits on a high hill, and is a Victorian Era gem. Now renovated, it awaits new owners. My father had his first teaching job in a high school next door. That building has been razed. Although only four when I lived here in town, I remember the five and dime store down the street. The counters were so low that I could see all the assortments of lipsticks, frilly handkerchiefs, and clip-on pearl earrings.

The original Common Man Restaurant is on Main Street. Common Man has become a well regarded major chain in New Hampshire.

BARNSTEAD

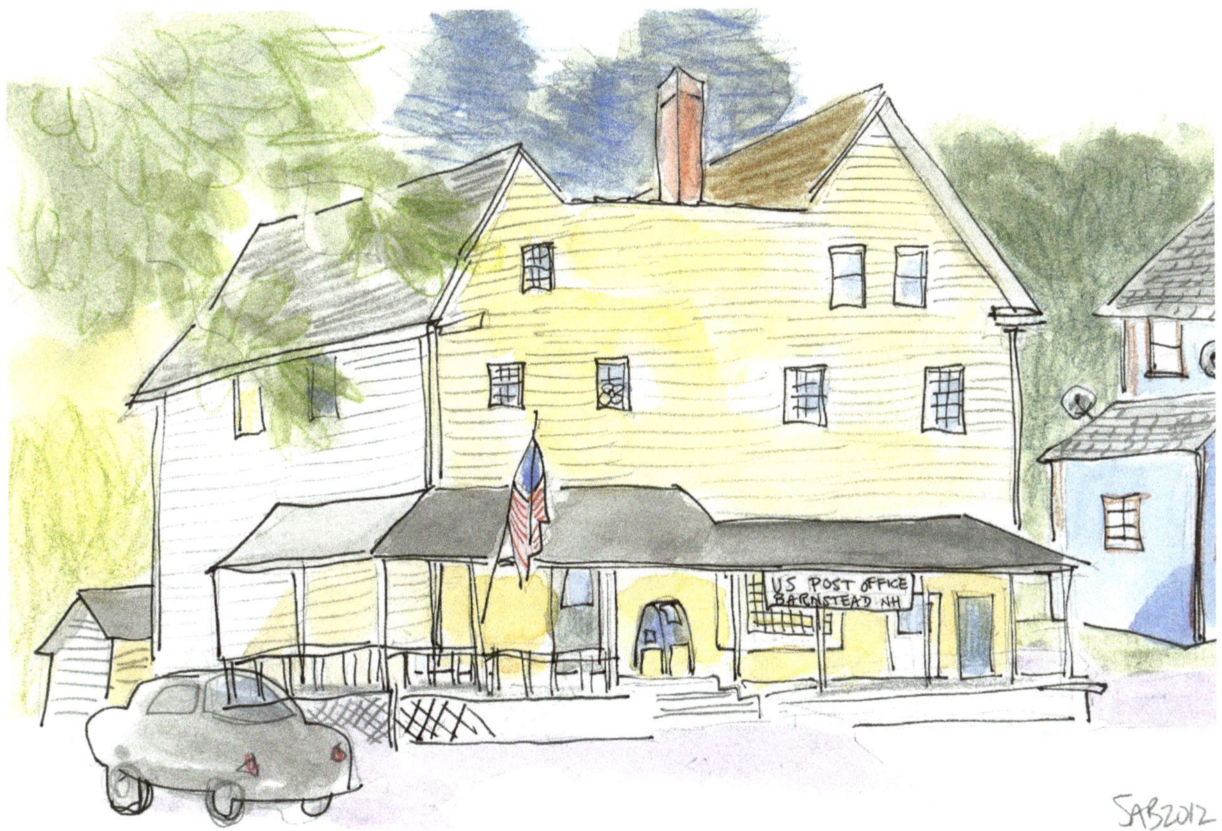

The Barnstead Post Office faces the town common, called the Parade, which is where the militia drilled.

The first settlers to Barnstead came from Barnstable, Massachusetts and Hampstead, New York in 1767, and they cleverly combined the two names.

The villages in town are Center Barnstead, Barnstead Parade, and South Barnstead. The land was good for agriculture, and the town was part of the sheep boom of the early 1800s. In 1830, it is said that 2,500 sheep roamed the hills and fields here. Mills proliferated along the Suncook River.

BARRINGTON

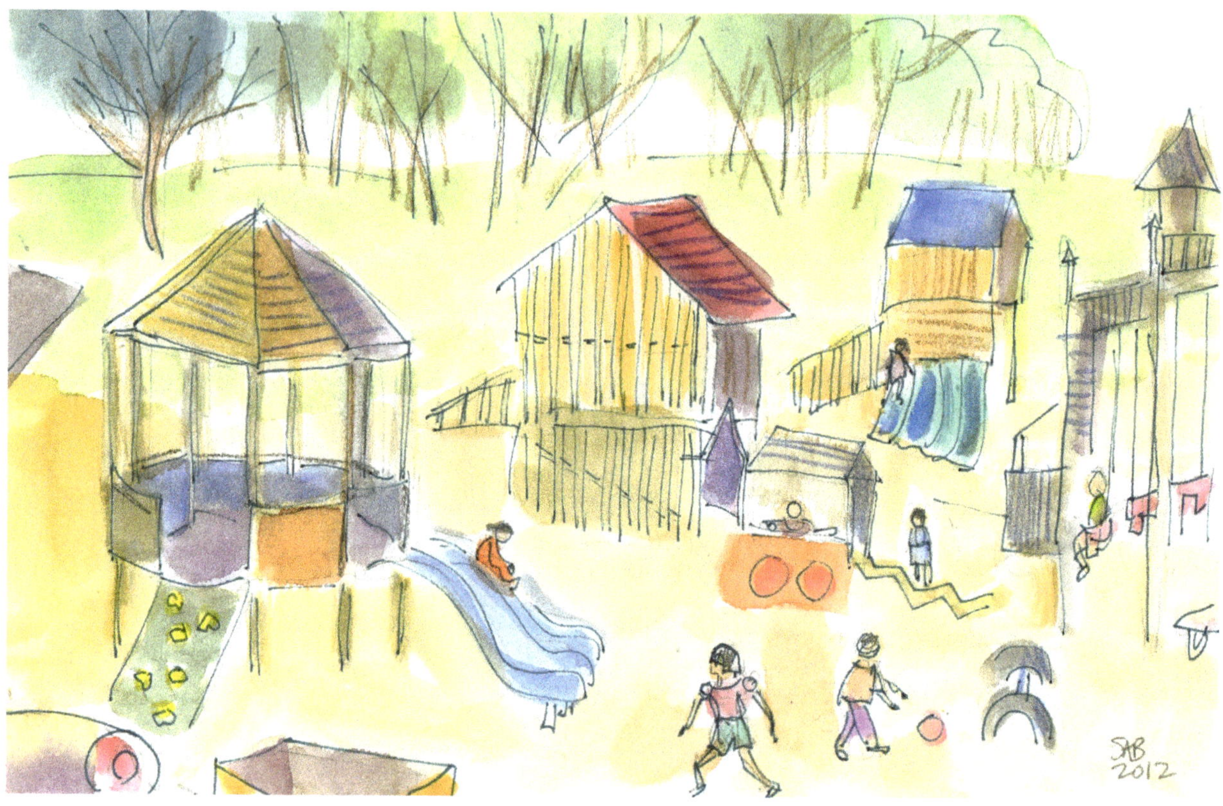

The Barrington Community Playground is a busy place. There were several parents there, supervising and having a Saturday afternoon chat.

I chose to just draw the children. The kids were enjoying the fun, adventure style, playground.

Barrington was incorporated in 1722 and named for a colonial governor of Massachusetts and New Hampshire. By 1810, it was the state's third largest town in population, and well known for its iron ore smelting.

Barrington lost half of its land when Strafford became a separate town.

BELMONT

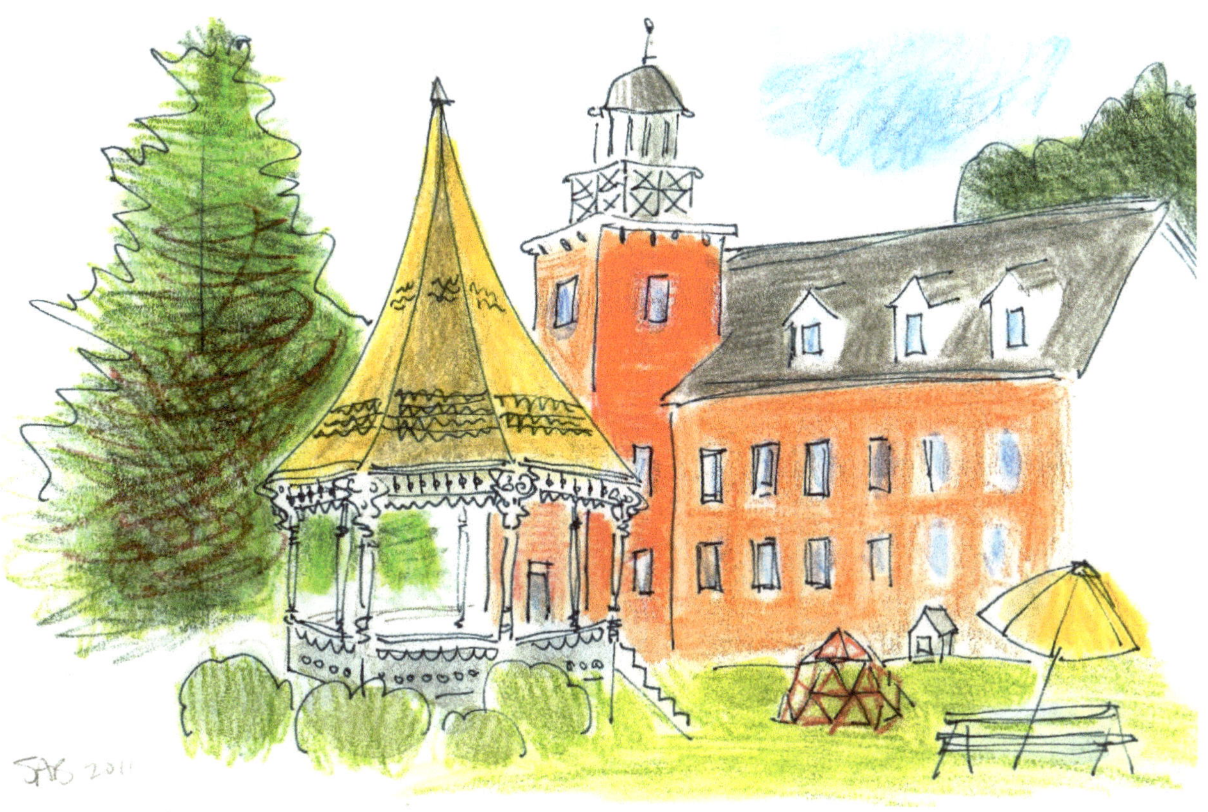

There are four Belmonts in New England. Reuse of town names is common here, often tracing to migration and settlement patterns.

Belmont is right in the center of the state. The mill building in the background, once the Belmont Hosiery Company, is now a community center and preschool. The children were called indoors before I could think of including them in the sketch.

New Hampshire is full of brick mills that have been repurposed to new uses. In the foreground is a very intricate bandstand, with lace-like white wooden trim and fancy patterns in the shingled roof.

BRIDGEWATER

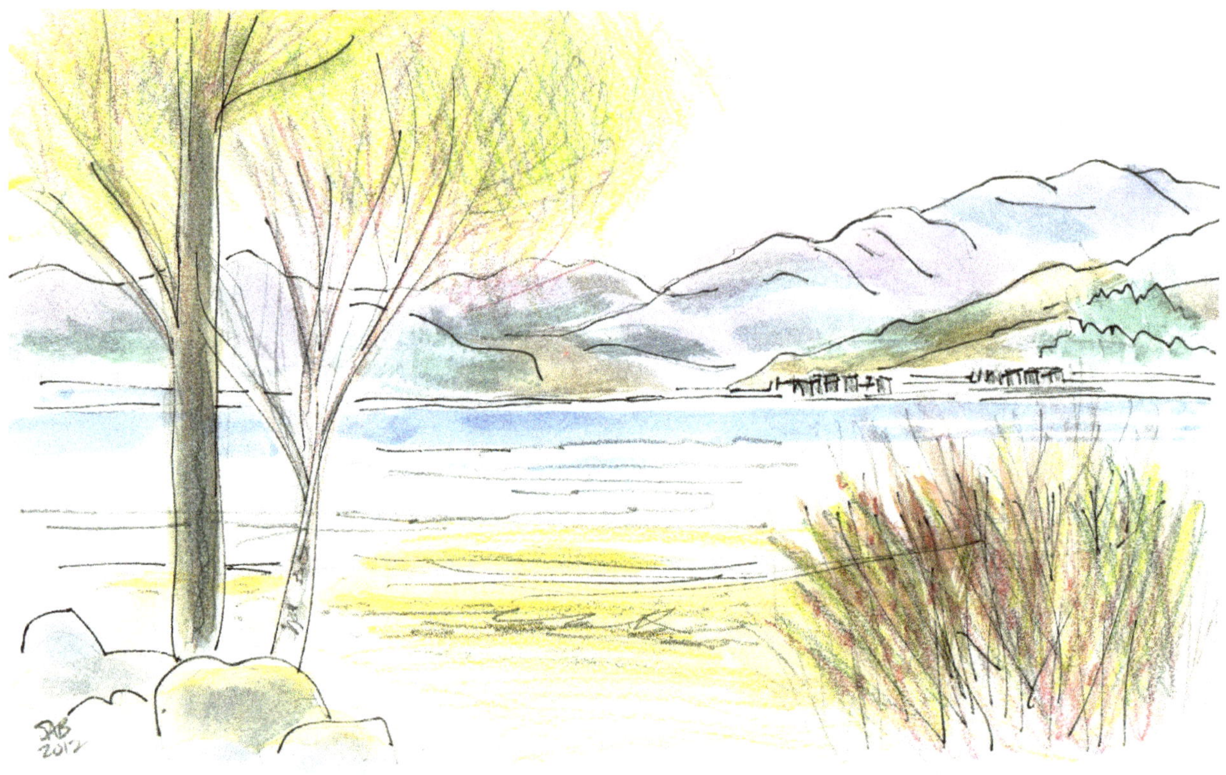

New Chester was the original name of this town. The land was later broken up into the towns of Bridgewater, Bristol, Hill, Danbury, and Wilmot.

This view looks west from the shores of Newfound Lake. The last remnants of the winter's ice were floating on the waves. The soft purple shades of the hills in the early spring are very appealing. New leaves are still tucked away, waiting and being cautious. Pines, firs, and hemlocks make a variety of green tones.

Starting at Route 3A in Bridgewater, take a drive around beautiful Newfound Lake.

BRISTOL

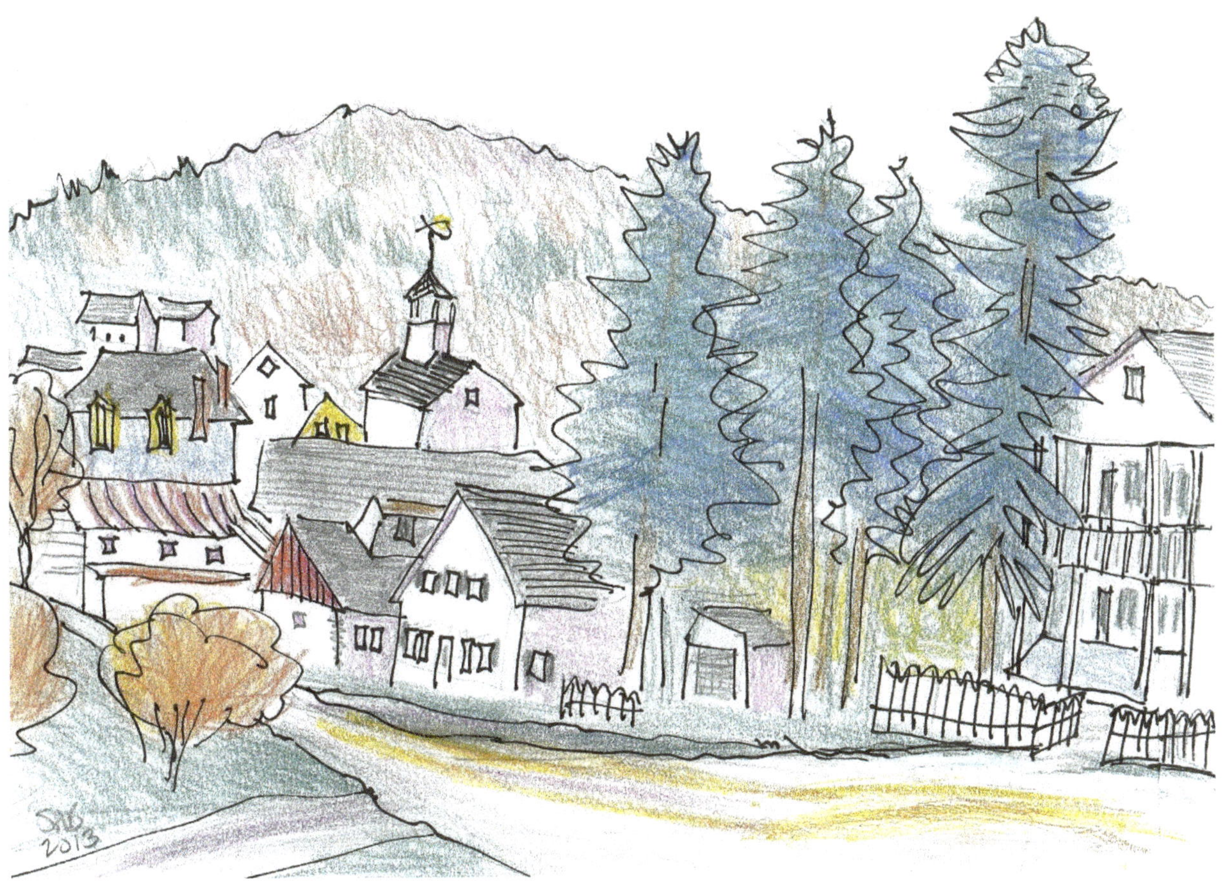

The Minot-Sleeper Library has a very nice new addition, a twin to the original building.

Bristol was settled in 1770 by Colonel Peter Sleeper and others. Its land includes the southern two thirds of Newfound Lake.

The name was chosen because the town has rich deposits of fine sand, like those found in Bristol, England. This product was used to manufacture bricks, called Bristol Bricks. I made a return trip to Bristol to capture the scene after the extensive redesign of the main square. South Main Street has a great view of the village, the background hills, as well as the homes and very tall evergreen trees near the old fire station.

BROOKFIELD

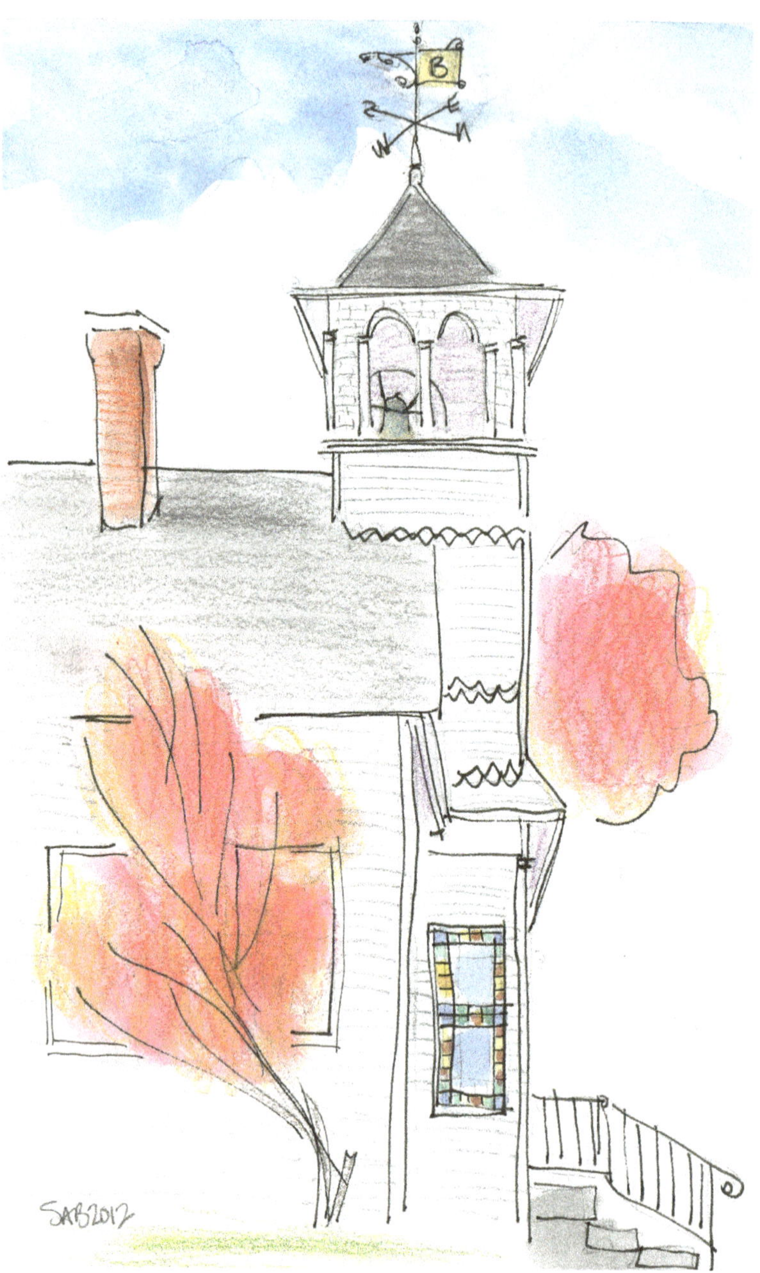

Brookfield, first called Coleraine, had a population of 712 in the 2010 census, with an area of 23.3 square miles (60 sq km).

Within the woodlands of this town run 136 miles of stone walls, which line the former agricultural fields of the 19th century. The Brookfield town house was built in 1915. As we drove up and parked, I looked to my right. No need to search for the best angle this time. The leaded glass window, wrought iron railing, and two gloriously colored trees made the perfect scene.

The ornate weather vane with the letter B cut out of the metal was a fine topper for the bell tower.

CENTER HARBOR

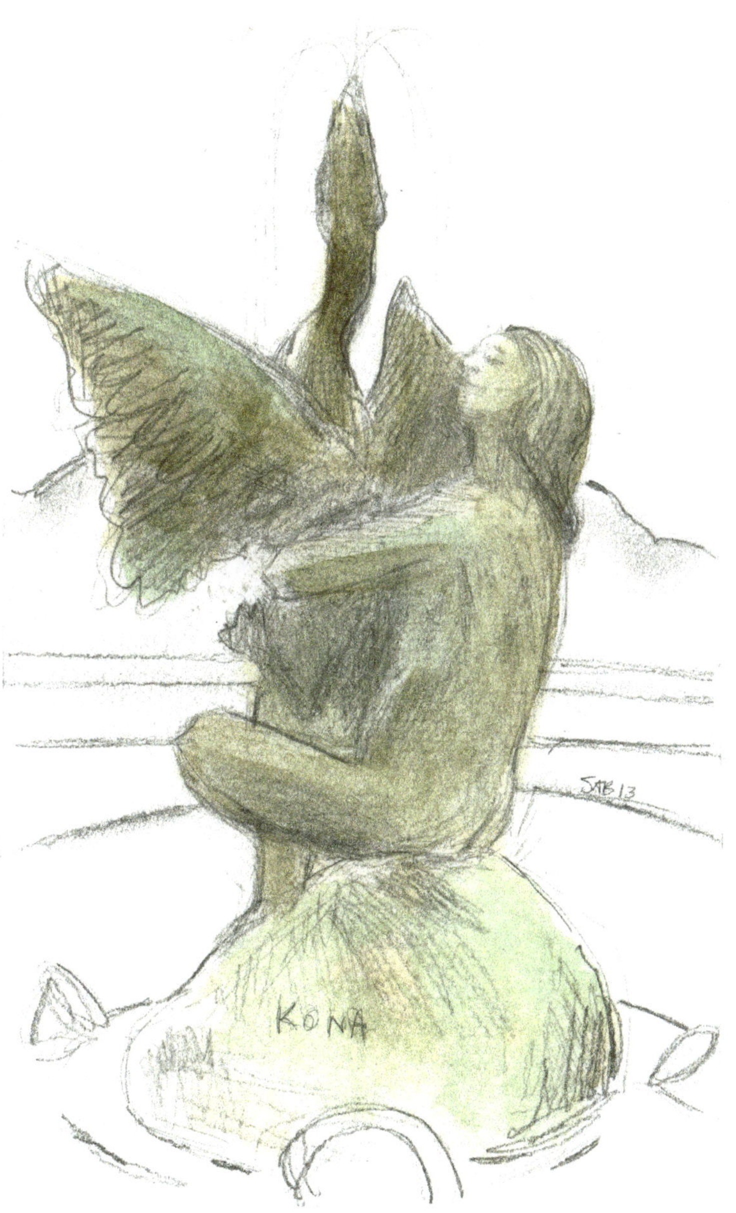

Center Harbor was a part of New Hampton until 1797. Its location close to water and mountains has made it a long time popular resort. The number of people in the area multiplies by seven during the summer months.

A fountain with a statue of an Indian boy and a goose stands in the middle of a busy intersection, a water trough for horses surrounding its base. The artist was S. Russell Gerry Crook, a student of Augustus Saint Gaudens, America's premier sculptor. Finished in 1907, it is dedicated to the cause of animals who need our help.

Center Harbor is the winter port of the M/S Mt. Washington, and "Ice Out" is officially declared when the Mt. Washington can make its first springtime circuit of the lake.

EATON

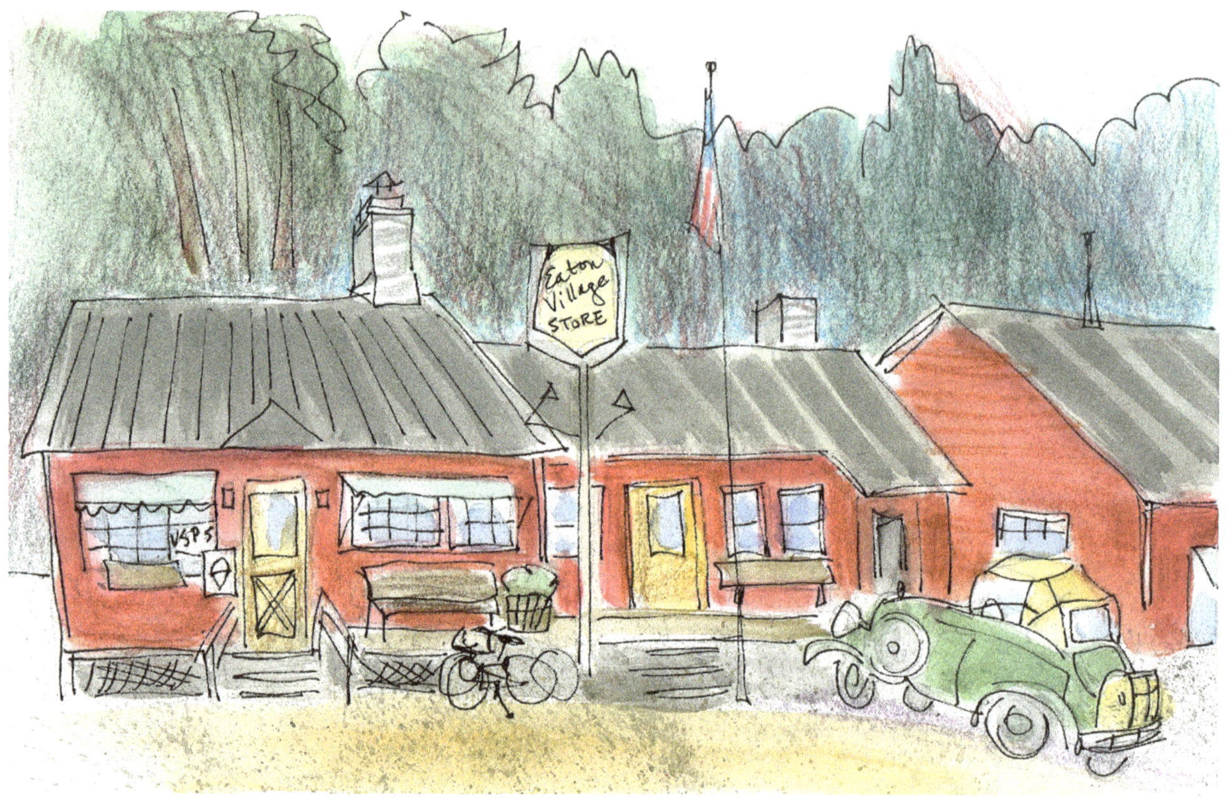

Eaton is a small town, with a population of only 400 people. Recently, the residents worked together and saved their village store. And they painted it 'barn red' again.

It houses the post office, a grocery store, and a restaurant. As soon as I started my drawing, a fine antique car pulled up. I sketched the car first, as there was no telling how long it was going to be posing for me. Luckily, it did stay put the whole time.

The Little White Church on Crystal Lake is a local landmark.

EFFINGHAM

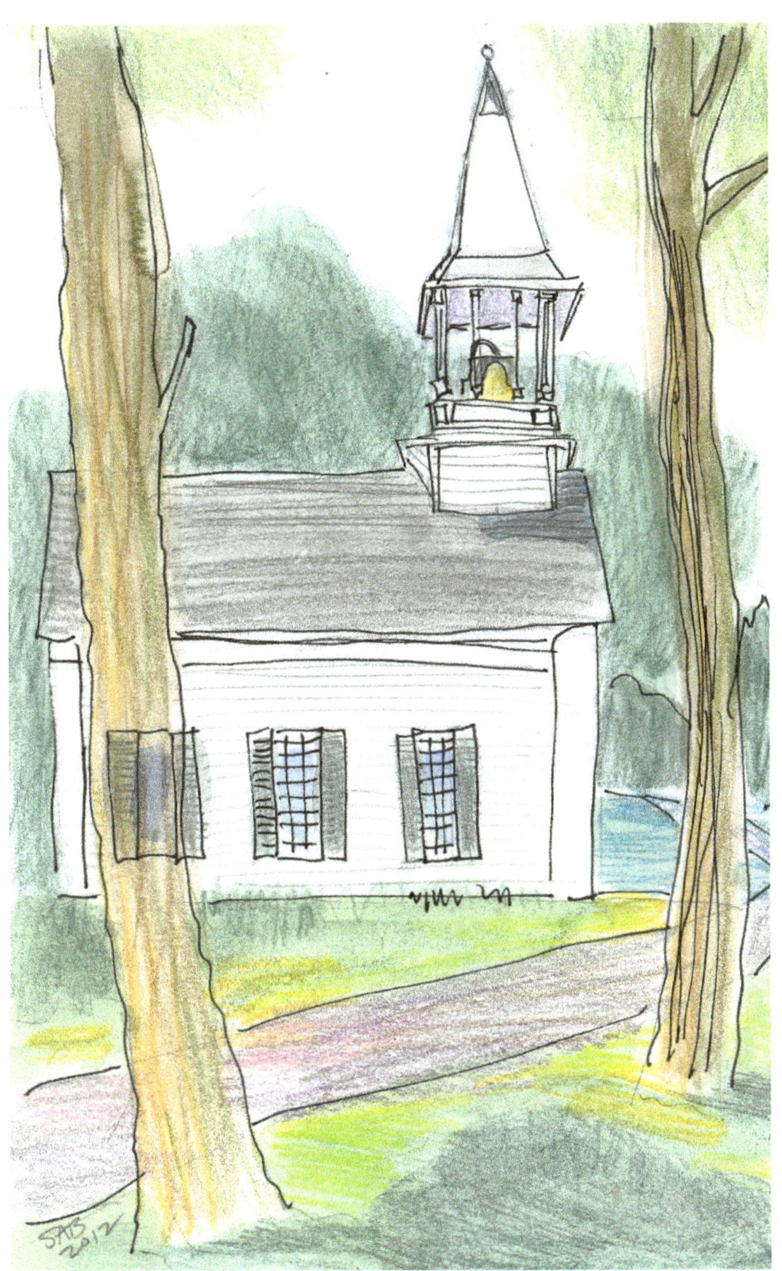

The town, named for the Howard family, the Earls of Effingham, England, was incorporated in 1778.

The villages are Effingham, Effingham Falls, Center Effingham, and South Effingham. The first 'normal school' in New Hampshire was started on the second floor of the Effingham Union Academy Building. A normal school trained teachers, who then trained the students to the norms or academic expectations.

The Effingham meetinghouse boasts a Paul Revere bell.

FARMINGTON

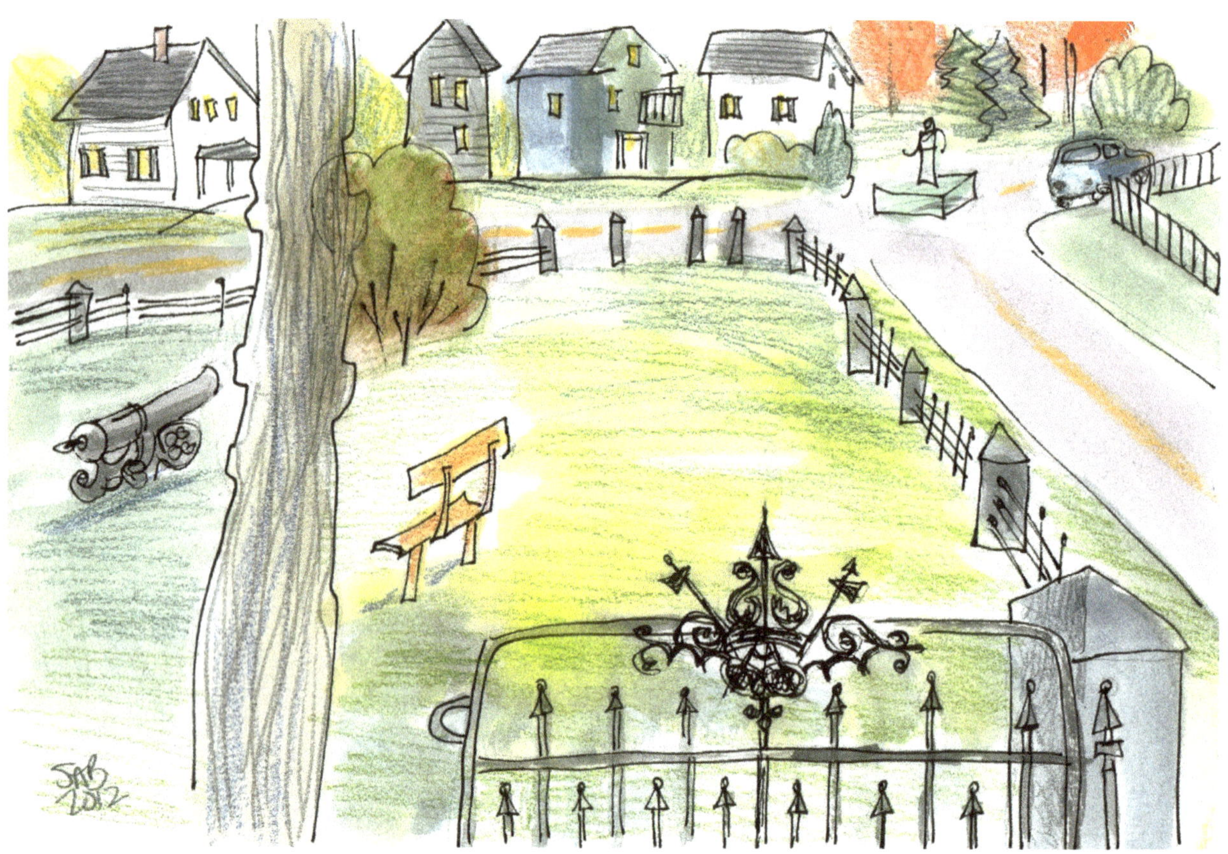

Originally the town was called Northwest Parish of Rochester. In 1800 Farmington was incorporated and a meetinghouse was built.

Initially I was attracted to the cast iron gate in the James Edgerly Park. It says "buckeye" and "patent" on it. My plan was to draw just the gate; then that plan expanded to all the fencing. Then I became interested in the bench, the tree, and the cannon. And then the road, the houses, and the green water pump in the middle of the intersection. Lastly, I inked in the little blue car where my husband was waiting for me.

Farmington and its mills were once known as "The Shoe Capital" of New Hampshire.

FREEDOM

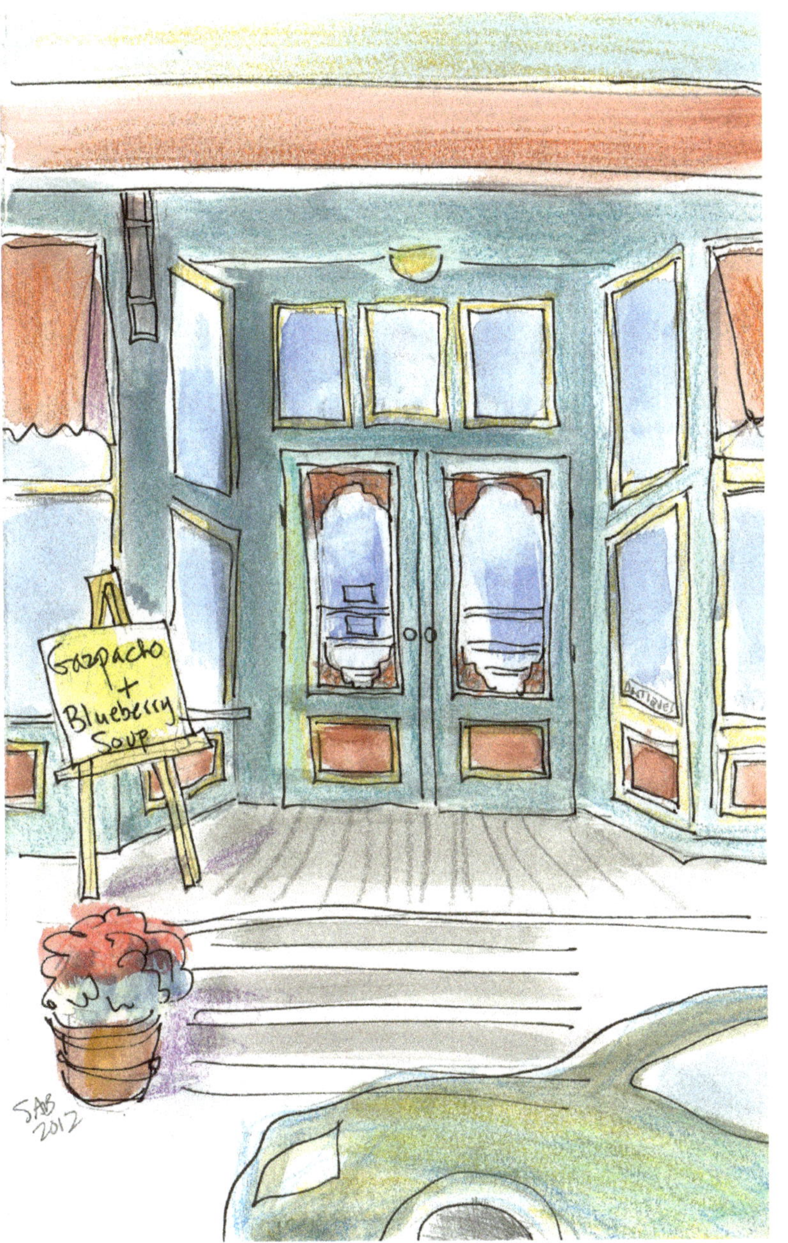

The Freedom Village Store was saved by the local residents.

Constructed about a century ago in the Victorian era, it thrived for a long time, and then went empty and forlorn. In 2009 the store was reopened as a non-profit space. It is a true community center, with food and art. And coffee, and on this day, gazpacho and also blueberry soup.

The quiet little town borders the state of Maine. Popular Ossipee Lake is in the southwest part of town.

The town of Freedom took its name when it broke away from Effingham, the town to the south.

GILFORD

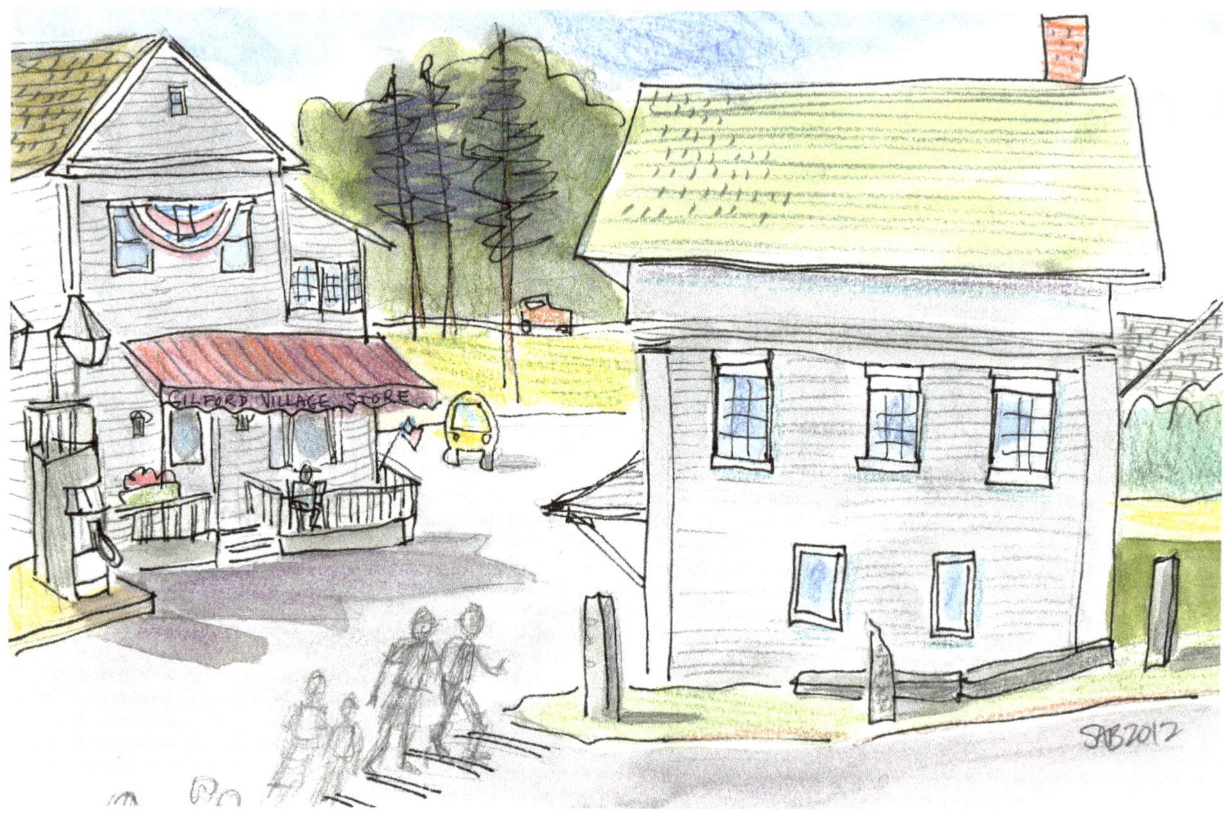

Gilford, first settled in 1778, was originally a part of Gilmanton called Gunstock Parish. Its current name commemorates the Revolutionary War battle of Guilford Court House in North Carolina.

School had just resumed in September when I drew this. I could not help but hear the conversations among the children as they walked home. It was pleasant to listen to their chatter as the drawing progressed.

Almost 30% of the town is water, the beautiful Lake Winnipesaukee.

GILMANTON

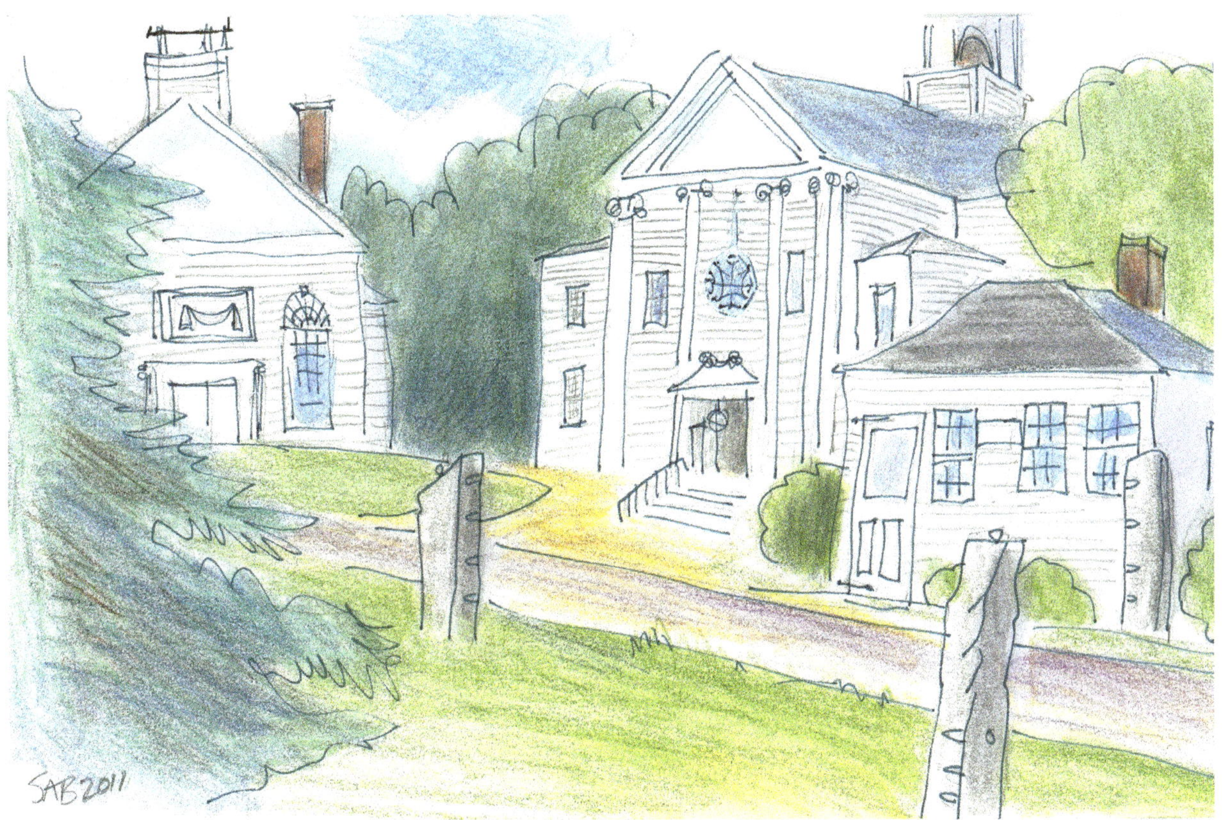

The town moved an antique barn from North Hampton and renovated it to become the new Gilmanton Year Round Library.

New Hampshire Routes 107 and 140 meet in Gilmanton Center. The tallest building in the center is the home of the town offices, built as the Gilmanton Academy in 1835.

On the left stands the Gilmanton Community Church, and on the right is Corners Library. Notice the granite pillars along the roadway. Too many to count, they seemed such a part of the place that I had to fit in three. They were once part of a fence. It is the Granite State, after all. Gilmanton Ironworks is a village in the town, although the industry is long gone.

HEBRON

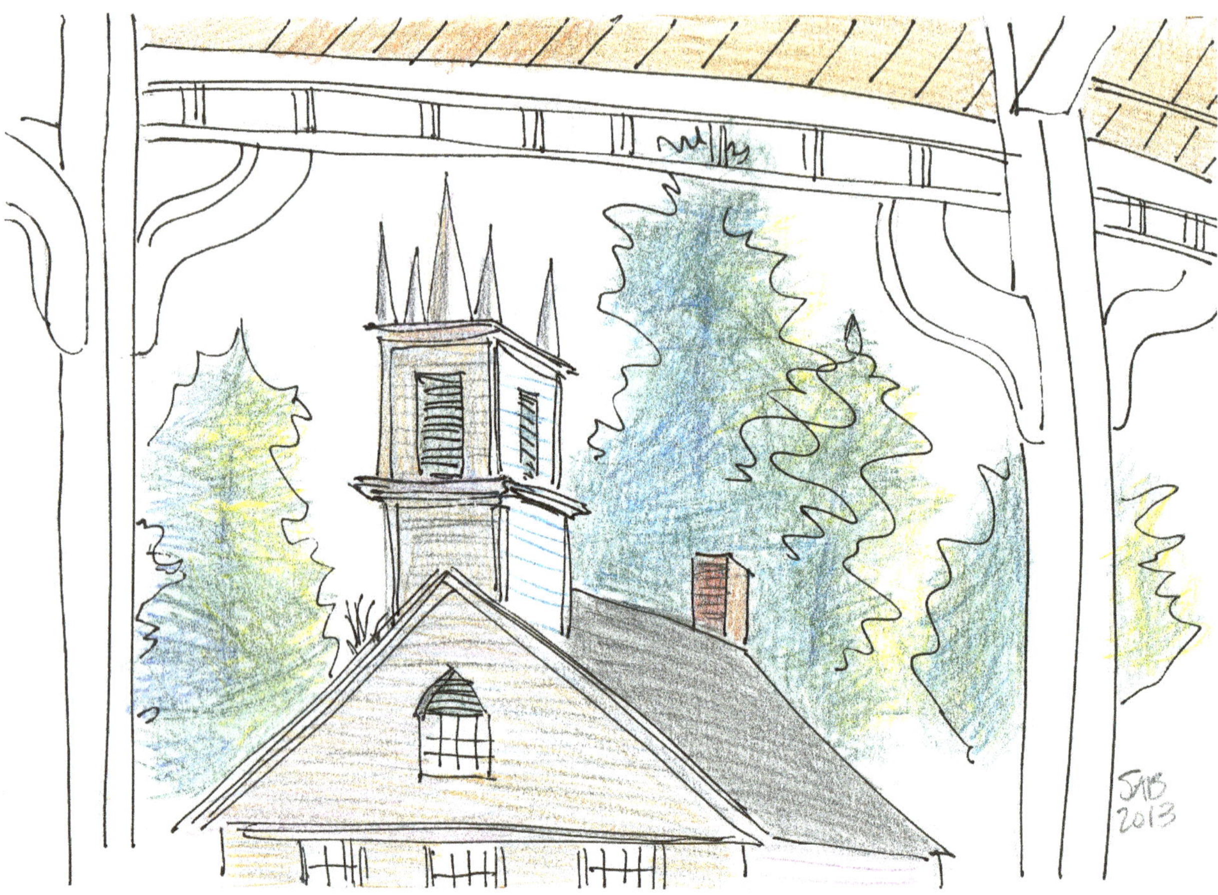

Hebron, at the northern border of Newfound Lake, was formed in 1791 from parts of West Plymouth and Groton.

Hebron common is surrounded by small, white, wooden buildings, including a church and the village store. No building is unusual or large, except for the town offices in the former Hebron Academy, drawn here. But a harmony exists, and there is a pleasant feeling of shelter in the 360 degree configuration of the structures. The Hebron Village Historic District was chosen in 1985 to be listed on the National Register of Historic Places.

The Newfound Audubon Center here, one of five in the state, studies seasonal bird migrations.

HOLDERNESS

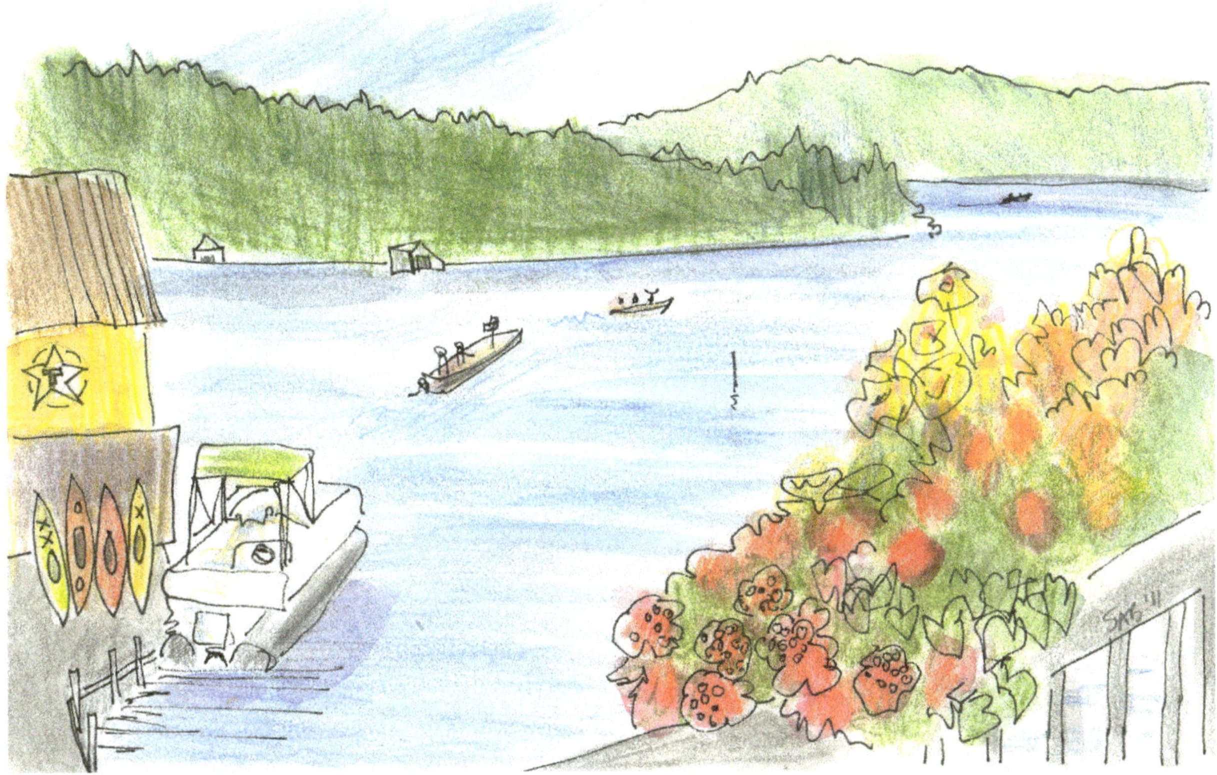

The town is home to the Holderness School and the Squam Lakes Natural Science Center.

The town was settled in 1763, and named after Robert Darcy, the fourth Earl of Holderness.

In 1868, the more commercial and manufacturing section of town separated and became Ashland. As we stood on the bridge overlooking Squam Lake, the bass boats with their hopeful fishermen were heading out, one after another. To secret coves perhaps. The film *On Golden Pond* was filmed on these waters. The local garden club has found a way to beautify the bridge with charming flower boxes.

LACONIA

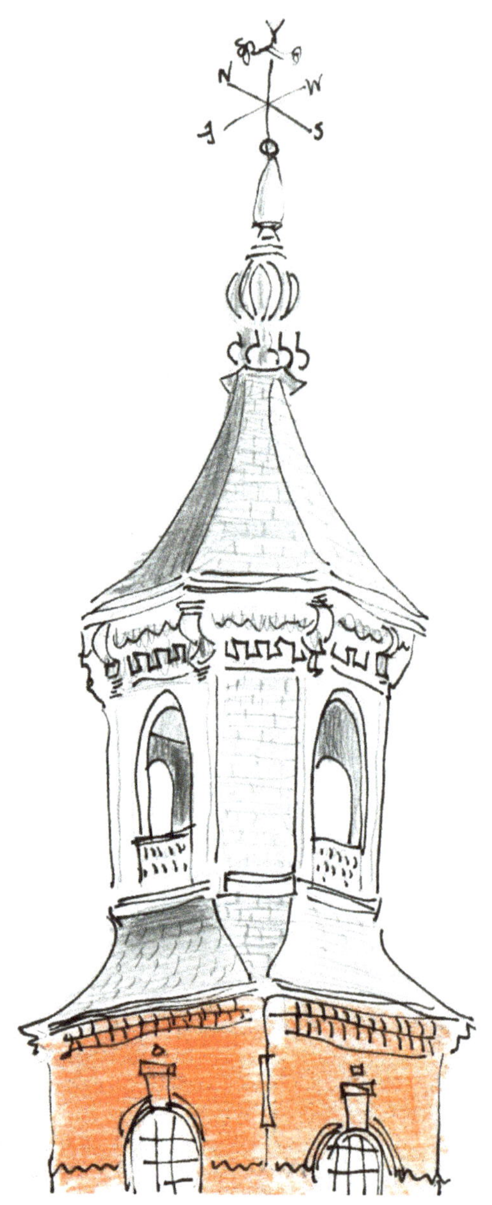

Laconia was settled in 1761 and was first called Meredith Bridge.

It includes the settlements of Lakeport and Weirs Beach. The Abenaki tribes had fishing nets, sometimes called weirs, at this location. The town is nicely situated between Lake Winnipesaukee and Winnisquam Lake.

The handsome brick and white trimmed tower of the Busiel Mill was a fine subject on a blue sky day. The adjacent Belknap Mill is now a great museum of the hosiery industry and staffed by knowledgeable guides. The town also manufactured rail, trolley, and subway cars at the Laconia Car Company.

Every June, Laconia hosts the popular "Bike Week" (motorcycle).

MADISON

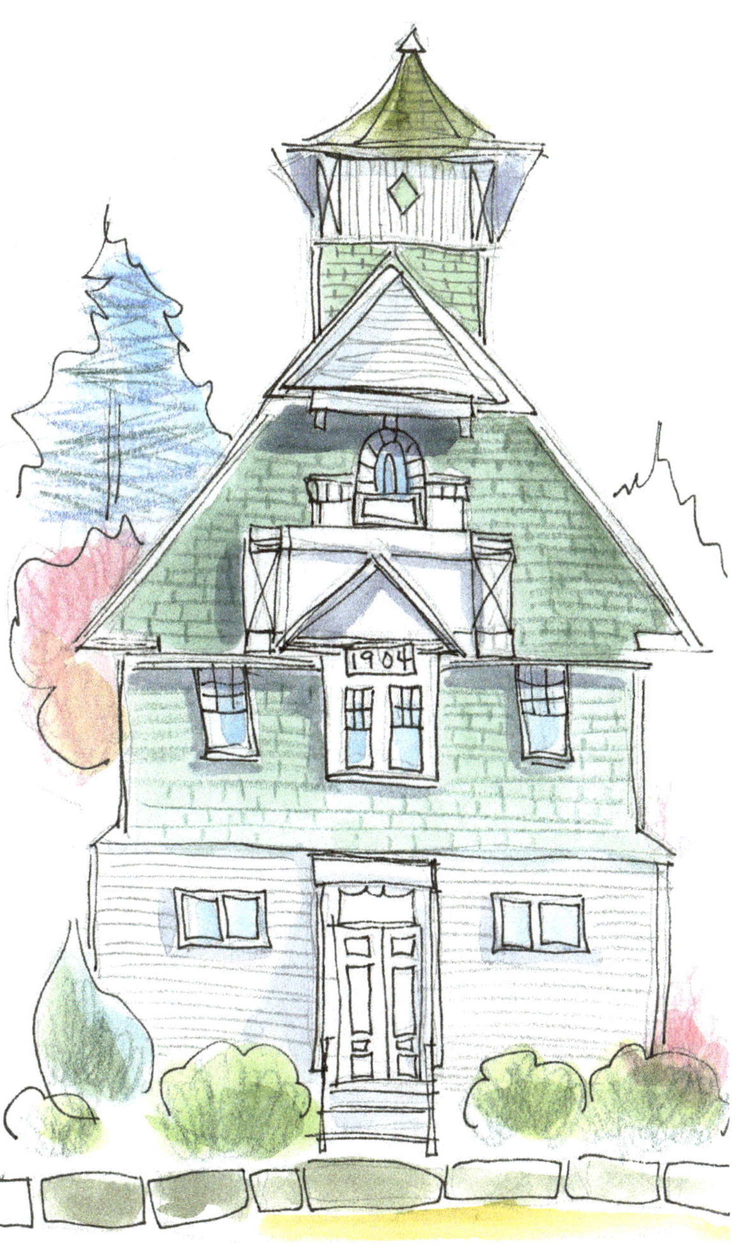

The look of the town offices and police station on the hill is appealing. Although unusually tall for Craftsman style, the wooden façade, shingles, and small and varied window shapes give it away.

This building was moved to the site. Ox teams, heavy-duty sleds, and helping hands were readily available to move buildings on snow-packed roads in the winter time, and this was much more affordable than employing a master carpenter to design and construct a brand new building.

Madison is well known for its enormous, erratic, glacial boulder in its own state park.

MEREDITH

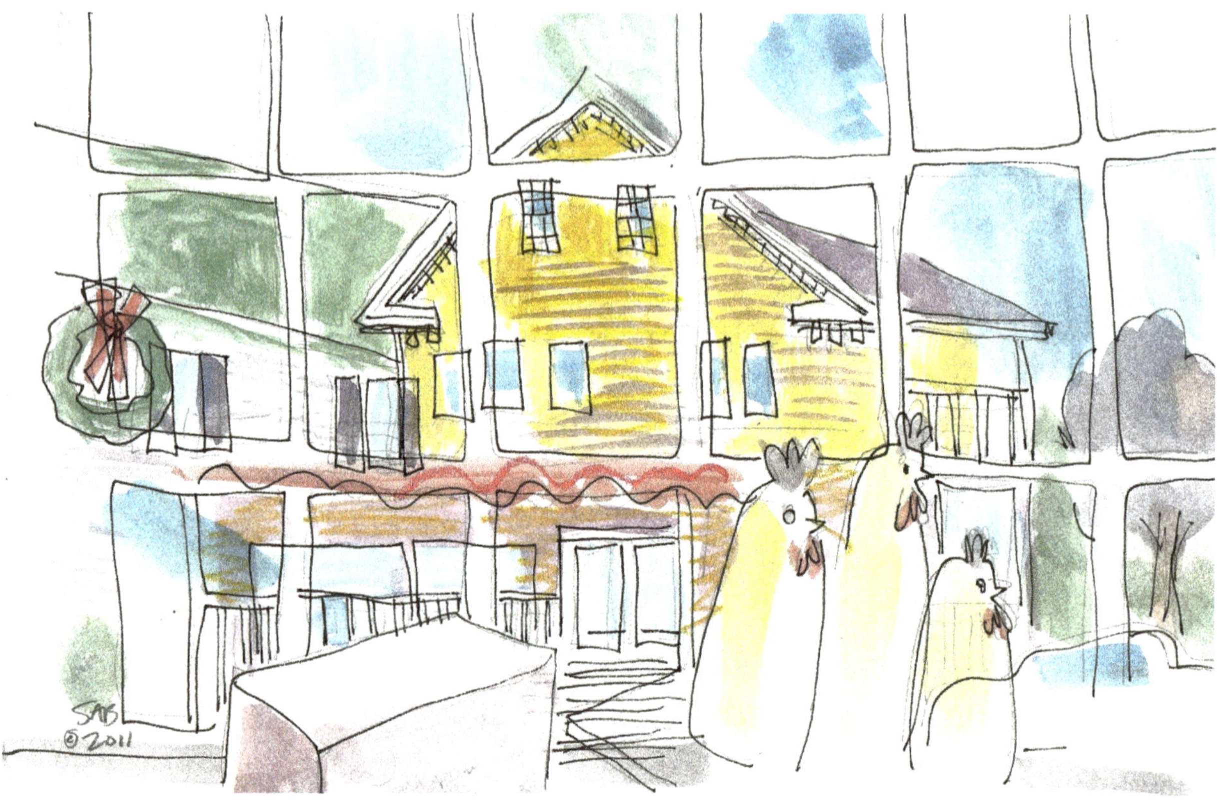

In 1849, when the railroad connected the town to the outer world, the summer resort era began. SS Mt. Washington, a steamboat built in 1872, ferried visitors around Lake Winnipesaukee.

Its modern counterpart still does. And a busy place it is, with a summer theater, children's museum, shops, hotels and restaurants. And plenty of opportunities to rent a canoe, kayak, or paddleboat. I do enjoy drawing through multi-paned windows, in this case a pharmacy turned kitchen supply store. The yellow house across the street is now a café.

Inter-Lakes High School serves the local students of Meredith, Center Harbor, and Sandwich.

MIDDLETON

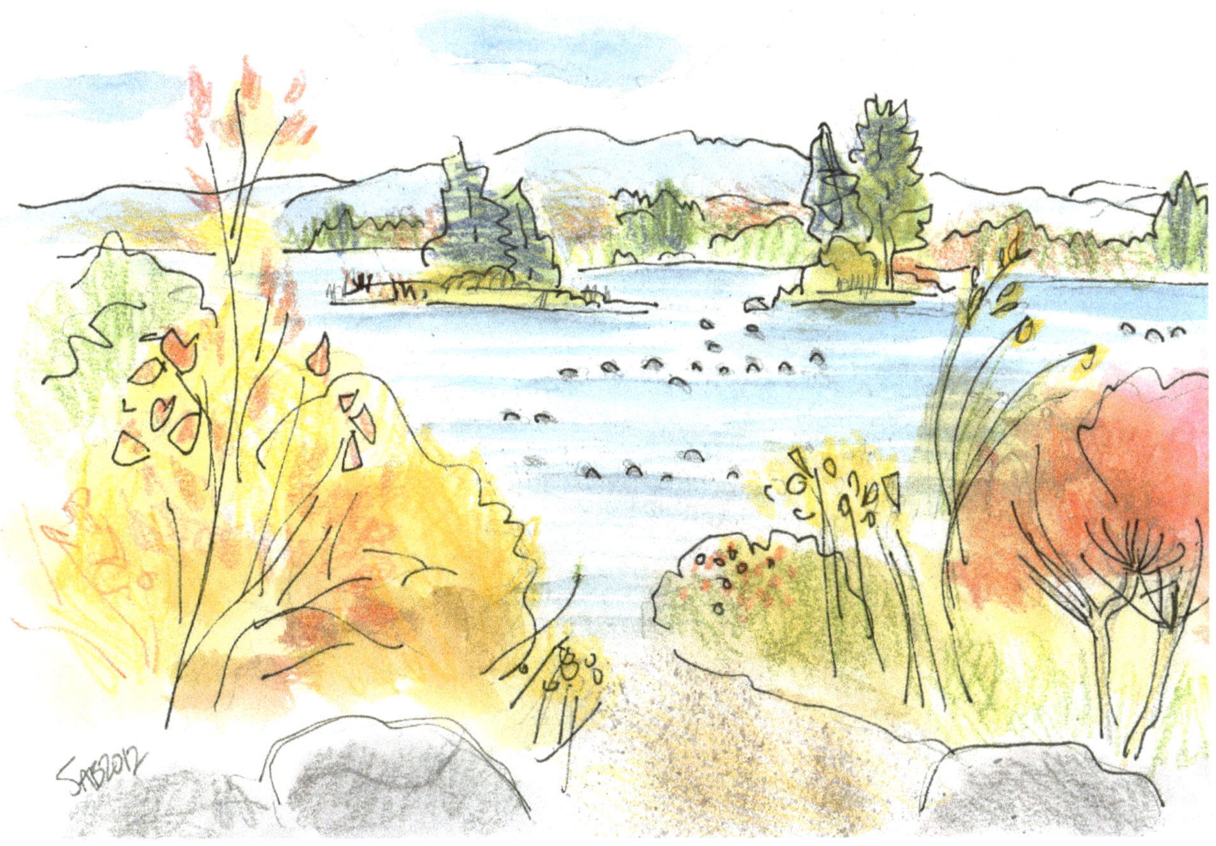

A well beloved 1811 landscape mural in the town hall is carefully maintained and appreciated as folk art.

This view of the lake really caught my eye. Such pretty little islands. And all those small rocks in the water, making quite a parade in Sunrise Lake. The fall leaves were starting to turn yellow, orange, and red.

Middleton was incorporated in 1778, and Brookfield split off six years later. The original settlers came from Lee and Rochester. The history of the town hall is unusual. It was built in 1795 and moved to its current site in 1812. Then it was jacked up, to add another story on the ground floor.

MILTON

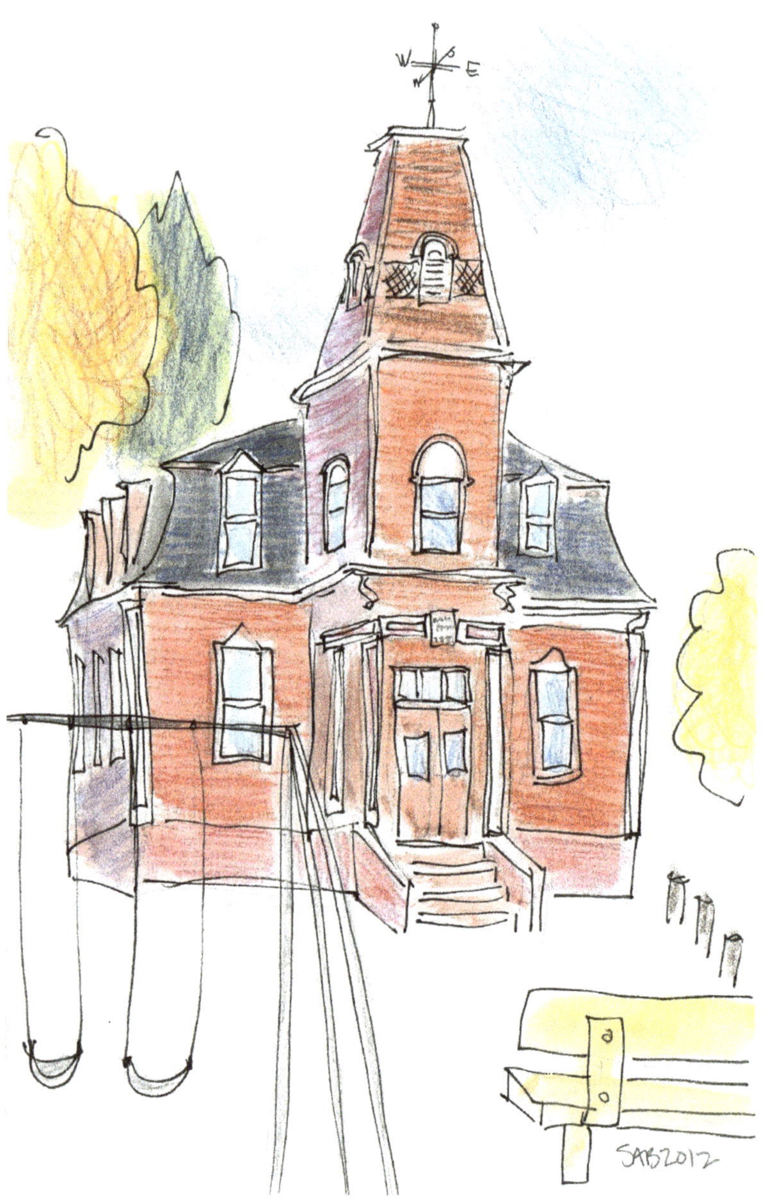

Milton, first a part of Rochester and called Northeast Parish, borders Maine. The mills on the Salmon Falls River manufactured woolen blankets, shoes, carriages, and lumber. And fiberboard lunch boxes and violin cases.

The Milton Free Library in Milton Mills was originally built as a school. This architectural style, imported from France, is called Empire. A social event was wrapping up in the library as we drove into town, and people were streaming out. I thought about including them in the drawing.

Milton is home to the New Hampshire Farm Museum. It occupies an old yellow farmhouse and several barns.

MOULTONBORO

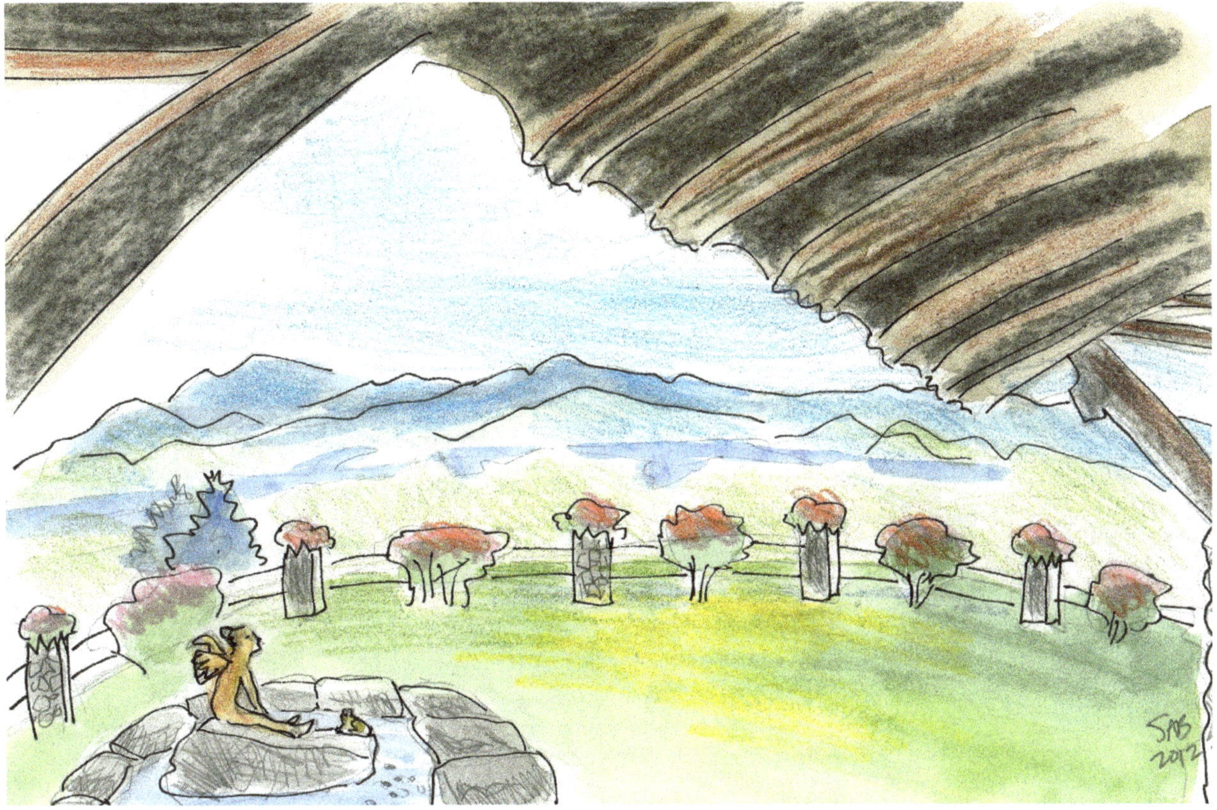

Poets Robert Frost and John Greenleaf Whittier were both summer residents in Moultonboro.

Lucknow is an estate in Moultonboro, sometimes called the 'Castle In The Clouds'. Its home and carriage house were built in 1914 in the American Craftsman style by Thomas Gustave Plant.

Plant made his fortune operating a shoe factory in Massachusetts. The Lucknow estate covers 6,300 acres. Its front garden overlooks all of Lake Winnipesaukee and the mountains beyond. It certainly was a challenge to depict both the foreground with the overhanging roof and small fountain, and the stunning panorama of the lake and beyond. Lucknow is now operated by a very dedicated non-profit group.

NEW DURHAM

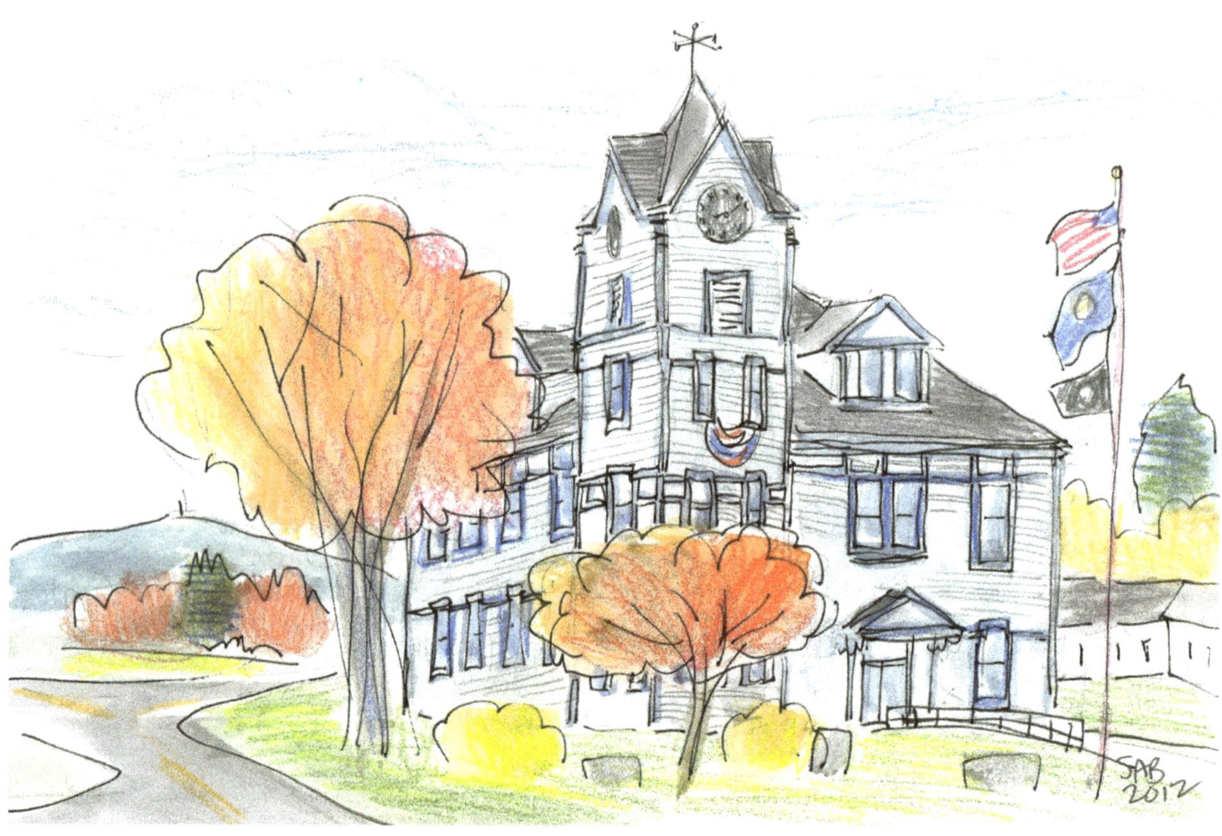

Town halls in New England serve as meeting spaces, voting places, and offices for the town's administrative systems.

New Durham's impressive wooden town hall was built in the 1890s and listed on the National Register of Historic Places in 1980. The New Durham Library is across the street.

The town was settled in 1750 by people from Durham, not that far to the south. Also in town are the Powder Mill Fish Hatchery and the Lions Club Camp Pride.

New Durham's Merrymeeting Lake, such a cheery name, is a habitat for nesting loons.

NEW HAMPTON

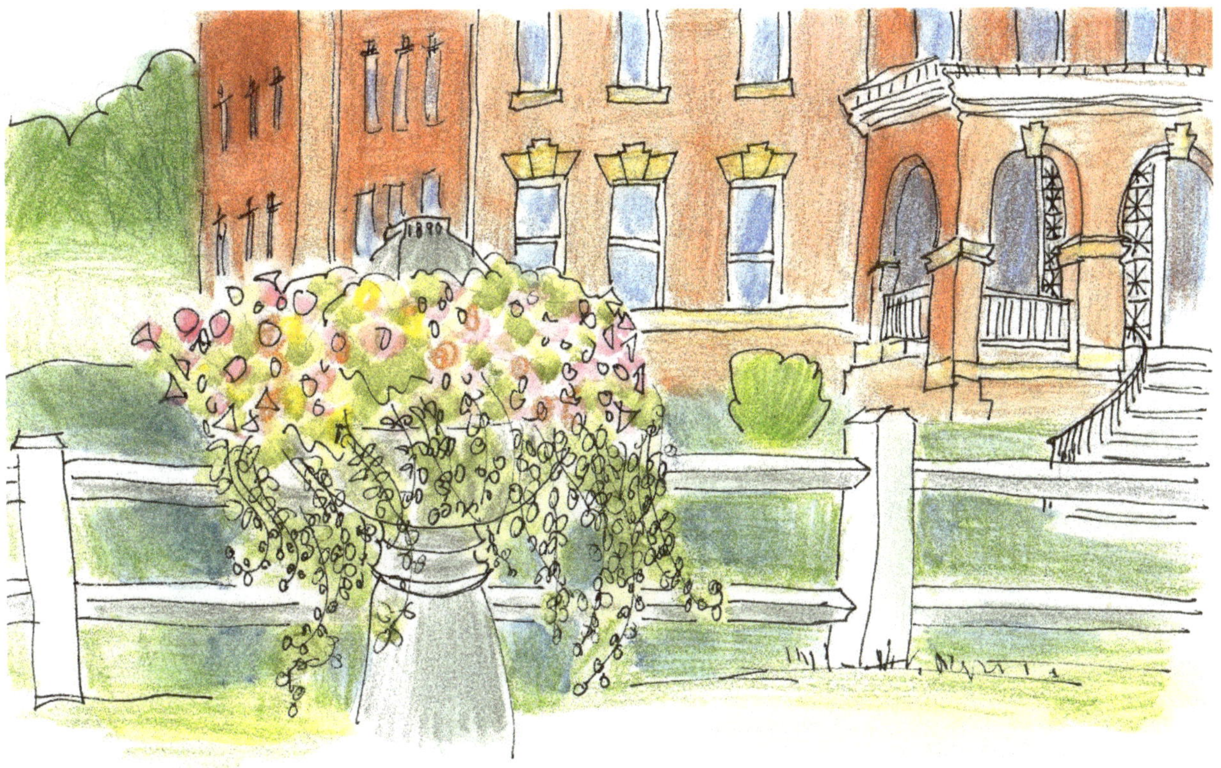

The Gordon-Nash Library is the only privately owned and run, but public, town library in New Hampshire.

The town was first called Moultonborough Addition. When incorporated in 1777, it became New Hampton. The first town meeting was held in the Dana Meetinghouse in 1801.

The well-regarded New Hampton School was started in 1821. The school was originally co-educational, then just for boys, and now has returned to accepting both. Currently it has about 300 students. The flower filled granite planter sits along the sidewalk in front of Lane Hall, 1919. My father-in-law came here for one year after high school, to boost his grades prior to application to college.

OSSIPEE

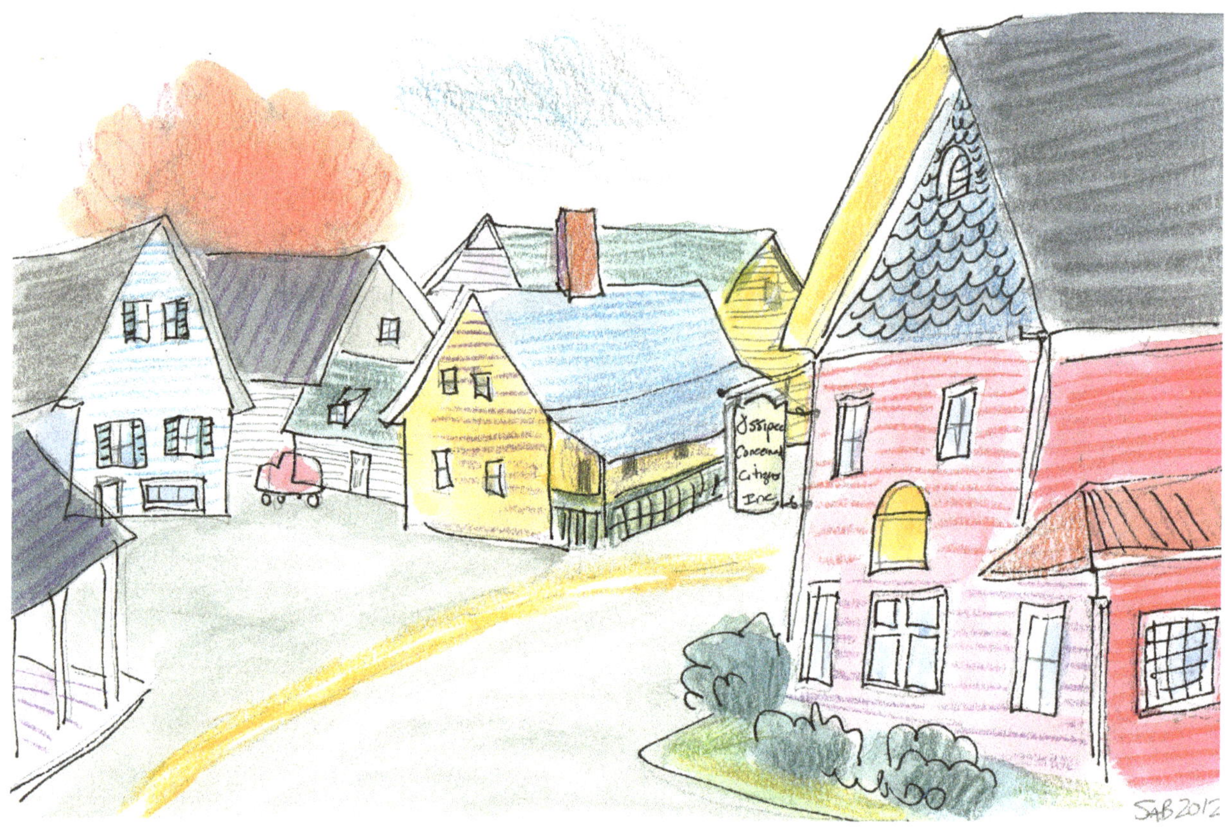

The town was once the site of a stockaded fort, built as protection from the Mohawks by the Ossipee, one of the twelve Algonquin Tribes.

These houses in Center Ossipee made a colorful composition. They were all built probably around 1880, when the railroad came to town. The railroad brought summer-long visitors to the lakes and mountains.

The Ossipee Mountains are a nearby mountain range, and part of a string of ring dikes, the remains of long gone volcanoes. On a topographical map they present a striking appearance, like a series of circles.

RUMNEY

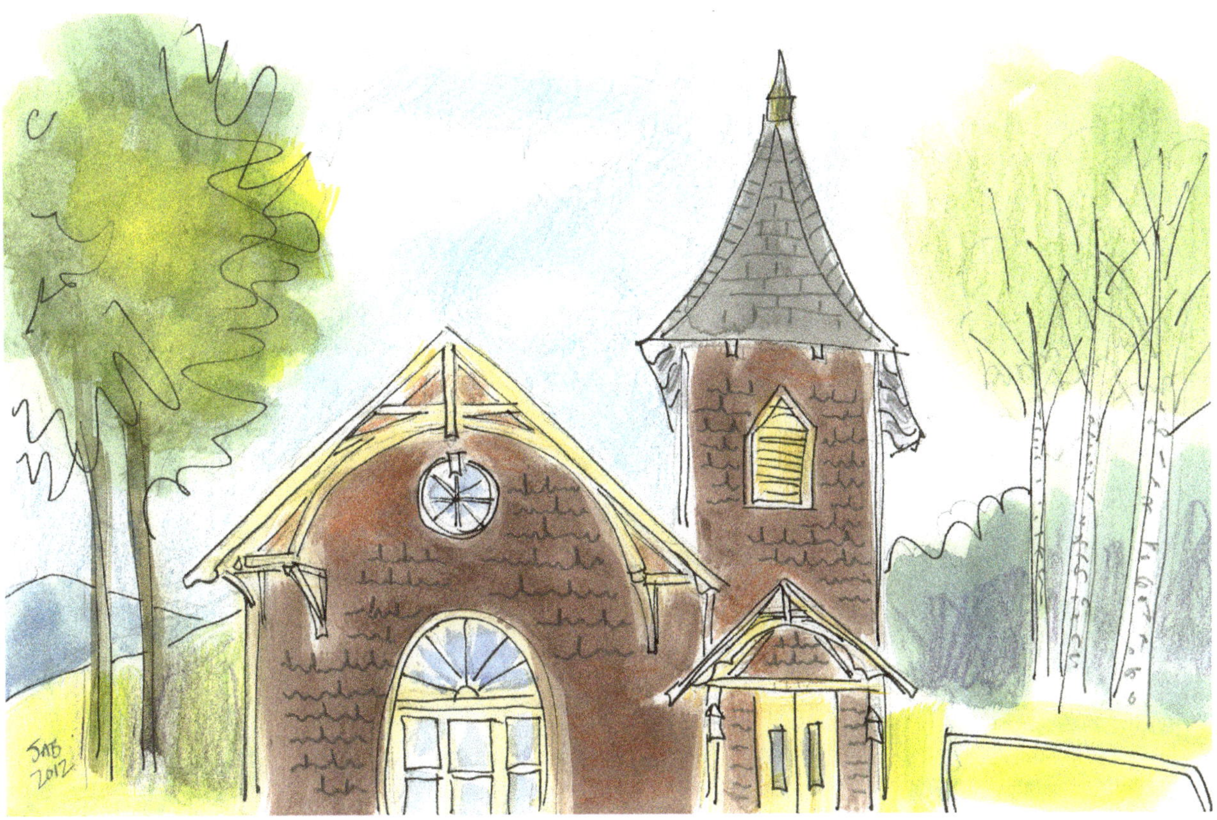

Rumney with a population of about 1,500 people is located on the southern edge of the White Mountain National Forest.

Fans of rock climbing come to Rumney Rocks on the south face of Rattlesnake Mountain. Other visitors enjoy the 350 acre Stinson Lake.

Settled in 1767, the villages of the town are Rumney Village, Rumney Depot, Stinson Lake, and West Rumney. The West Rumney Community Church was built in the Craftsman Style and retains the brown stained shingles of that era. The exterior wooden bracing is attractive too.

SANBORNTON

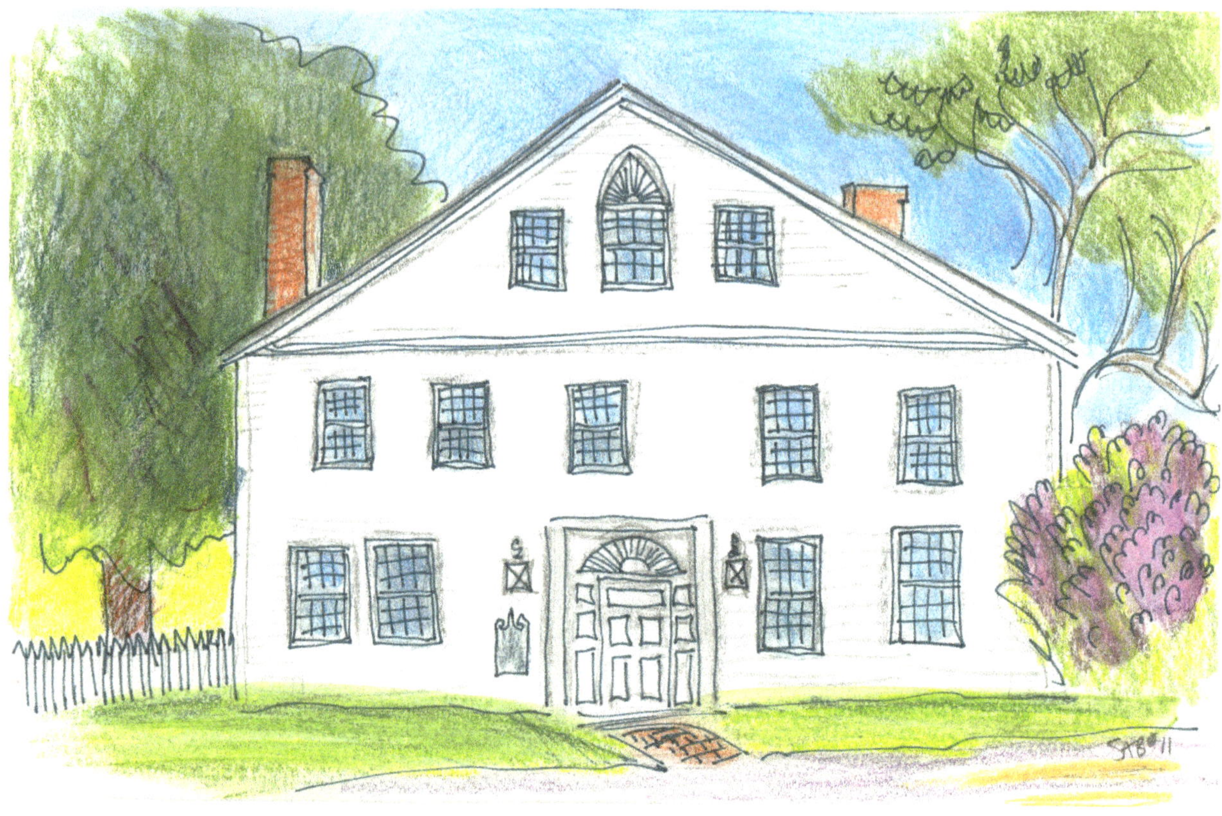

The town of Sanbornton is very close to the middle of the state. Outlet shopping opportunities abound near the interchange at Route 93. But just a mile or two away from modern life sits this old inn and tavern, circa 1800.

The Sanbornton Historical Society takes care of it. Inside are a museum and public meeting rooms, where we've attended several interesting historical presentations. In one of these rooms is a bar, with bars on it. To keep the bartender and the liquor safe from thievery. It serves as an historical artifact nowadays.

The spring day was unusually warm, and the scent of the lilacs drifted across the narrow lane.

SANDWICH

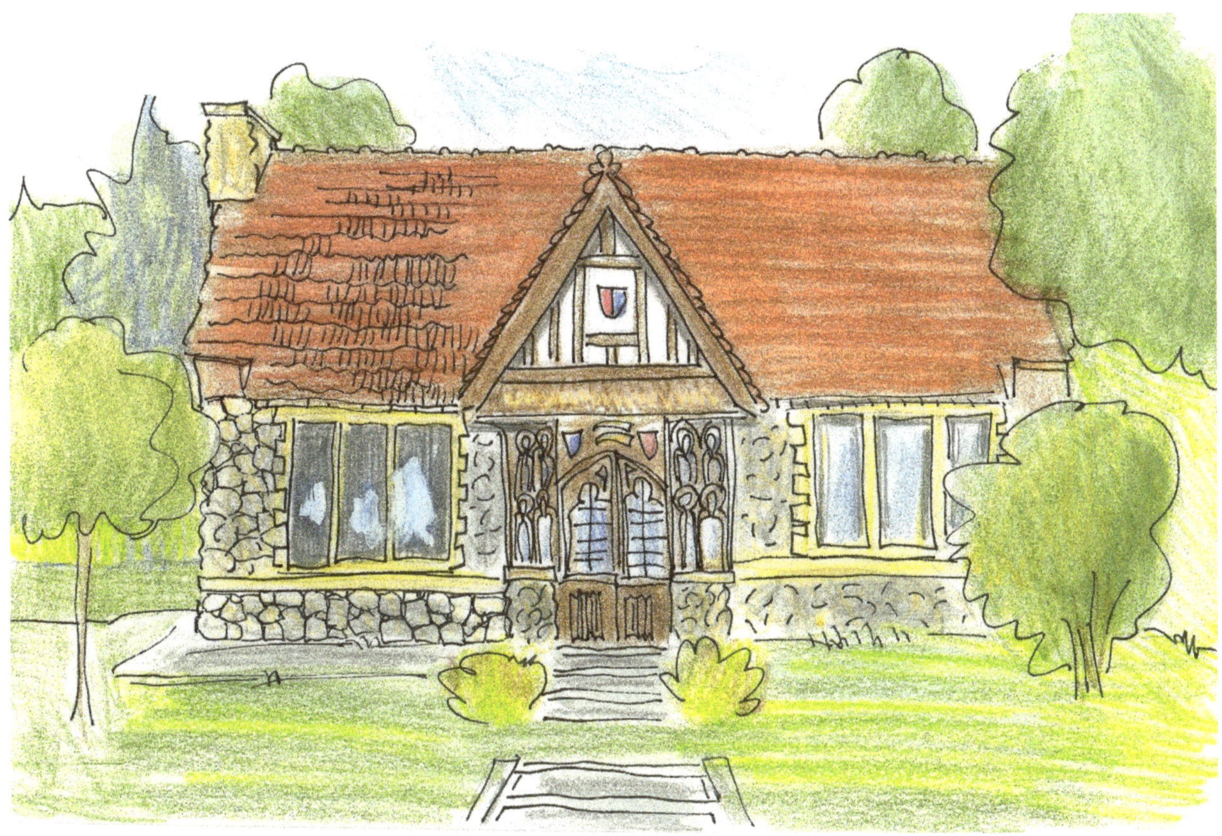

Sandwich is right between the Lakes Region on Squam Lake and the White Mountain Region to the north.

Sandwich is a town of 84 square miles and a population of under 1400 people.

Among a small cluster of white frame houses sits the unusual Samuel H. Wentworth Library, a building comprising a rich selection of materials: red tile roof, gray fieldstone walls, stained glass windows, and lots of shields and heraldry. Its presentation is very Old World, but with a modern wing off to the back. The well respected League of New Hampshire Craftsmen began in Sandwich in 1920 and was then called Sandwich Home Industries.

STRAFFORD

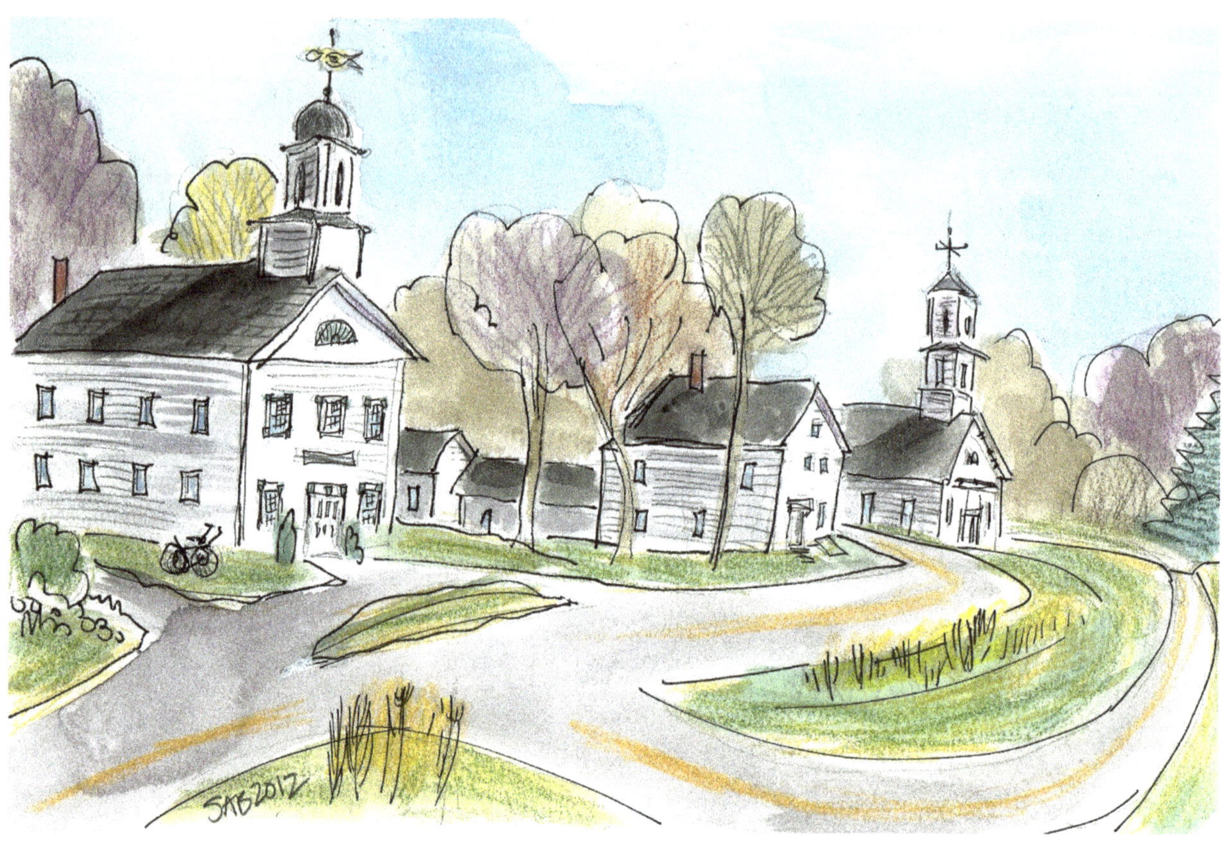

The building on the left with the old plow on the lawn is Austin Hall, the home of the Strafford Historical Society Museum and formerly the Austin Academy. It is no longer a school but has recently been restored as a community meeting space.

The windows and doors are decorative and unusual. The building on the right is the 3rd Baptist Church. The building in the middle is a private home, which exhibits the 'connected' building style of central New England architecture.

I paced around for quite a while in the long grass to find just the right place to draw the curves in the roads.

TAMWORTH

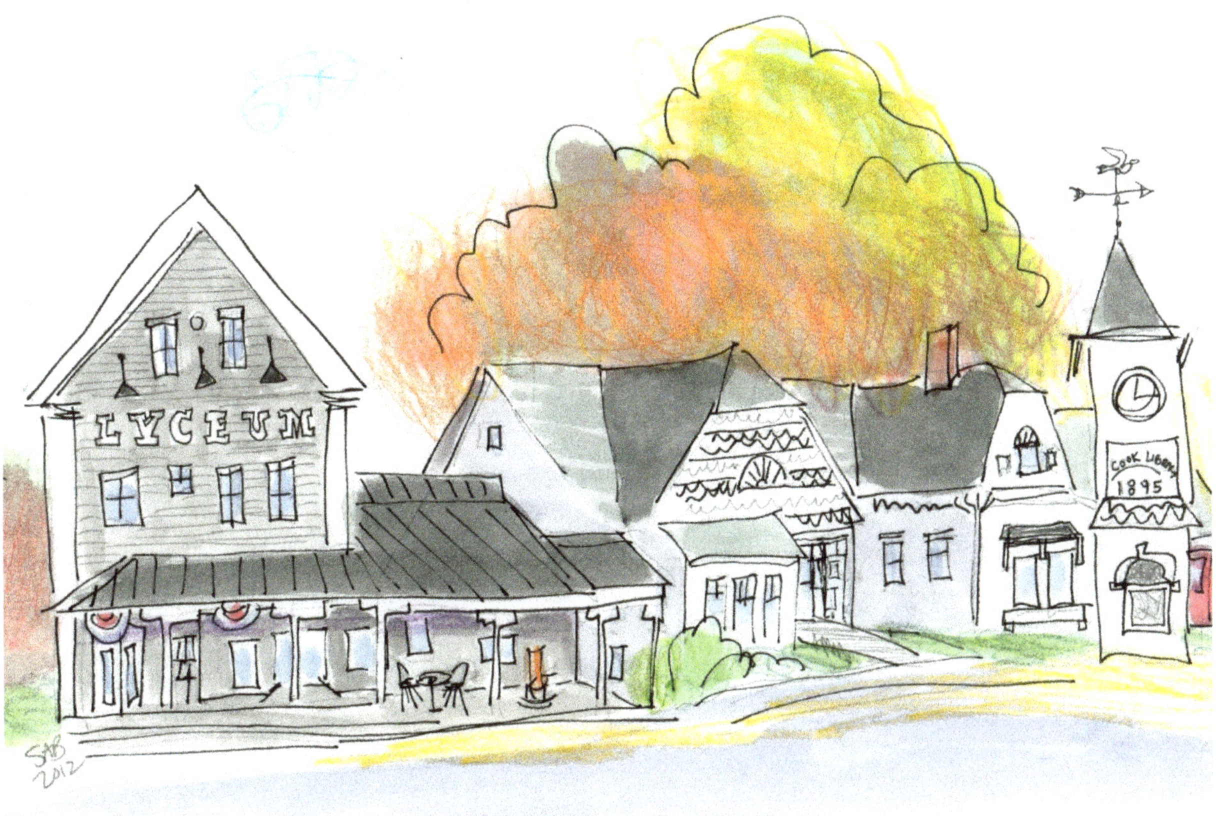

Artists are often inspired by the view of Mt. Chocorua from Tamworth.

With a population just under 3,000 people, Tamworth extends out to include four villages—Chocorua, South Tamworth, Wonalancet, and Whittier.

In Tamworth village itself a general store called the Lyceum, with a welcoming porch, sits next to the Cook Memorial Library. Across the street from the library is the Barnstormers Theatre, a summer stock playhouse. Francis Grover Cleveland, the son of President Cleveland, loved theater and established this one in 1931. Just a bit further up the road is the Remick Country Doctor Museum and Farm.

TUFTONBORO

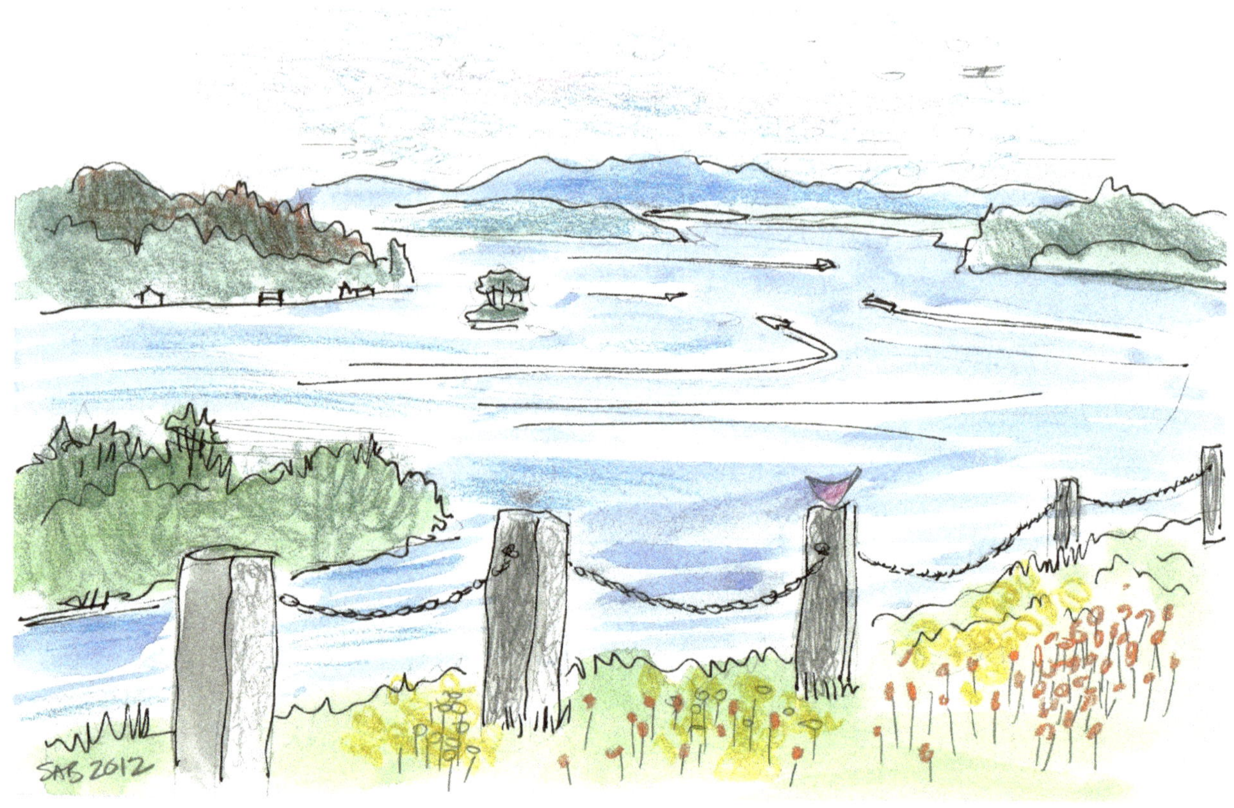

Bordered on the southwest by Lake Winnipesaukee, Tuftonboro has several villages: Tuftonboro Corner, Center Tuftonboro, Melvin Corner, Melvin Village, and Mirror Lake.

The land was once owned by just one man, John Tufton Mason, who then parceled it out. It was settled around 1780 and incorporated in 1795. The side lawn of the United Methodist Church has a great view, high over the lake.

The many boats on Lake Winnipesaukee looked like water bugs, and I drew the tiny biplane too.

WAKEFIELD

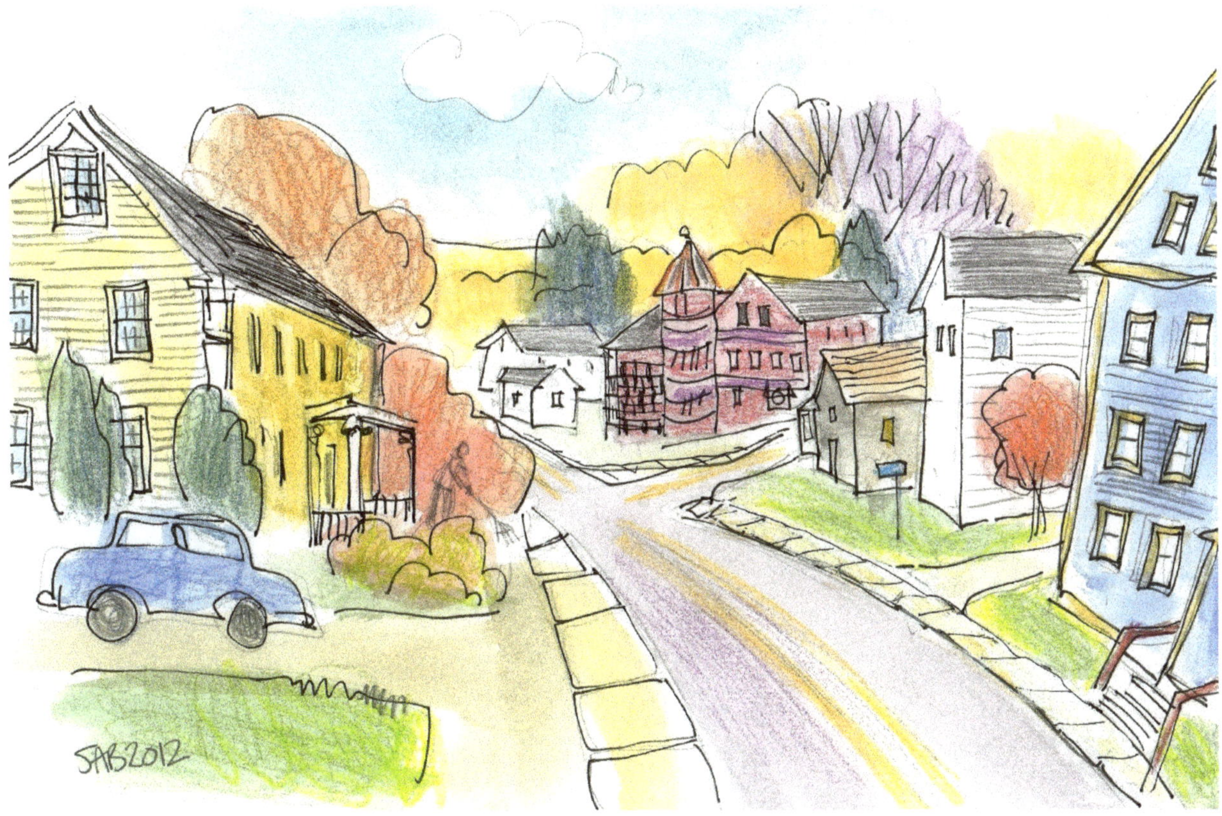

Wakefield has ten ponds and lakes, four of which span the border with Maine.

These brightly colored buildings caught my eye on a gray and overcast day. The pinkish-purple house has a turret, one of my favorite things.

The villages in the town are Wakefield Corner, East Wakefield, North Wakefield, Sanbornville, Union, Woodman, and Province Lake. The town was a stage coach stop between the seacoast and the White Mountains. When the railroad came to the town, the population center shifted, as it did in many other towns. Sanbornville became the retail district.

WOLFEBORO

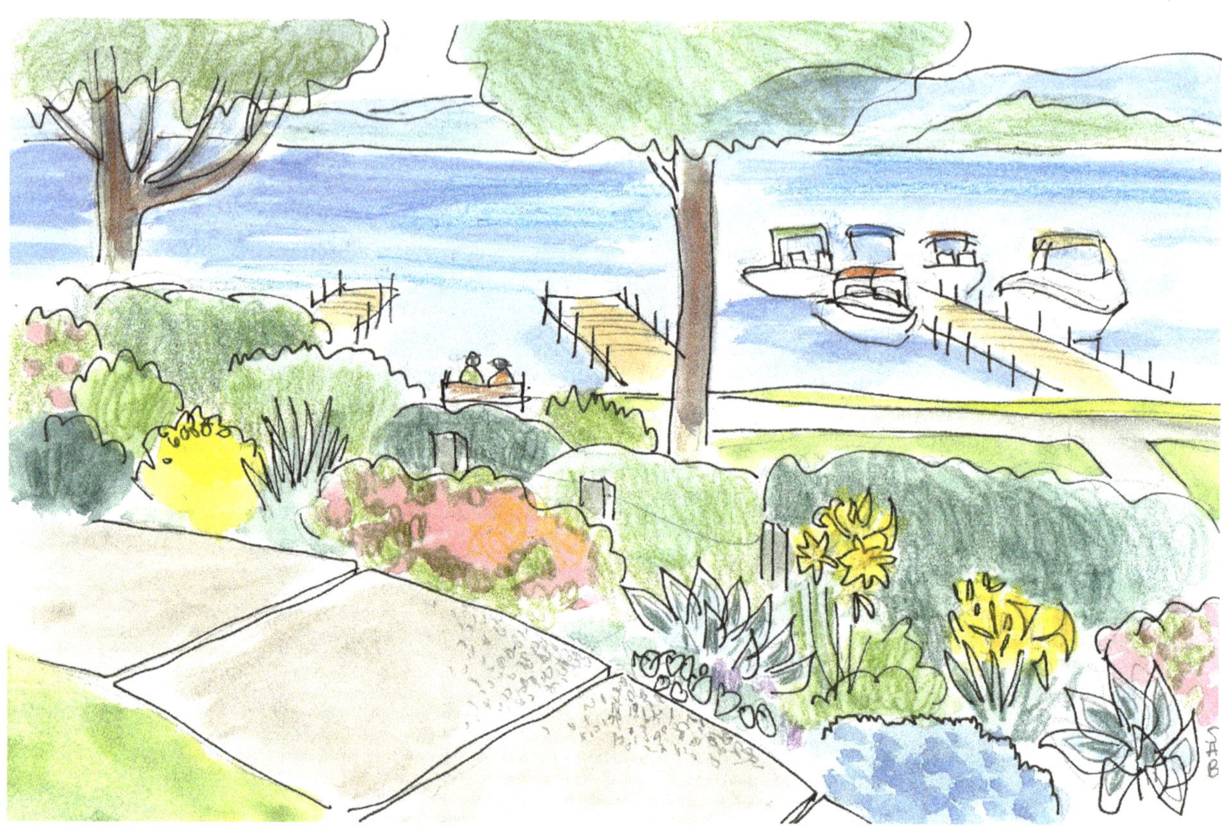

Wolfeboro sits between Lake Winnipesaukee and Lake Wentworth. Settled in 1770, it was named for the British General James Wolfe.

A small, charming, resort town, I found many vistas begging to be drawn. After strolling along Main Street, window shopping, this lovely park invited us in. A set of semi-circular terraces led from the street to the lake's edge. Some parts were in full sun, some in shade. The garden was all very carefully designed and well maintained.

It was the last day of school when we were here, and noisy, excited students were all about.

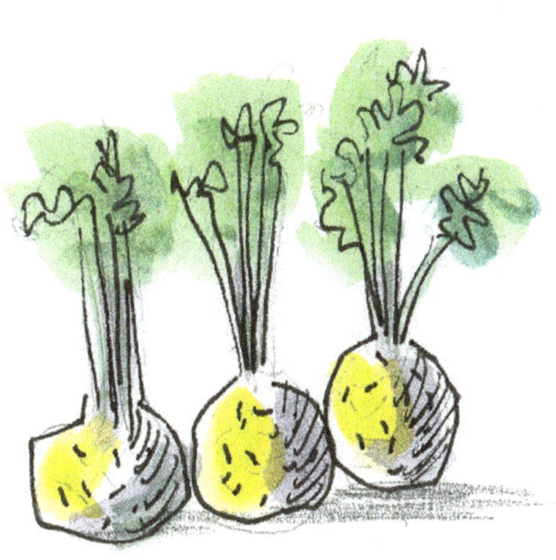

Merrimack Valley

ALLENSTOWN

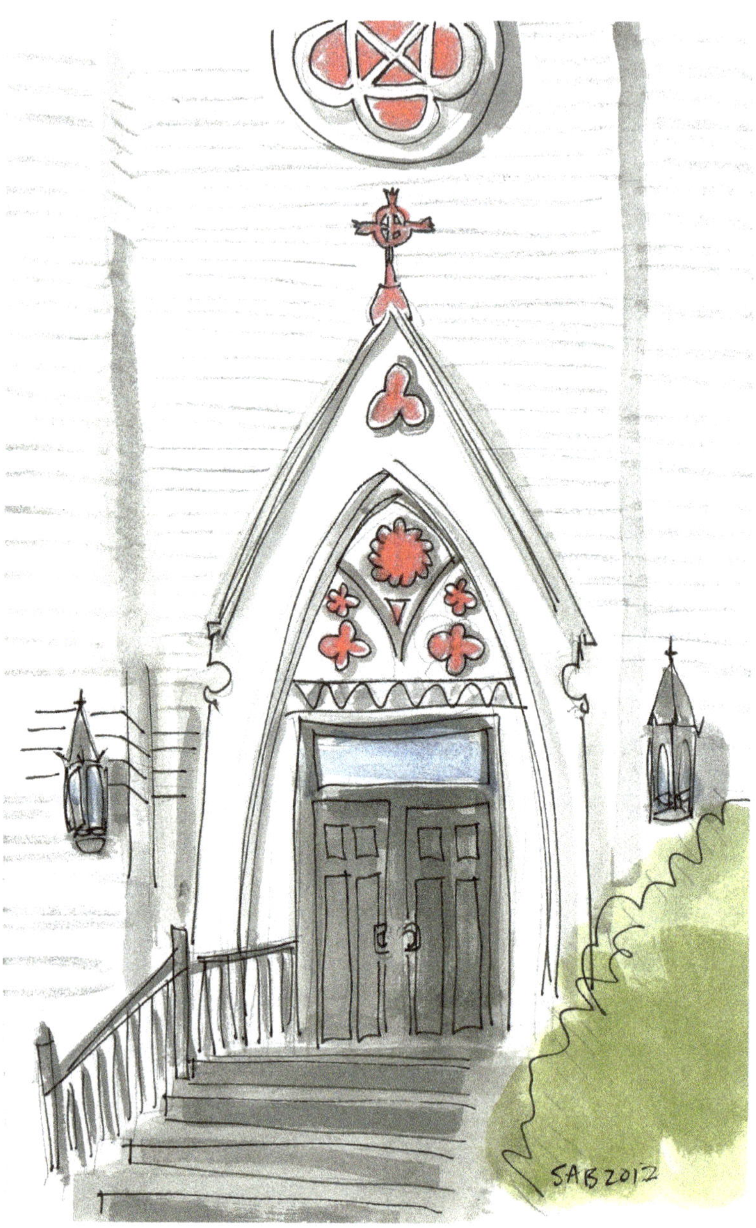

Allenstown was granted in 1721, but not incorporated for over 100 years. Part of the town includes the village of Suncook.

The red and white paint scheme of St. John the Baptist Catholic Church in Allenstown is eye catching. The signs at the church memorial on the side street are in English and French, an indication of the lingering influence of the mill workers from French Canada.

Robert Frost expanded his poetic themes of botany and nature by hiking along the banks of the Suncook River.

Over half of the town is the Bear Brook State Park.

AMHERST

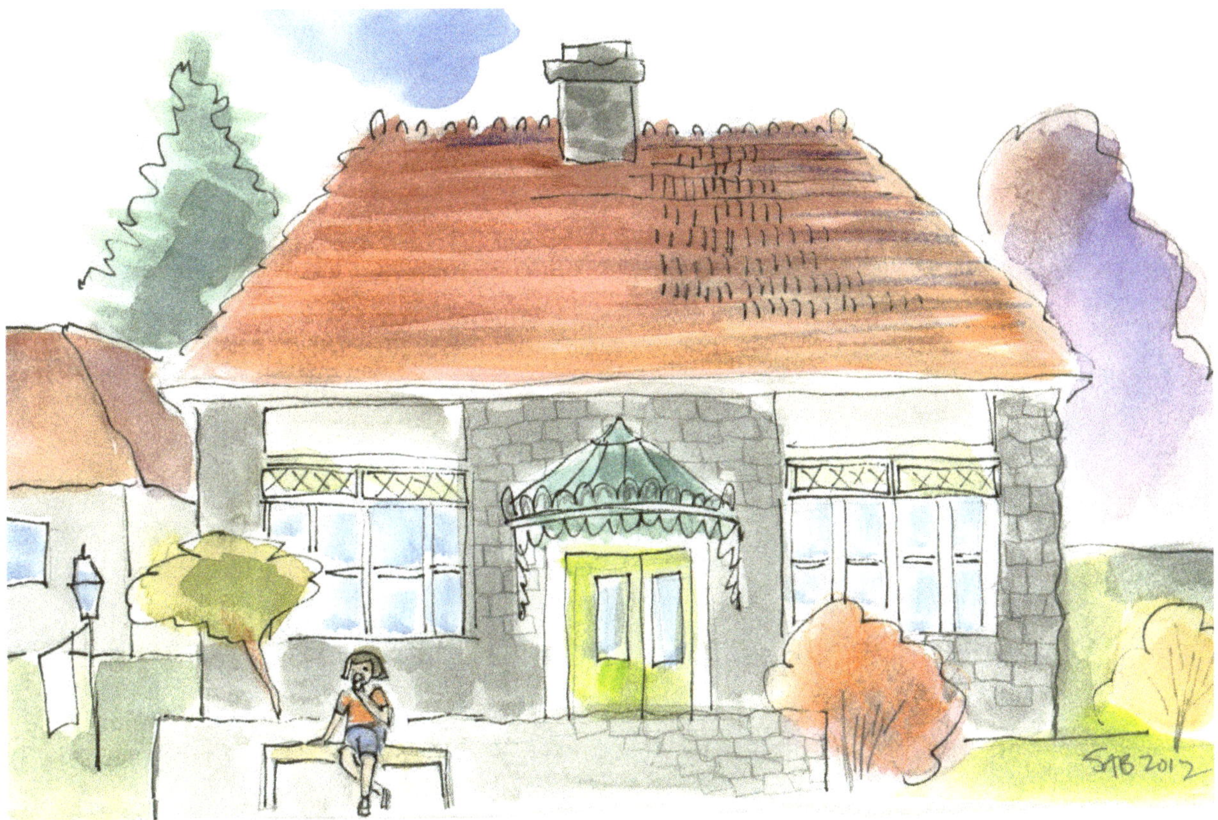

The library was hosting an ice cream social the day I was there.

Amherst has a lovely, harmonious, village green with dozens of Federal style homes, churches, and town office buildings surrounding it. Originally granted in 1728 to veterans of King Philip's War, the town charter of 1760 named the town Amherst after British General Lord Amherst. (King Philip was the name the British used for a powerful native chief, not a European monarch.)

The library is off to the side of the green, and it's a fine stone structure dating to 1892. The façade is especially attractive with its copper and green glass details, as well as Mexican roof tiles. The modern addition is off to the left.

AUBURN

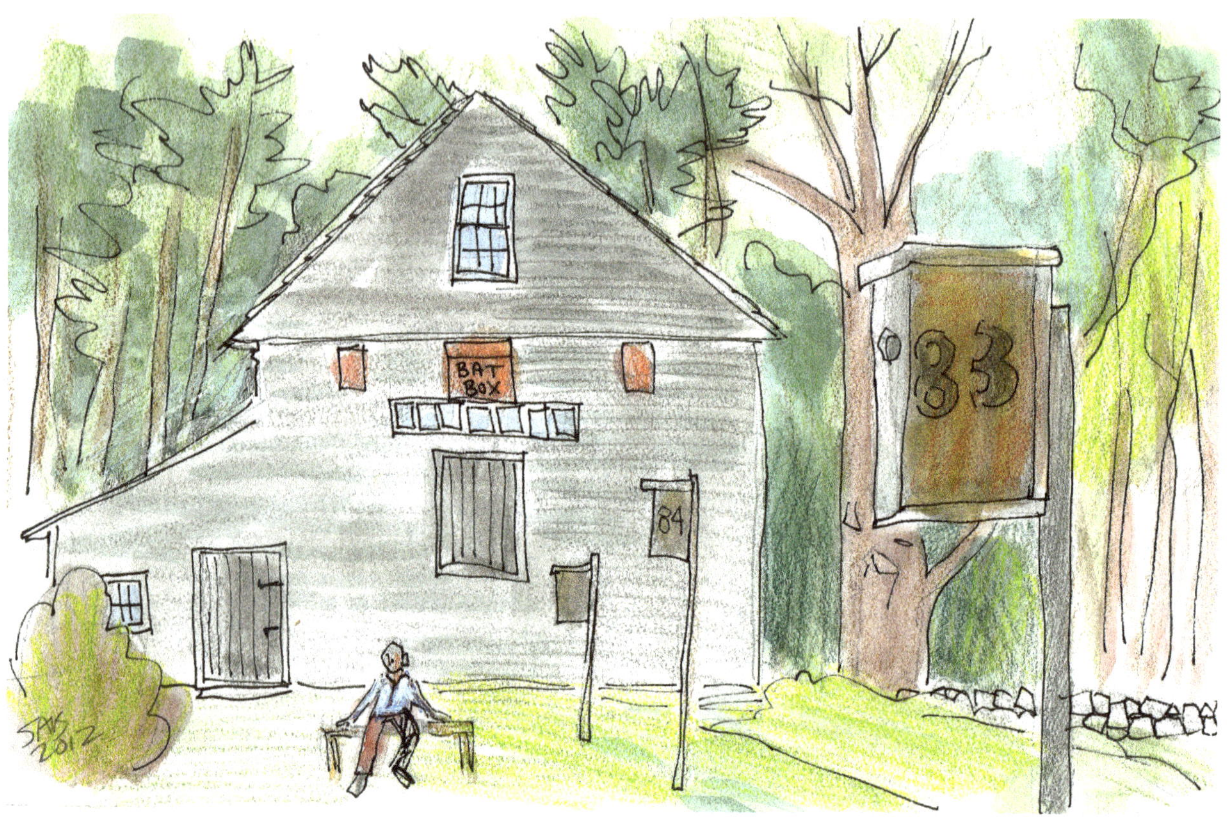

Auburn is a town of about 5,000 people, just east of Manchester. The town's name derives from a popular 18th century poem by Oliver Goldsmith.

The town land nearly surrounds Massabesic Lake, which is the water supply for Manchester and other towns. Limited boating recreation is allowed, and weekly yacht races do take place in the summer. At the Audubon Center, 85 or more wooden nesting boxes give homes to bluebird families.

I'd love to be in town for the annual rubber ducky race on the lake.

BEDFORD

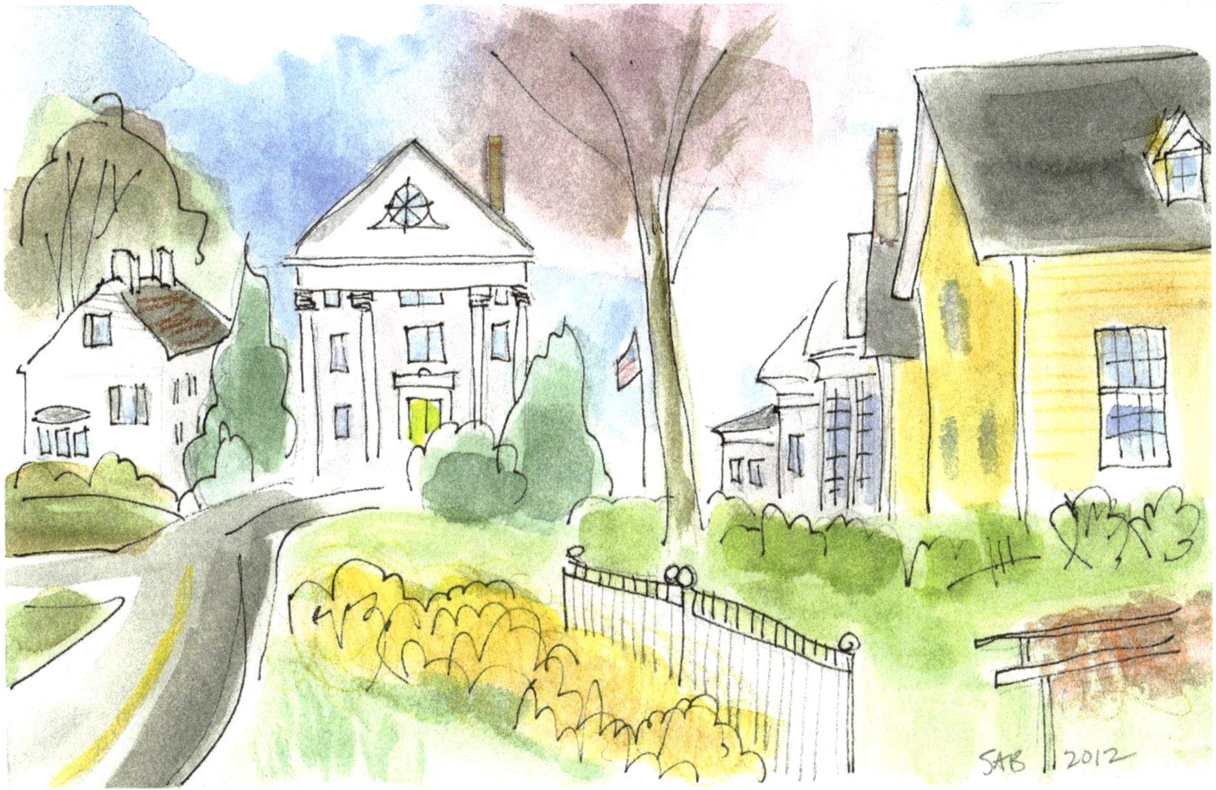

The large yellow forsythia bush is a sign of early spring.

I often notice similar looking towers, rooflines, and ornamentation in neighboring towns.

Pattern books and readymade gingerbread trim were easily available for builders in the 1800s. In Bedford Center I stopped to add to my drawing several times as I walked along. The town hall, which includes the Narragansett Grange No. 16, is in the center. The yellow and the white buildings are private homes, and there are small glimpses of the town library.

BOSCAWEN

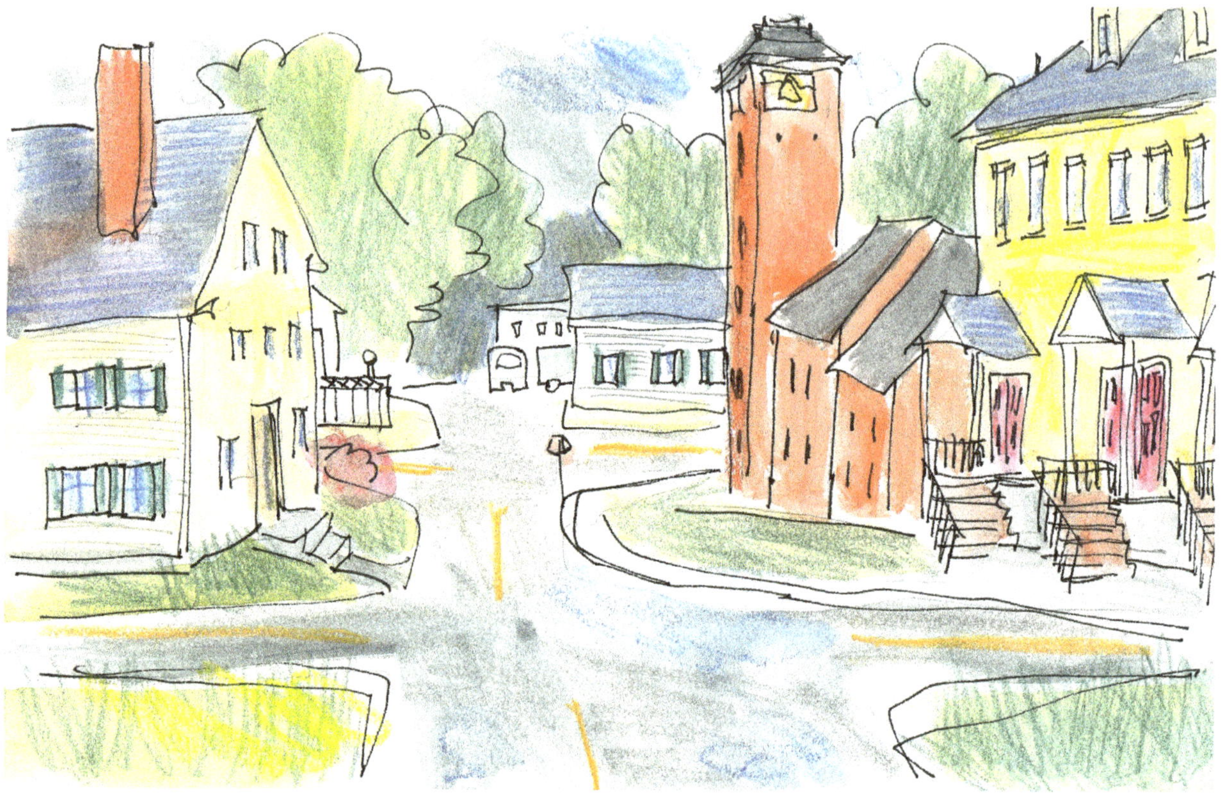

With a population of about 4,000 residents, the town is located just north of Concord between the Merrimack River and the Contoocook River, spanning both sides of Route 93.

The fire station is the building in the center, with its brick tower for drying hoses—which also provides a home for the fire bell at the top. On the right is some original mill housing, with its matching doorways. The Merrimack River is at the bottom of the hill behind the trees. At the river's edge were flour, textile, and lumber mills, and a tannery.

The puddles in the street indicate the weather this day.

BOW

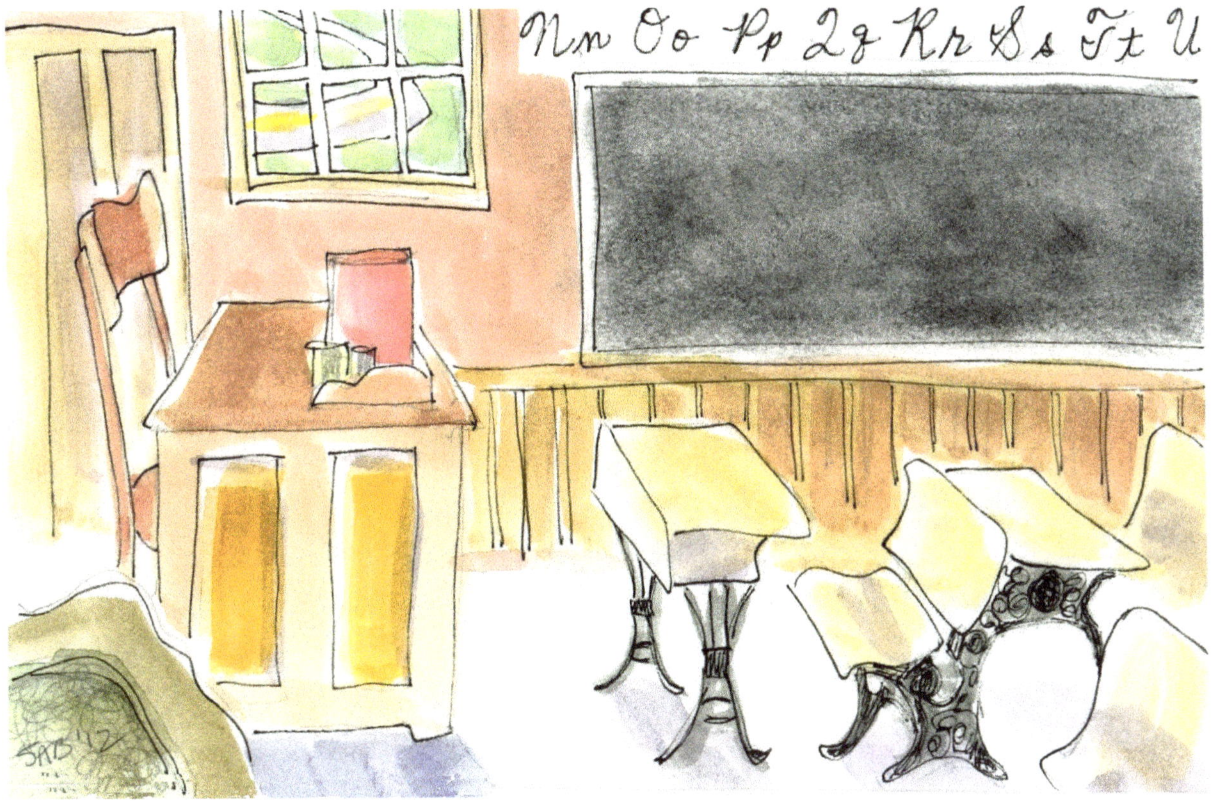

Bow takes its name from the sharp turn or bend in the Merrimack River.

This town, with a population of about 7,600 people, has had various names and several boundary changes since the early 1700s.

For many years, the land was claimed by both Massachusetts and New Hampshire. The Bow Center Schoolhouse was built in 1894, and now the town's modern schools are nearby. Take note of the black slate writing board. The lettering above this chalkboard is called the Palmer Penmanship script, taught only in North America. It is a distinctive loopy style that still challenges most students.

BROOKLINE

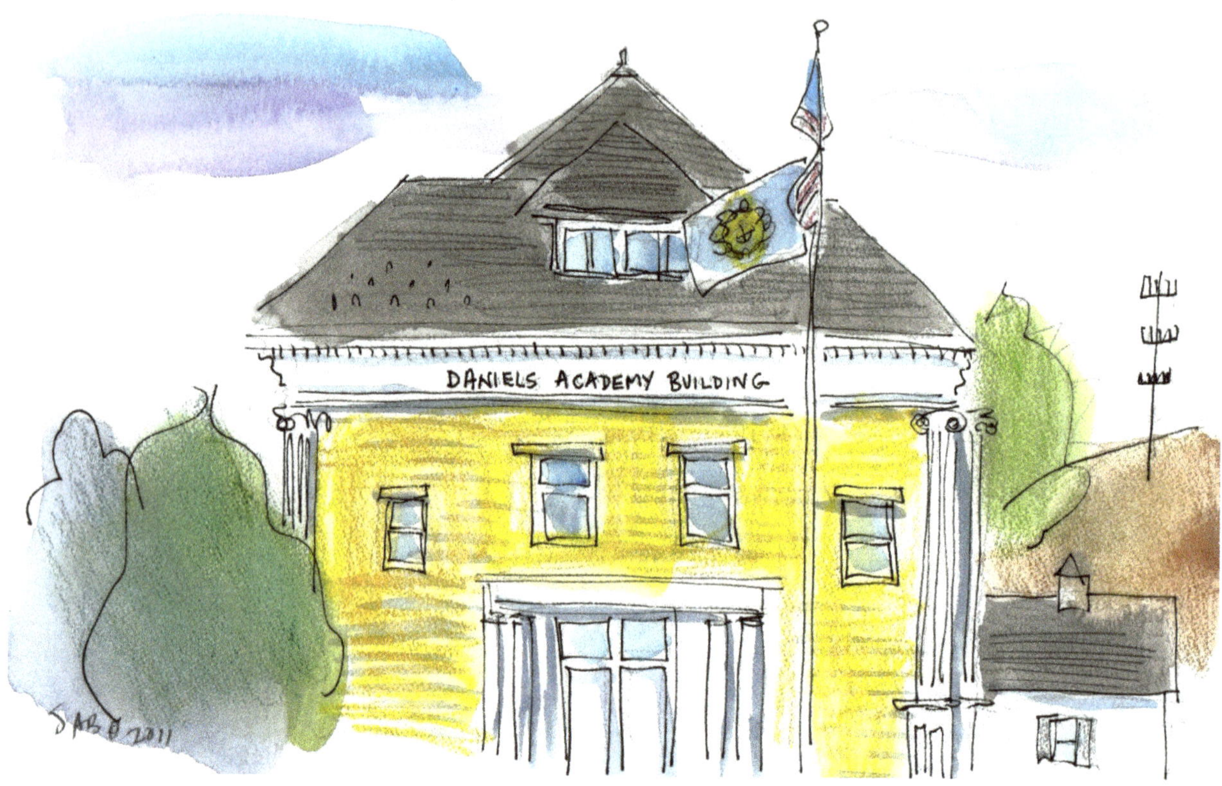

Brookline borders the state of Massachusetts in the south. The town was once a part of Dunstable, Massachusetts, and then was settled as West Hollis, New Hampshire.

Early settlers came from Brookline, Massachusetts and chose its current name. This large square building is the town offices. The former home of the Daniels Academy, it was founded in 1905 for girls and boys. It looks dignified and solid and well worth repurposing. The Andres Institute of Art in town specializes in sculpture workshops.

If I see a yellow building in a town, I am there like a moth to the flame.

CANDIA

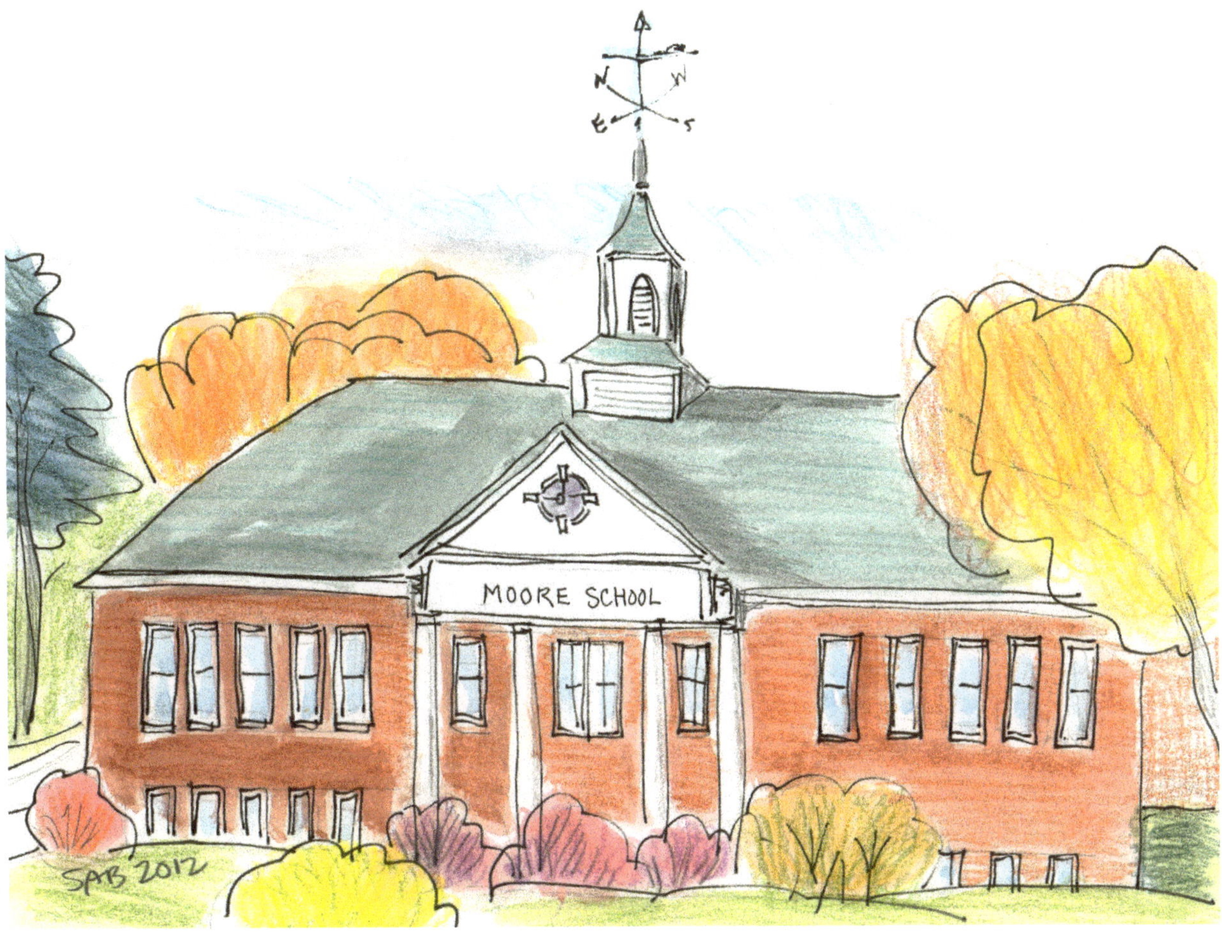

We have taken our daughter and our young granddaughter to the well known petting zoo named Charmingfare.

The Henry W. Moore School, a very solid looking building, is located in Candia Four Corners. Like so many towns in the state, Candia has had many names. Settled in 1743 as part of Chester, it was once known as Charmingfare, meaning a bridle trail. Historians are uncertain of the origin of the final name of the town.

When I draw, I remember whom I meet, the weather, and what I had for lunch. In this case, lunch was delicious pizza from the nearby restaurant on the other corner of the intersection.

CANTERBURY

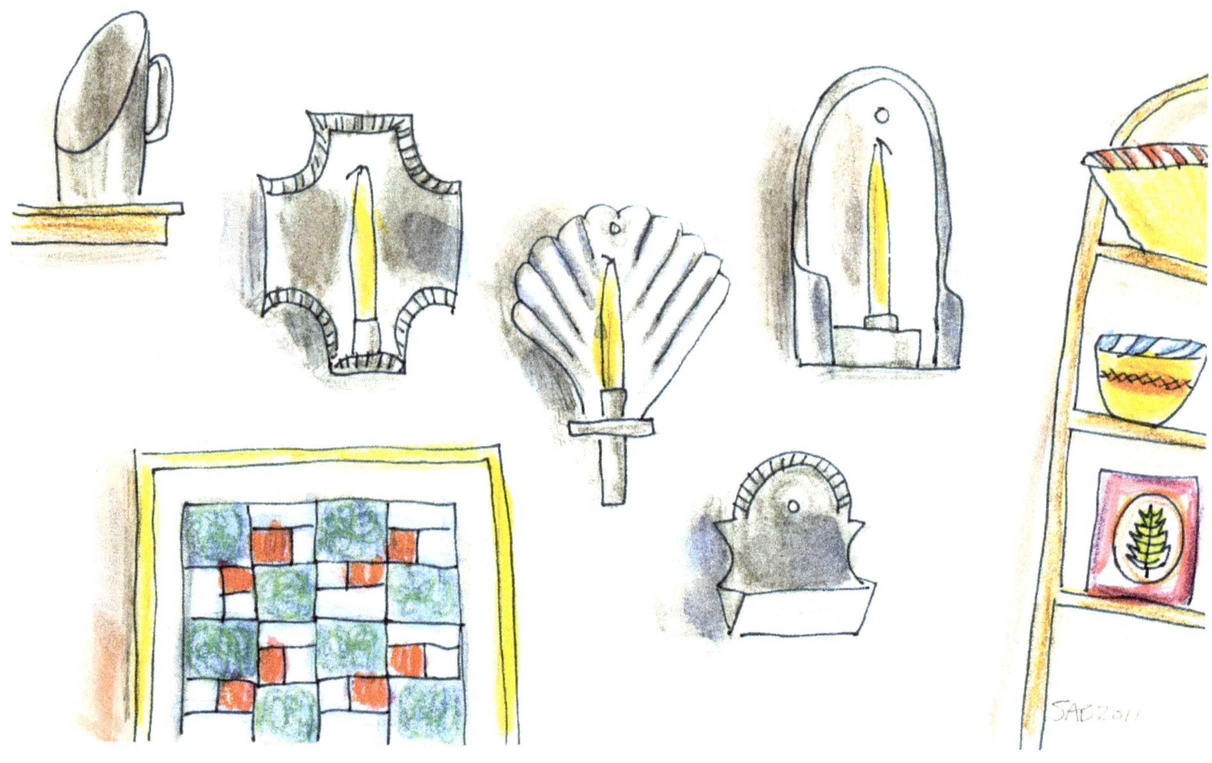

The town center is an attractive cluster of white frame buildings. The Elkins Public Library is in a new building, but artfully designed to fit in with the old.

A large Shaker Village of 25 buildings is located in the eastern side of Canterbury. Shakers were a Protestant sect that flourished in the 18th and 19th centuries in the U.S. and England. I drew the replicas of Shaker tinware, quilts, and other crafts that are for sale in the village.

Several New Hampshire Humanities Council presentations have taken place in the library, including a modern day sighting of Abraham Lincoln.

CHESTER

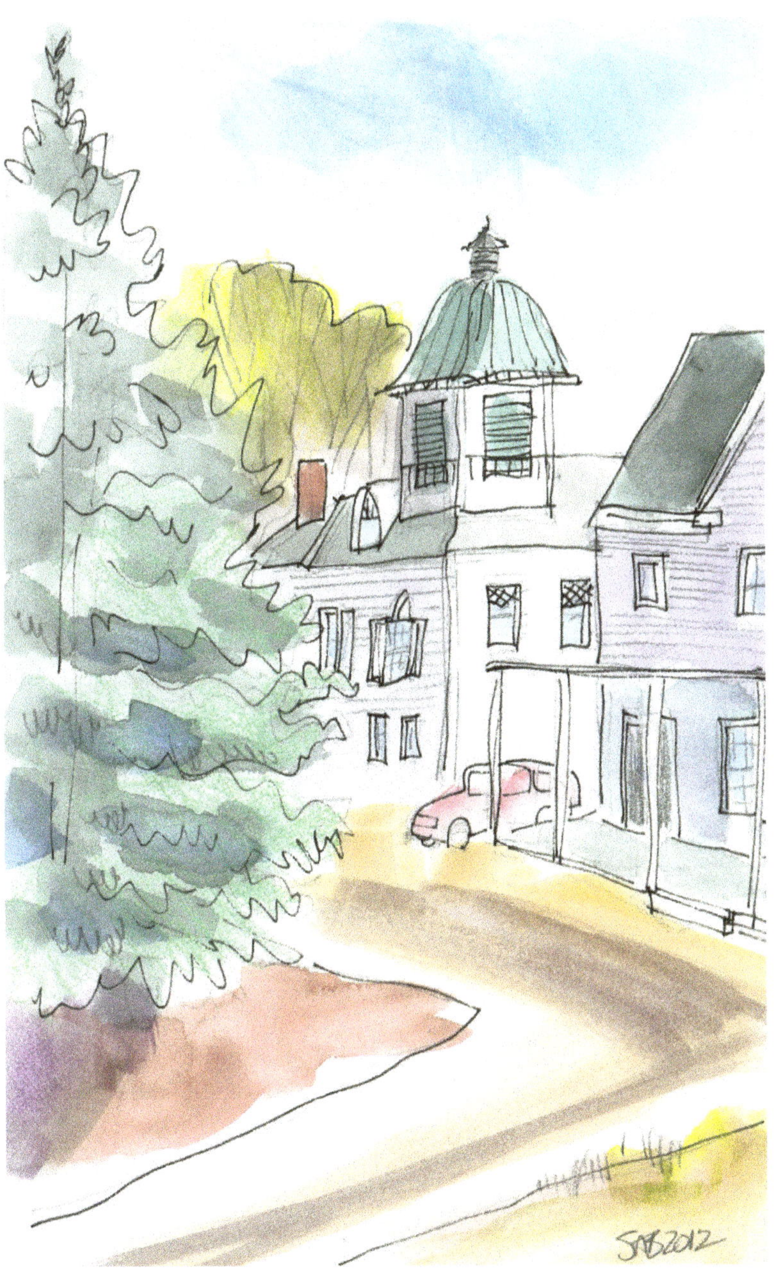

The Stevens Memorial Hall, a Colonial revival style of 1910, has a lovely copper green cupola.

The imposing building is also home to the town's Historical Society. It is spacious enough to hold all the community's events. Next to it on the right is the town post office. I did give more than equal space to the beautiful blue spruce growing at the edge of the road too.

Chester once included Candia and parts of Hooksett. The noted sculptor Daniel Chester French was a summer resident for a time.

A graveyard nearby will appeal to some history buffs with its old slate markers.

CHICHESTER

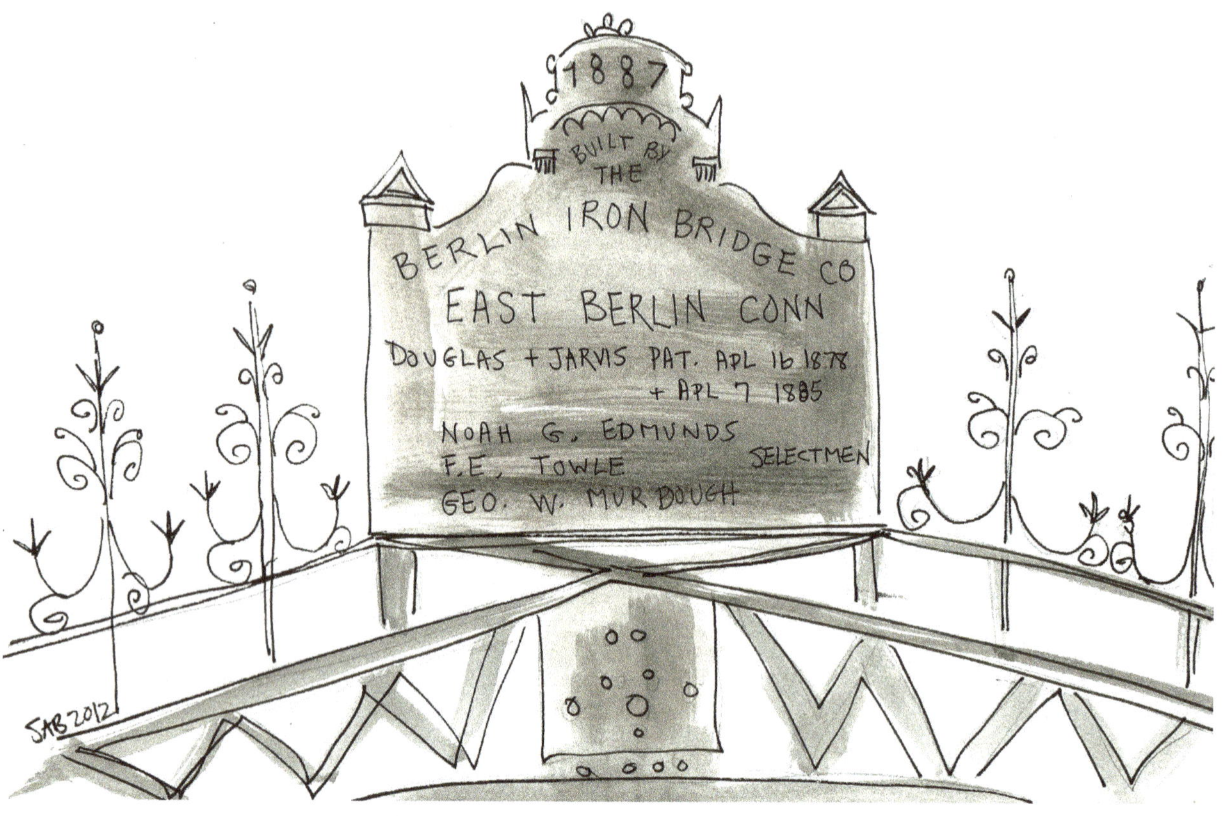

Most towns in New Hampshire either have native names like Suncook or Merrimack, or Anglo-Saxon names like this one, Chichester, named for an English earl.

My drawing is just the signcap of the Pineground Bridge, of a parabolic lenticular design. I looked that up for any readers who are bridge engineers. It was in use from 1887 through to 1981. It has been replaced by an adjacent modern bridge, and restored and available for pedestrian use. The bridge can be found on Depot Road, just off of Route 28.

I just love architectural flourishes like this spiraled wrought iron.

CONCORD

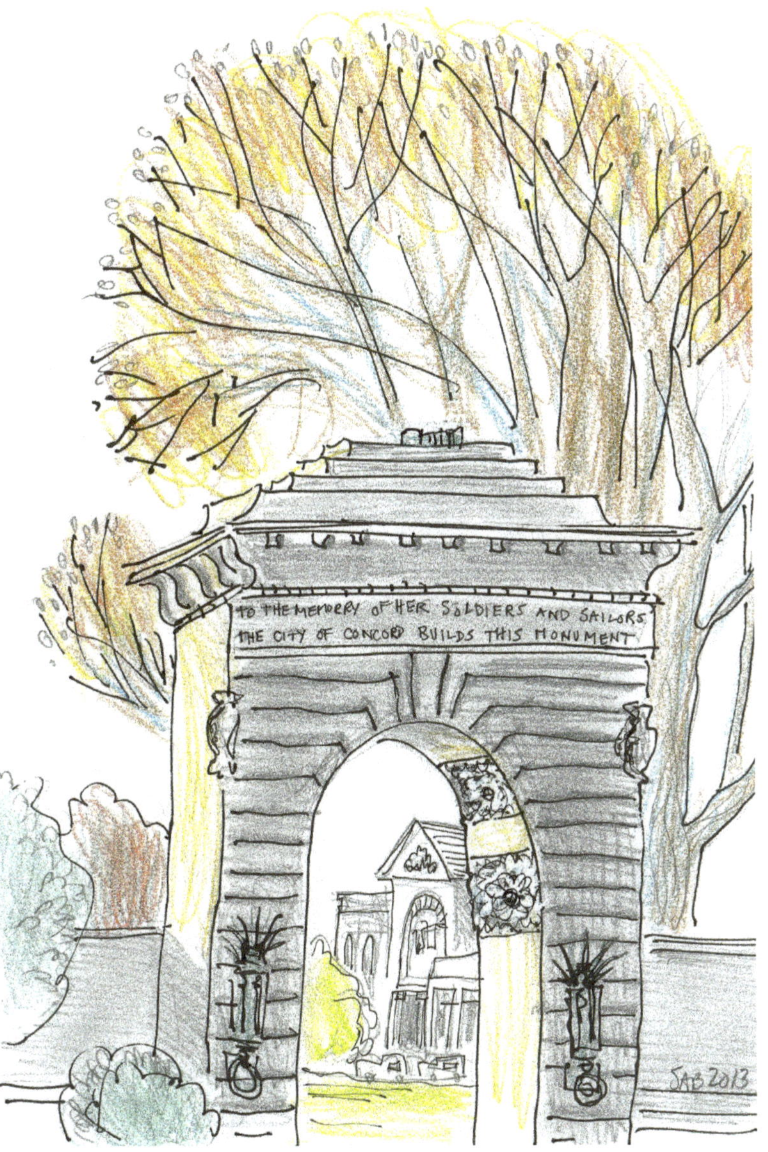

Our state capital city, along the banks of the Merrimack River, was home to a branch of the Abenaki Native Americans named the Pennacook. They farmed the fertile flood plains and strung nets across the rapids.

Europeans arrived in 1725. Their village was originally incorporated as Rumford. It had long lasting boundary disputes with the town of Bow. When the conflicts were settled, the town took the new name of Concord, meaning peace and harmony.

The city has a population of about 43,000 people. When I was young, my family lived next to White Park, a wonderful urban recreational space.

On a blustery late fall day, I sketched the Civil War Memorial Arch on Main Street in front of the Capitol Building. Ten thousand people attended the dedication ceremony in 1899.

DEERFIELD

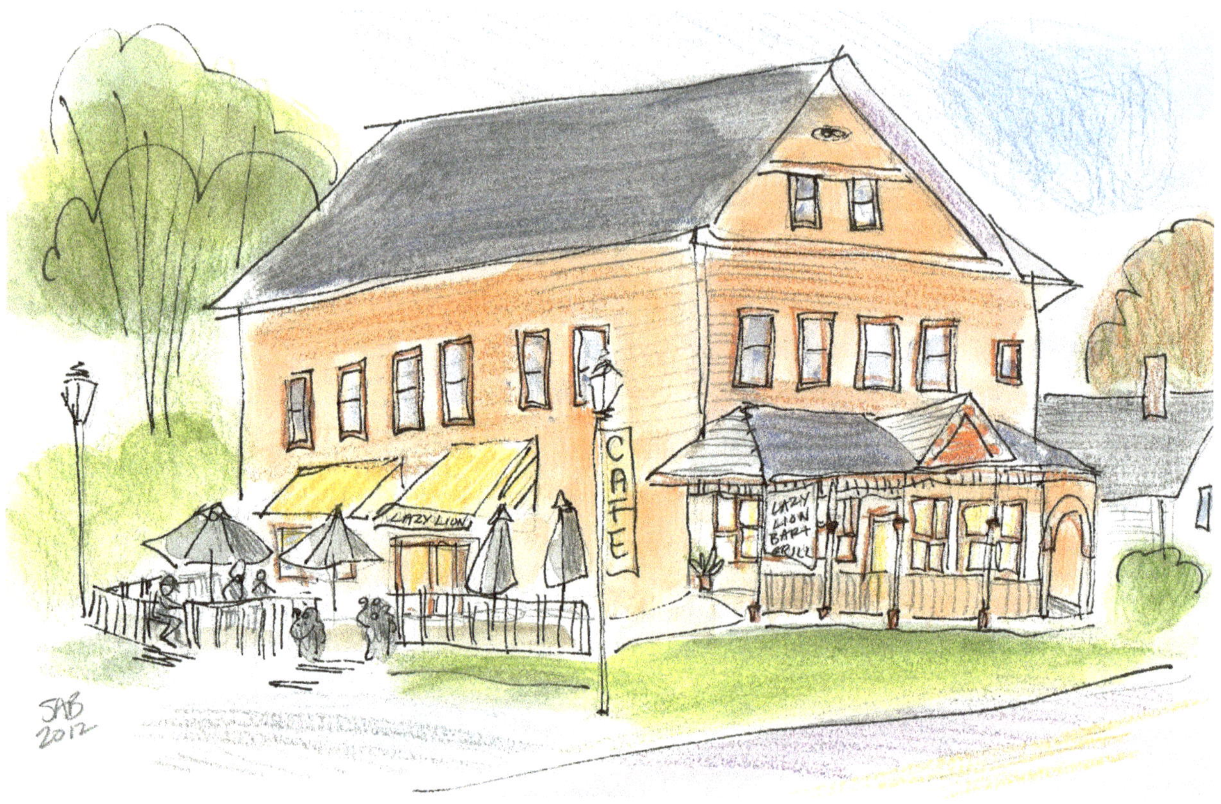

We rounded a corner in Deerfield, NH, and this orange building popped into view. When I saw the words Lazy Lion Café, I took heart.

We could have a bite to eat, and I wouldn't have to draw on an empty stomach. The former G. L. Wentworth store is another general store for my collection. Many people know this town for its longstanding and popular agricultural and family fun Deerfield Fair. Part of town is called Deerfield Parade. Militia trained here for the Revolutionary War and the Civil War.

Quiet and picturesque, Deerfield is tucked away between the busy Routes 4 and 101.

DERRY

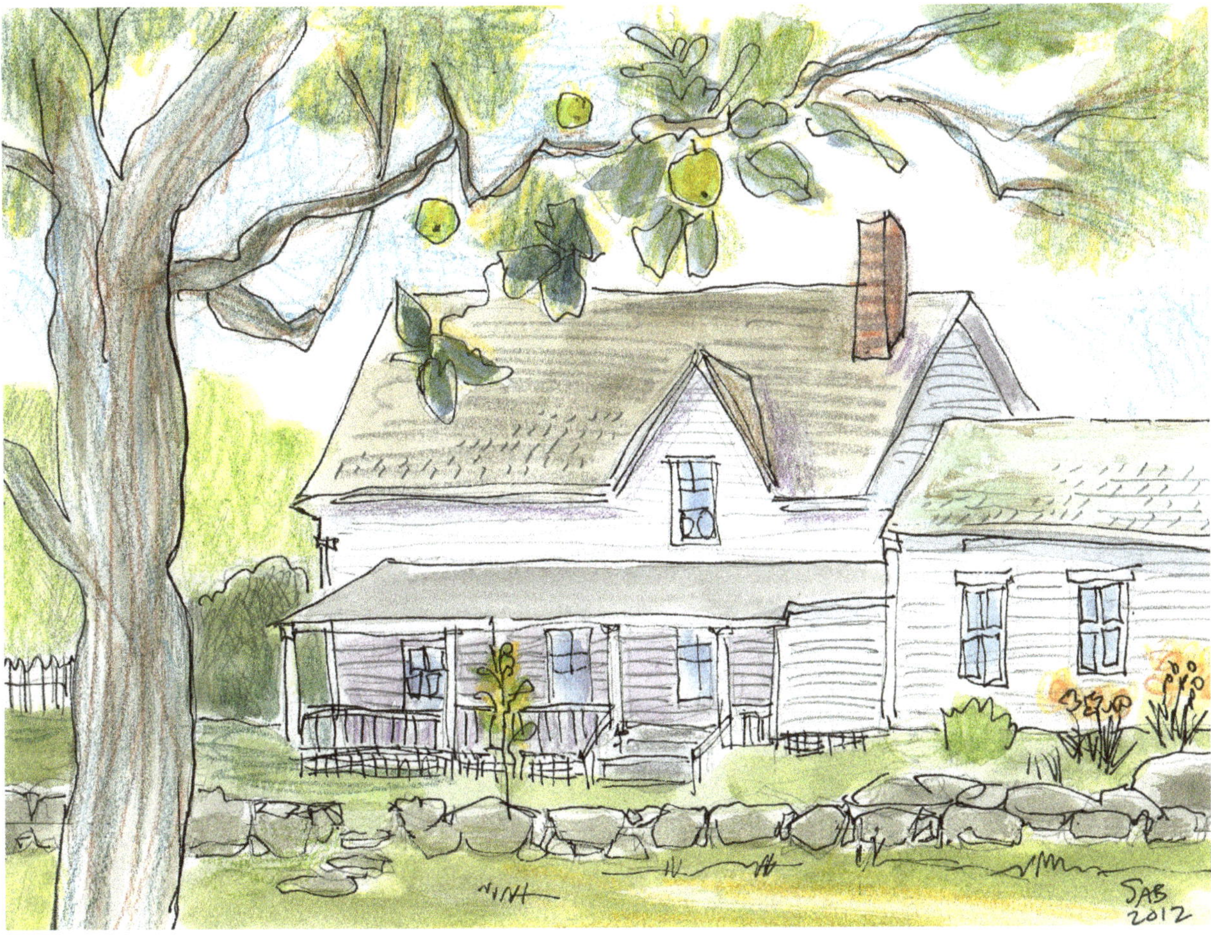

While I was drawing the Frost farmhouse, a cameraman from the *New Hampshire Chronicle* TV program was capturing the whole process on film.

From 1900 to 1911, the award winning poet Robert Frost lived in this farmhouse on the edge of town with his wife Elinor and their small children. He wrote many of his best known poems here, and others that he wrote elsewhere were inspired by memories of this place.

Frost's grandfather bought the farm for him and his family on the condition that they agree to live there for ten years. Soon after that, the family was off to England. The grounds and the house are open to the public, and the knowledgeable staff is known to freely recite Frost's poetry.

DUNBARTON

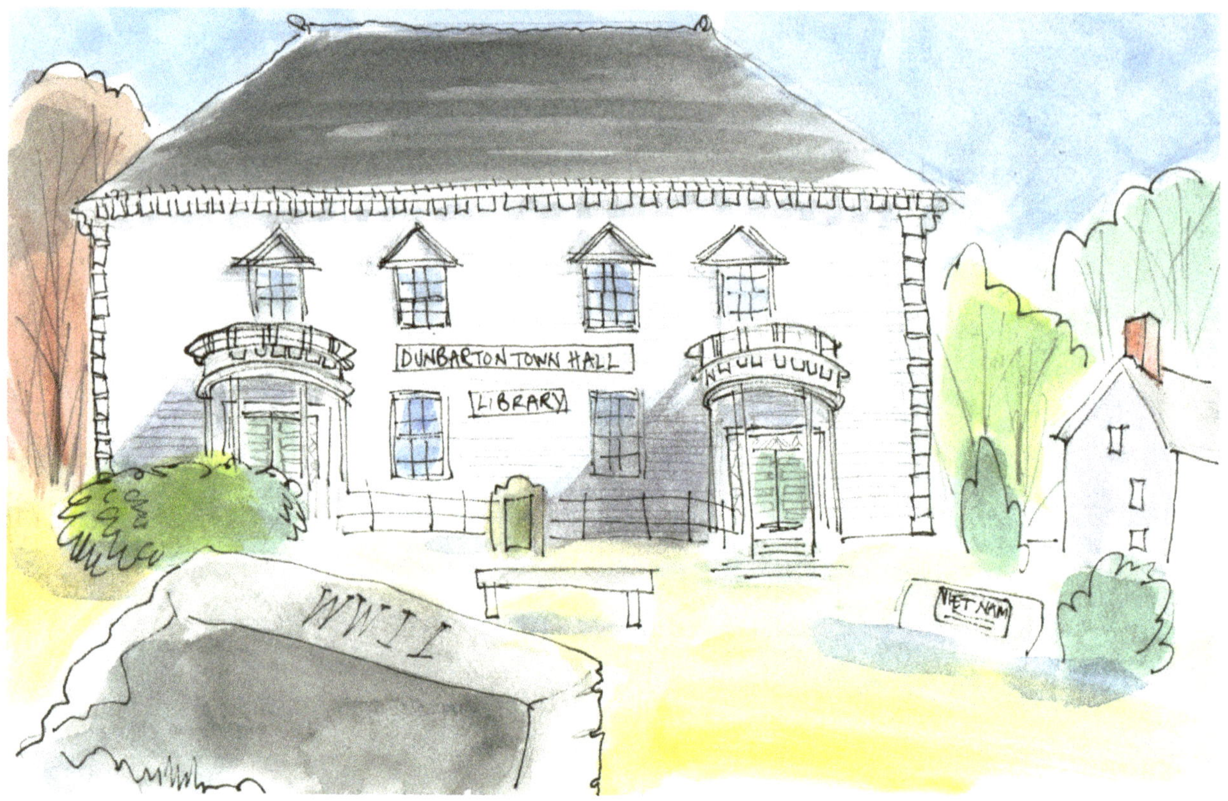

This large ornate white wooden building is right in the center of the common. It is the town's library and town hall, built in 1908 to replace an earlier one that burned.

The large twin doors with roof railing were lovely, and the bright sunshine and shadows helped me to draw them. Surrounding the doors there are complex leaded windows in clear glass. This structure has a refined dignity. A fund-raising effort is ongoing to restore the top floor for public use. Several monuments on the lawn honor veterans.

The town takes its name from Dunbartonshire in Scotland, birthplace of Archibald Stark, an early settler and the father of Revolutionary War General John Stark.

EPSOM

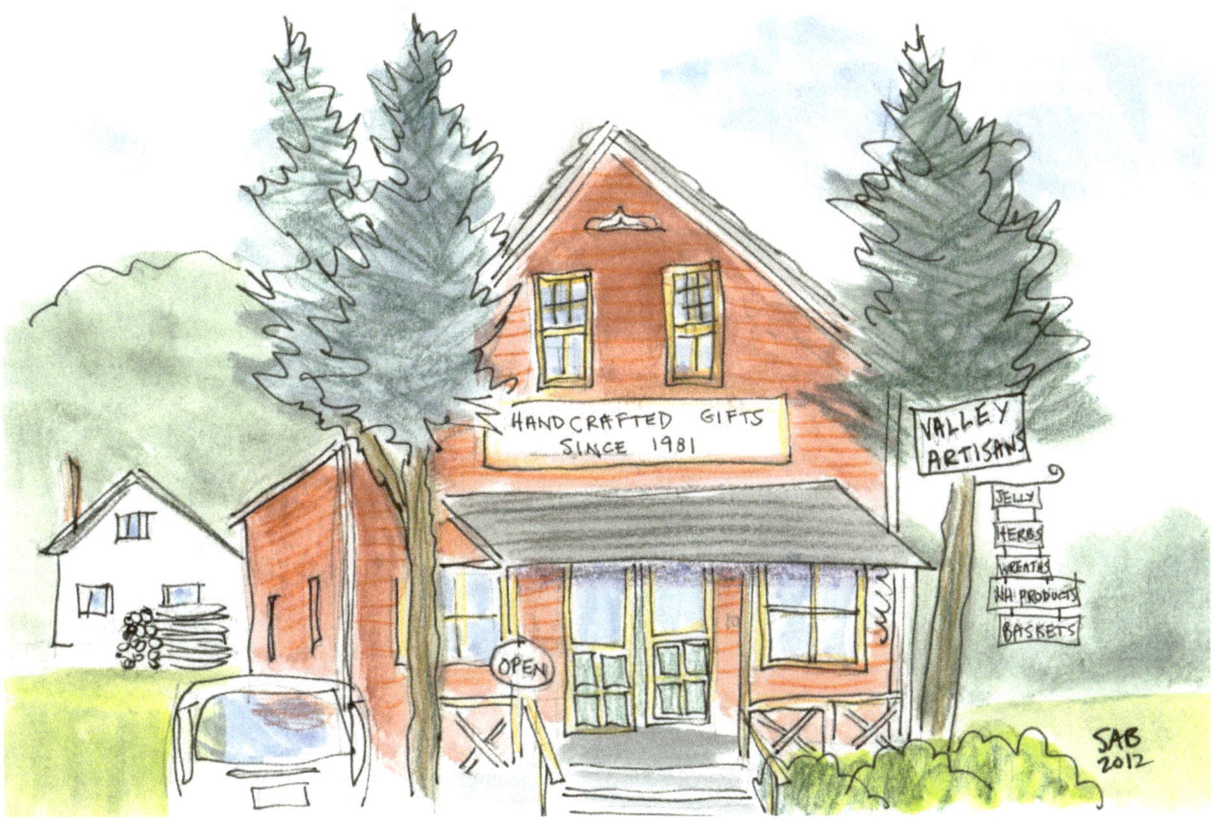

This building, just a few feet from the road, looks to me like an old general store, complete with a welcoming porch.

The town was incorporated in 1727 and named for Epsom, England.

Recently the town has been making some changes. In 2006, a new library was built, and the old building was turned into the town Historical Center. The Old Freewill Baptist Church Meetinghouse, built in 1861, was moved in 2007 to a spot right near the new library. These buildings and the town offices are all in one location and are the new center of town.

FRANKLIN

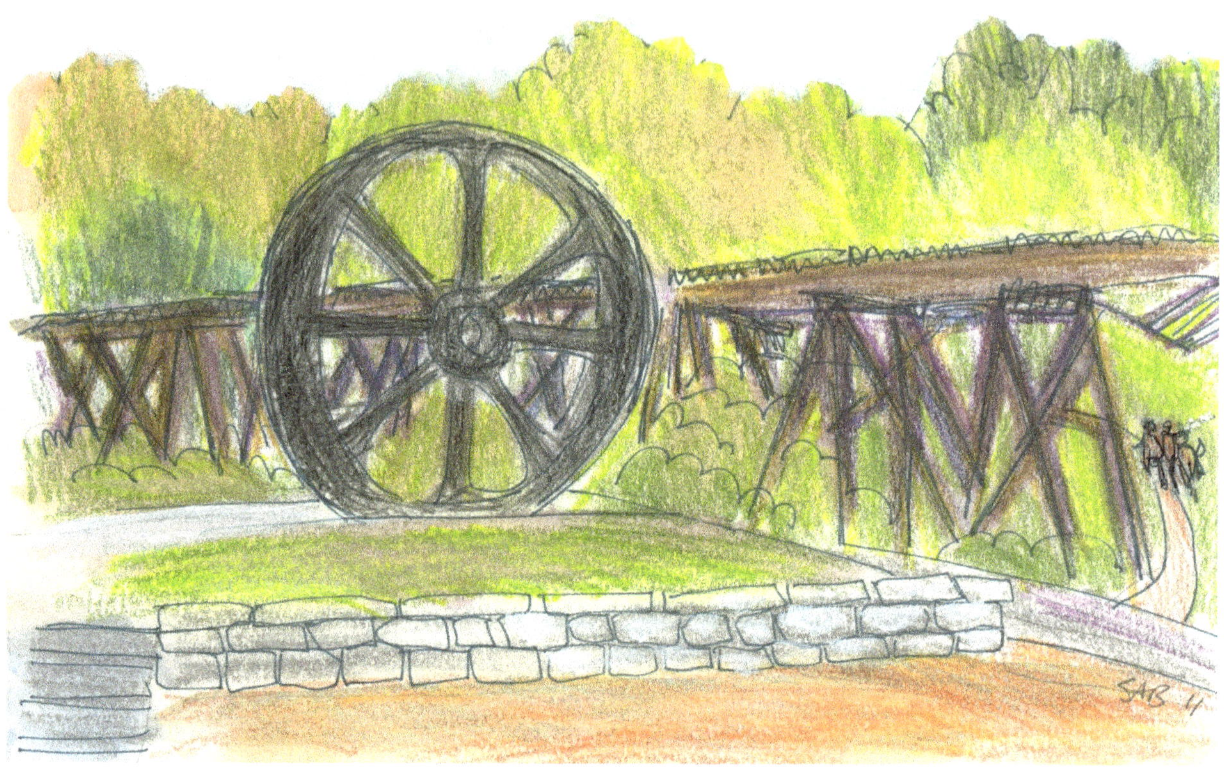

Franklin was formed in 1820 from four neighboring towns. The Pemigewasset and Winnipesaukee Rivers merge here to form the Merrimack, which flows through northeastern Massachusetts to the Atlantic.

These rivers powered the Industrial Revolution in this part of New England. The history of the town includes saw mills, grist mills, fulling and yarn mills, doors sashes and blinds, woolens, hosiery, and paper. The town has a splendid Carnegie library, as well as a combination opera house and town hall. Trestle View Park is a remembrance of the era of the mills.

Across the street to the far right, you can see start of the five mile long Winnipesaukee River Trail.

GOFFSTOWN

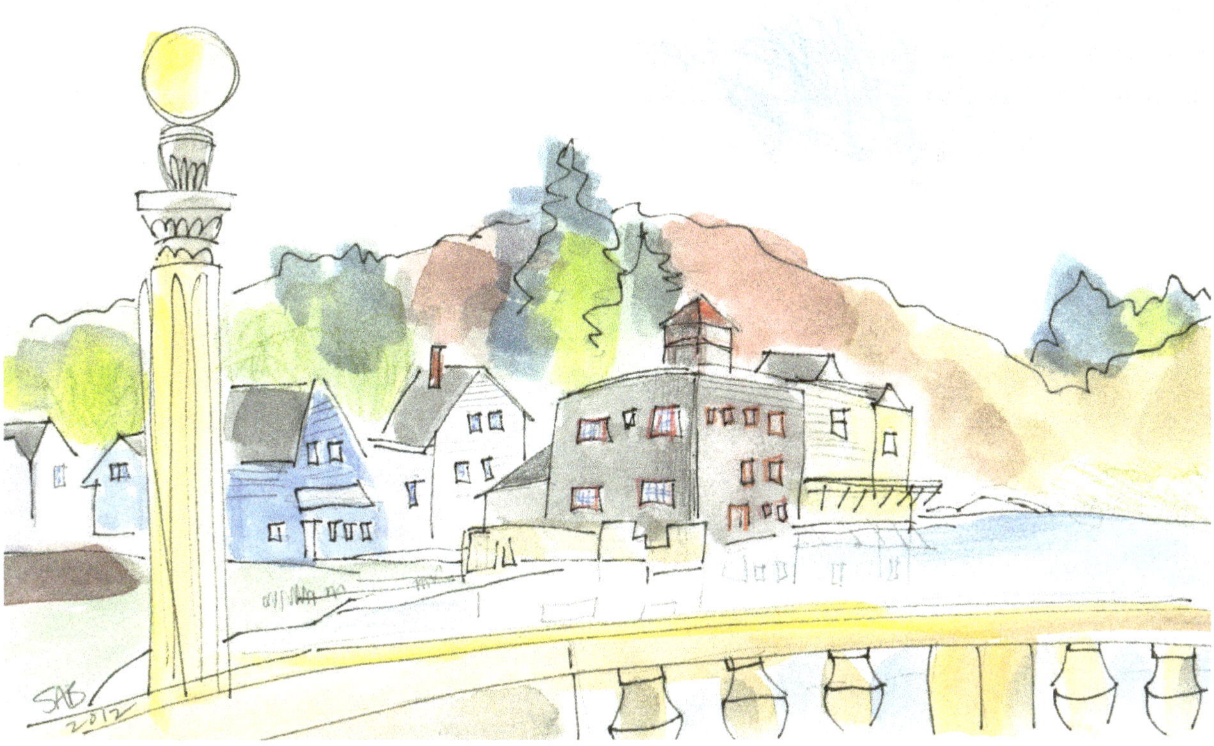

Goffstown is well known for its Lions Club popcorn cart.

Many of the buildings along the Piscataquog River are former saw mills and textile mills. An old postcard picture shows a wooden covered bridge spanning the river.

In the early 1900s, the Incline Railway was built by the Otis Elevator Company to the top of one of the Uncanoonuc Mountains. A five story hotel was built to feed and house the brave tourists and skiers. Television and radio towers are the only structures now on the steep slope. And speaking of TV, the Benedictine liberal arts college in town, Saint Anselm's College, is known for sponsoring political debates among presidential candidates in New Hampshire's first in the nation primary elections.

HOLLIS

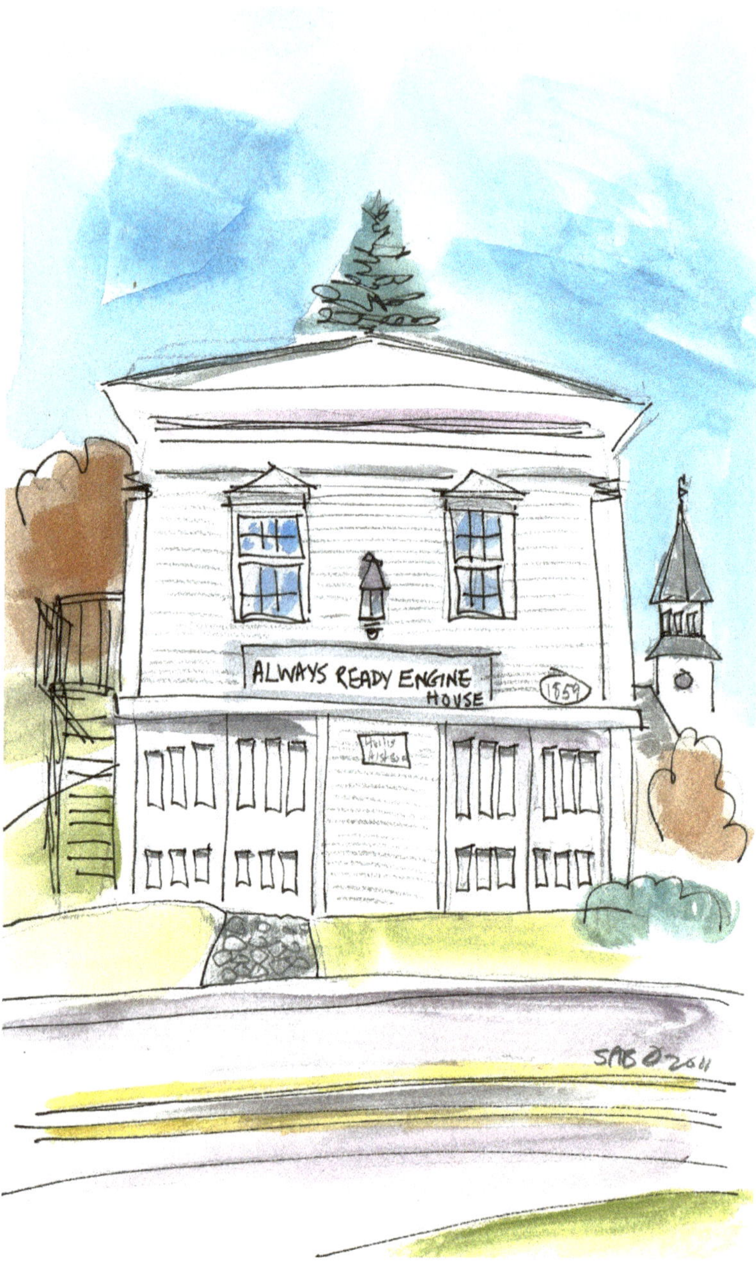

The square, boxy, white building is the former fire station, now the home of the local Historical Society. It was home to a horse drawn carriage and hose.

The tower in the background belongs to the town offices located on the common. The little tree appears to be atop the fire station roof, but it is merely centered behind it. The Hollis Social Library was being clad in a gleaming new copper roof the day I was there.

Hollis is well known for its large old apple orchards.

HOOKSETT

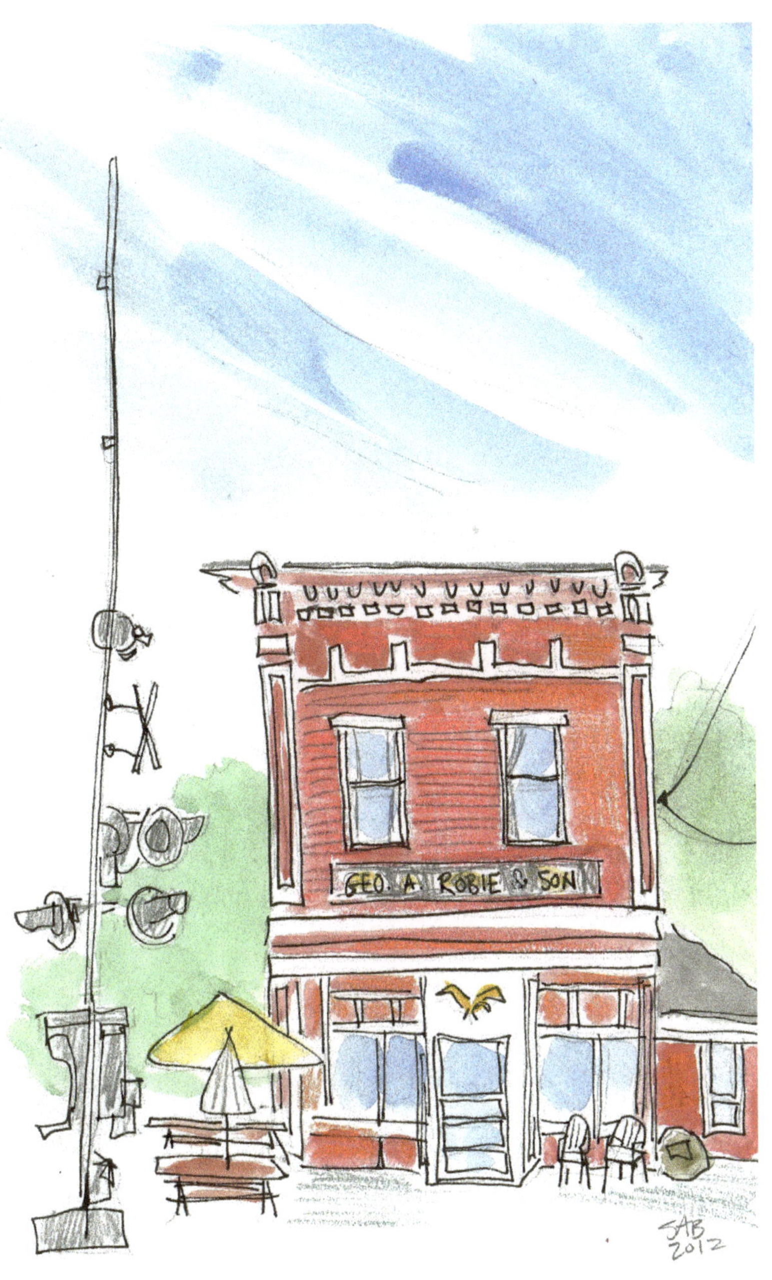

General stores are the traditional meeting places for the townspeople and those running for elected public office. The sign above the door says 'Geo. A. Robie & Son'.

This was a family business for 110 years. It sits right along the railroad tracks in Hooksett Village and has been a stop for presidential candidates since the 1950s. The walls inside are lined with political buttons, photos, bumper stickers, and the like. At one time the business received merchandise by barge from the Merrimack River, and it also served as the town's post office.

We got all turned around the first time we tried to find this store because we were on the wrong side of the Merrimack River.

HOPKINTON

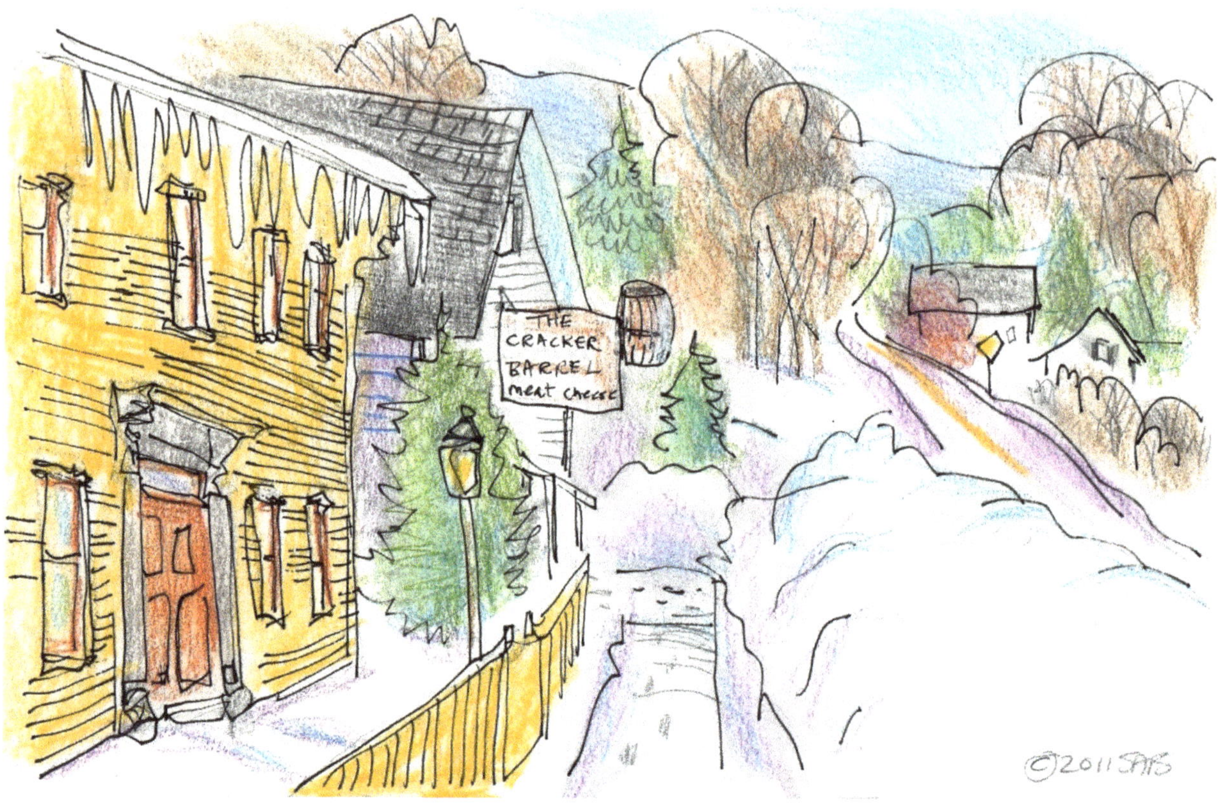

Hopkinton has three districts; Hopkinton Village, Contoocook, and West Hopkinton. Contoocook is the most commercial.

I drew the Theophilus Stanley Tavern (1791) in Hopkinton Village very rapidly, as it was extremely cold that day, well below zero in fact. I did add the colors at home, I admit. Many houses in this area are painted white. A yellow one contrasts nicely with the enormous piles of snow along the road. The tavern, recently restored, is now a private residence.

The Cracker Barrel Corner Market is a town institution.

HUDSON

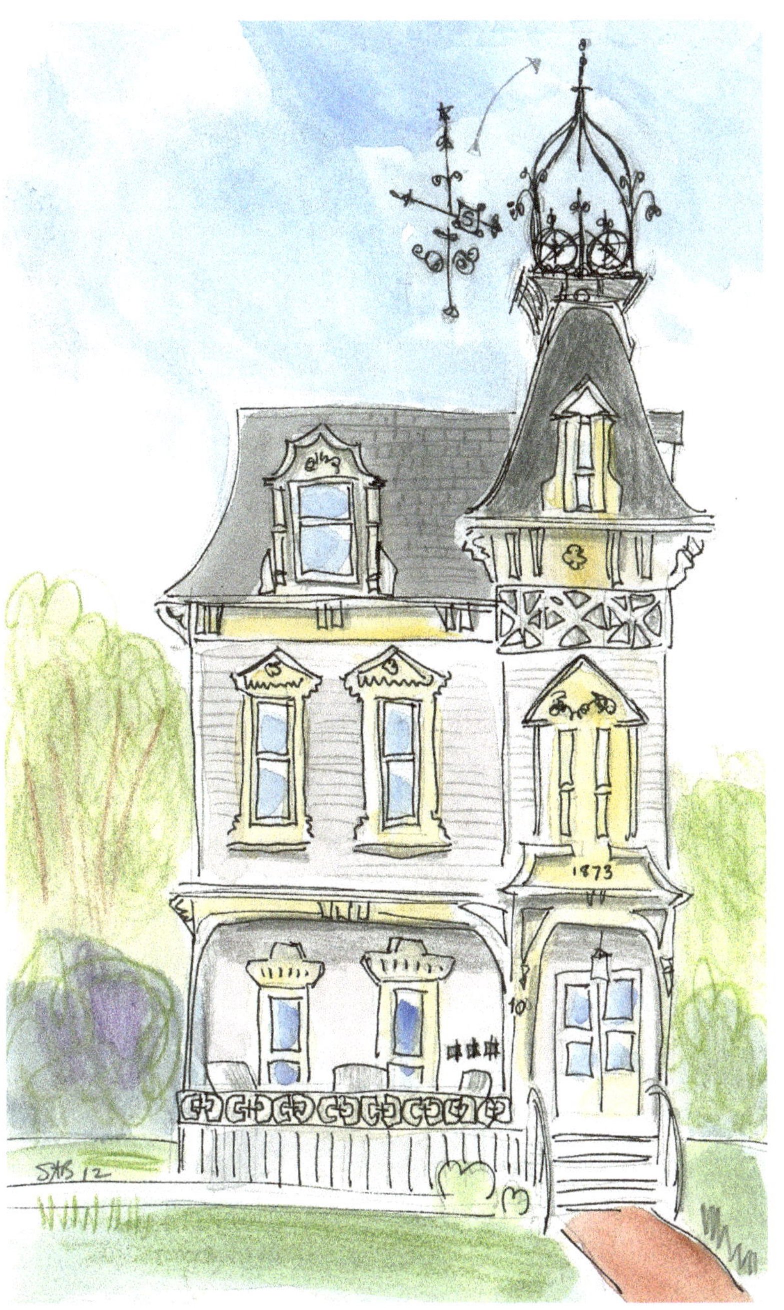

Hudson, with a population of 25,000, is quite a large place by New Hampshire measures. It is directly across the Merrimack River from the major city of Nashua, and also on the border with Massachusetts.

The land here was claimed by both states for a long time. The border between the two states was finally settled upon in 1741. An early prominent family was the Hills, and their summer home is now the Historical Society. The Alvirne High School originates from a Hills family donation. Many people remember Benson's Wild Animal Farm. Me included.

The amazingly intricate wrought iron top of this Victorian era house called me to draw it, despite the fact that I knew it would overflow the paper's edge.

LITCHFIELD

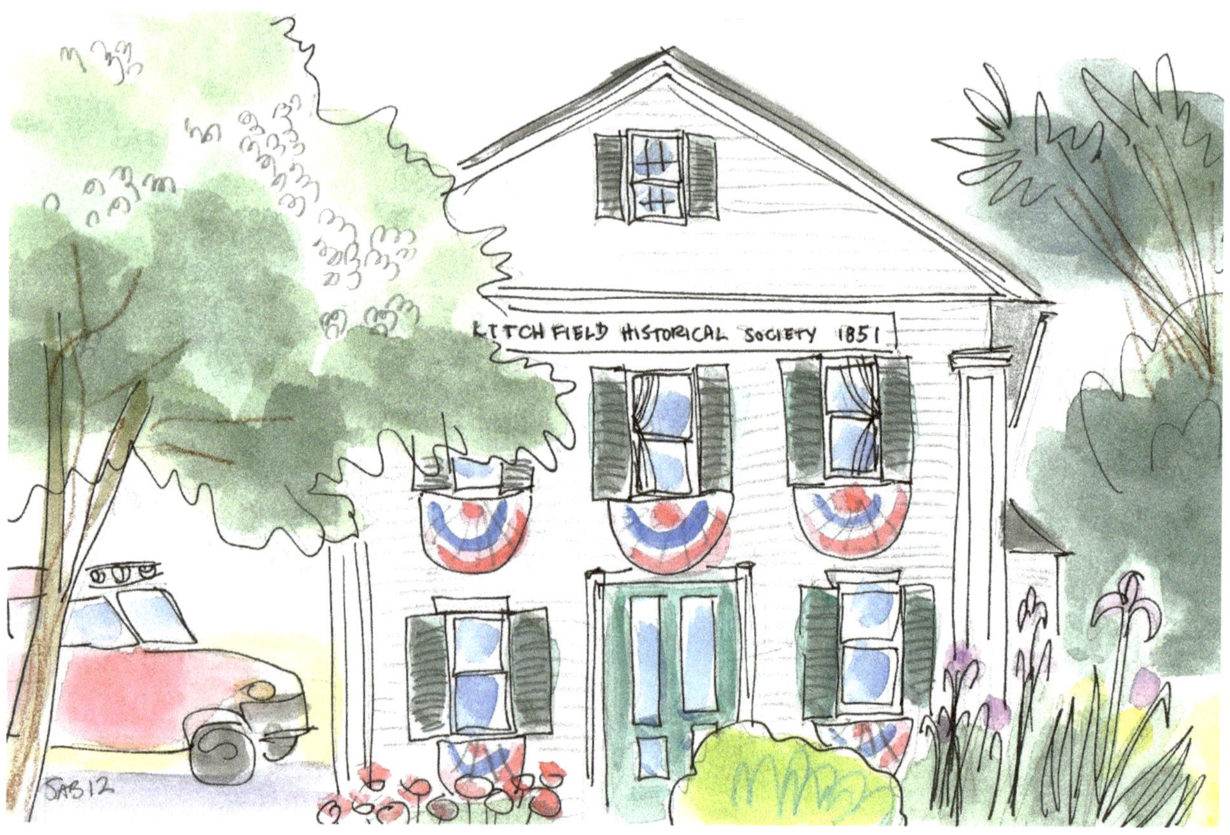

Litchfield is a small but growing town along the Merrimack River, nestled between Manchester and Nashua. We saw lots of rich brown soil, ready for this year's crops to be planted.

The land next to rivers is always very fertile, and the town is known for its produce farms. The white wooden frame building is the home of the Litchfield Historical Society. The Memorial Day bunting will most likely remain until Independence Day. The town's library, the Aaron Cutler Memorial Library, is a very handsome brick and granite structure.

Flowering trees and an iris garden are sure signs of spring in New Hampshire.

LONDONDERRY

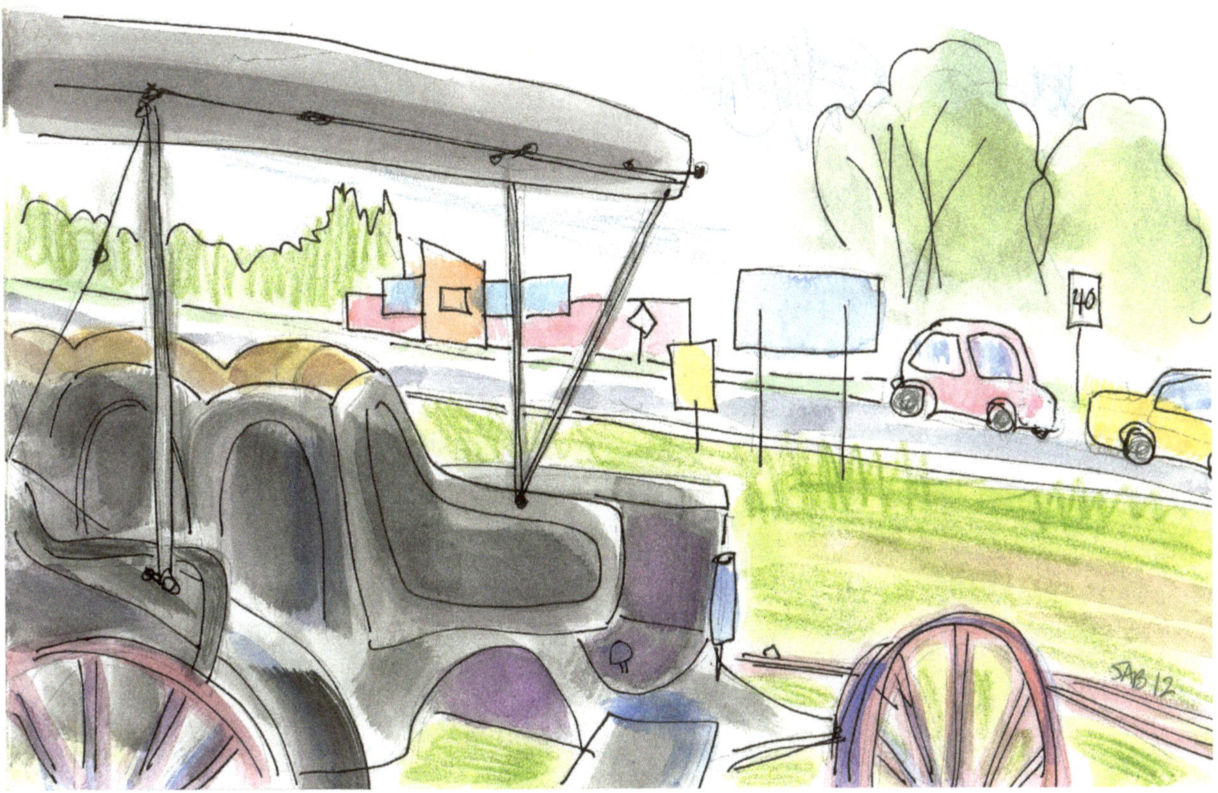

The old vehicle seemed to gaze out towards the modern busy highway and crossroads.

The town was settled in 1718 by people from Northern Ireland. The land along the Merrimack River was fertile, and the farms flourished.

The town and area are still known for apple orchards. Londonderry shares a northern border with Manchester, and some of the Manchester-Boston Regional Airport is on town land. We ate on the terrace at The Coach Stop, overlooking the front lawn. The carriage on the lawn was in wonderful condition, and it looked like it had had a lot of loving restoration.

LOUDON

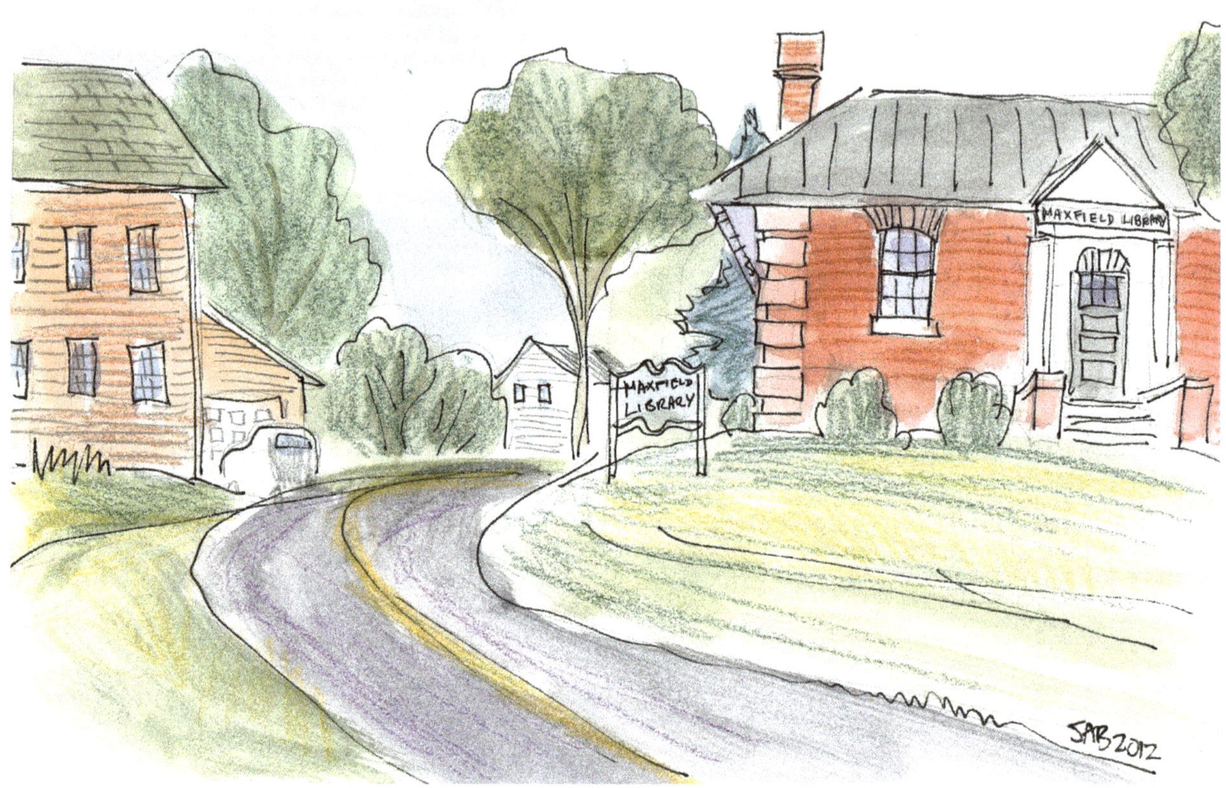

Loudon is a town east of the state capital of Concord. Here on the bend of the road is the brick Maxfield Public Library.

I do love to draw curves in the road (sort of like a racetrack), and the yellow paint stripe that always accompanies them. The private home on the left is an unusual, pumpkin-like color. Near this corner is an old general store with a porch full of rocking chairs.

Loudon is the home of the New Hampshire Motor speedway, which hosts America's oldest motorcycle race.

MANCHESTER

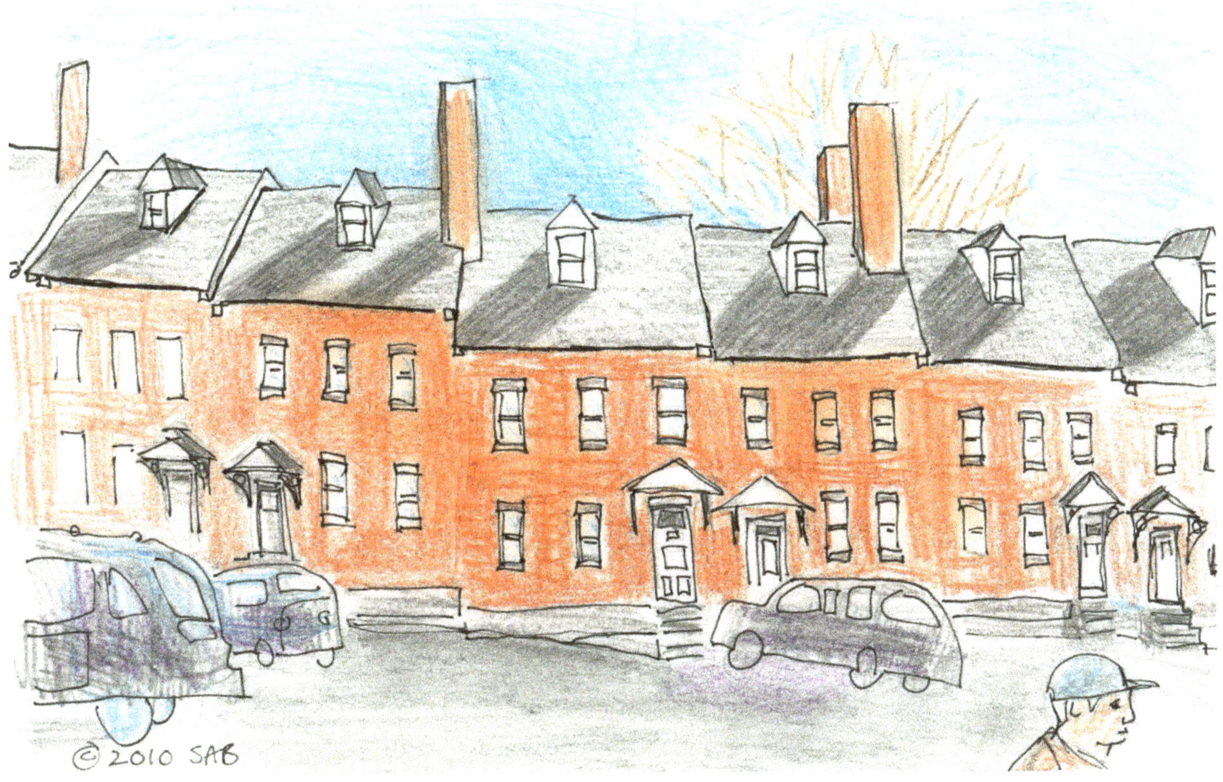

On a cold but sunny winter day, I sketched the shadows on the roofs of the corporations – housing built by the mill owners for their workers.

Manchester is the state's largest city, with a population just over 100,000 people. The Merrimack River bisects it.

Originally called Derryfield, the name was changed to Manchester in 1810 as a purposeful echo to the first great industrialized city in the world, Manchester, England. At this time, a canal and lock system had been built next to the river and a mill called Amoskeag Cotton and Woolen Manufacturing had been established. By 1846, it was the largest mill in the world, with over 4,000 looms. The mills closed in 1935, but the mile-long buildings are now put to new uses.

MERRIMACK

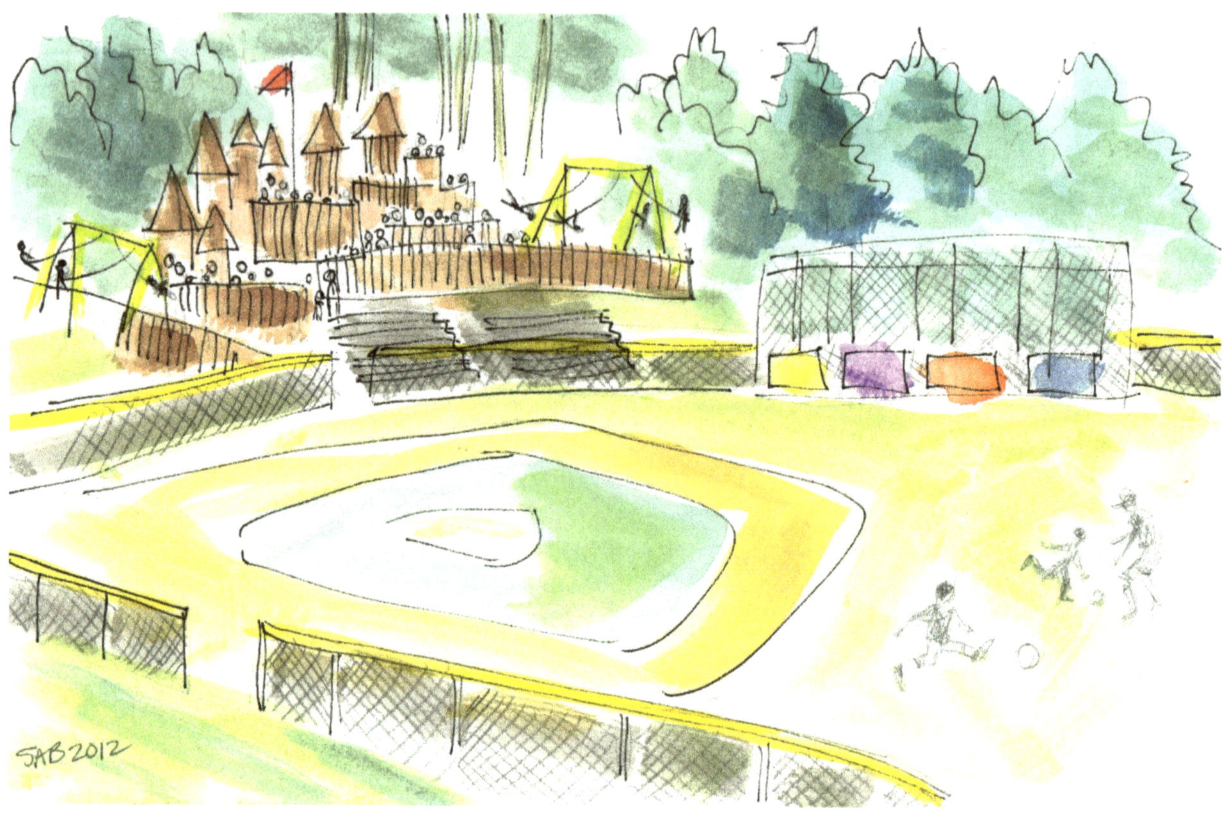

We drove to Merrimack, bordering the river of that name, on one Sunday in March when the weather was unseasonably warm.

But there were no leaves yet on the trees, and the grass was still hibernating. Twin Bridge Park in Merrimack was absolutely filled with happy families enjoying the sunny day. The baseball diamond was still waiting for the season, but look at the castle-themed playground. The kids are flying on the swings!

For the history minded person, visit the home of Mathew Thornton, signer of the Declaration of Independence.

MILFORD

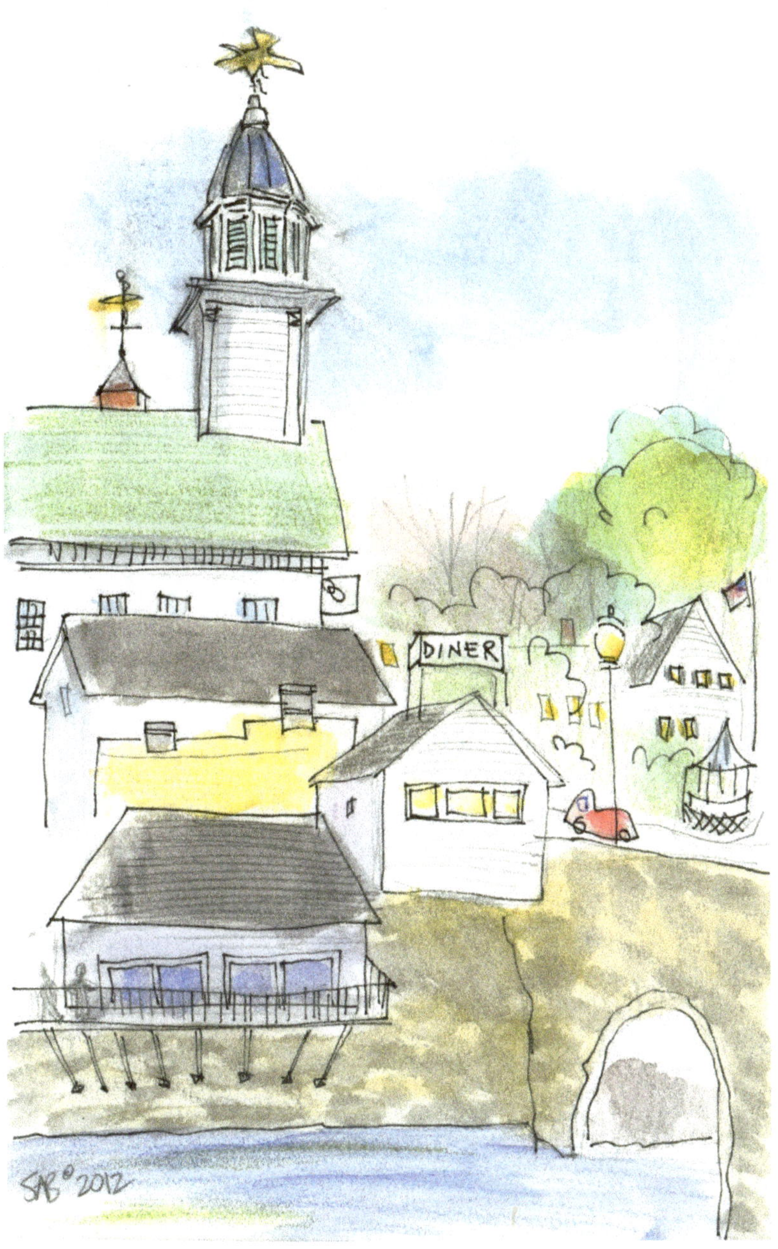

Milford was once a part of Amherst, but broke away in 1794. The small building on the left hangs over the Souhegan River. It is part of the long established Red Arrow diner.

In the background I drew the town oval and the Pillsbury bandstand. The gold eagle is atop the Odd Fellows Lodge, a world-wide fraternal and benevolent organization. The phrase 'odd fellows' refers to its origins in England. Minor trades that didn't have their own guilds formed this one. Milford once had many granite quarries.

My father's family came from Quebec to work in New Hampshire's quarries.

MONT VERNON

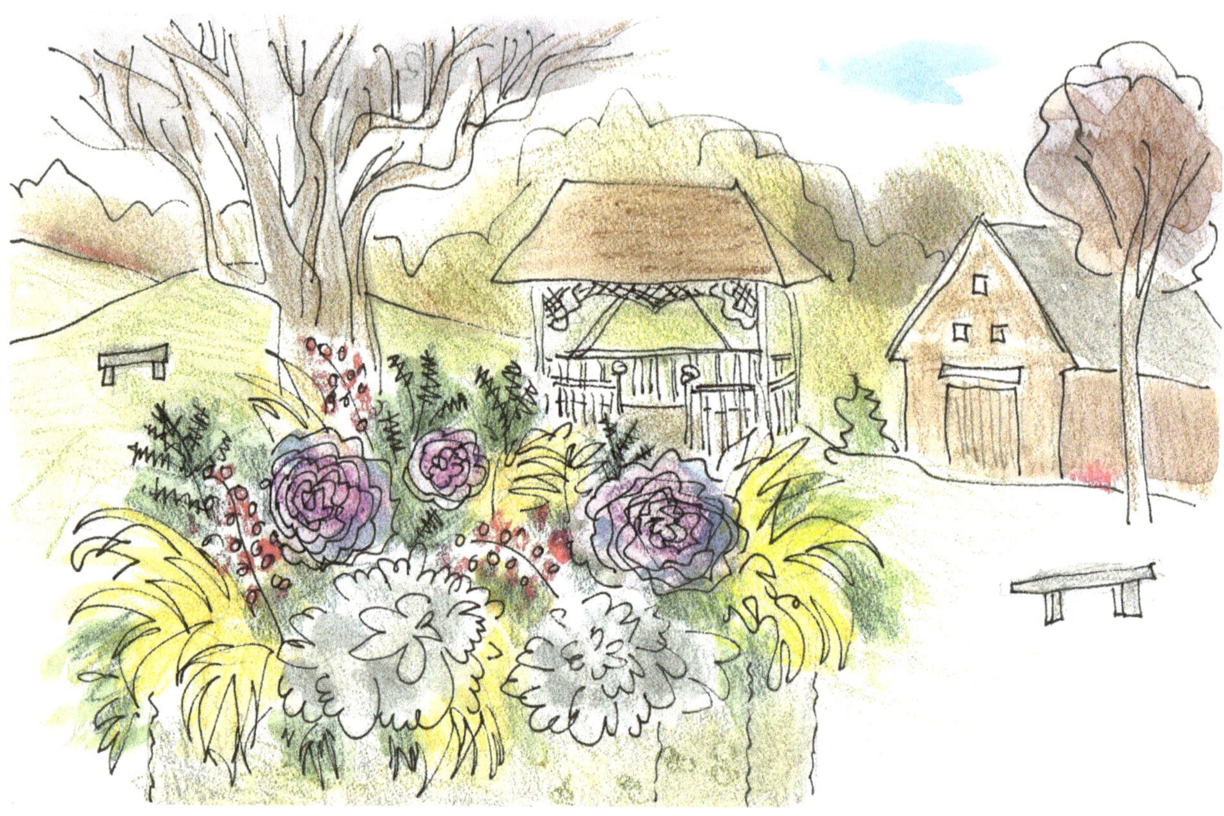

The town is on the crest of a very steep hill. Like many New Hampshire towns with a great vista, large hotels were built for summer residents.

The hotels are all gone now, but Mont Vernon's fine location is making it a great residential community, close enough for an easy commute to nearby cities. I drew the town green on a brisk winter's day. This winter arrangement in a horse trough was made for public enjoyment. It showed real style, solid design, and fine knowledge of plants. The three purple, rose-like plants are kale, which loves cold weather.

The town was named after the home of George Washington, Mount Vernon

NASHUA

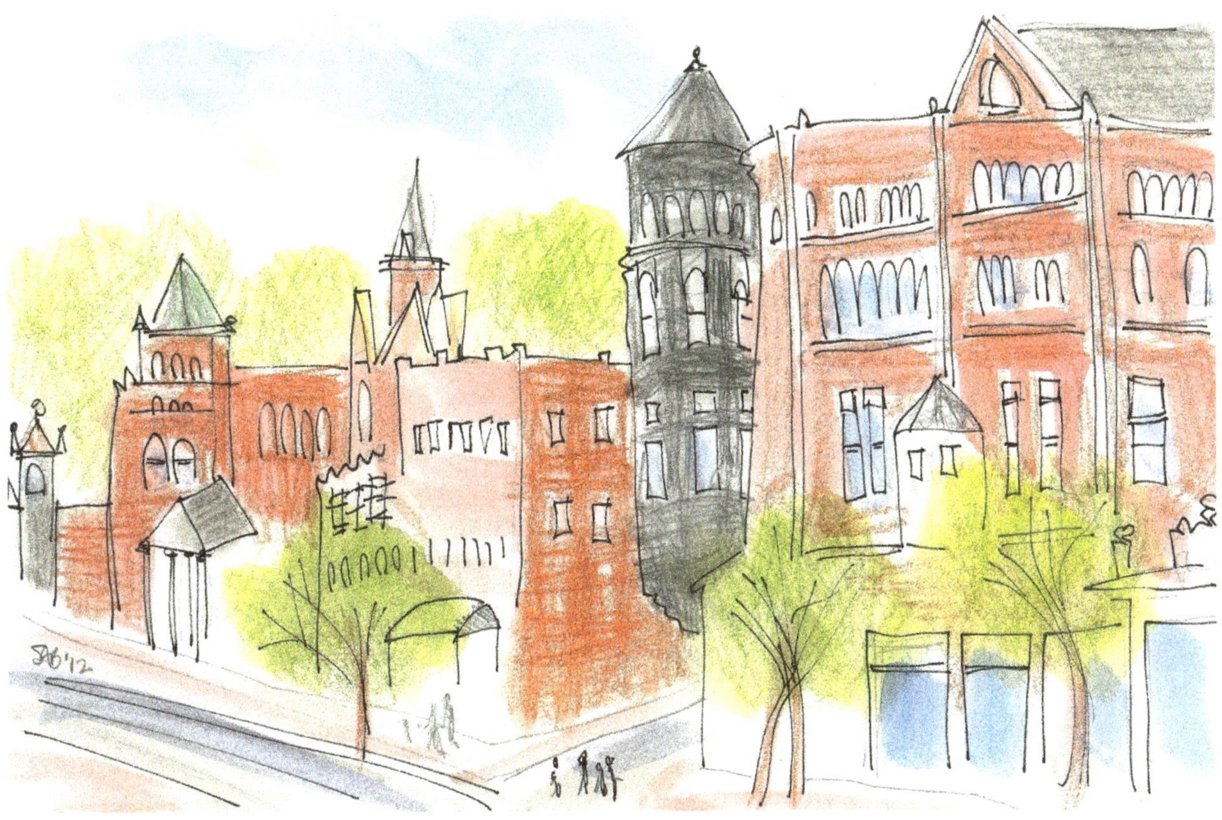

Drawing towers and turrets appeals to me, and Nashua, New Hampshire's second largest city, abounds with them.

When I was a child, Nashua was a major shopping destination for our family. It had department stores, a true sign of urban life.

One of the department stores had a system of pneumatic tubes. You handed your cash to an employee, who fed it along with the bill of sale into a tubular canister. This went into a pipe and whoosh, away it went. You could watch it whiz around and up until it reached the cashiers on the top floor. They made change and sent it all back again.

NEW BOSTON

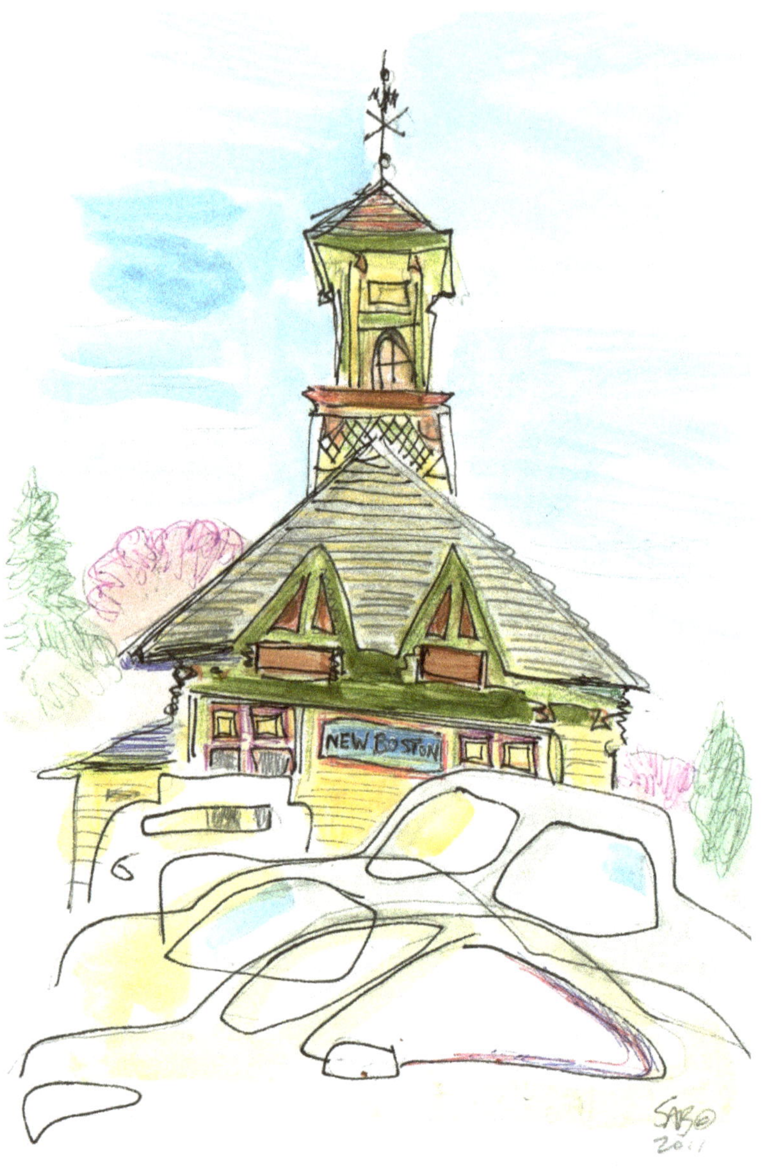

New Boston, settled by families from Boston in the 1700s, has an unusual central core. Many of the buildings, including a general store, a hardware store, many homes, a bandstand, and the fire station are in ornate Victorian style.

This is due to a fire in 1887 that destroyed 40 older buildings. The town center has a cohesive look. New Boston is a town that I glimpsed often in my childhood. Mind you, we never stopped. We were on our way north to Bradford. Finally, many years later, the day came to stop, get out, stroll around, and then draw this old fire station.

The old Dodge's General Store is back in business with new owners.

NORTHFIELD

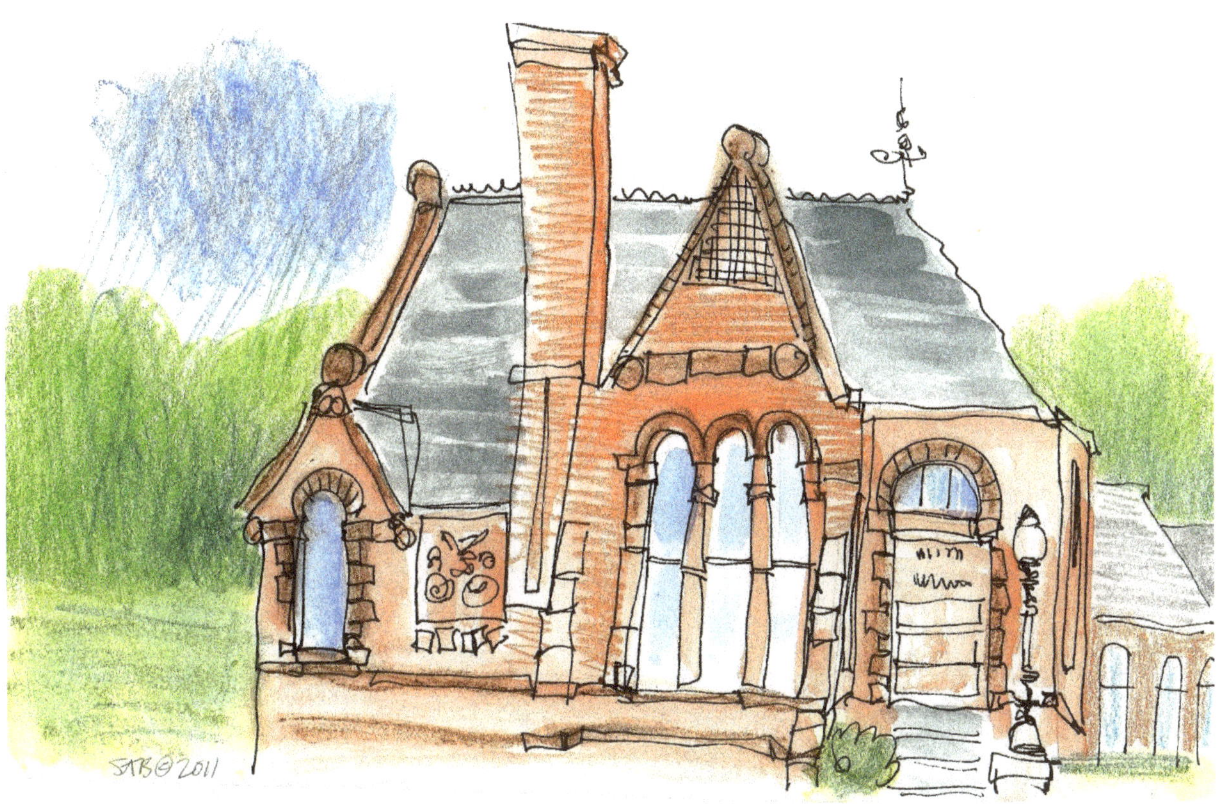

It was an early spring day when I drew this, and bucketing down rain.

The town was formed in 1780, as a breakaway from Canterbury to the south. This building is the 1905 Hall Memorial Library, shared with the town of Tilton.

I do so love late Victorian tour de force brick edifices—such a combination of masterful solidity and frivolity, with a dash of brio! As with many buildings of this era, there is a new addition out the back. That way it doesn't spoil the looks of the original architecture. And this one was done in a tasteful and harmonious fashion.

NORTHWOOD

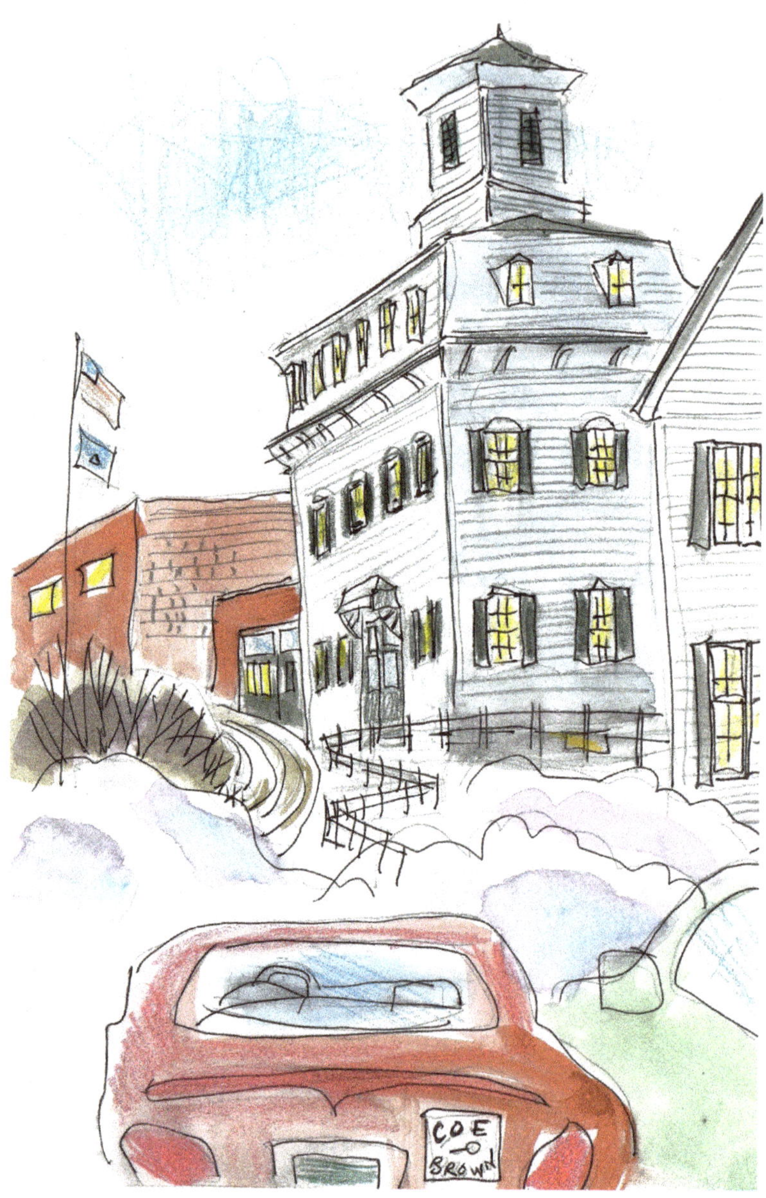

I chose to draw a side view of Coe-Brown Northwood Academy. The academy is a public high school, originally founded as a private high school in 1867. That's a rather common situation here in New Hampshire.

Named for two benefactors, the school welcomes students from Northwood and surrounding towns. It sure is a vertical old wooden building, with high piles of snow lining the parking lot. The red car is included because I do like the color. And because it has a Coe-Brown magnetic sign attached to it, which updates the image to the present times.

Northwood's commercial life hugs along Route 4, built in 1800 to connect Portsmouth to Concord.

PELHAM

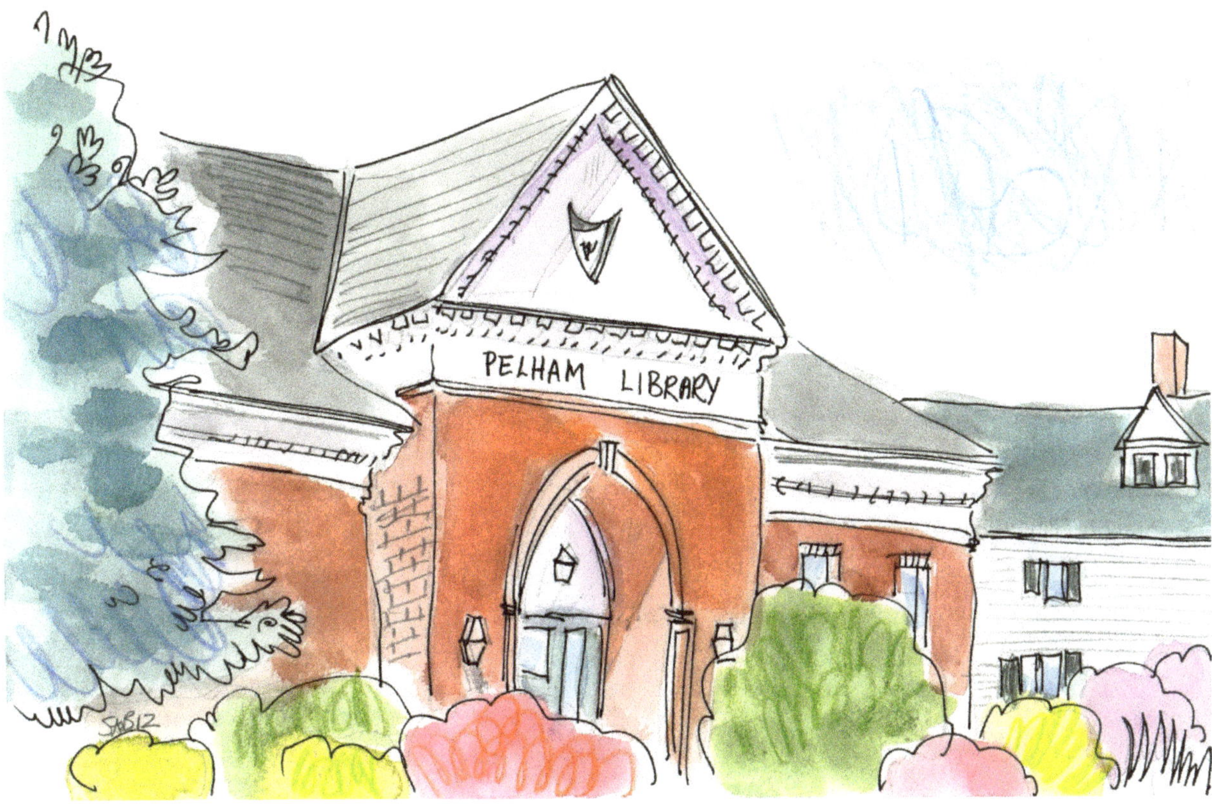

Pelham has built many outdoor sports facilities including an 18-hole disc golf course.

For years and years, my memory of Pelham was the place where I went to Girl Scout camp in the 1950s.

Camp Runnels is still there, providing summer fun for girls aged nine to twelve. The former Pelham Library is now the Pelham Historical Society. The new Pelham Public library sits nearby on the village green. The arch, the shadows, and the gorgeous garden in the front of the doorway inspired me to paint this scene.

PEMBROKE

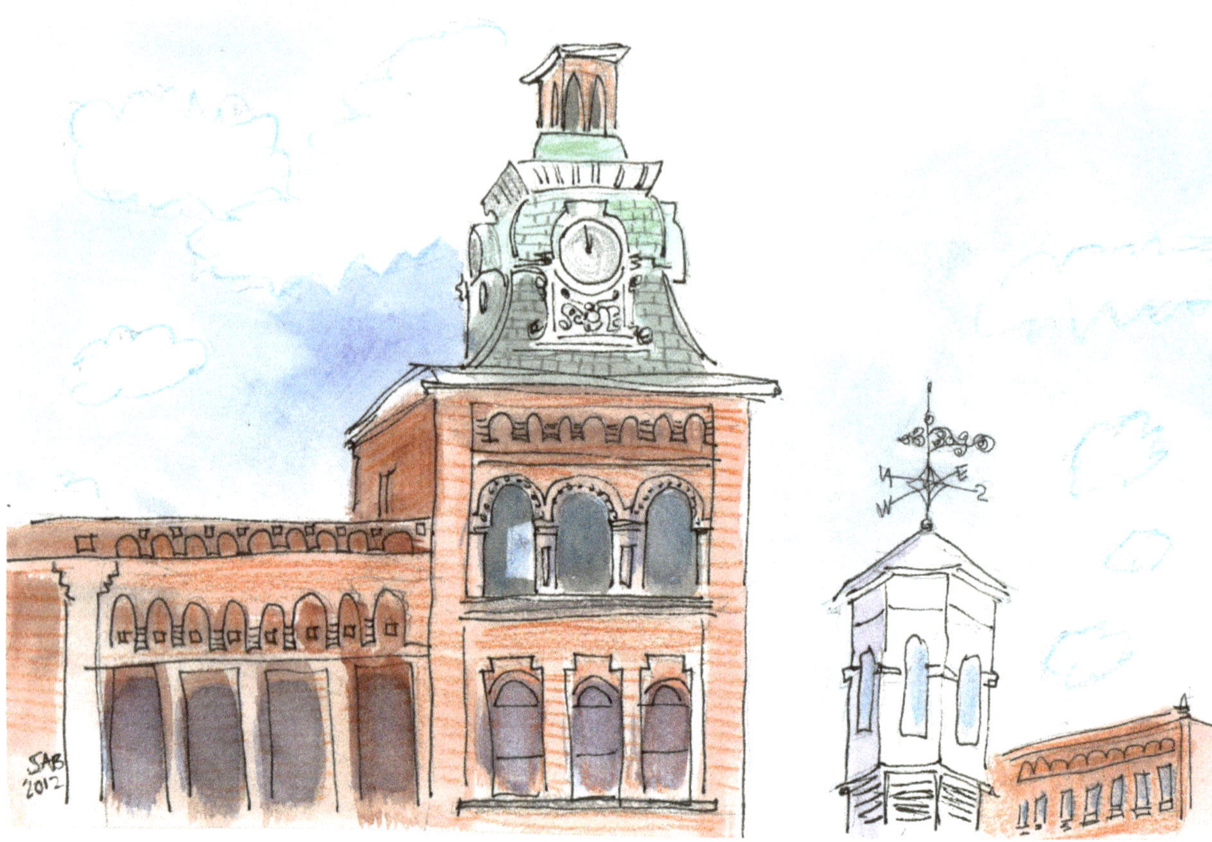

The village of Suncook lies partially within the town of Pembroke. Architecturally, it is an intact mill village.

The water power was harnessed by the 1730s. By 1900 the Pembroke Mill, Webster Mill, and China Mill employed 1,500 workers, most from Quebec, Canada, who made printed cotton cloth. Now the mill buildings are used for housing and small businesses. Cloth manufacturing moved to the southern states, and then to other countries. But the sturdily built brick towers remain. General LaFayette toured the village in 1824. A plaque and a poem honoring the man are here for all to read.

The old clock tower building is now the Emerson Mills Condos.

PITTSFIELD

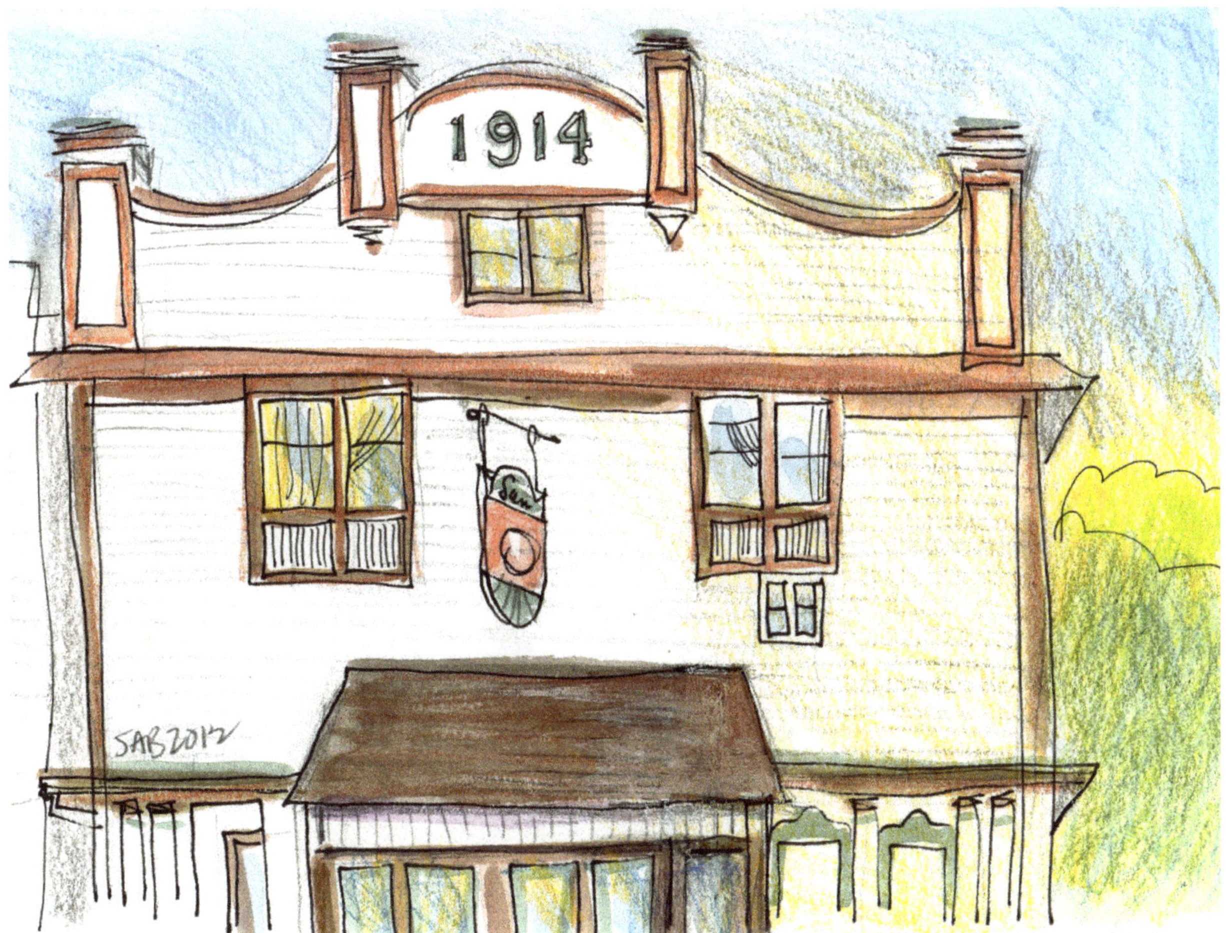

The town of about 4,000 people is bounded by the Suncook River. The name was chosen to honor William Pitt, a Prime Minister of Great Britain.

When I look at one of my drawings, I can always remember the weather. On this day it was hot, dry, and sunny.

Most of the early settlers came from Hampton on the Atlantic coast. My sketch is the old movie house in the downtown. When it was built, it was the place to go to see a silent film, and later a talkie. Think of the excited townspeople who lined up weekly to see the latest stories and stars straight from Hollywood. Since 1968, the Pittsfield Players Scenic Theater has put on performances here.

RAYMOND

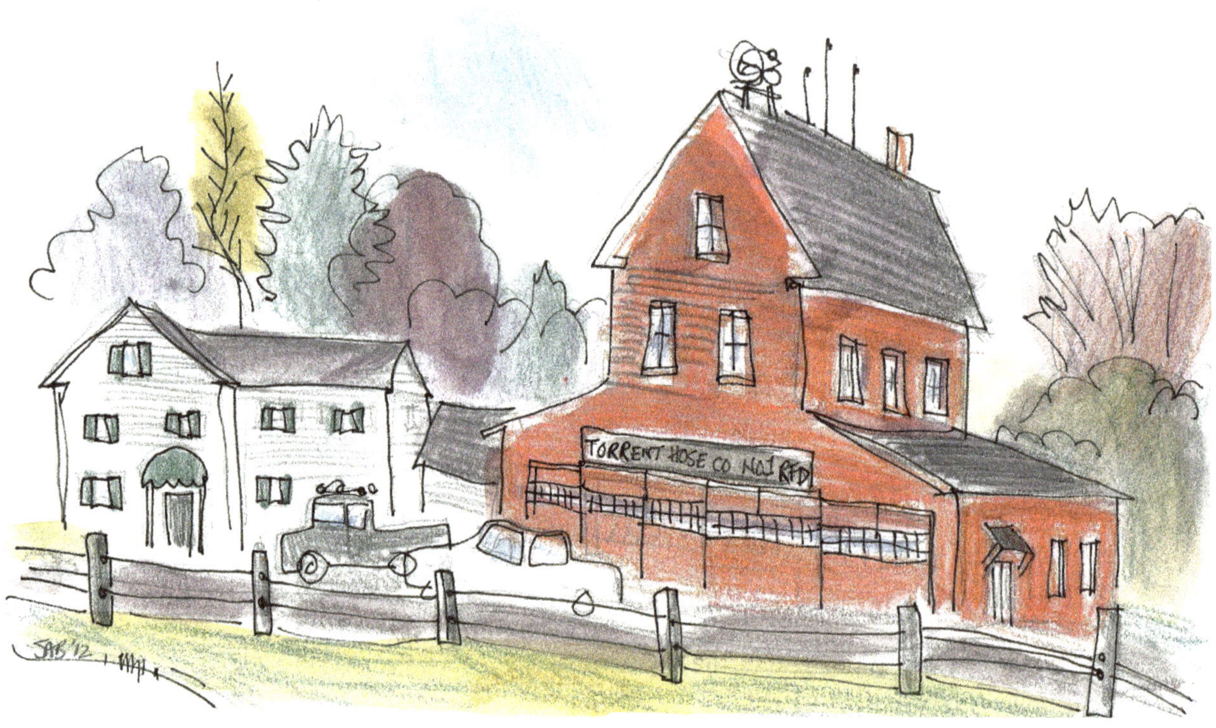

The sign on the red building says "Torrent Hose Co. No 1 RFD". It is the fire station in the town center.

Clearly it is an old house, repurposed and expanded horizontally, and perhaps raised up one story as well. This view is from the town common and the Lyman Memorial Park. The settlement was once called Freetown, but upon incorporation it was renamed Raymond. Although it is good to have highways bypass the little towns, you never see the towns and have no sense of where you really are.

The town has a lovely little Carnegie library, the Dudley-Tucker Library.

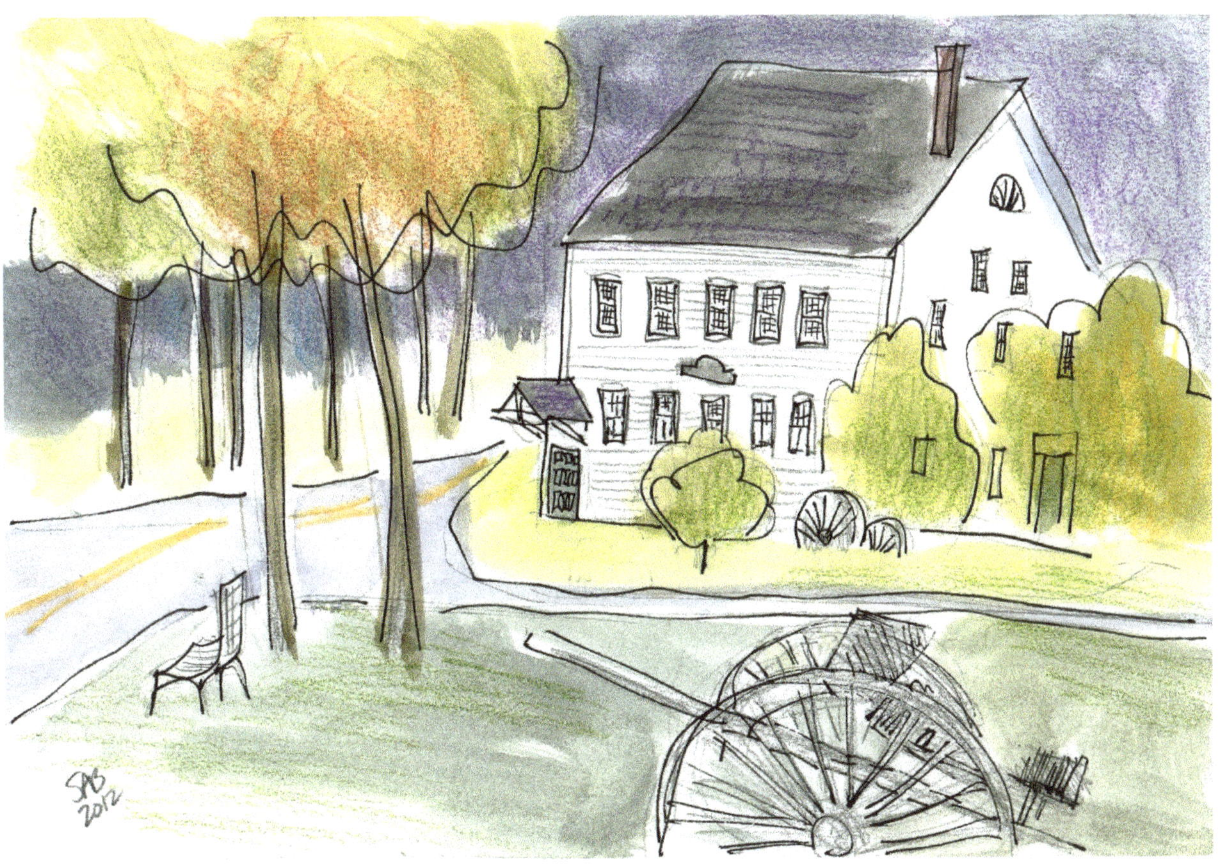

Canobie Lake Park was built in 1902 by the Northeast Street Railway Company to encourage weekend trolley excursions.

The Veterans' Park in Salem was lit by the yellow aura of a streetlight. I drew the cannon the best I could, considering the low light and my lack of expertise in sketching military hardware.

The white frame building is the Salem Historical Museum in the former town hall. Two millstones are set upright in the lawn as a decoration. Salem is also known for an unexplained series of rock structures dubbed America's Stonehenge, and for Rockingham Park Race Track.

TILTON

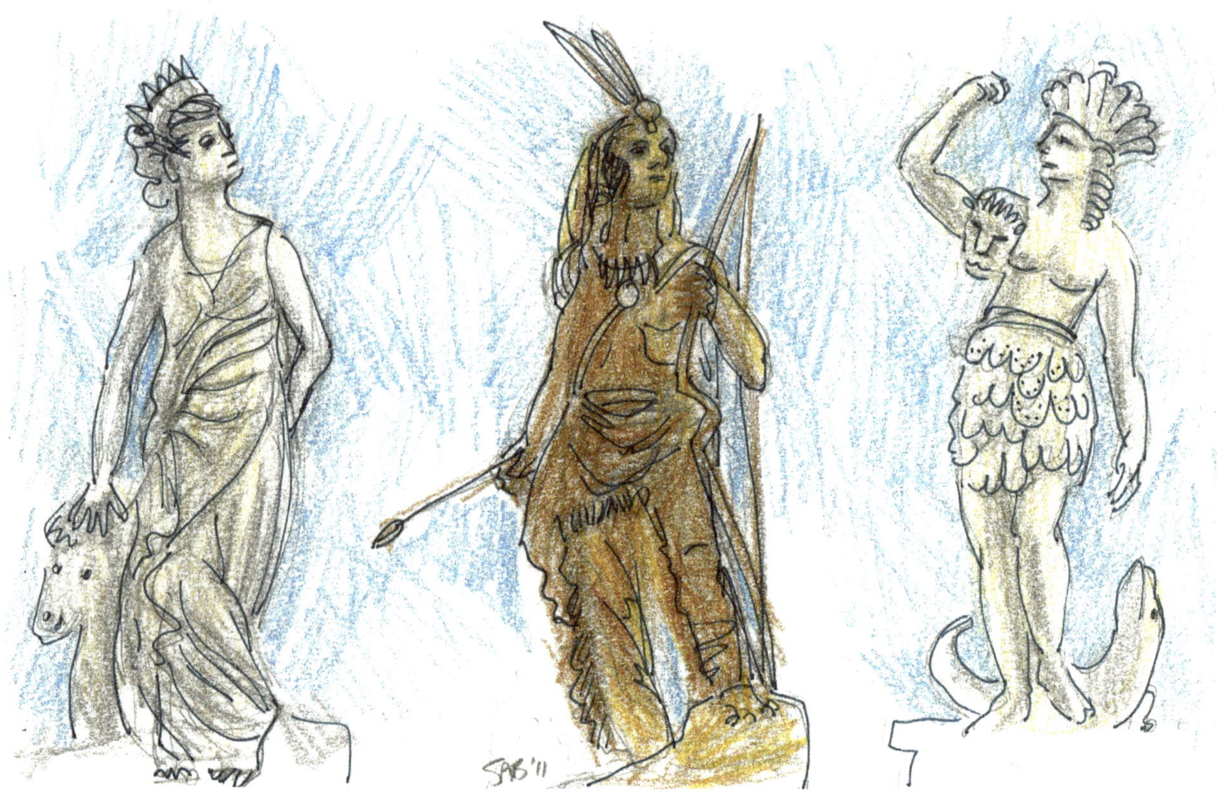

If you walk along Main Street in downtown Tilton, these three statues (here drawn as if adjacent) will greet you.

On the far left is a marble "Miss Tilton", the middle is a bronze Squantum chief, and on the far right is an "Indian queen", also in marble. Up the hill from Main Street is the campus of the well-regarded Tilton School, established in 1845.

Smitty's Cinema is a popular place to see a film, with its armchair seating and full restaurant menu.

WEARE

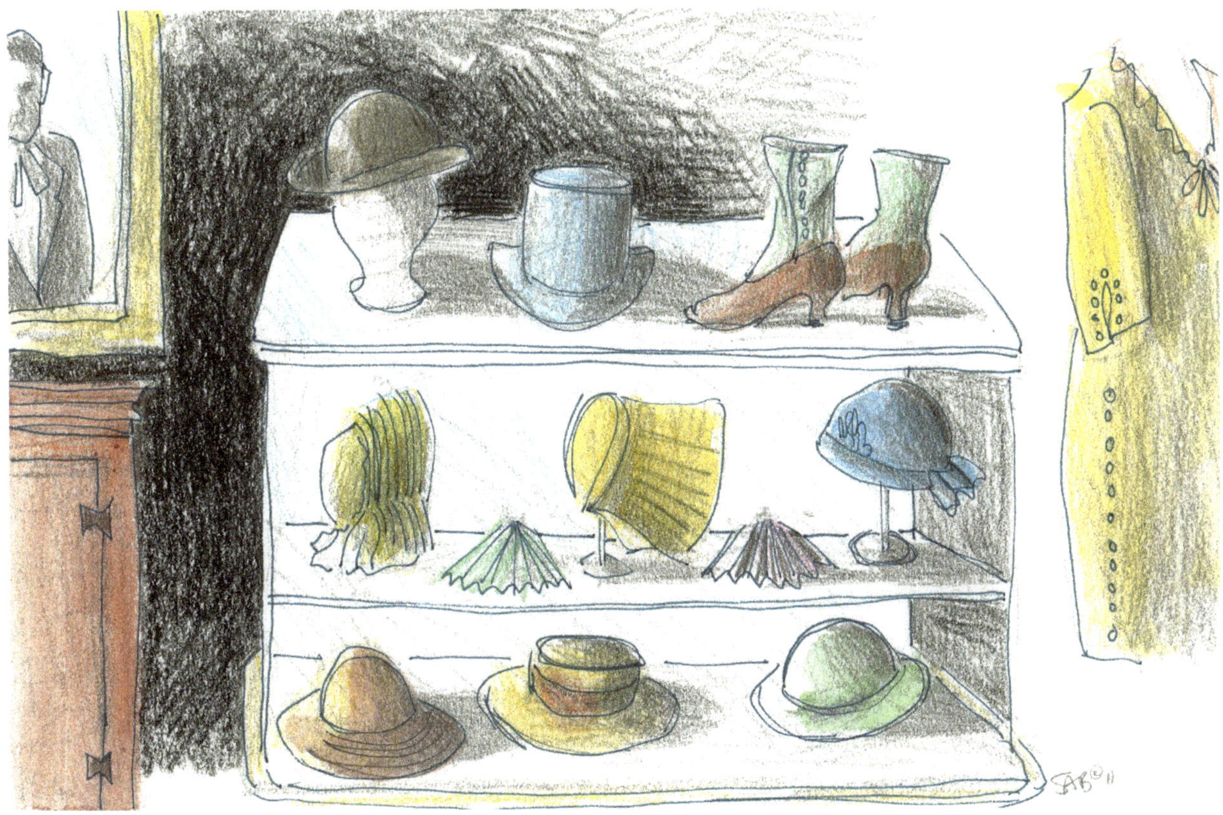

The display case at the Historical Society caught my attention with its fashionable shoes as well as a satisfying variety of hat shapes.

Jokes aside, where is Weare?

The town of 8,000 residents is equidistant between Concord and Manchester, and to the west. It was incorporated in 1764 and named for its first Town Clerk. On the day I was roaming around with my sketchbook, I was admiring the façade of the Stone Memorial Building, designed by the famed Manchester architect, William Butterfield. I was spotted by a woman who had a key to open the door for me. She very kindly let me in and advised me that photography is prohibited. I reached for my pencil.

WINDHAM

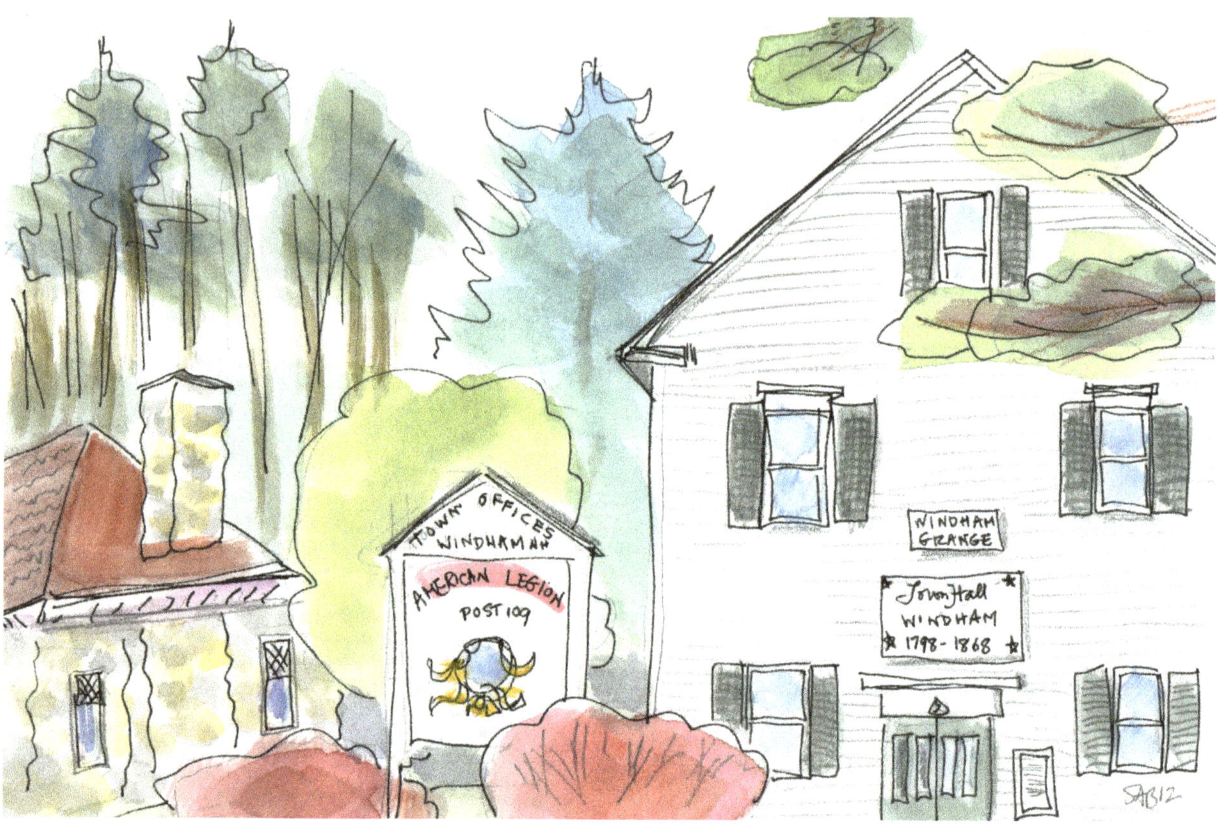

Derry, Londonderry, and Windham were once all one region and called Nutfield. Windham was established as a place name in 1742, just after the settlement of the border battle between New Hampshire and Massachusetts.

I drew the town hall including the town offices, and the Armstrong Building, a town museum. The latter is the old Nesmith Library. The contrast between the wood frame structure, the rough fieldstone one, and the tall pines inspired the composition. The Grange and the American Legion meet in the town offices building.

A town landmark, the Searles Castle, 1915, is used for weddings and receptions.

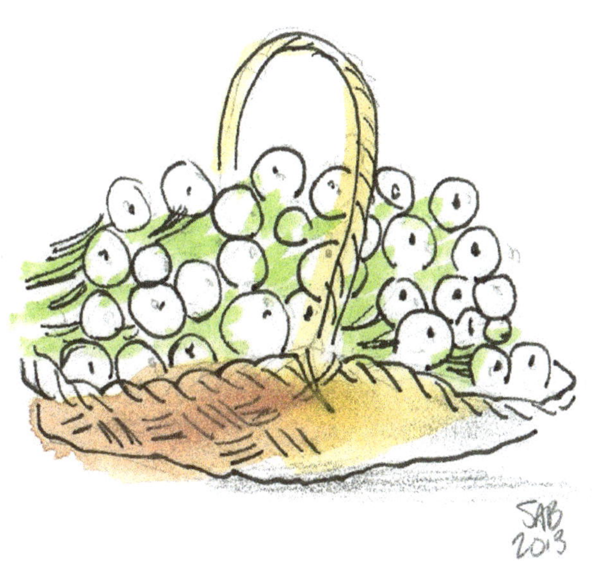
SAB
2013

Monadnock

ACWORTH

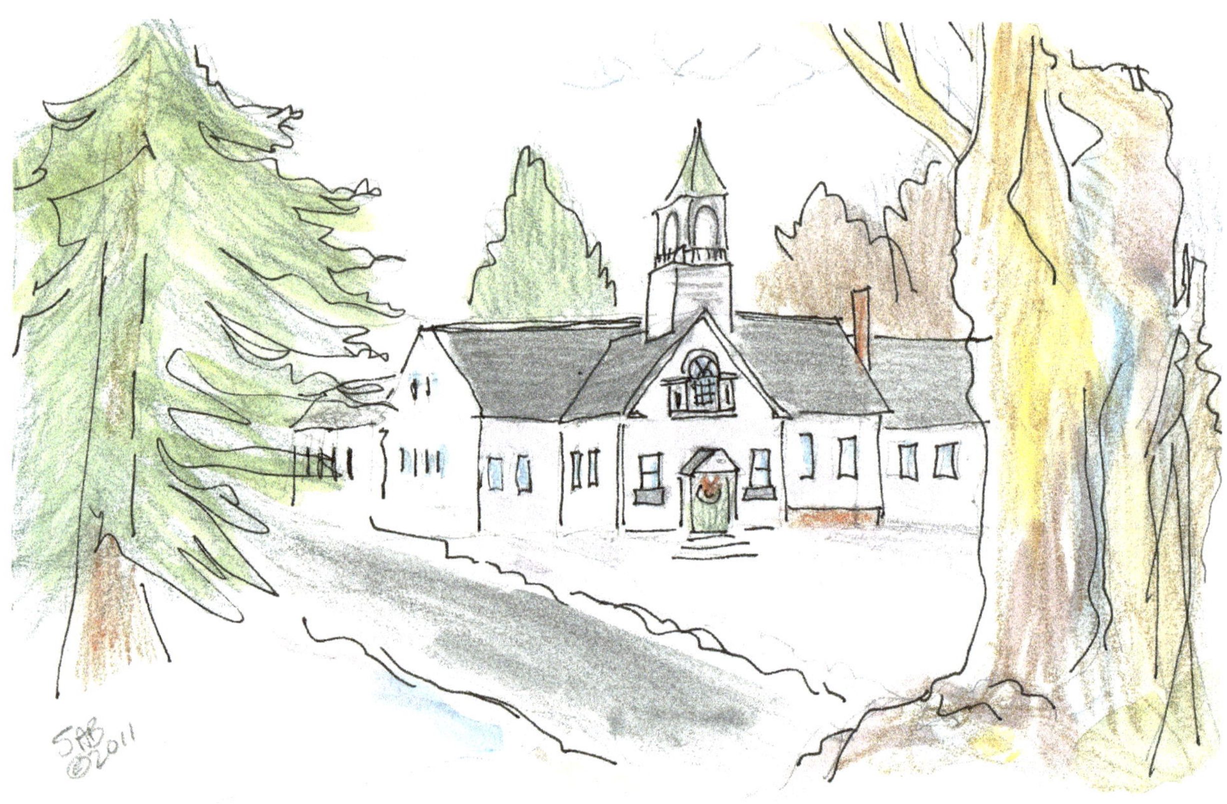

The town common is a lovely setting for a tall church and a lineup of ancient, knobby trees.

I drew the Acworth Elementary School because I liked its central door and holiday wreath. The town library was funded by resident Ithiel Silsby and is registered as a National Historical Landmark. The first time we tried to get to this town, we drove in a circle and never got there. We shortly thereafter bought an atlas!

It was extremely cold on this day, with crunchy snow and still air.

ALSTEAD

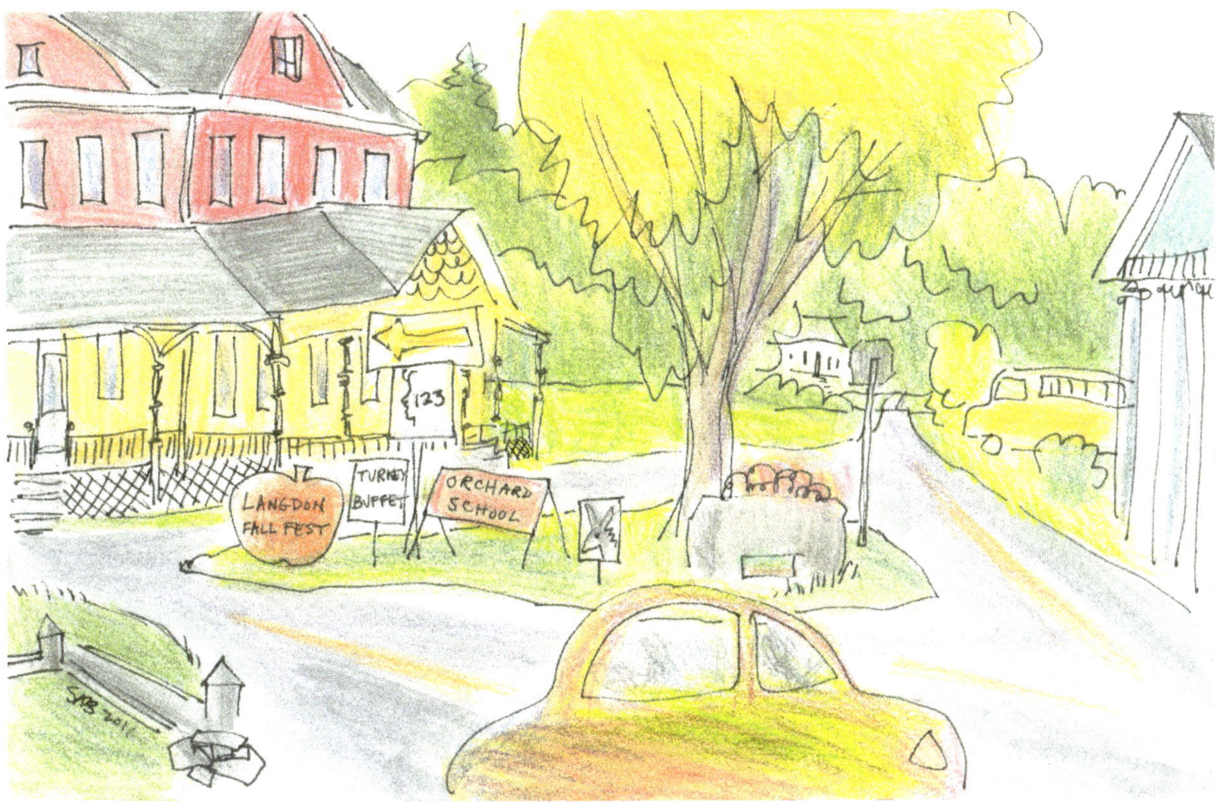

The History Channel provided funding for the town to produce a book about the 2005 flood and aftermath.

The corner of Mechanic Street and Main Street is a busy place any time of the year. In the autumn, signs just grow there like planted shrubbery.

The signs remind the locals of all the annual fall events coming up. Only the dates change from one year to the next. The building behind the tree was probably an inn, now a private home. The very front edge of the Shedd-Porter Memorial Library peeks out on the right. John G. Shedd, a former Alstead resident, was the president of Marshall Field's, the famous department store in Chicago.

ANTRIM

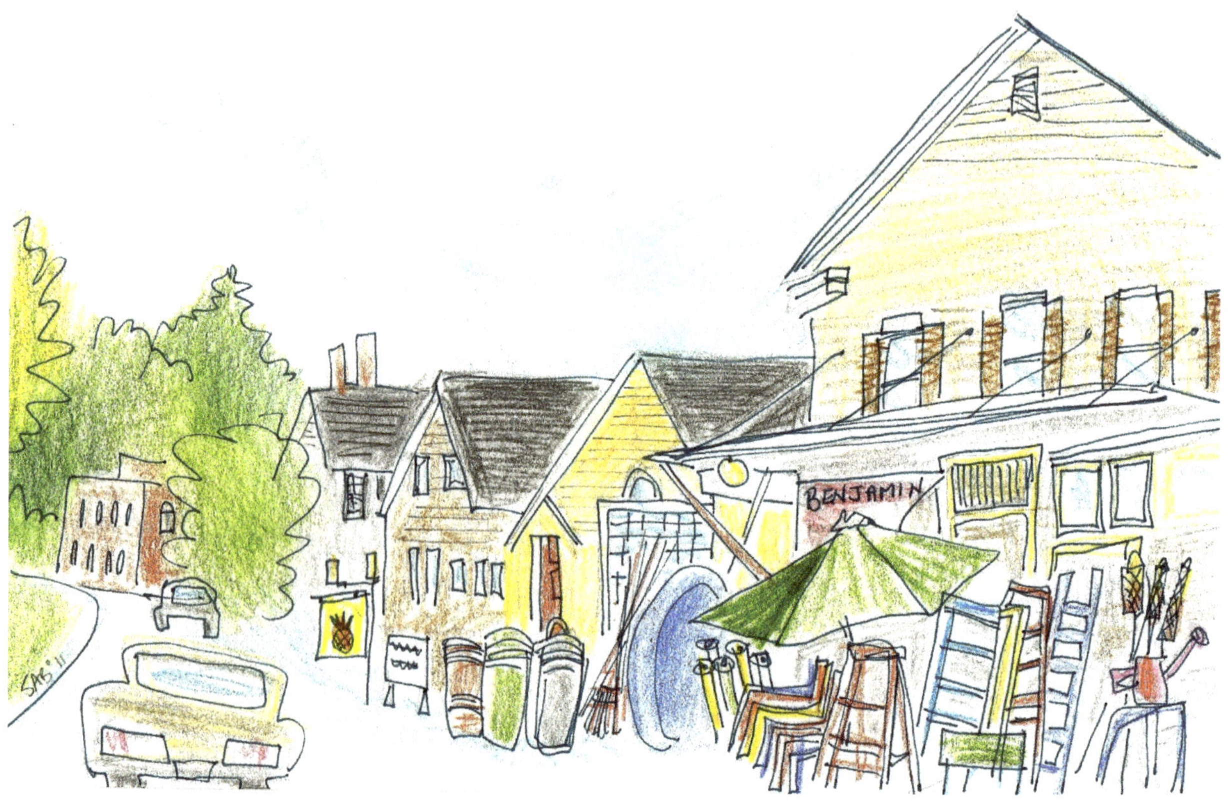

County Antrim, the town's namesake, is found in Northern Ireland. That was the native home of Philip Riley, on whose land the town was built.

These buildings, early to mid 1800s, are of wood except for the brick mill on the left. My sister and I have often remarked how attractive the displays are in front of this hardware store. I think the eye likes patterns, and it doesn't seem to matter too much if the design is fine art, or carefully stacked chairs.

Antrim was once the home of Camp Sachem, a Boy Scout camp attended by my husband.

The mills in Antrim produced cutlery for a couple of hundred years.

BENNINGTON

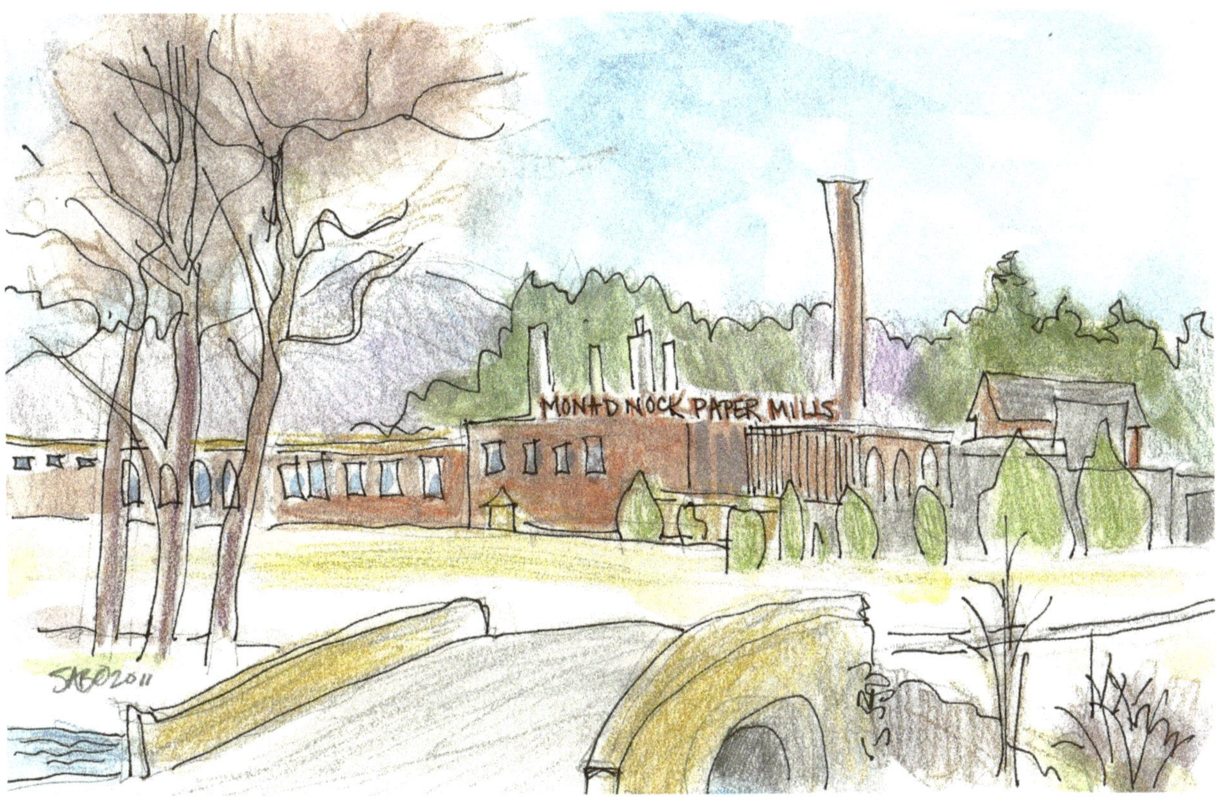

Monadnock is the name of a nearby mountain, and in native language means an isolated single peak.

The long, brick, Monadnock Paper Mills stretch along the valley in town. New England used to be full of paper mills, but this is one of the few left. It has over 300 products and an excellent history of green practices.

The Contoocook River, which drops 70 feet in a mile and a half here, flows under the bridge. The water power was also used to manufacture cutlery in the village. The town was incorporated in 1842 from parts of Deering, Greenfield, Hancock, and Francestown.

CHARLESTOWN

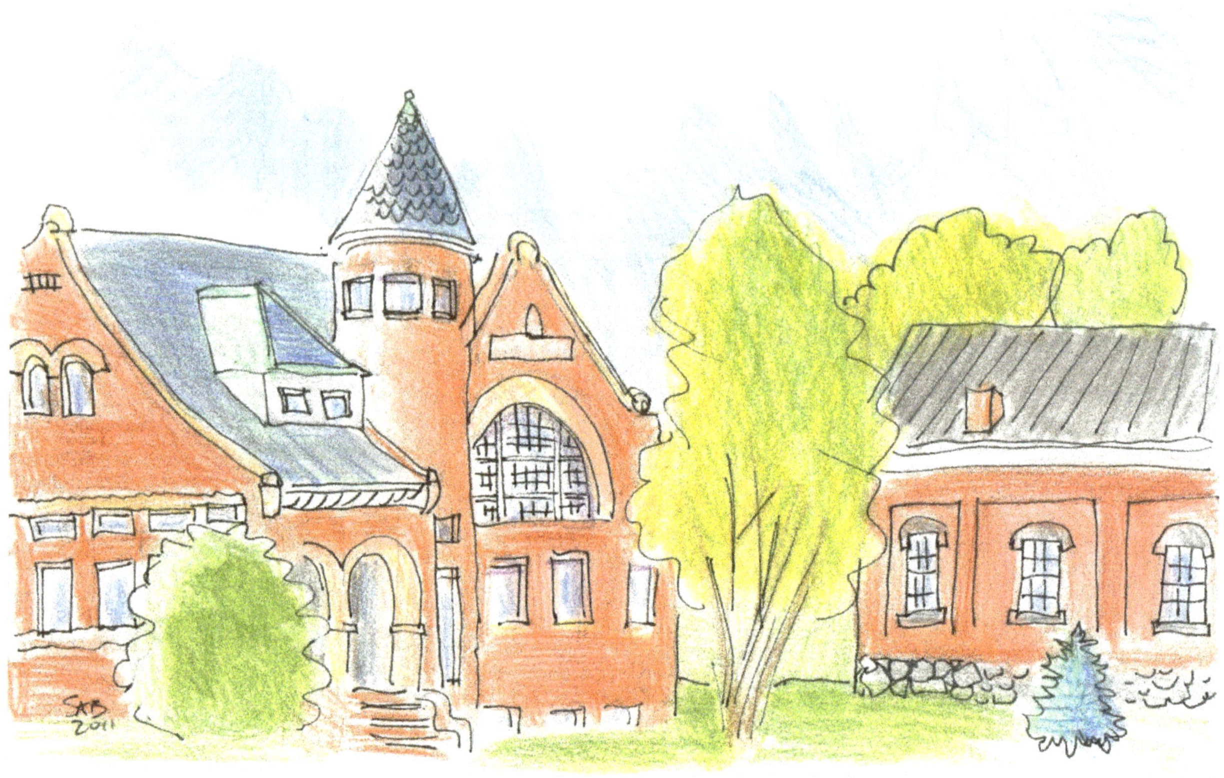

With just over 5,000 people, Charlestown is south of Claremont and follows the state border along the Connecticut River. The broad Main Street has the air of a boulevard, lined with historic homes.

Sixty-three buildings along this street are named in the National Register of Historic Places. The handsome, brick, Silsby Free Library sits on the left, and the town offices are on the right. The funds for the library were donated by the same philanthropist as the library in nearby Acworth. For two years (1781-1782) Charlestown was a part of Vermont.

Fort at Number 4 is a reconstructed stockaded community, open for tours.

CHESTERFIELD

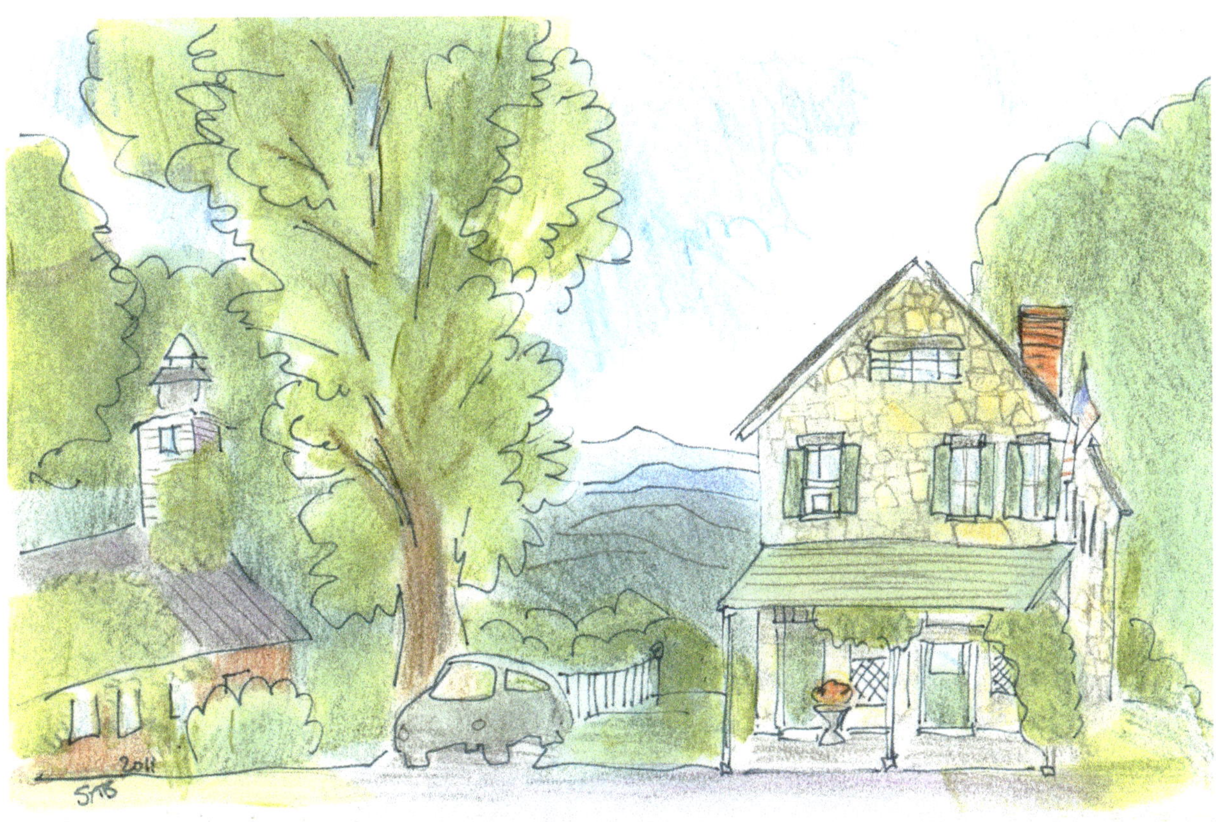

This corner of Chesterfield is a stone village. The stone is warm, yellow-gray granite, locally quarried.

Vermont can be seen in the far distance, across the Connecticut River.

This stone building with a green roofed porch is the town's post office. I made sure to include the plants growing near and onto the structure. The Chesterfield Public Library, across the street and also of stone, is a welcoming place. I learned there that the older wooden buildings had burned, and that the town wisely decided to replace them with stone. The town also includes the villages of Spofford and West Chesterfield.

DEERING

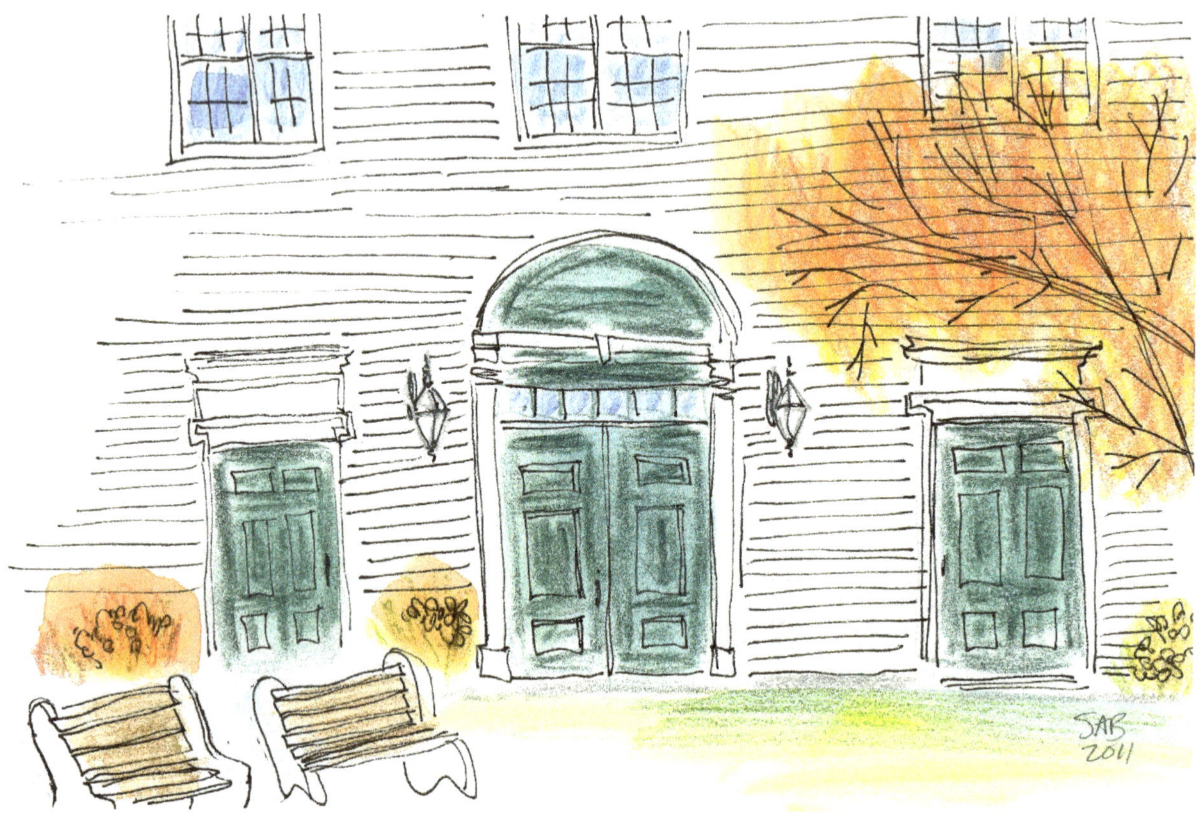

I decided to focus on the twin front doors of the Deering Town Hall, erected in 1788. From 1788 to 1829 the building was used as a meetinghouse for both civic and religious groups.

Autumn colors are so beautiful against a white building.

In 1819, New Hampshire passed the Toleration Act, requiring the separation of church and state. The Congregational Church members were required to construct their own building. Completed in 1830, the church sits across the road. Now a quiet place of homes and farms, Deering once used the town's rivers to power 2 sawmills, 1 gristmill, and a textile mill. Try to imagine the loud noise of it all.

DUBLIN

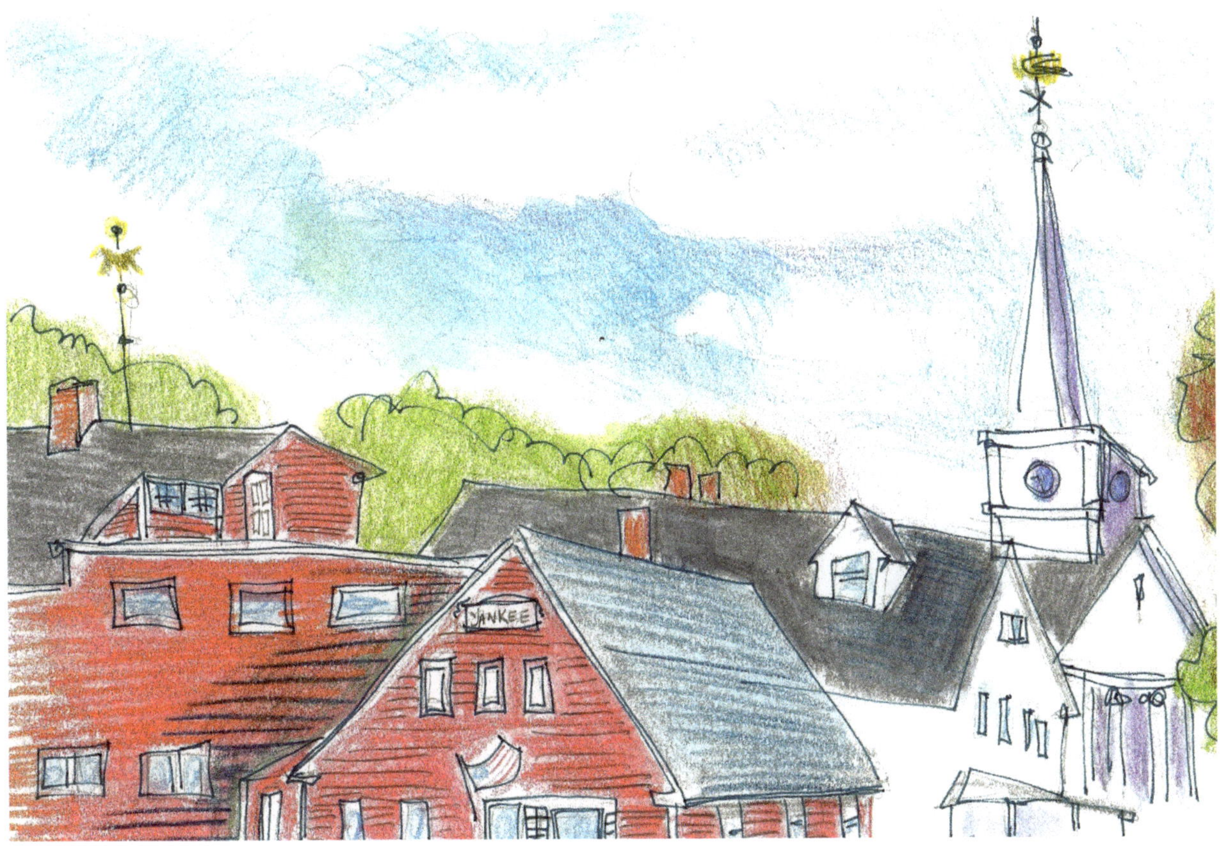

The northern slopes of beautiful Mount Monadnock lie within the town boundary.

Governor John Wentworth incorporated the town in 1771. The land was farmed and orchards were planted. In 1870, the mill village of Harrisville separated from the town.

The tall steeple of the Dublin Community Church on the right contrasts with the low, horizontal building on the left. The red building is the home of *Yankee Magazine*. Across the street sit the town hall and municipal offices, and the town library.

FITZWILLIAM

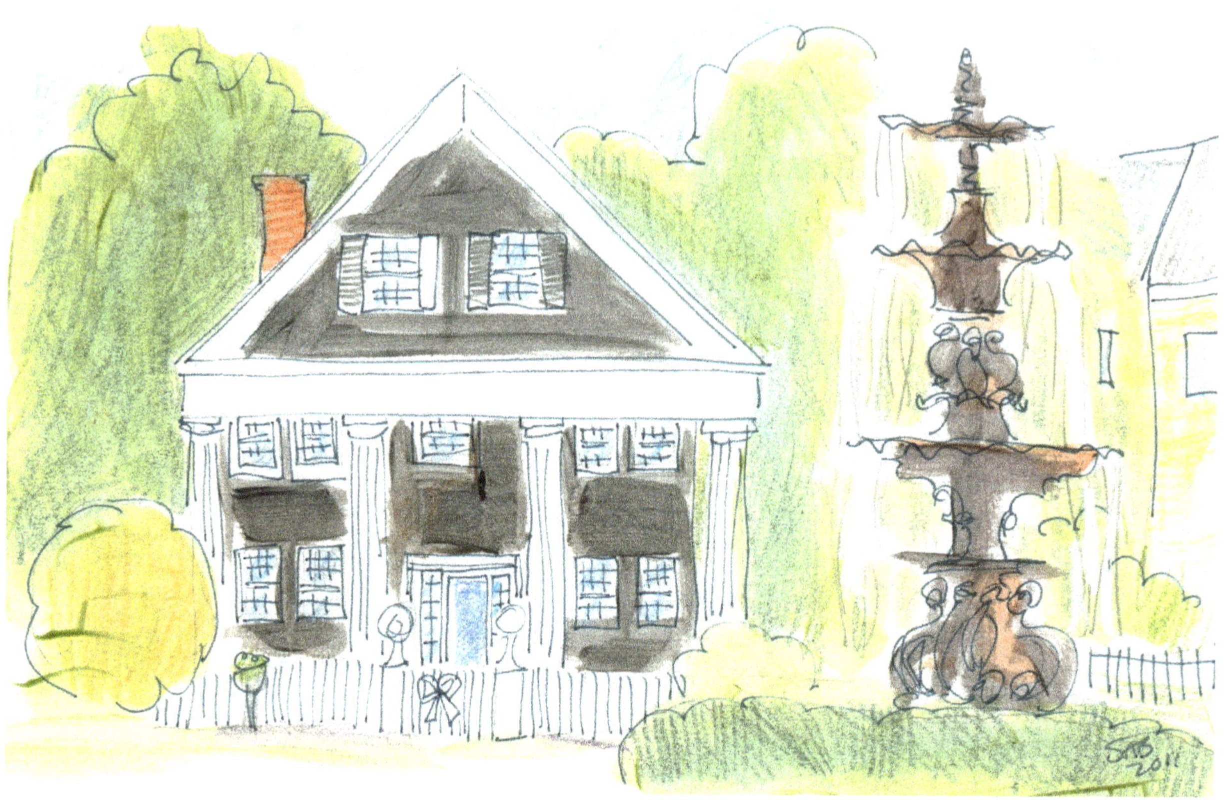

Fitzwilliam, population about 2,500, has a lovely town common and an agreeable ambiance.

Governor John Wentworth incorporated the town in 1773 and named it for his cousin, William Fitzwilliam. Early industries included a granite quarry, a woodworking mill, and textiles. The town common is listed in the National Register of Historic Places, and this includes mention of twelve buildings sited around the space. The ornate metal fountain, beautiful and delicate, is probably Victorian. To the left of the fountain I included the unusual gray and white frame house.

I'm sure a July visit to the 16-acre Rhododendron State Park would be wonderful.

FRANCESTOWN

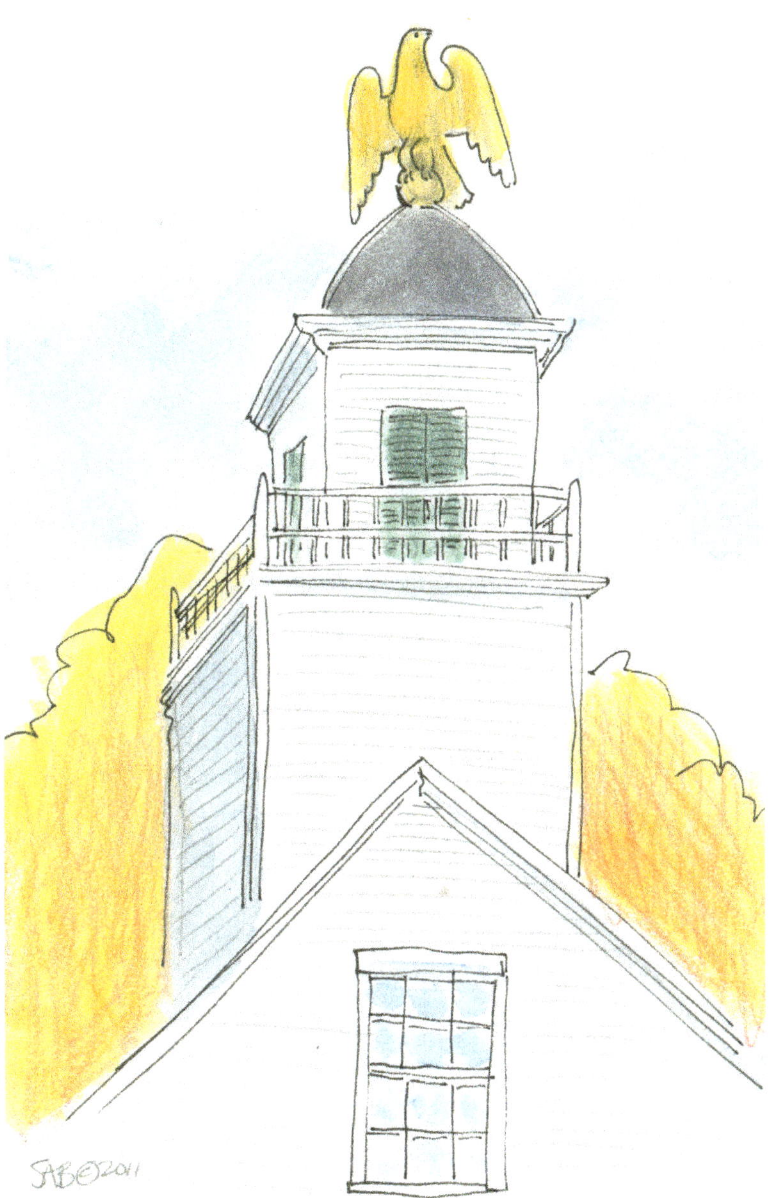

The eagle is atop the Francestown Academy steeple. I am very likely to draw any eagle I find on a building or statue.

A private school from 1801–1921, it is maintained today as a town hall and community meeting space. The students came from quite a distance and boarded in the town. They went on to study law or medicine or theology. One student, Franklin Pierce, became the 14th President of the United States. At one time the town was world famous for the quality of its soapstone, which was used in the manufacture of stoves and sinks.

The town once collected tolls for use of the Second New Hampshire Turnpike, at one cent per mile.

GILSUM

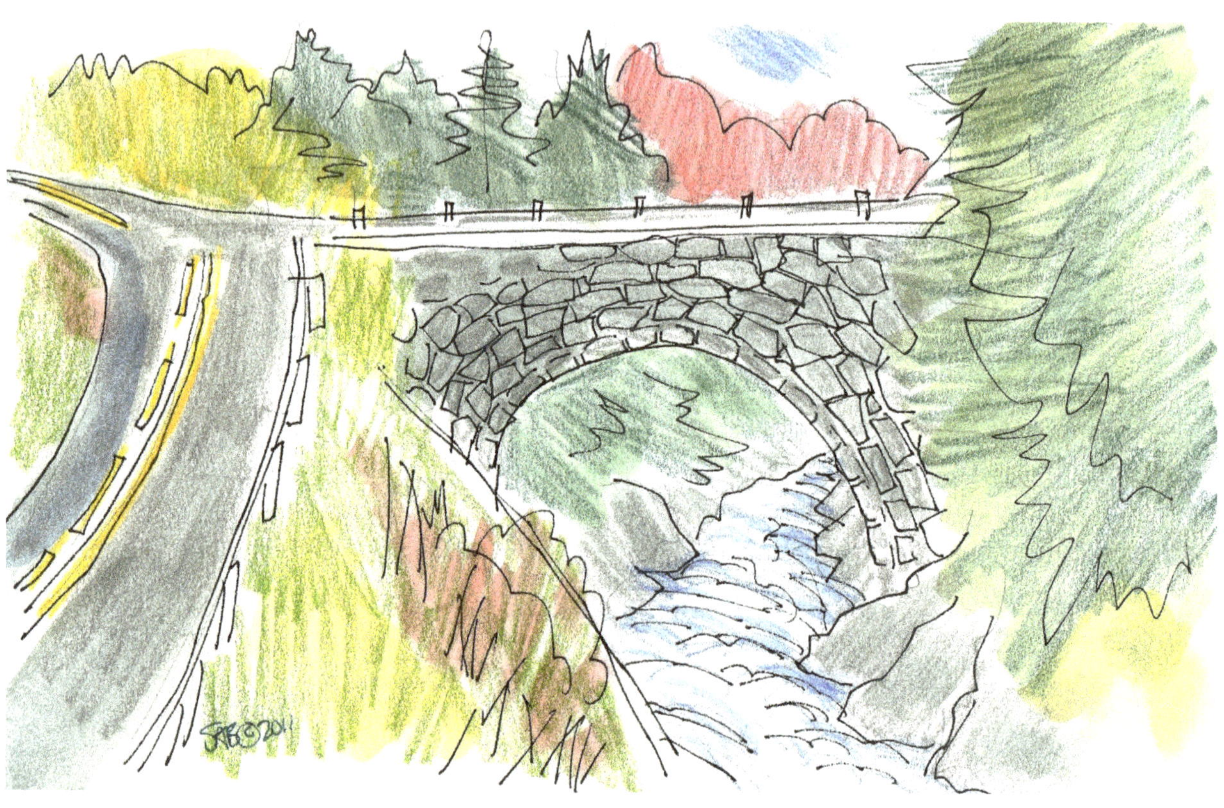

One early Fall day we took a drive with the goal of sketching this bridge in Gilsum. My engineer husband marveled at the bridge's dry-stone or mortarless construction. It has been holding steady since 1860. The Ashuelot River rushes along 36 feet below.

High quality crystals are mined in the area, and in fact a gem show was taking place in town when we were there. The Gilsum name is a combination of early land owners' names, Samuel Gilbert and his son-in-law Thomas Sumner.

I made sure my footing was very secure on the steep hillside before I focused on the drawing process.

GREENFIELD

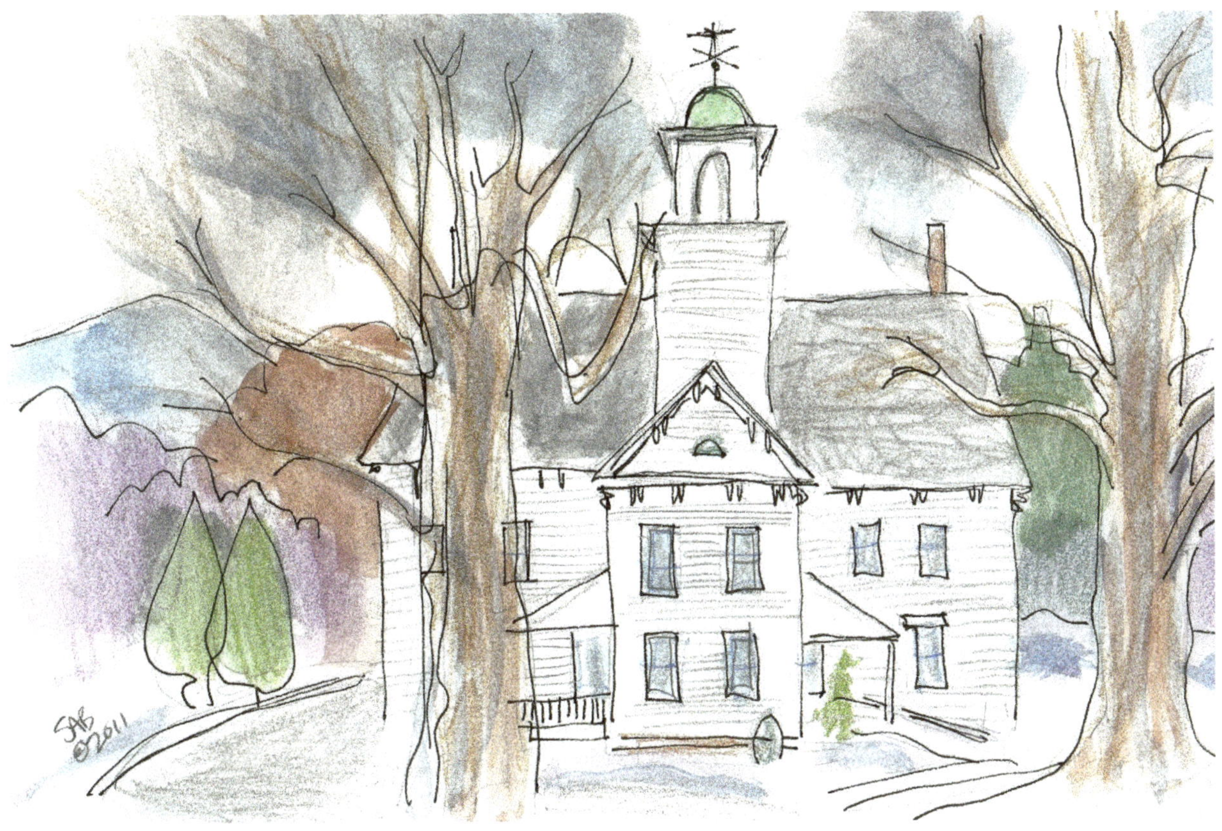

Drawing in the winter months can be a chilly event, but I enjoy it because of the long vistas through the trees.

The area was originally known as Lyndeborough Addition. In 1791, the residents petitioned to separate, choosing the new name of the town to emphasize the fertile land.

The town hall is an attractive wooden structure facing the green. An extremely large old church, a general store, and private homes complete the village center. This town is well known for its Crotched Mountain Rehabilitation Center, initially started to help children with the residual effects of polio.

GREENVILLE

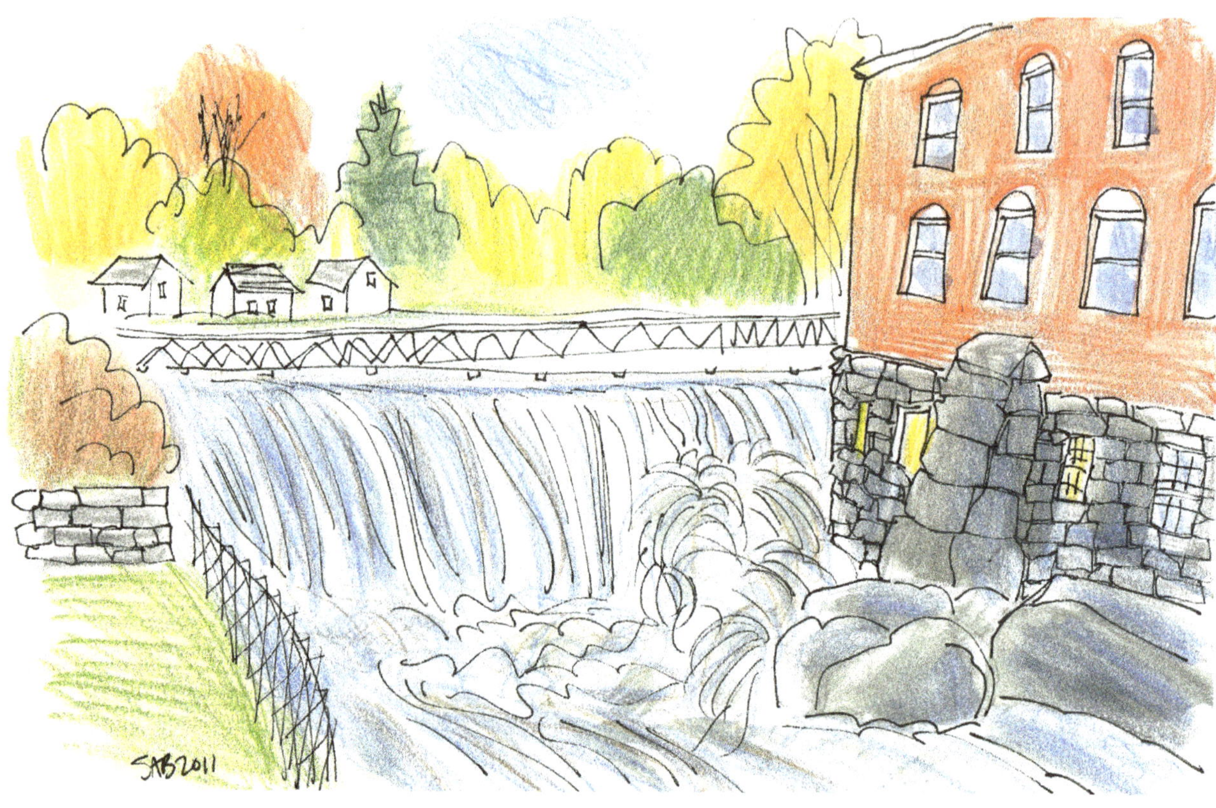

Once called Mason Village, Greenville was incorporated in 1872. The High Falls on the Souhegan River powered the cotton and woolen mills during the 1800s and the early 1900s.

New Hampshire mills lost the industry to the southern states when water power became less important in the manufacturing process. Most of the mills are now reused for other purposes. They were built to last and are structurally strong. Some of the mills in this town have been converted to housing for the elderly.

As it was misting heavily when I drew this, the paper was a little soggy when I finished.

HANCOCK

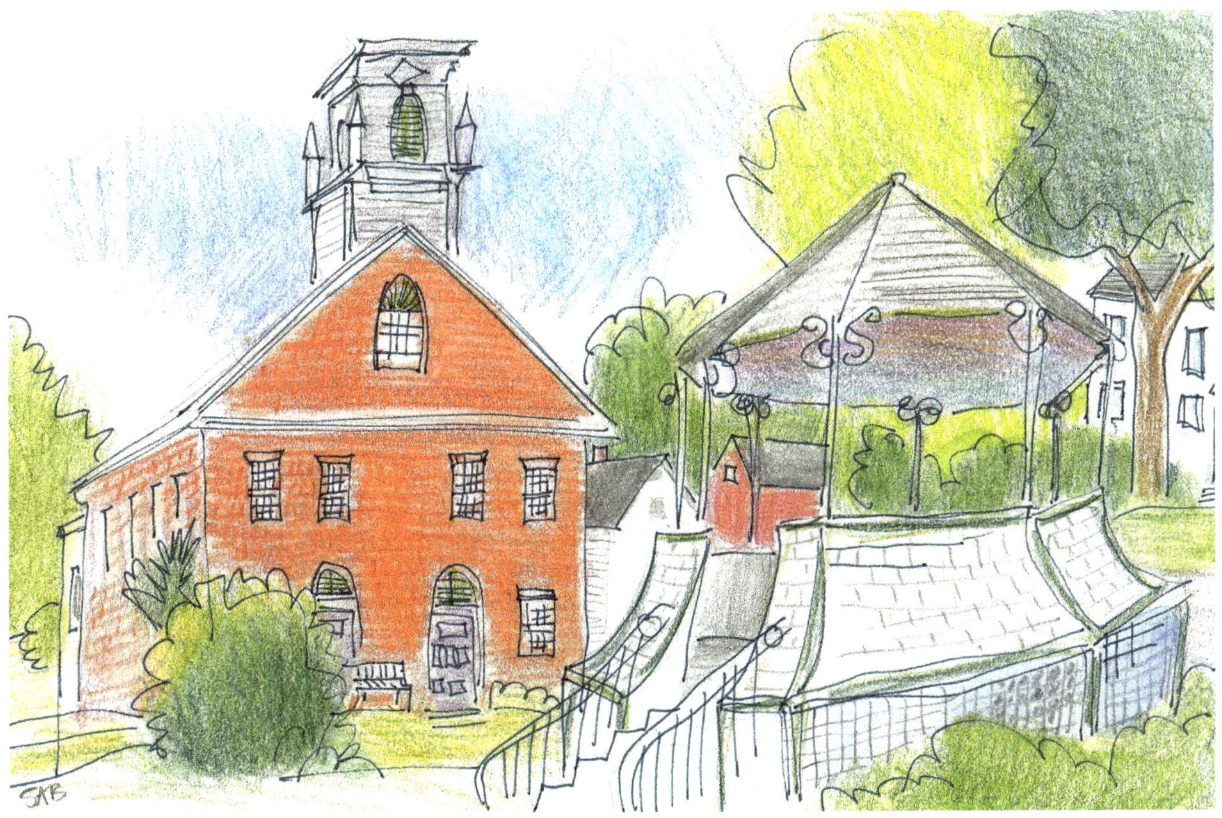

This wooden shingled bandstand is an unusual design, and I had to sketch it.

The village itself is a quiet, one street place - perfect for a stroll. The town, set off from Peterborough in 1779, was named for its famous resident John Hancock, a signer of the Declaration of Independence.

The brick Hancock meetinghouse is on the left with its twin front doors. Other buildings along the Hancock Village Historic District are private homes, the town library, an inn, and two stores.

HARRISVILLE

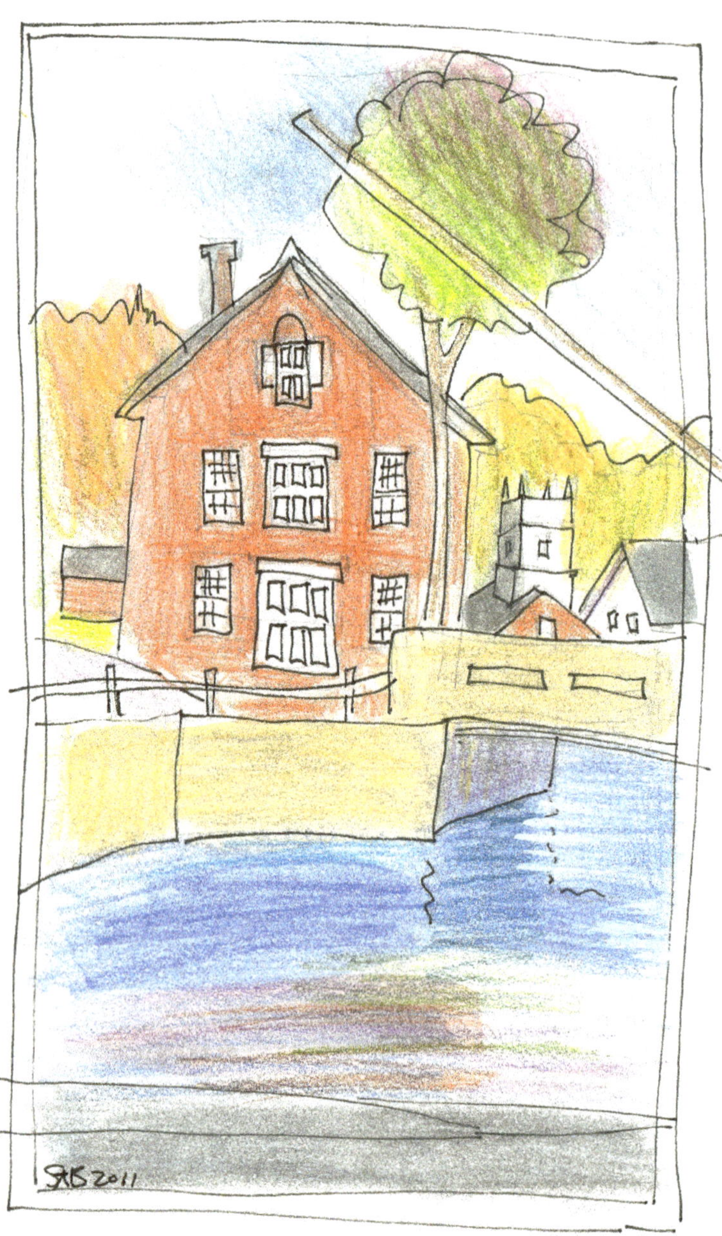

Harrisville, not far from Keene, is an intact textile mill village. The town has retained its brick mill buildings, churches, school, and village store.

The highest quality yarn is still being made here. The Knitting and Weaving Centers at Harrisville Designs sell supplies and finished woven items, and also have classrooms and instruction on the second floor. This view, through a window there, looks out on a bridge and the mill pond. The square-towered building in the rear is the town library.

The Colony family has owned the mills, called the Cheshire Mills, from the 1800s and established Historic Harrisville in 1971.

The old mill race thunders under the Harrisville Designs building, as a constant reminder of the power of fast moving water.

HINSDALE

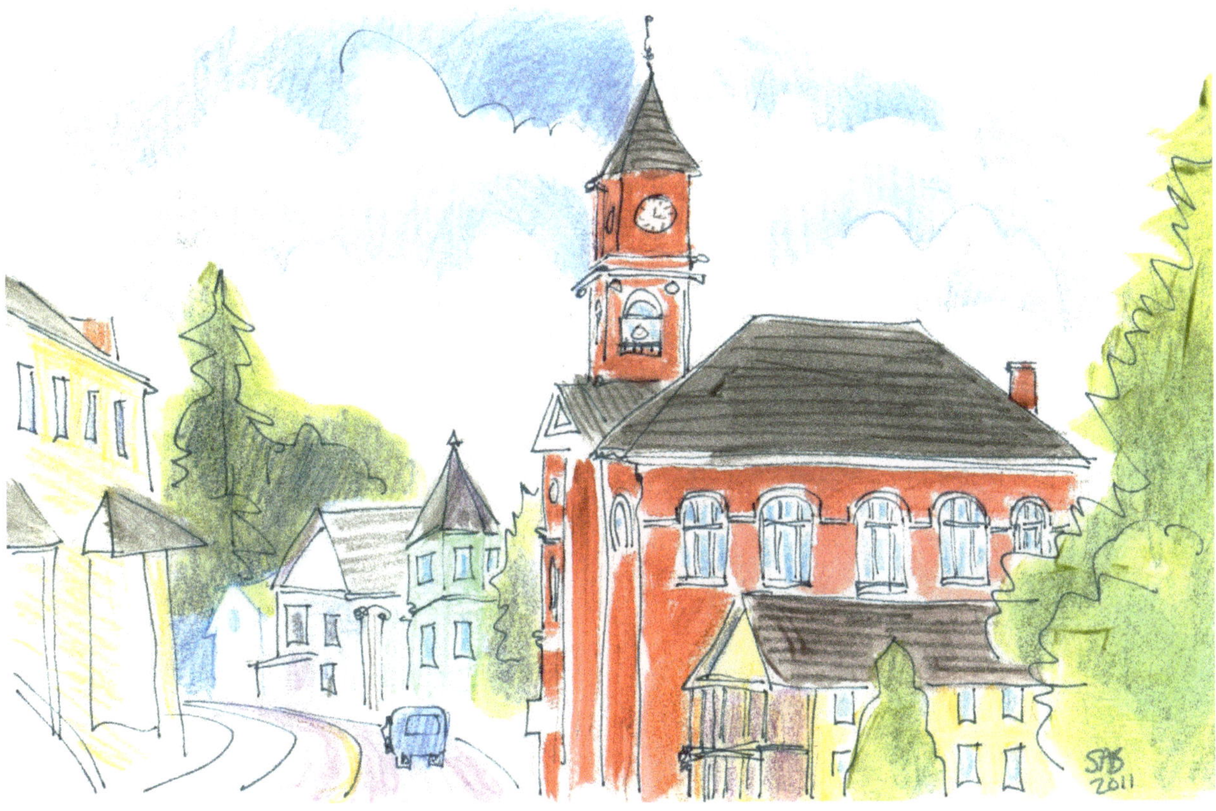

Hinsdale resident George A Long received a patent in 1875 for his steam propelled vehicle, an early automobile.

The small town of Hinsdale occupies the southwest corner of the state, following along the Connecticut River at New Hampshire's three-way junction with Massachusetts and Vermont.

The red brick building is the town hall, built in 1900 in a time of great prosperity. The far smaller yellow building is the town post office, the oldest in the country. The Newhall and Stebbins company made lawn mowers and grass trimmers in Hinsdale from 1860 until 1962.

JAFFREY

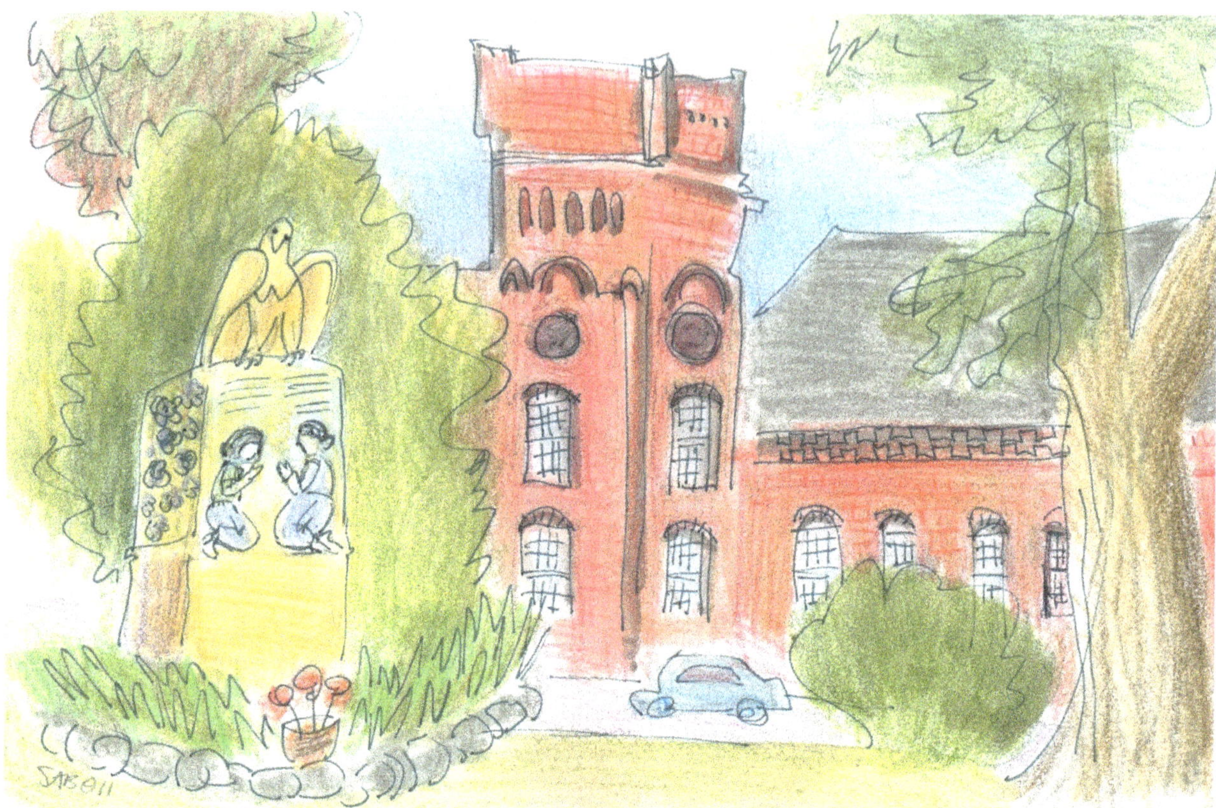

The World War II memorial on the town common is unusual and very moving. The highly detailed figures in glazed ceramic depict a young woman on the left and an older woman on the right.

The women, wife and mother of a soldier, are kneeling in prayer. The Danish sculptor Viggo Brandt-Erickson made this tribute to the Gold Star Mothers in 1949 when he was a resident in town. The building on the right is a former mill and now has been redesigned as new housing.

Since the 1840s tourists have been coming to Jaffrey to climb Mount Monadnock.

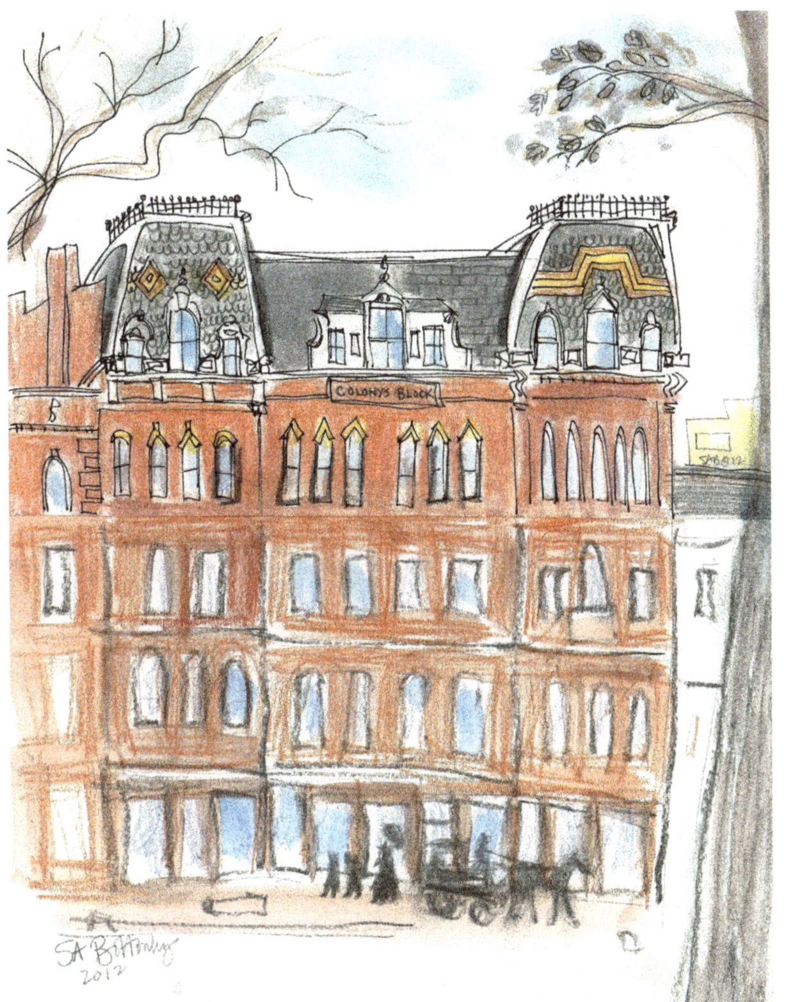

Colony's Block is a landmark on Central Square. Brick with granite trim, the building boasts a decorative slate Mansard roof. Its French Second Empire architectural style became very popular around the world.

I just love how it seems symmetrical at first glance, but isn't. It was built in 1870 after the original one burned in 1865. Of course, the scene of people, with horse and cart, came from my imagination. A former Colony family mansion serves as the very beautiful Keene Public Library, and the family name features strongly in nearby Harrisville.

The students of Keene State College make up 25 % of the population of the city.

LANGDON

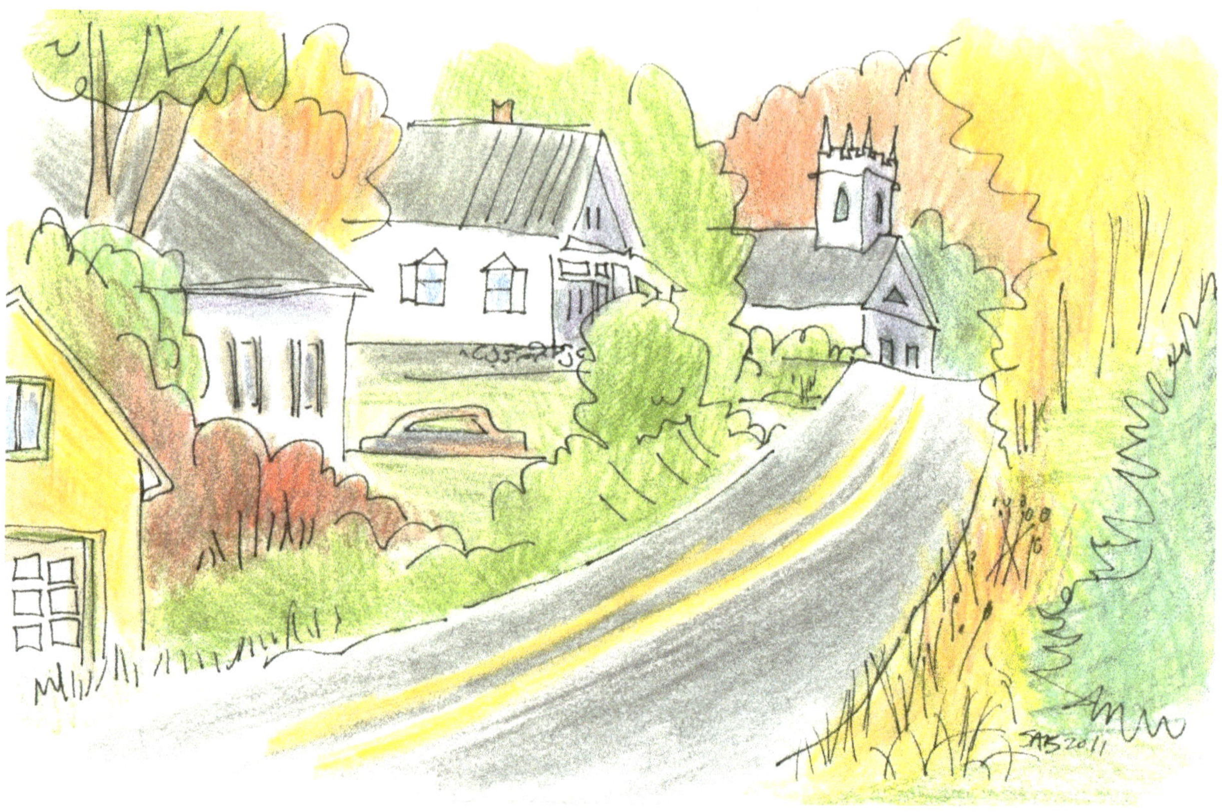

From what I can tell, this is downtown Langdon. It has a small population of about 700 people.

The town, named after Governor John Langdon, was incorporated in 1787. I just loved the curve of the steep hill with the buildings on the left parading up the hill. The Congregational Church at the top is partially obscured, but looks grand anyway. Langdon is home to the Fall Mountain Regional High School, serving eight towns.

The Prentiss Bridge in town is the state's shortest covered bridge at 34 feet.

LEMPSTER

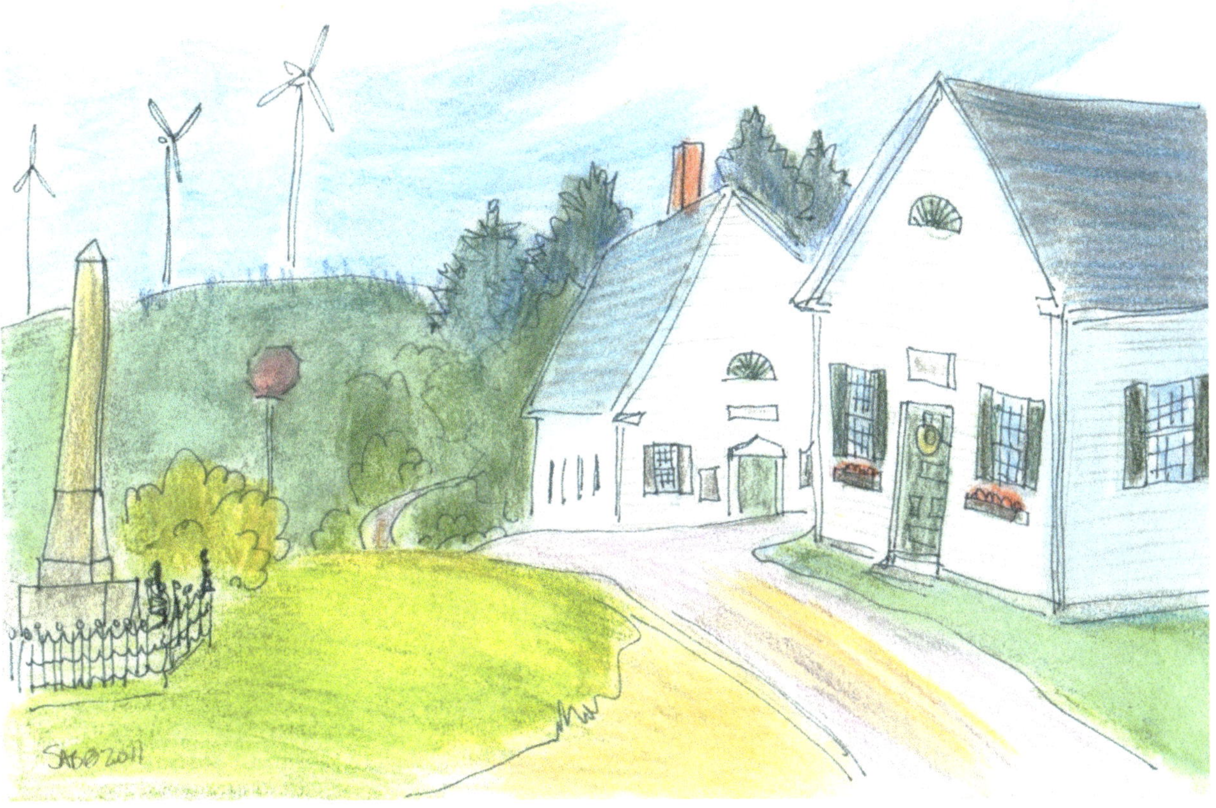

The 12 wind turbines on Bean Mountain have been generating power since 2008.

The curves and contours of the land at the East Lempster crossroads are pleasing to the eye. The Miner Memorial Library is on the far right, and the other building is the town offices.

The unusual name of the town is thought to be a spelled out version of the pronunciation of the town of Leominster in England. The town hall, to the left of the monument and out of the picture, houses many a historical oddity such as a winter hearse on metal runners.

LYNDEBOROUGH

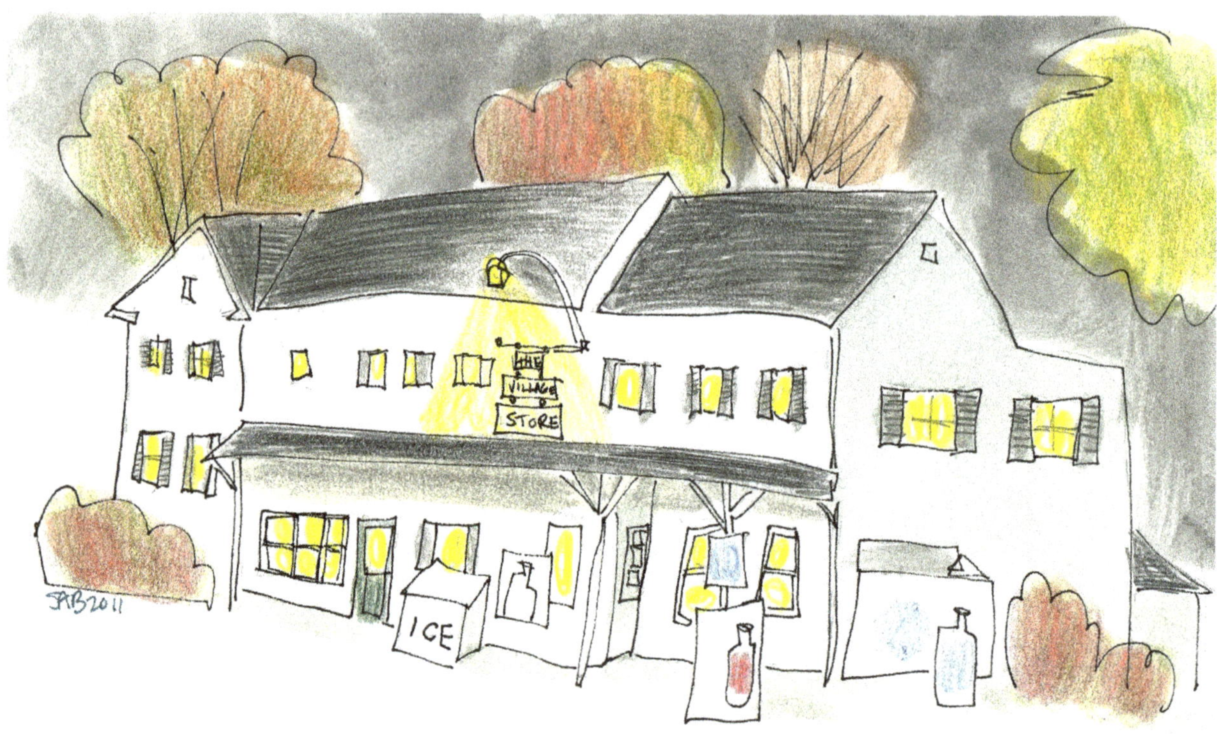

The settlement was originally known as Salem-Canada. The land was granted to war veterans from Salem, Massachusetts who participated in the colony's first war with Canada.

The land was later regranted to others, one of whom was Judge Benjamin Lynde, chief justice of Massachusetts, however he never became a resident. The general store in Lyndeborough (pronunciation Lineborough) caught my eye. This building likely started out as the far left section. Or maybe the far left and the far right were joined with the middle part. This sort of thing is not uncommon. Buildings grow, and buildings get moved.

Drawing at night adds drama to a scene.

MARLBOROUGH

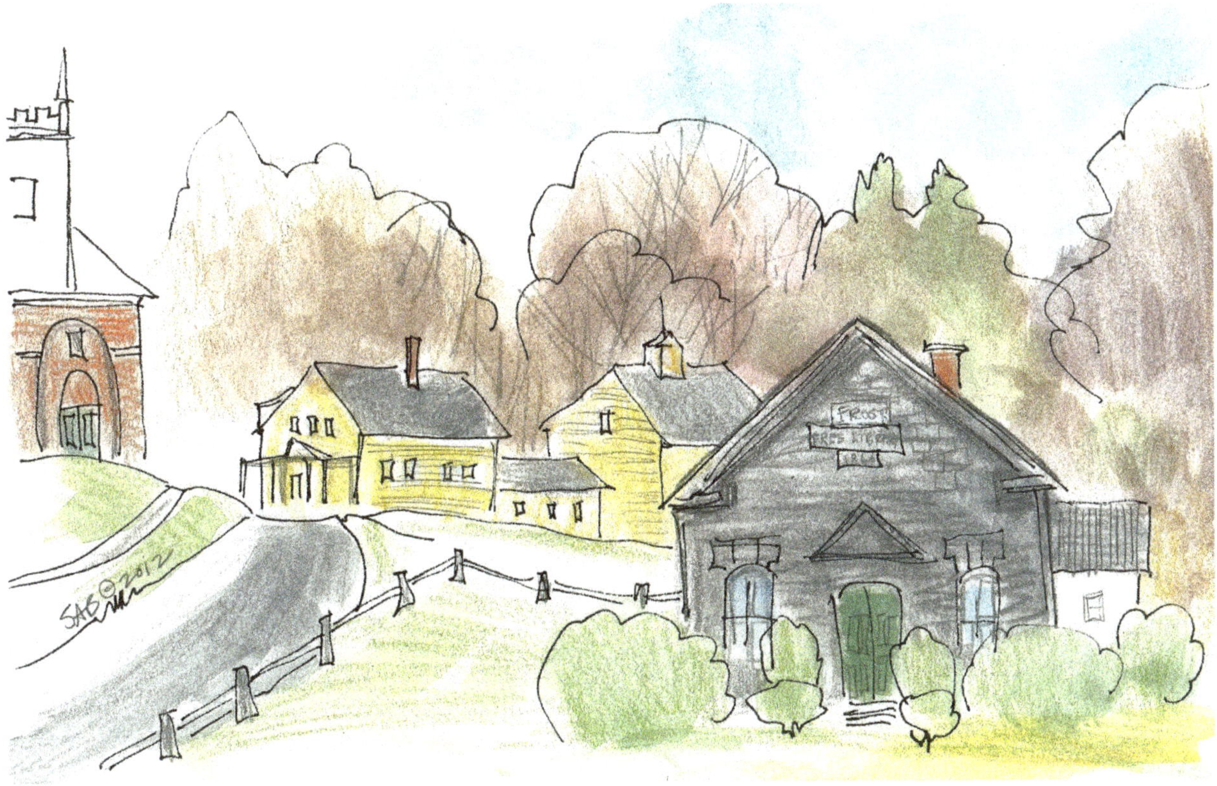

Behind is a New England style farmhouse. The home is attached to a smaller building, and then connected to the barn.

First called Monadnock Number Five, then Oxford, early settlers came from Marlborough, Massachusetts. Local dark gray granite was used to construct the Frost Free Library.

Rufus S. Frost, born in town, became a U.S. representative from Massachusetts. The word 'free' means that it costs nothing to go in and read and borrow the books. Until the mid-1880s, there were only 'social libraries'. The elite of the area would pay a fee to become subscribers. As a move towards democracy, towns began to establish the free library system.

MARLOW

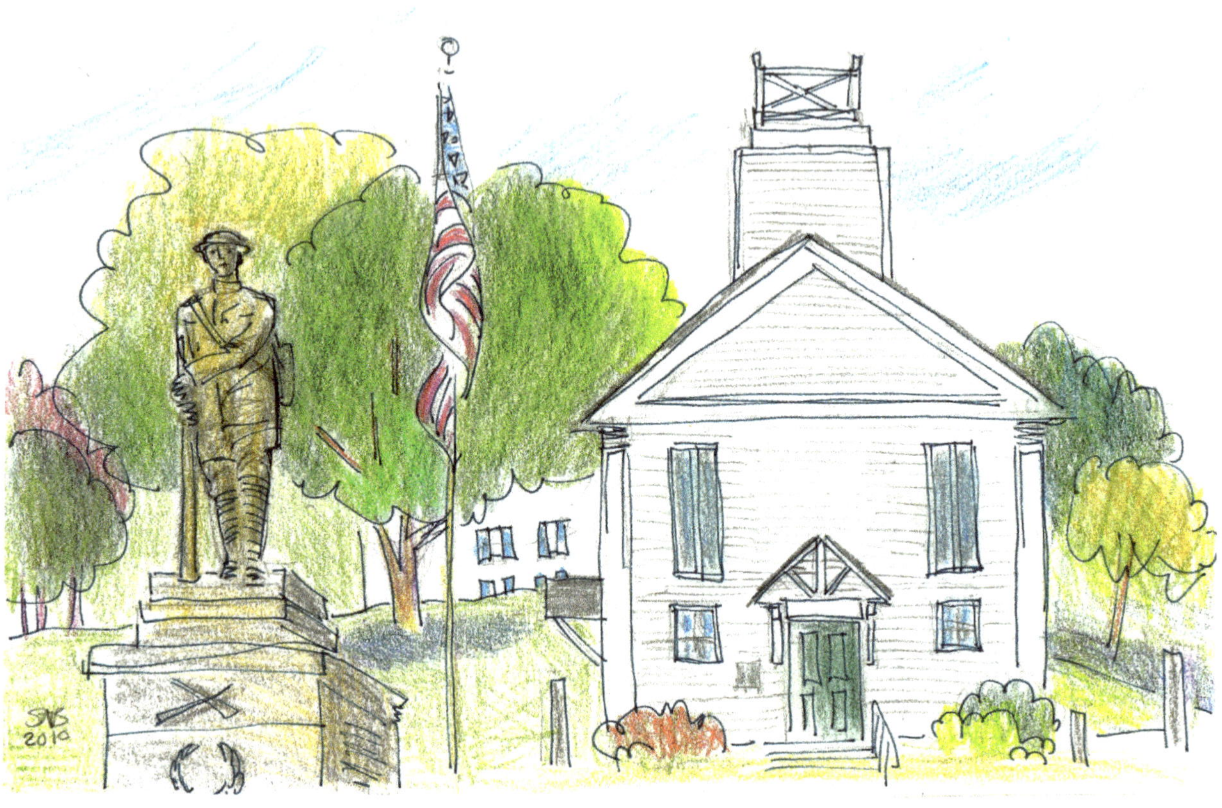

Although I have no aptitude for making three dimensional art, I enjoy looking at it and drawing monuments and sculpture of all kinds.

In Marlow I stood in the road to get the best angle to draw the War Memorial and Jones Hall. While the monument lists soldiers from the Revolutionary War onwards, the statue itself depicts a soldier from the First World War. The building to the right is Jones Hall which serves as the town hall and, with a side entrance, the town library.

My grandfather, a stone cutter, was skilled enough to take hammer and chisel to marble. I so admire the skill of a person who can make a sculpture such as this one.

MASON

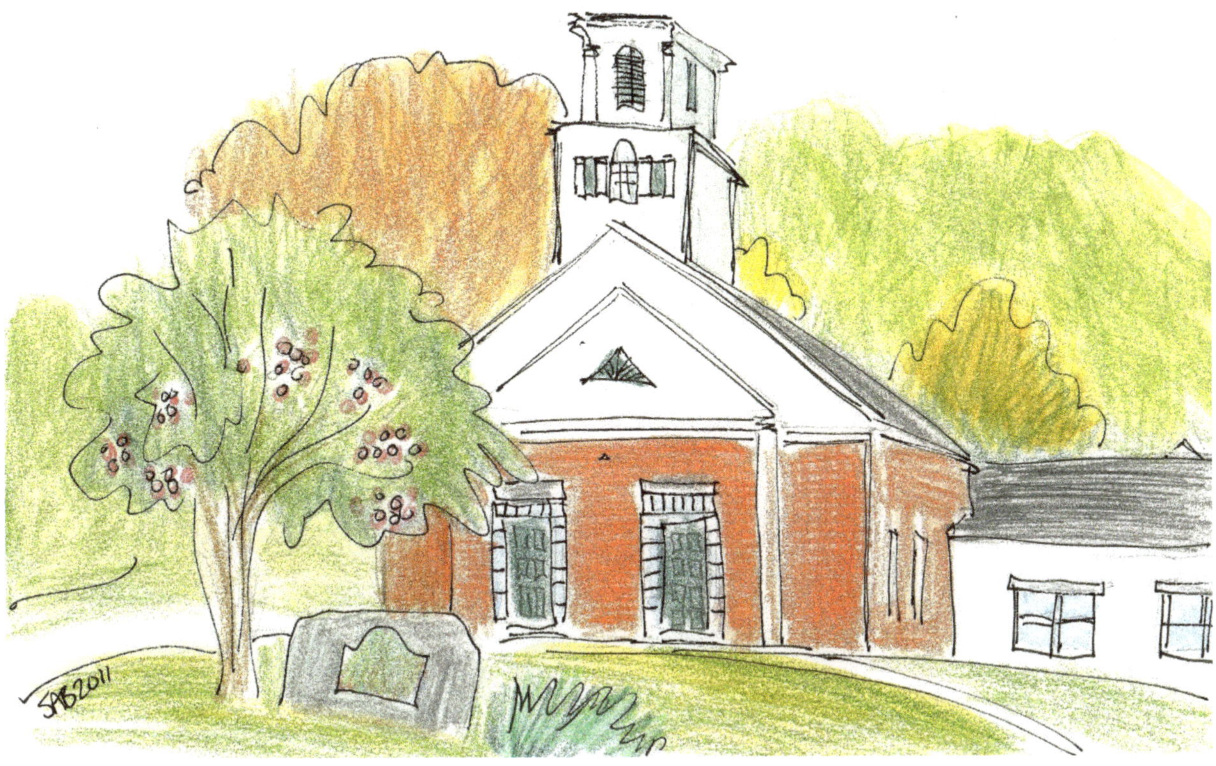

Mason resident Uncle Sam Wilson, supplier of beef to the U.S. Army, is believed to be the origin of America's symbol.

The Mason Elementary School on Darling Hill Road is at the intersection of five narrow country roads.

The new wing is to the right. The two front doors, a sign of an old building in New Hampshire, have beautiful windows surrounding them. It was dusk by the time I got here, so they were all aglow with interior light. In 1768, Governor John Wentworth named the town after the founder of New Hampshire, John Mason.

NELSON

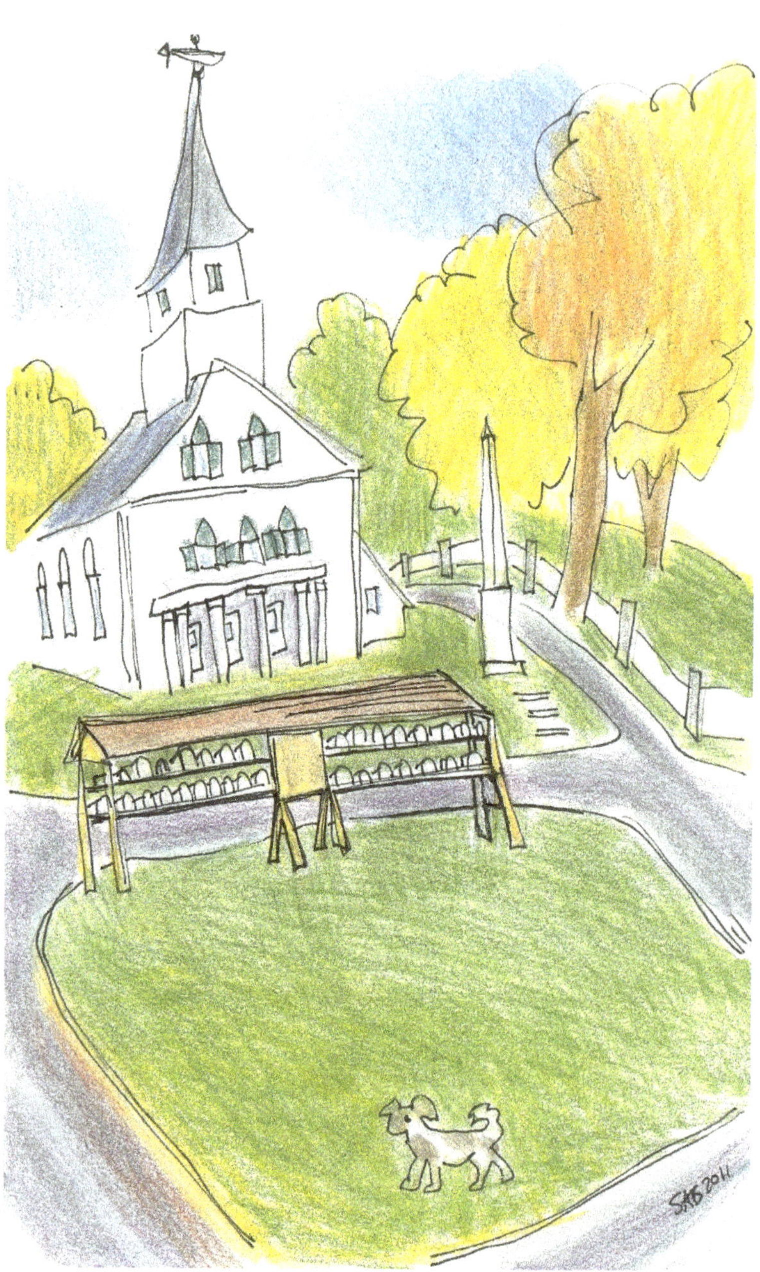

Nelson is not far off of a major highway, Route 9, but it seems like a place unto itself. Originally incorporated in 1774 as Packersfield, the current name was chosen in 1814.

The Nelson Congregational Church and an obelisk war memorial are at the top of the green. The double row of metal mailboxes, roofed against the weather, is a creative solution to the lack of a town post office. Nelson is well known for musical events: contra dancing in the town hall and the Apple Hill Center for Music.

My dog Hank is taking a little walk on the green. He was my sketching travel companion that day.

NEW IPSWICH

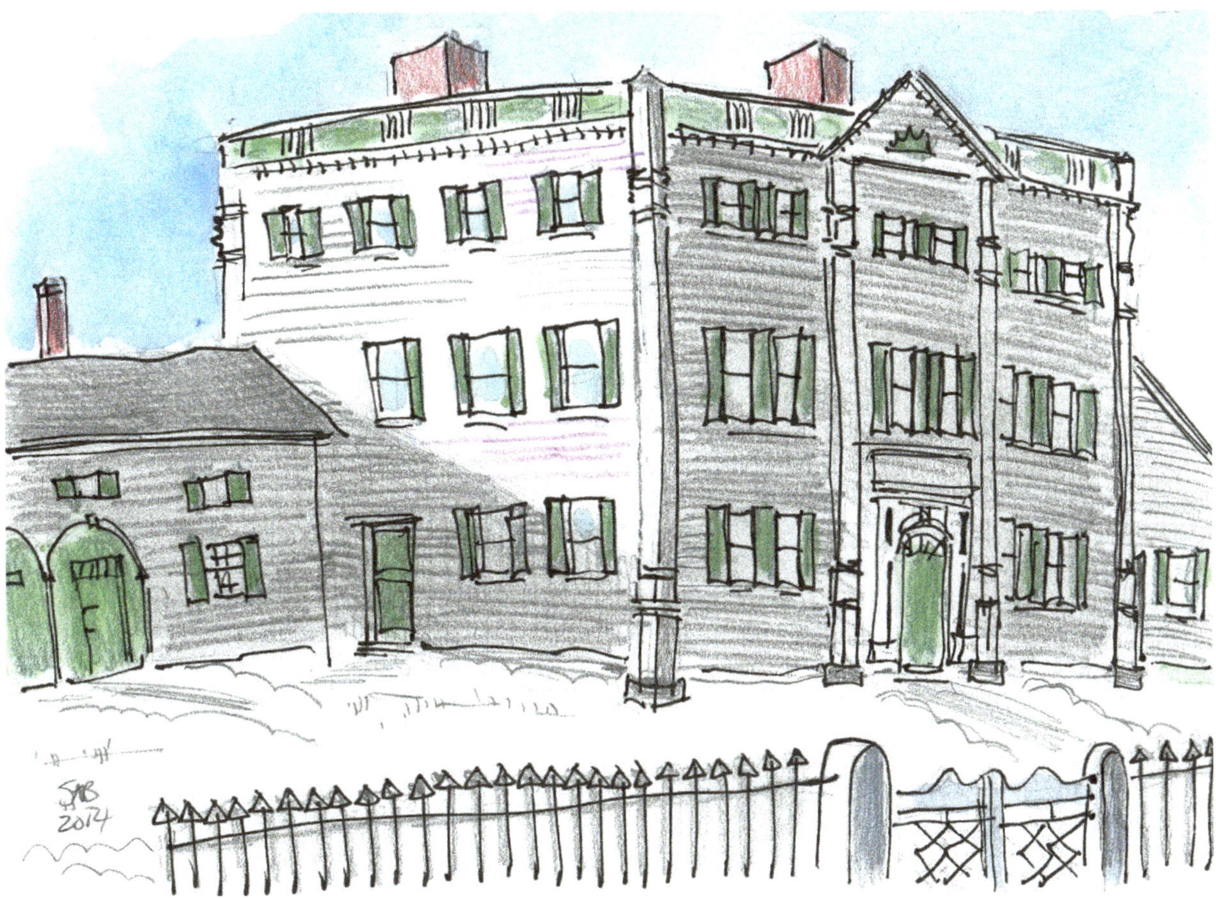

The town, with a population of about 5,000, sits right on New Hampshire's southern border.

A Merchant Ivory film entitled *The Europeans*, based on a novel by Henry James, was filmed here in Barrett House in 1979. The house was built in 1800.

It was granted as Ipswich in 1735 to 60 people from Ipswich, Massachusetts. In 1766, it was regranted as New Ipswich. The Souhegan River provided the water power for New Hampshire's first woolen mill here in 1801. The mills brought prosperity to the town, and many business owners built fine homes.

PETERBOROUGH

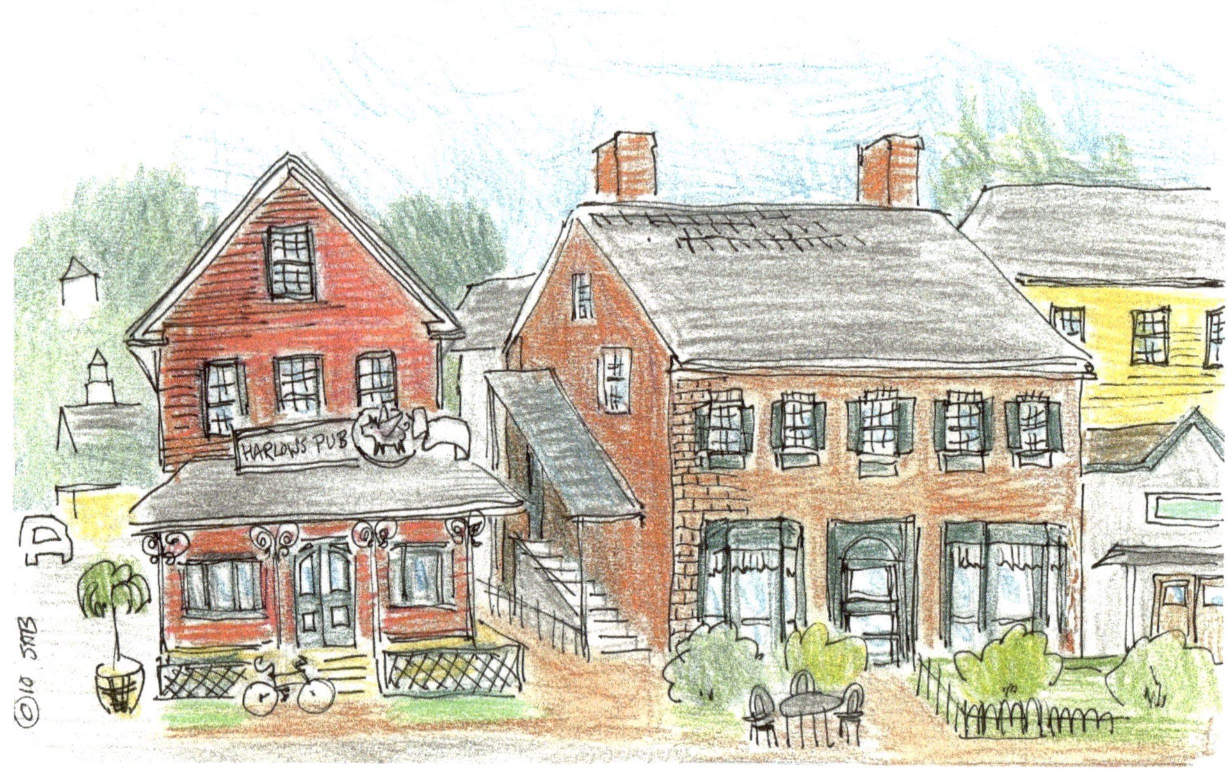

Grove Street, with its row of brick and wood frame structures, is a bustling place in Peterborough.

In 1938 Thornton Wilder wrote the play *Our Town* in fictional Grover's Corners, based on this town and others nearby. A summer stock theater, the Peterborough Players, has been around since 1933. The Sharon Art Center in School Street offers the best craft sales room anywhere. Peterborough is home to the famous McDowell Art Colony, founded in 1907.

Be sure to visit charming Depot Square, home to 14 locally owned businesses.

RICHMOND

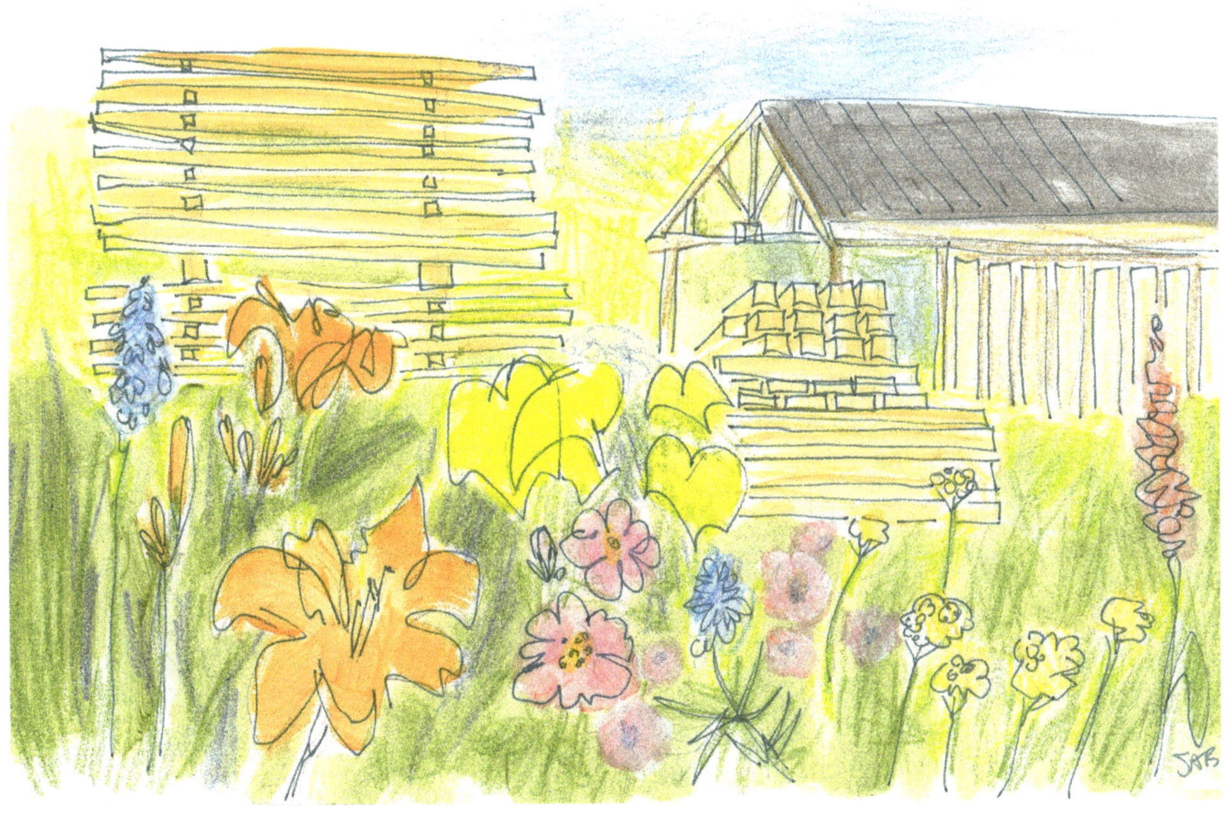

The Richmond Community United Methodist Church, built in 1837, has a beautiful brick Greek Revival façade.

The town was settled in 1757 by families from Rhode Island and Massachusetts. Four Corners is where I stopped the car to walk for a bit.

Around a bend, I noticed an abundance of flowers growing along the roadside. And the scent of the recently sawn pine boards hung in the air. Something about the pines and the blooms brought me right back to my childhood days of wandering in fields and woods. The flowers are orange day lilies, white yarrow, wild grapes, and wild roses.

RINDGE

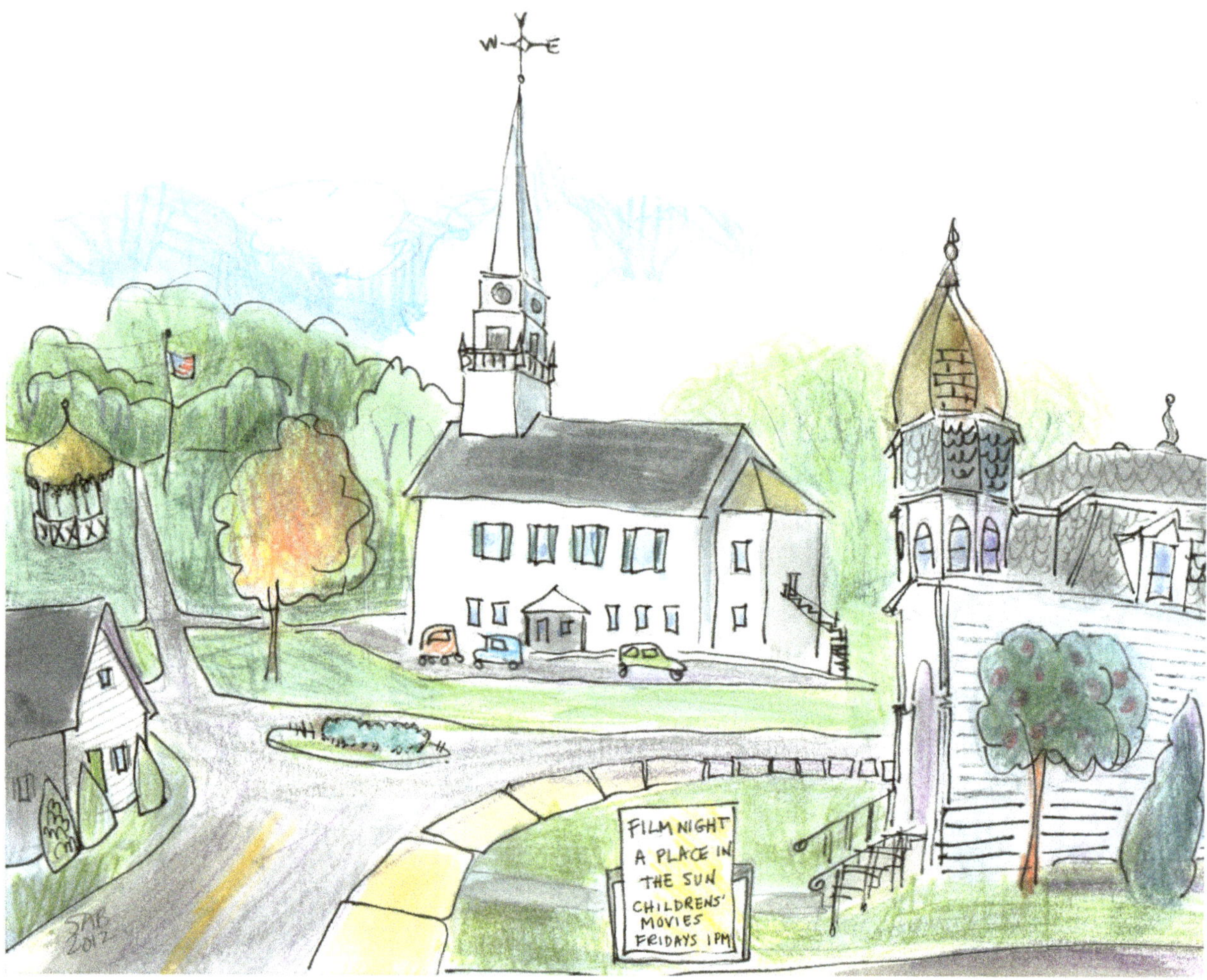

Standing on the sidewalk in front of the library, I drew quickly as the skies darkened.

I had already walked up the hill to the bandstand on the far left. When designing my composition, the bandstand was included even though it is really out of sight. The large white building in the center is the town hall. Built as a meetinghouse in 1796, it was acquired by the town in 1839. The town rents out the second floor to The First Congregational Church.

Rindge is perhaps best known as the home of the Cathedral of the Pines.

ROXBURY

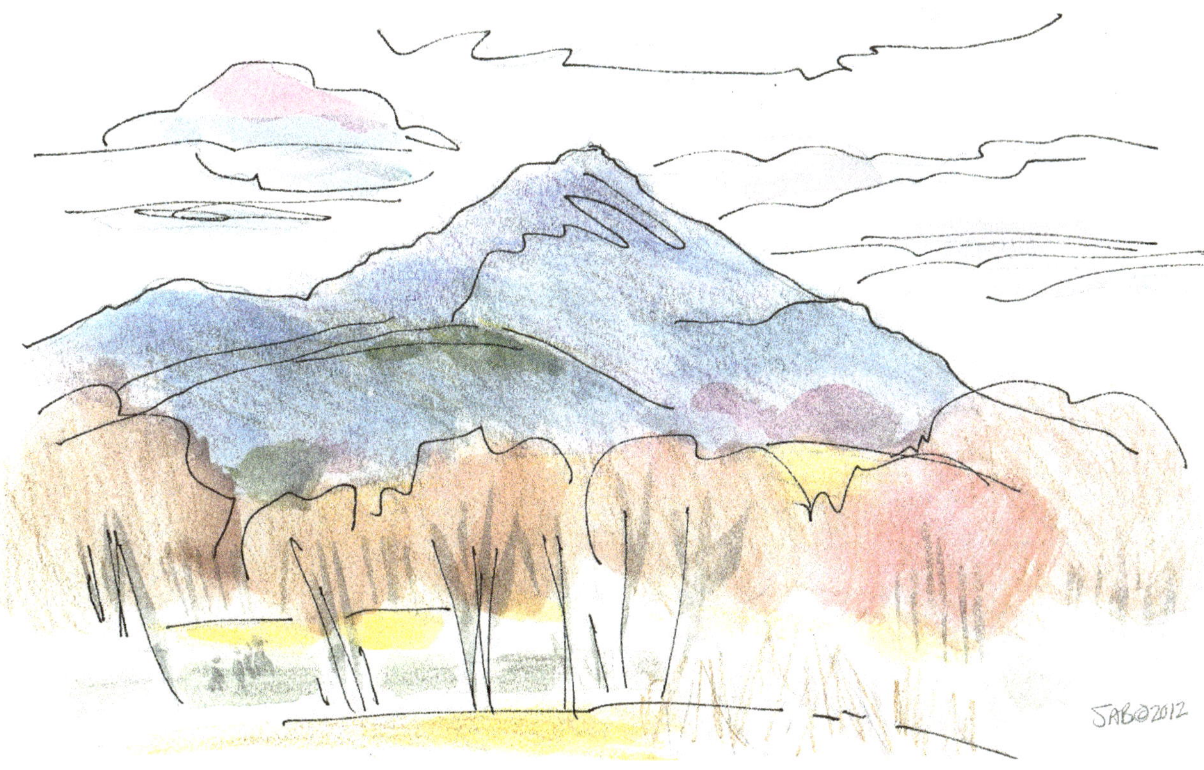

Otter Brook Lake was constructed in 1958 by the Army Corps of Engineers to control flooding.

The town was incorporated in 1812, from the neighboring towns of Nelson, Marlborough, and Keene.

We came from the direction of Marlborough, up steep hills, and onto dirt roads. A line of beautiful pheasants then crossed the road in front of us. When I saw this vista looking back toward majestic Mount Monadnock, I reached for my pencil.

The artist Joseph Ames was born here, as was his poet and inventor brother Nathan. Another native of Roxbury, Cyrus Wakefield, became a businessman and philanthropist in Wakefield, Massachusetts.

SHARON

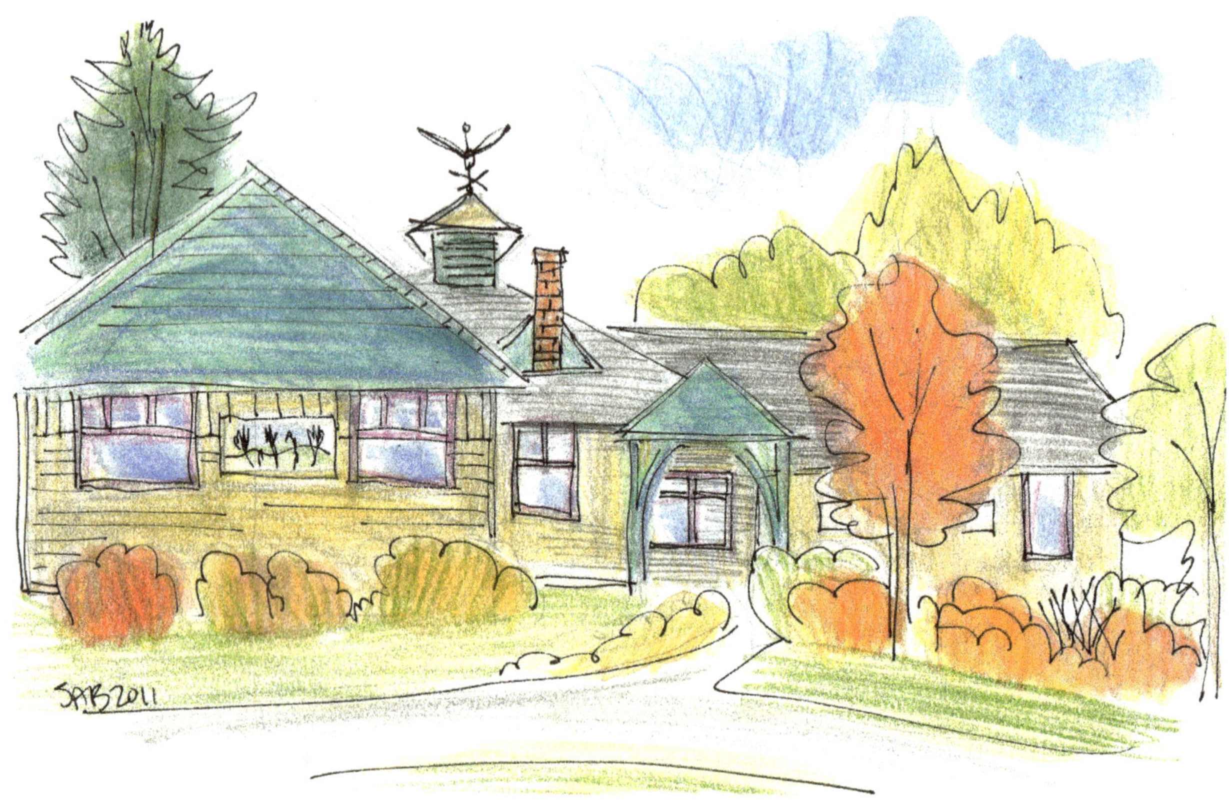

A multitude of arts and crafts classes are available at the Sharon Arts Center education building, shown above. The Sharon Arts Center's sales and exhibition space is located in nearby Peterborough.

Sharon has a population of fewer than 500 people. The town seal features a one-room brick schoolhouse, which has been in continuous use since it was built in 1832. Besides the education of the town's children, the small building has been used by church groups. Currently, town officials meet there.

Sharon, originally a part of Peterborough, was incorporated in 1791.

STODDARD

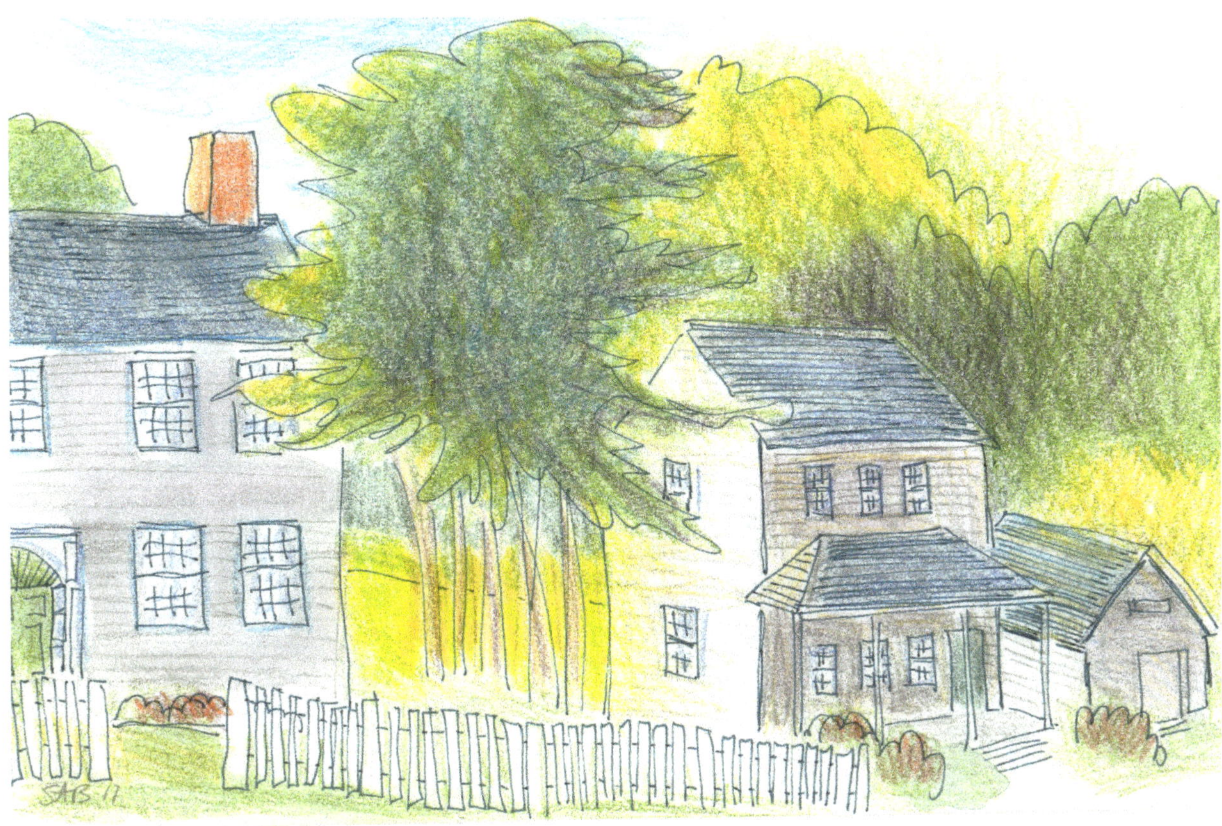

Just off of Route 9, at the Antrim town line, stands the double arched, mortarless bridge.

Stoddard is a quiet village these days, but from 1842 to 1873 it was an active center of hand blown glass.

Four glass manufacturers employing 800 people turned out colored glass bottles using local sand. The mineral deposits in the sand naturally created amber, green, and red colored glass. These items are highly prized and collected today. After the Civil War, machine-made clear glass was in demand, and the glass industry moved elsewhere. This trio of wooden frame buildings in the village center are a private home, the Historical Society, and the Hearse House.

SULLIVAN

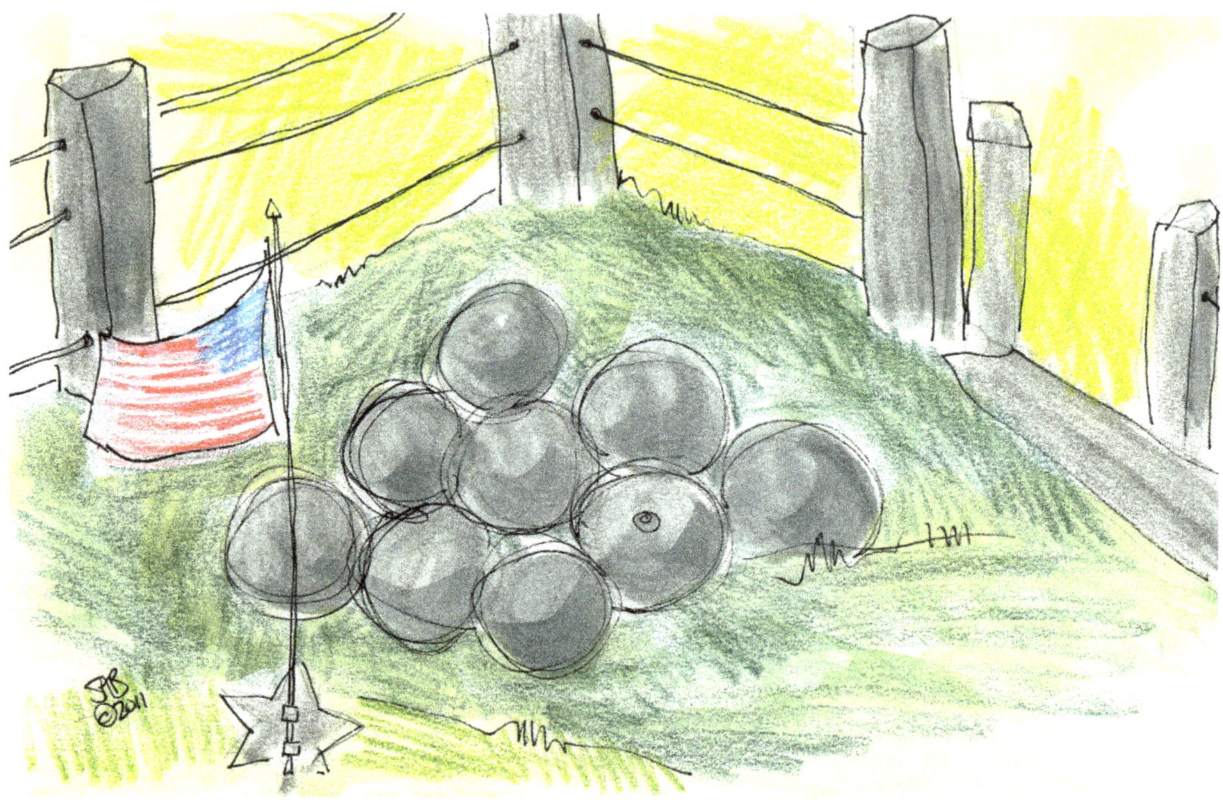

Sullivan was incorporated in 1787 from parts of the neighboring towns of Gilsum, Keene, Nelson, and Stoddard.

The town does have a very fine, tall steepled, Congregational church. But I was taken with the small war memorial across the street from the church: an obelisk, a granite and iron railed fence, and a pile of cannon balls. It evoked an emotional response, so I painted them, and included the flag in the star holder. Sullivan was the first town in the state to build a memorial to those killed in the Civil War.

The town seal has a depiction of this war memorial on it.

SURRY

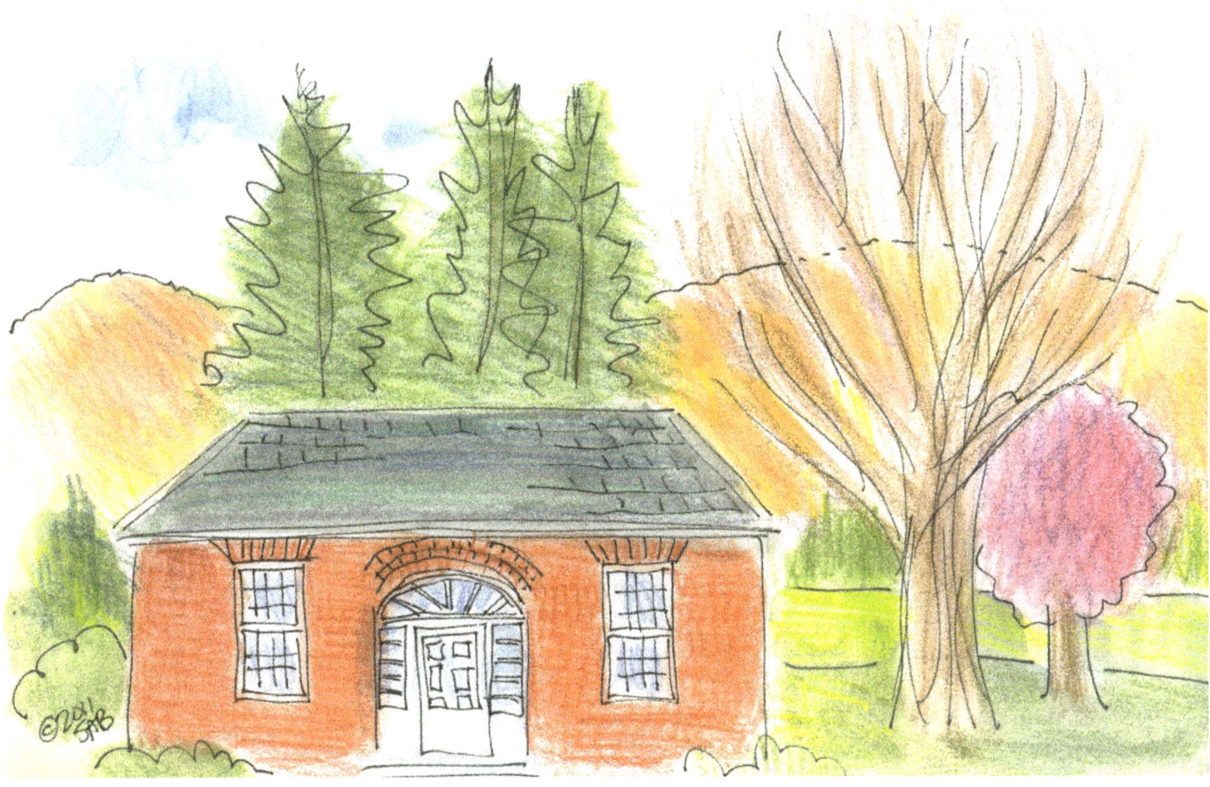

Surry takes its name from Charles Howard, Earl of Surry, England.

The town, chartered in 1769, is still a small place with a population under 750 people.

The Reed Free Library was sketched on a very warm day in the fall. In the background is Surry Mountain, once mined for copper, gold, and silver. I love historical markers that tell you these things. You see the fall colors on the hills, yellows and reds of the maples and birch trees. The pink one is my version of a copper beech tree in full sunlight.

SWANZEY

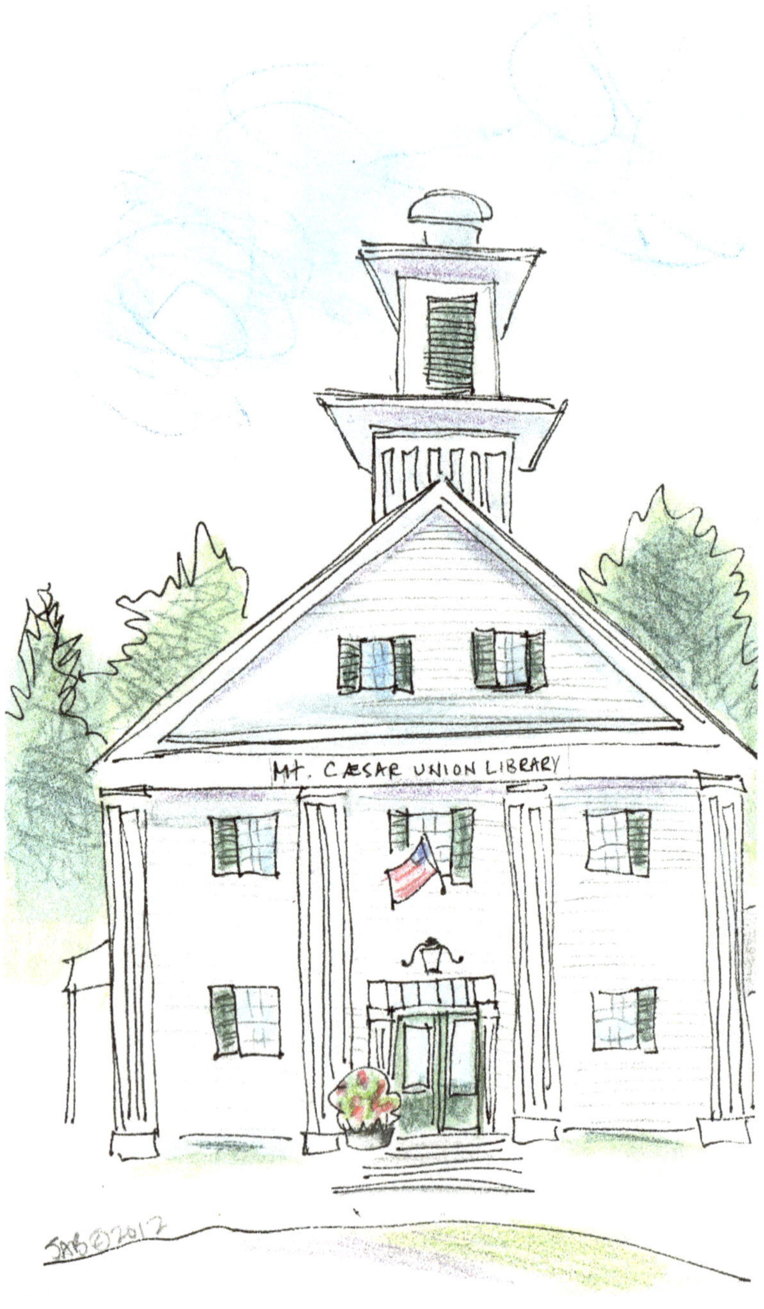

The town of 7,300 people is just to the south of Keene and is 43 square miles in area.

Perhaps this is why the town has two libraries, one in the west side of town, the other in the middle. The Mount Caesar Union Library on Route 32 was my drawing assignment on a very cold winter day. The imposing structure, with its white clapboards, green shutters, and columns, is an unusual design for a town library. Mount Caesar, a local mountain of 962 feet elevation, takes its name from the freed slave Freeman Caesar.

The town is rich in covered bridges: there are four of them.

TEMPLE

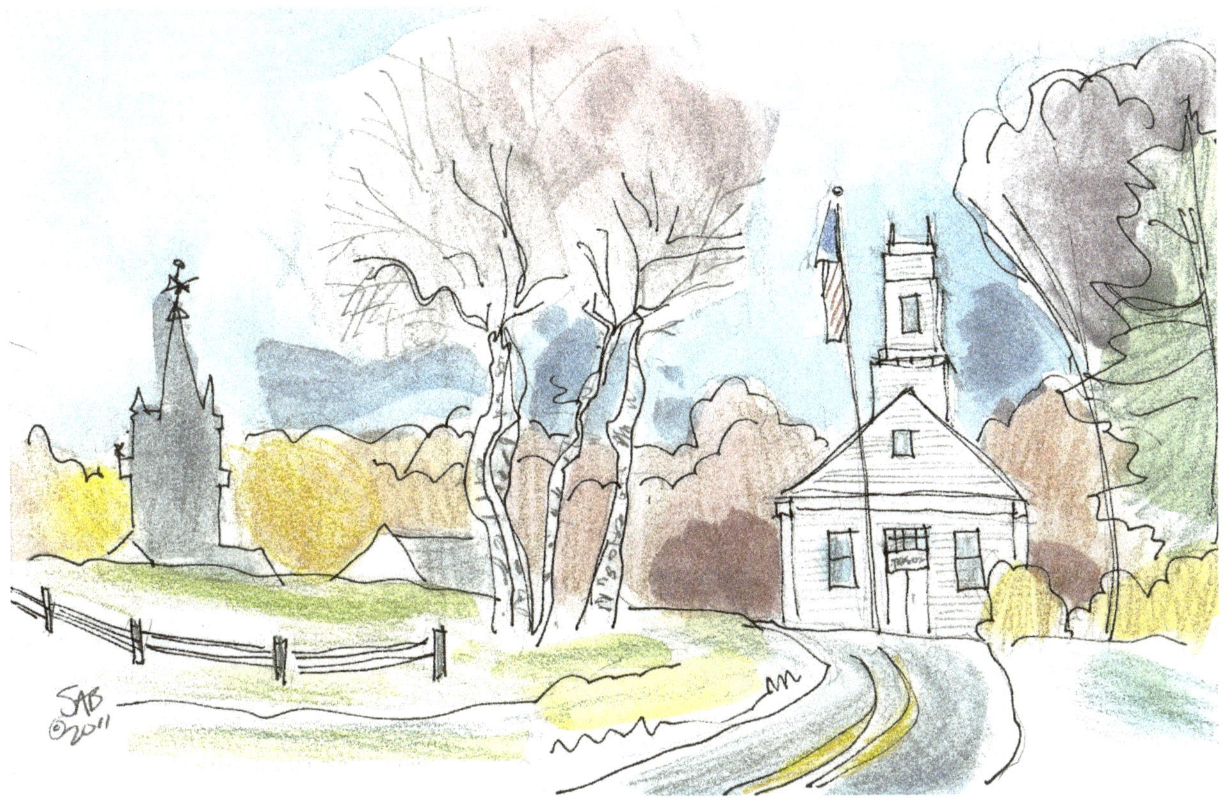

The birch trees were an especially charming part of the town common.

A small town with a population of about 1400 people, Temple is near the border of Massachusetts. Until incorporation in 1768, it was known as Peterborough Slip.

The white building is the town hall and Miller Grange. Weekend contra dancing, often known elsewhere as square dancing, takes place here. Early evening sessions for families are offered. On another musical note, the Temple Band lays claim to being America's oldest town band. Its first performance was in 1800 for George Washington. That is quite a brag. Surrounding the town green are a church, a general store, a post office, an inn with a restaurant, and a graveyard.

TROY

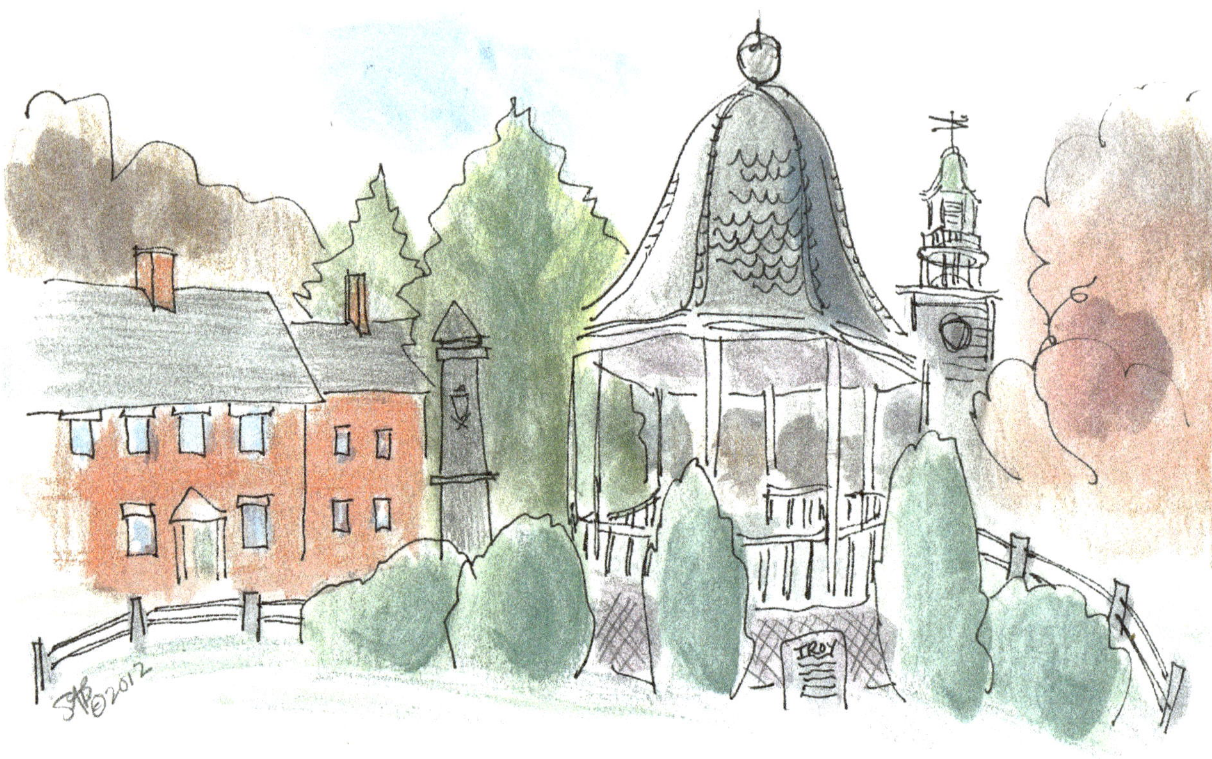

Troy's very attractive common is circled with a granite post and iron railing fence. The bandstand has presence with its bell curve and top ball and spike.

To the far right is the town hall and offices building. The obelisk is a monument to the men of the town who served in the Civil War. The brick buildings have a pleasingly solid style of architecture that has enduring character.

Troy Mills manufactured horse blankets for over 100 years.

WALPOLE

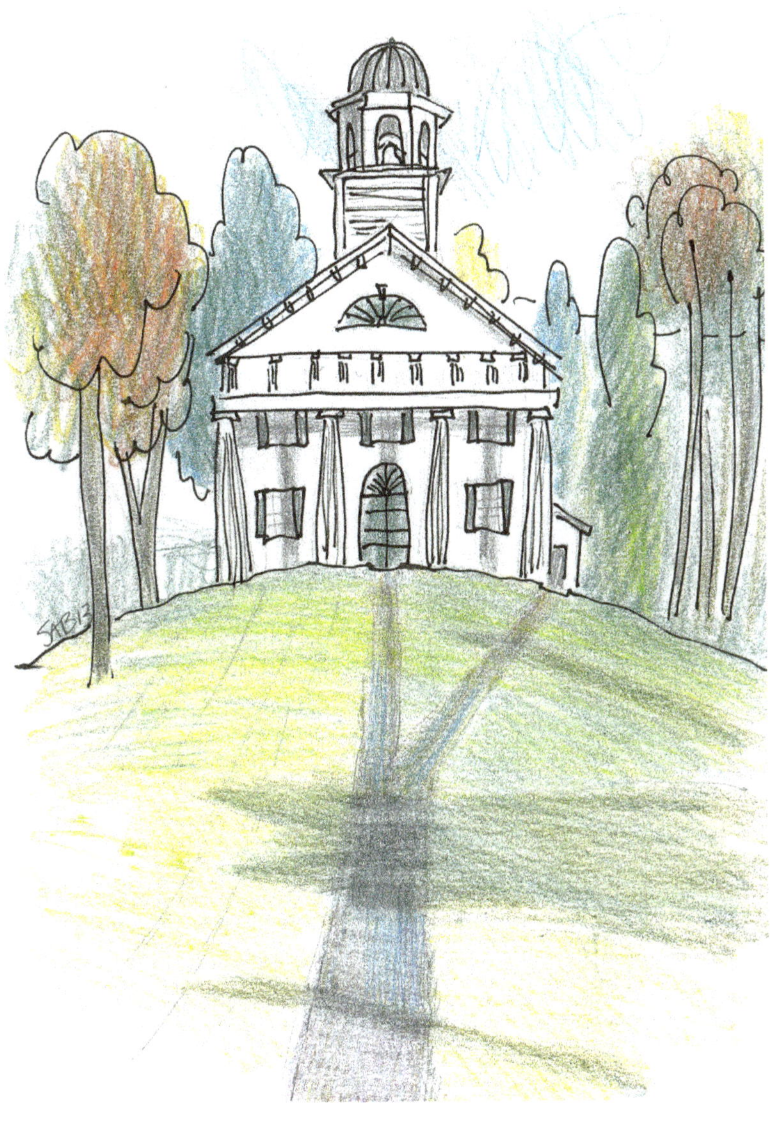

Walpole is an attractive village in the western part of the state along the Vermont border. Incorporated in 1761, the name was chosen in honor of Sir Robert Walpole, the first Prime Minister of Great Britain.

The town green is a long rectangle surrounded by white buildings, both private homes and community buildings. There's a lively mix of shops, pubs, restaurants, and a craft gallery. The Walpole Historical Society, which I drew, is located in the former Walpole Academy building. The town continues to be a center for writers, artists, and other creative people.

When we come to Walpole, we enjoy our hot chocolate at L. A Burdick's.

WESTMORELAND

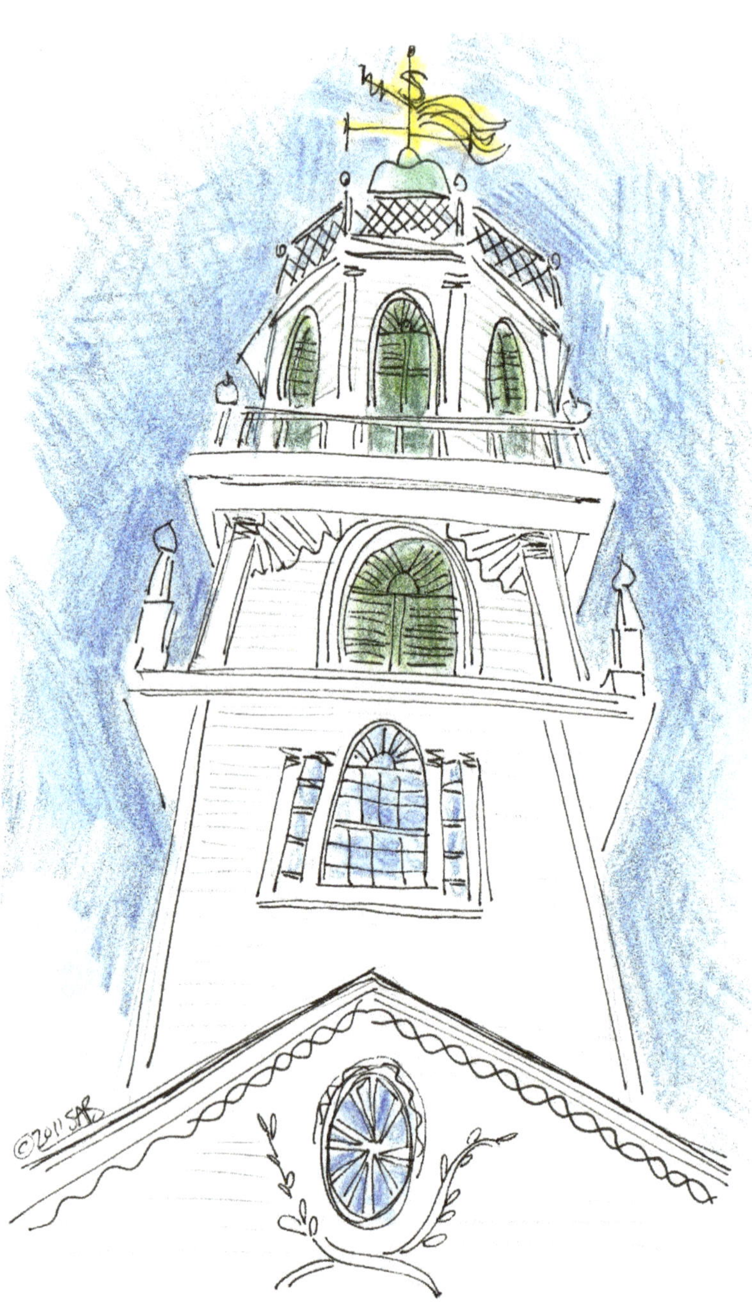

The town border follows the Connecticut River. Early European settlers came up the river by canoe from Northfield, Massachusetts.

Originally named Great Meadow, then Number 2, the town was regranted in 1752 by Governor Benning Wentworth, who chose its current name. Parkhill Meetinghouse was first built in 1762, and the current appearance of the beautifully ornate building dates from 1824. It was moved to this spot from a nearby location as the population of the settlement shifted.

My partial sketch of the meetinghouse shows many details that are indistinct in a photograph.

WILTON

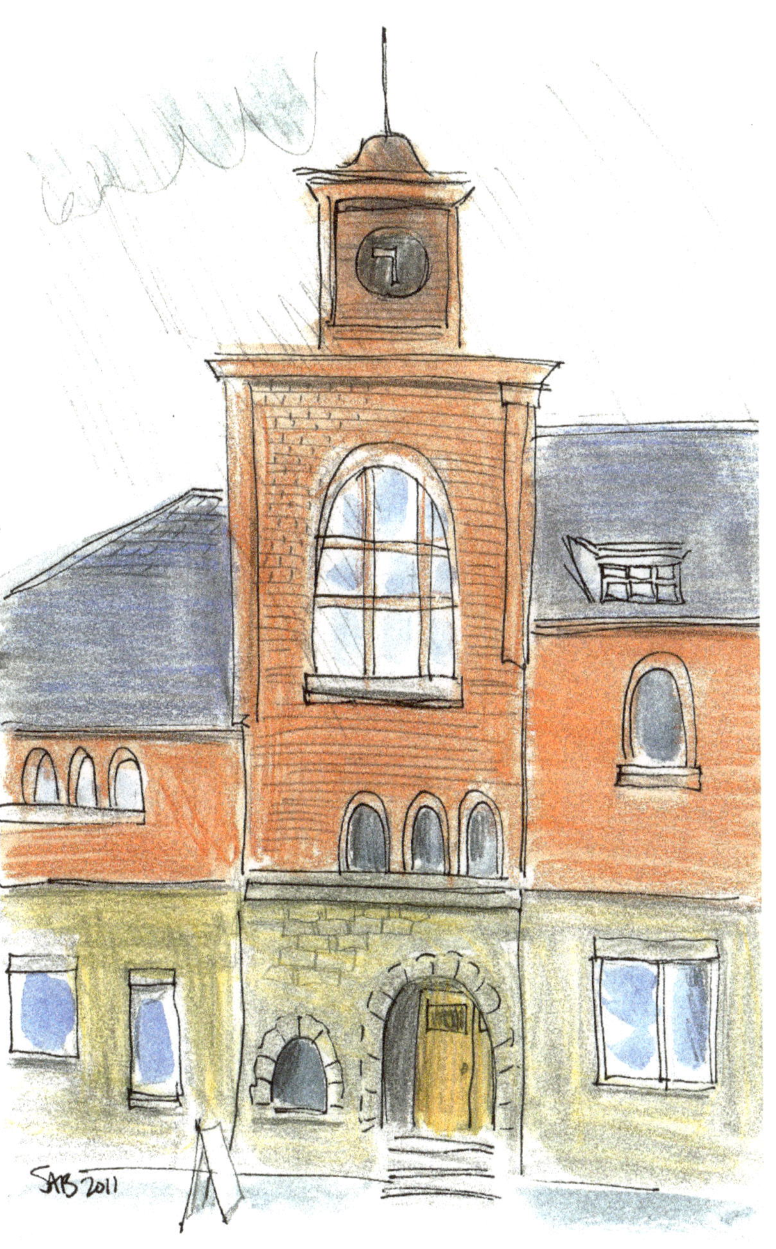

Walking along Main Street, I passed a yoga studio, small restaurants, and shops. The door to the 1886 Wilton Town Hall Theater was on my left.

The theater hosted travelling shows and vaudeville entertainment in its early days. Then silent films came. Now it is an arthouse theater. The little sign out on the sidewalk indicates the upcoming film.

The Souhegan Wood Products company has been located in the old Souhegan Textile Mill since the 1940s. Some other mills have been repurposed as housing and artists' studios.

If I lived closer to Wilton, I would be a regular at this theater

WINCHESTER

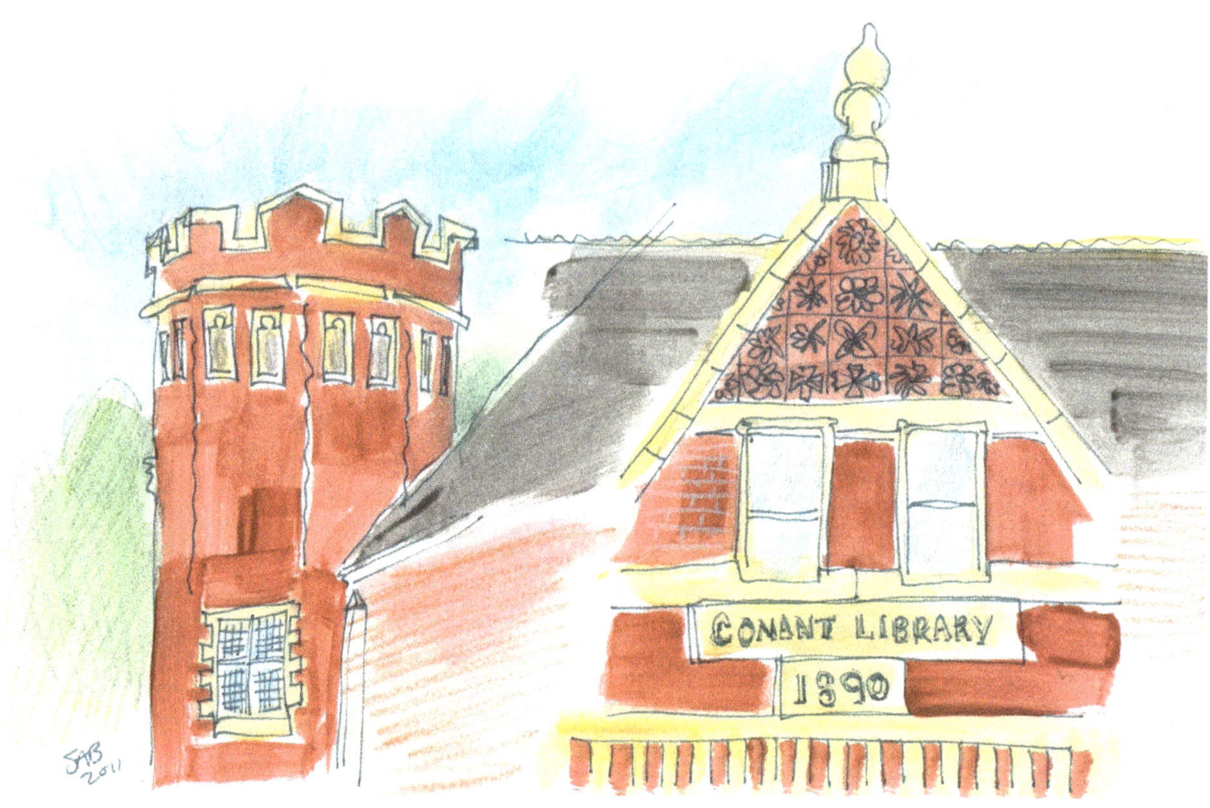

Winchester is just to the east of Hinsdale. The drawing is a composite of views of two buildings that are next door to each other, the town hall and the library.

The town hall, the tower on the left, was built in 1880, and the very ornate library followed in 1890. Enjoying the architectural flourishes on each so much, I drew parts of both. The town was named in honor of Charles Paulet, 3rd Duke of Bolton, 8th Marquis of Winchester (UK), and constable at the Tower of London.

I may return for the annual Pickle Festival in September.

WINDSOR

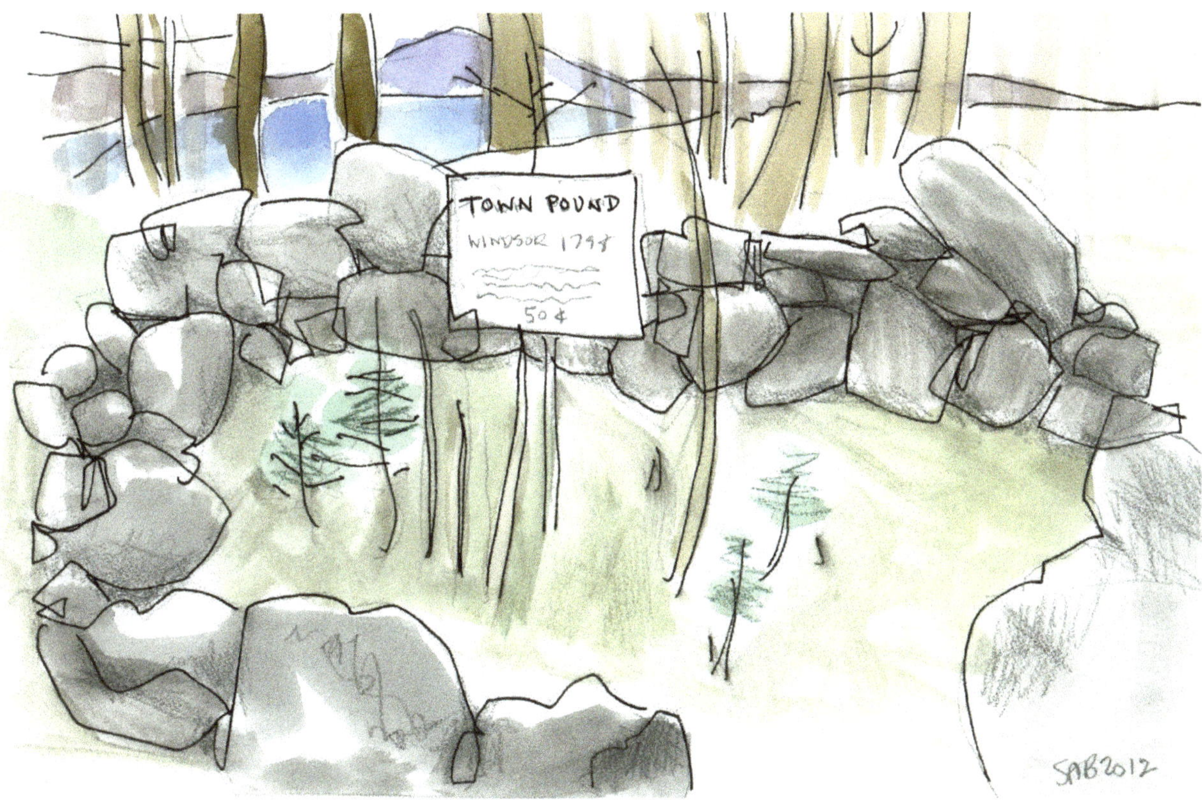

I liked how I could see through the woods to the lake and mountain.

The tiny town of Windsor, just west of Hillsborough, has a population of about 200 within about 8 square miles.

It was known originally as Campbell's Gore. A gore is a wedge shaped piece of land, often set off by itself as other boundaries are drawn. Three summer camps are long established in this rural setting. I drew the stone-walled town pound, an enclosure for farm animals that have become loose and wandering. The sign in the center has a date of 1798 and notes that the fee for claiming an impounded animal was 50 cents per day—quite a large sum by the standards of the time. Little volunteer evergreens are sprouting in the center.

North Country

BERLIN

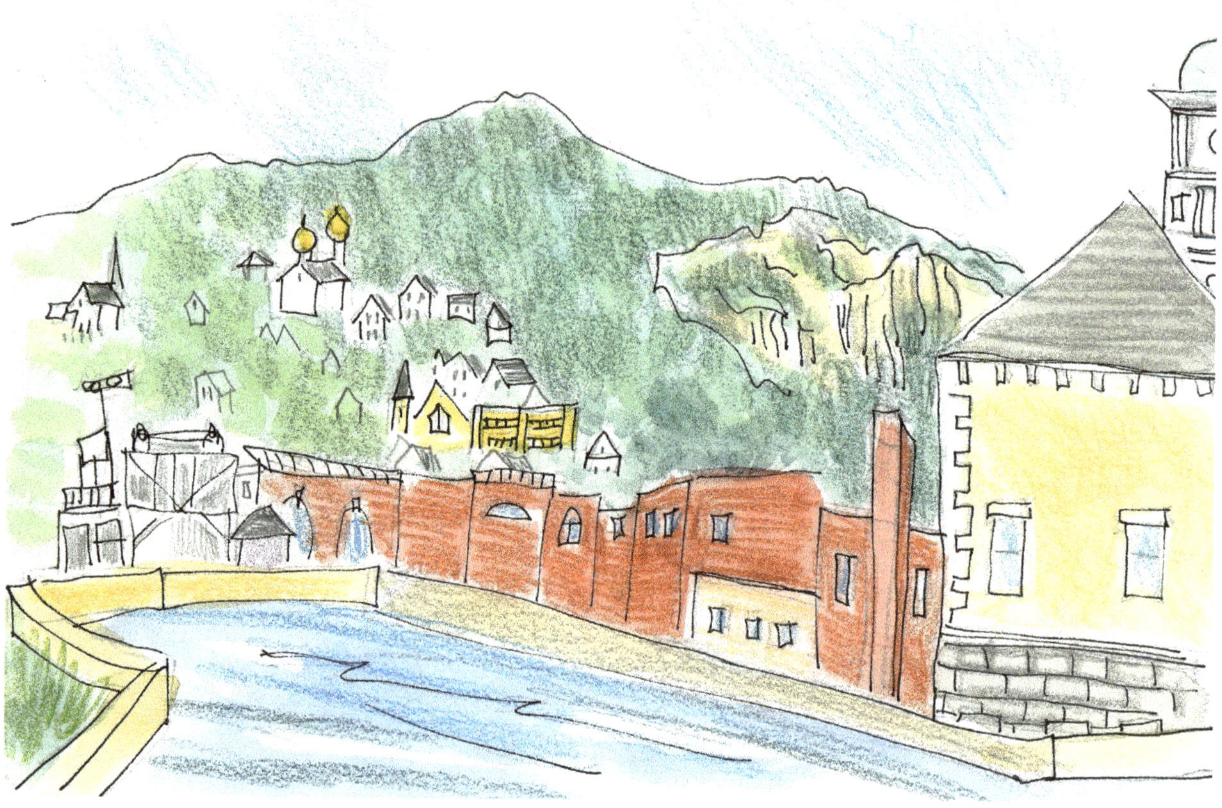

The name of the town dates from 1829. Prior to that time early settlers called it Maynesborough.

The mountainous area is heavily forested and, as a result, the European settlers developed logging, and wood and paper industries on the Androscoggin River. The workers came from Russia, Norway, Italy, Sweden, Ireland, Germany, and French Canada. Sixty five percent of today's residents claim a French-Canadian ancestry. Each immigrant group had its own social services, including churches and meeting places. I drew one half of City Hall, Main Street, and a canal built for the paper industry.

Several churches and a school dot the very steep hillside.

CLARKSVILLE

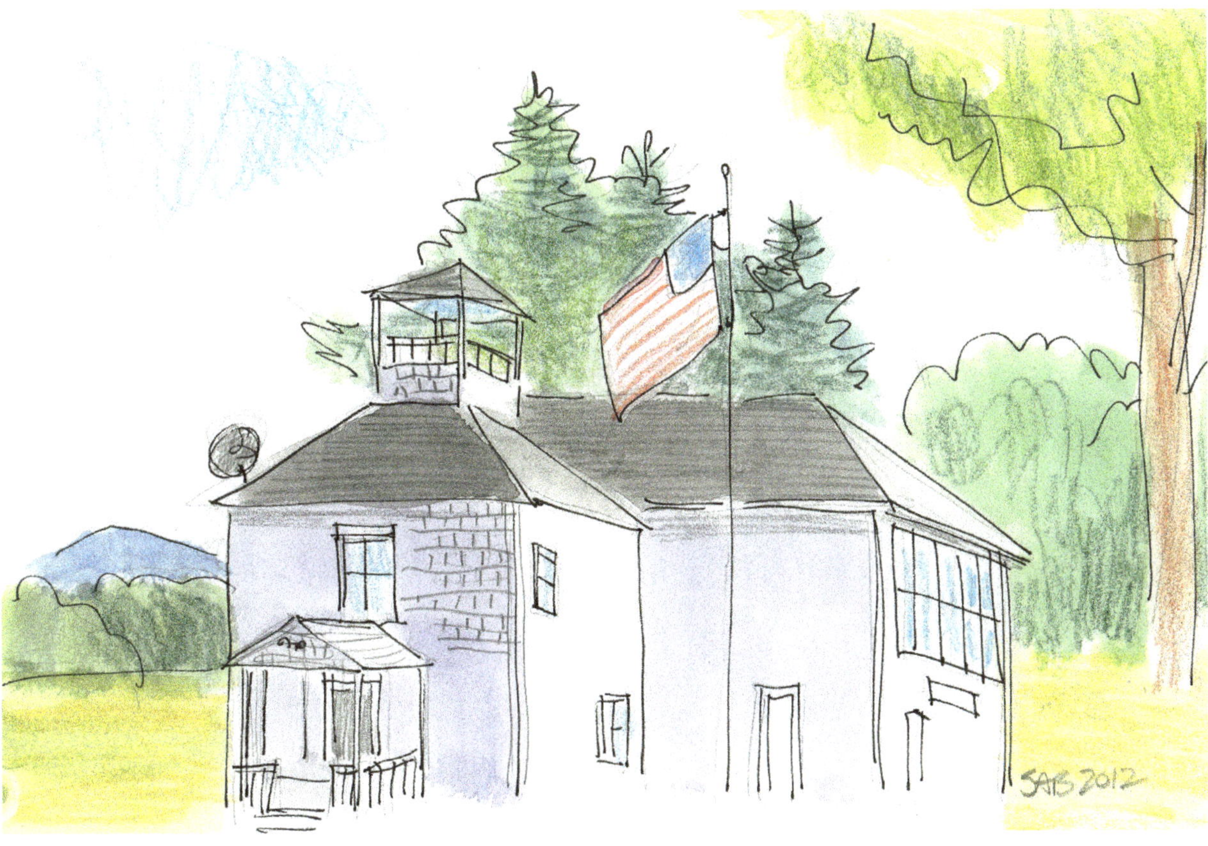

In the 1800s, the town industries produced potato starch and maple sugar.

From 1853 to 1872, this town was called Dartmouth College Grant. The college sold off sections of the land as a way of raising money.

The land was bought by Benjamin Clark of Boston and Joseph Murdock of Norwich, Vermont. The Clark family cleared the land for settlement, a momentous task. Lake Francis is the northern border of the town, and the western border is the Connecticut River.

This private home was originally a sawmill in Stewartstown. It was moved after World War I to house the Clarksville Dairy Company. From 1935 to 1968, it was the town school.

COLEBROOK

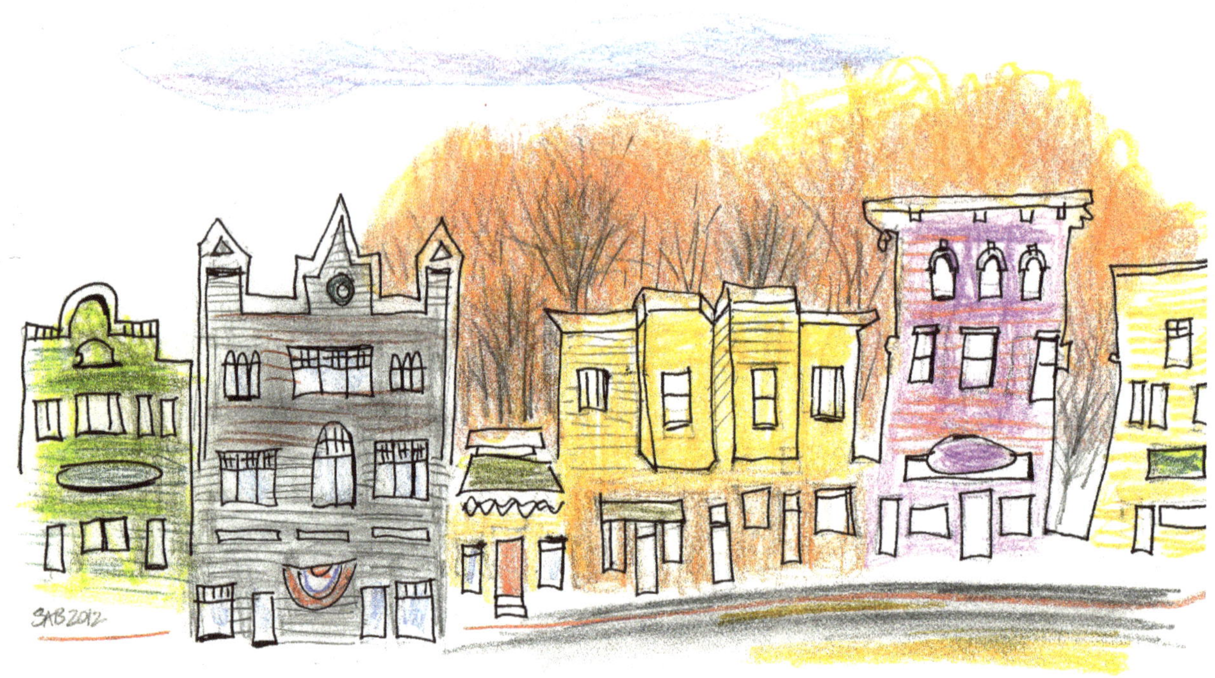

The town was first named Dryden and then became known as Colebrook Town. In 1796 the name Colebrook was selected to honor George Colebrooke, chairman of the East India Company.

Early industries were potato farming and whiskey distilled from the potatoes. When a road through Dixville Notch was completed, the farmers and businessmen in town were able to find markets for their products in Portland, Maine. Dairy farming and tourism are the two major industries now for the town of 2,400 residents. The park and picnic area at the base of Beaver Brook Falls is an active place for families.

The lineup of wooden false front buildings on Main Street was unusually colorful. I was spotted drawing them, and the rumors began.

COLUMBIA

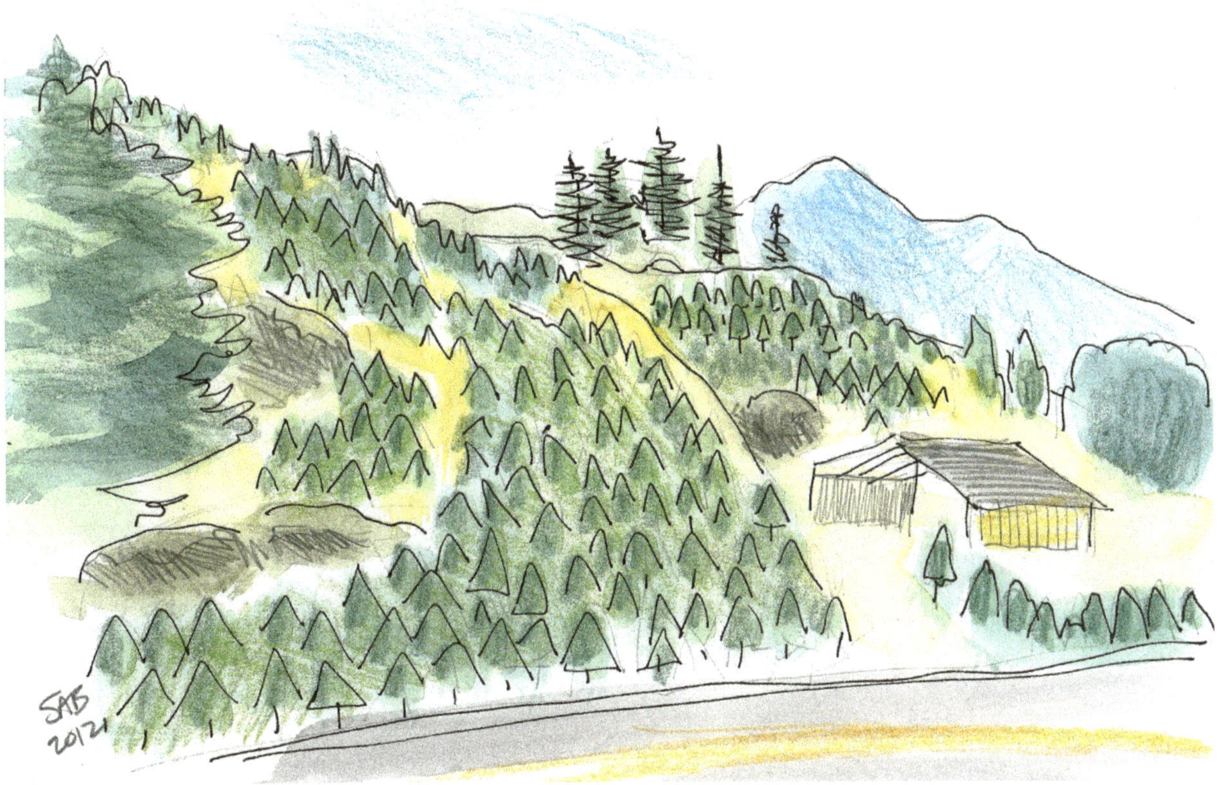

My eye enjoys patterns, and I am very likely to draw any repeated shape, such as these young trees.

Like many towns in the state, Columbia has had a series of names. First, it was Preston, then Cockburn Town. It became Columbia in 1812, just before the start of the war with Great Britain. Early residents made their money from lumber, potato starch, and maple sugar.

I drew the conical fir trees marching over the steep hills like so many rows of toy soldiers. Each one is destined to become a family's Christmas tree. Eight to ten years pass from seedling to full cutting size. Today's customers demand a perfect shape, which means annual pruning.

DALTON

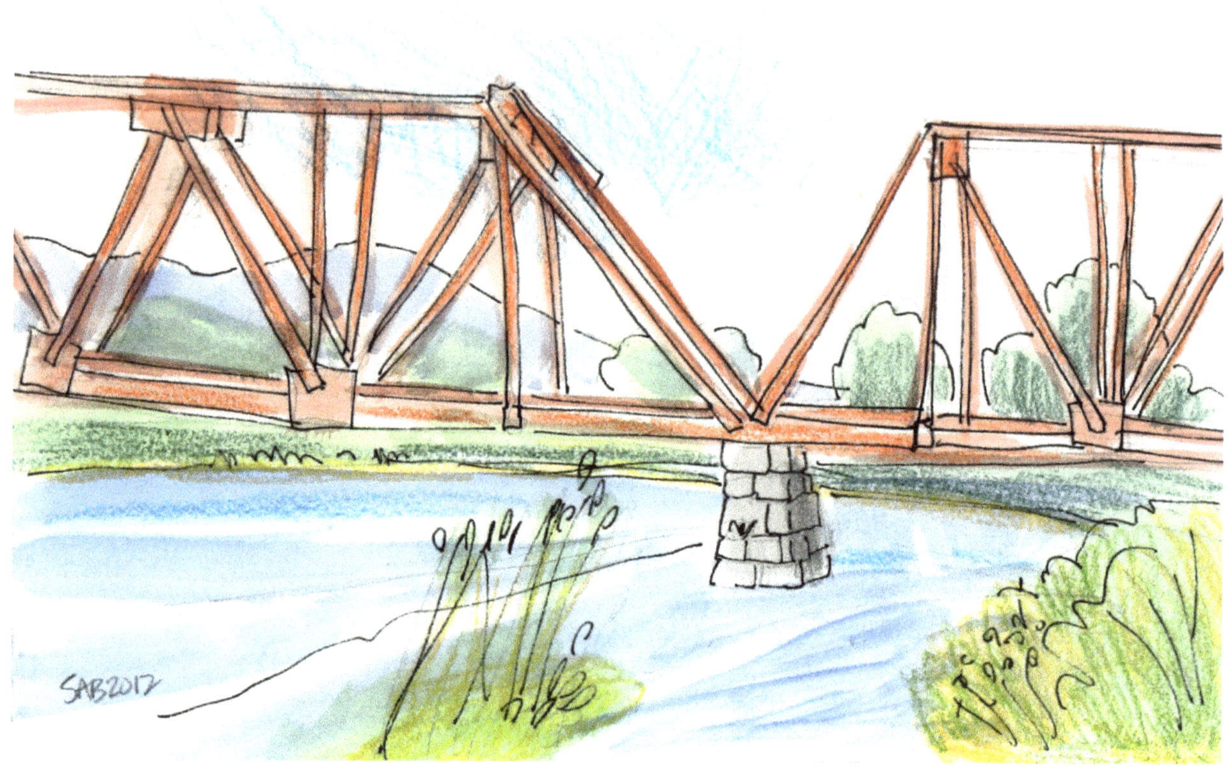

This is one of many New Hampshire towns with a population of under 1000 people. First it was named Chiswick, then Apthorp, and then in 1784, Dalton.

The railroad bridge crosses the slowly flowing Connecticut River into bordering Vermont. The town of Gilman is on the opposite bank. It was very peaceful here on this hot and sunny summer day. I remember the birds chirping in the grass as I drew.

Dalton has a multi-purpose municipal building which houses the town hall, the police, as well as the library.

DUMMER

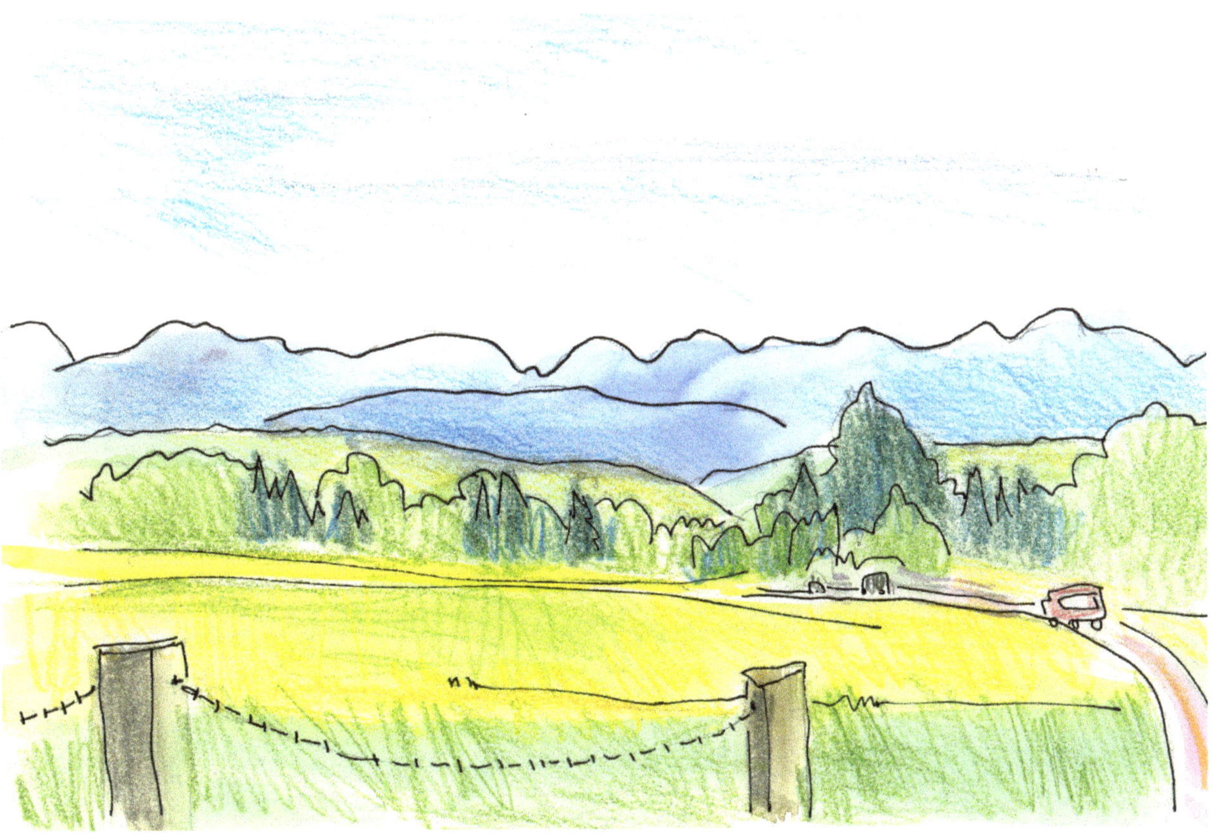

The Pontook Reservoir is a popular recreation site.

My artist's eye appreciated this view from Route 16, looking east. The fence makes a foreground, the flat fields and meadows make the middle ground, and the blue mountains make lovely layers in the background. The curve in the road leads your eyes into the picture frame.

Dummer was granted in 1773, but it was not settled until 1812. The first settler with his family was William Leighton from Farmington. The Upper Ammonoosuc River provided power for sawmills, leading to growth in population. The town was named for a governor of Massachusetts.

ERROL

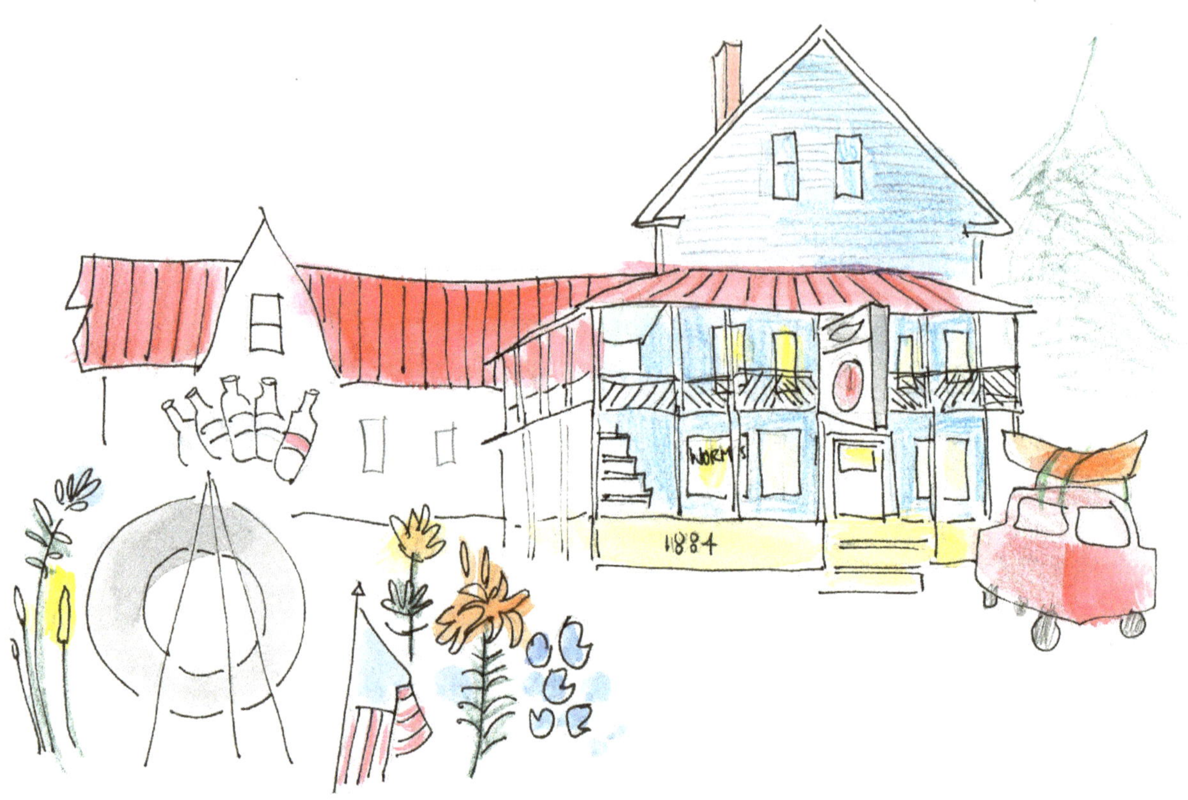

Errol is a small town north of the White Mountains, with a population of 300 people. The town was named for Scotland's James Hay, 15th Earl of Errol, in 1774.

The soil was considered poor, but suitable for hay, oats, and potatoes. Sawmills processed the ample lumber supply. Today the area is known for fishing, hunting, and snowmobiling. Other tourists paddle their canoes in the many secluded lakes. The kayak atop the car, in front of the Errol General Store, will feature in a day's adventure on the water. The flowers, flag, and round wreath form a small war memorial across the street.

Two camping areas in the town are the Androscoggin Wayside Park and the Mollidgewock State Park.

LANCASTER

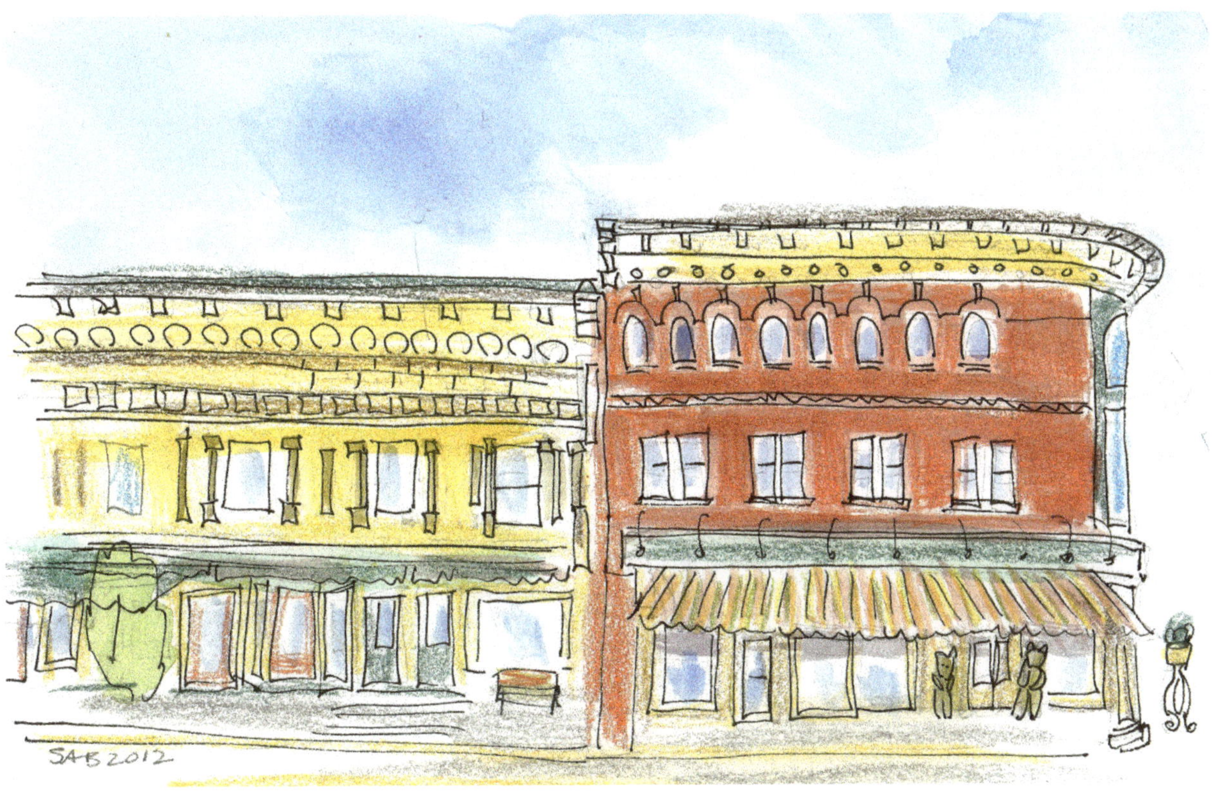

The town of Lancaster edges the Connecticut river. Fertile and flat meadows along the water provide good agricultural soil.

The circa 1900 urban block with its exuberant flourishes appealed to me. Benches, planters, and carved wooden bears rounded out the scene. The blistering July heat nearly wilted me while sketching this. The weather and temperature are two memories that always return to my mind when I look at one of my drawings.

Lancaster resident Senator John W. Weeks worked very hard to get congressional backing to create the White Mountain National Forest in 1910.

MILAN

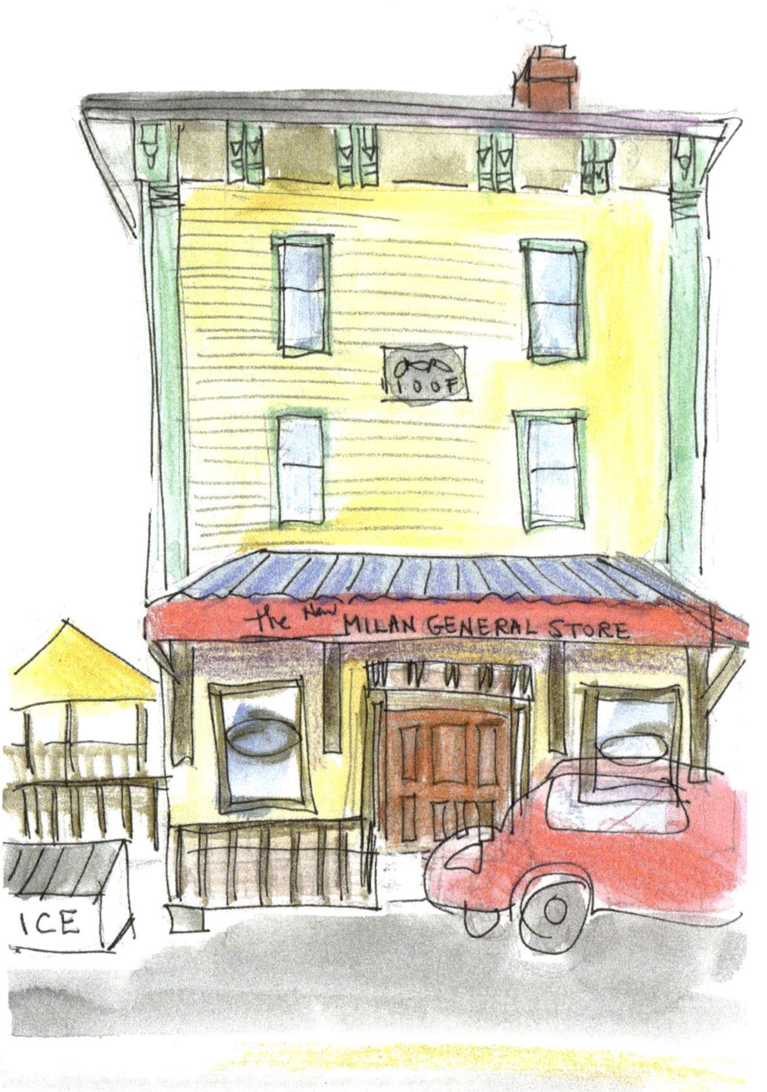

Milan, with the stress on the first syllable, is a small town. It is near the much larger town of Berlin, also with stress on the first syllable.

I was struck by the unusual color combination in this storefront. The name sign is very new and modern. I forgot to include the word 'Inc.' in the sign. Like so many buildings in the state, it is constructed of painted wood. The letters on the small sign mean Independent Order of Odd Fellows, indicating that this building was once used as a meeting hall.

Milan has a beautiful town library, with red tile roof, built of brown brick with elaborate ceramic decorative touches.

NORTHUMBERLAND

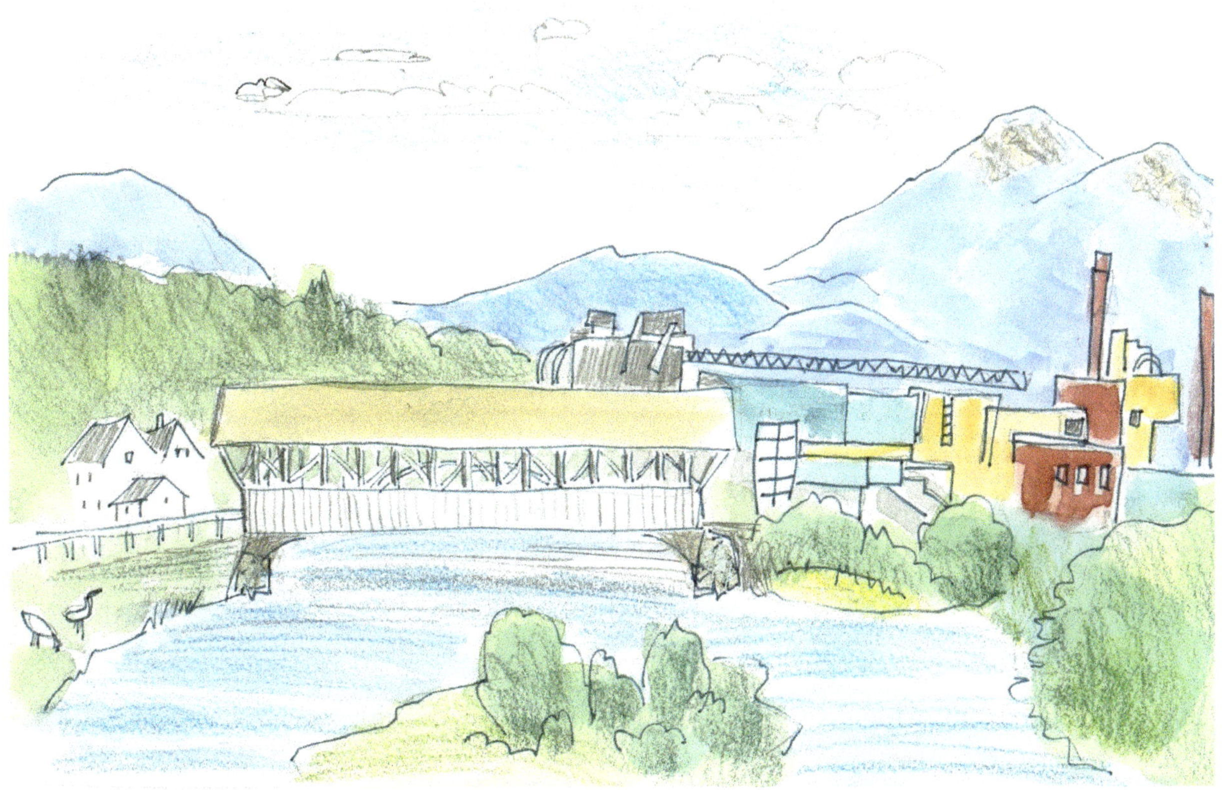

The rocky capped mountains on the right are the Percy Peaks.

Groveton is a village within the town of Northumberland. Some maps show one name or the other, but not both. The river is the Upper Ammonoosuc.

The paper mill in the right side will be dismantled soon, and the long-time paper making industry will close up shop in this town. So this drawing is a kind of record of time and place. That in itself is another reason to sketch a scene. We met some nice employees of the town library who enjoyed showing us maps and scrapbooks of the history of the settlement.

PITTSBURG

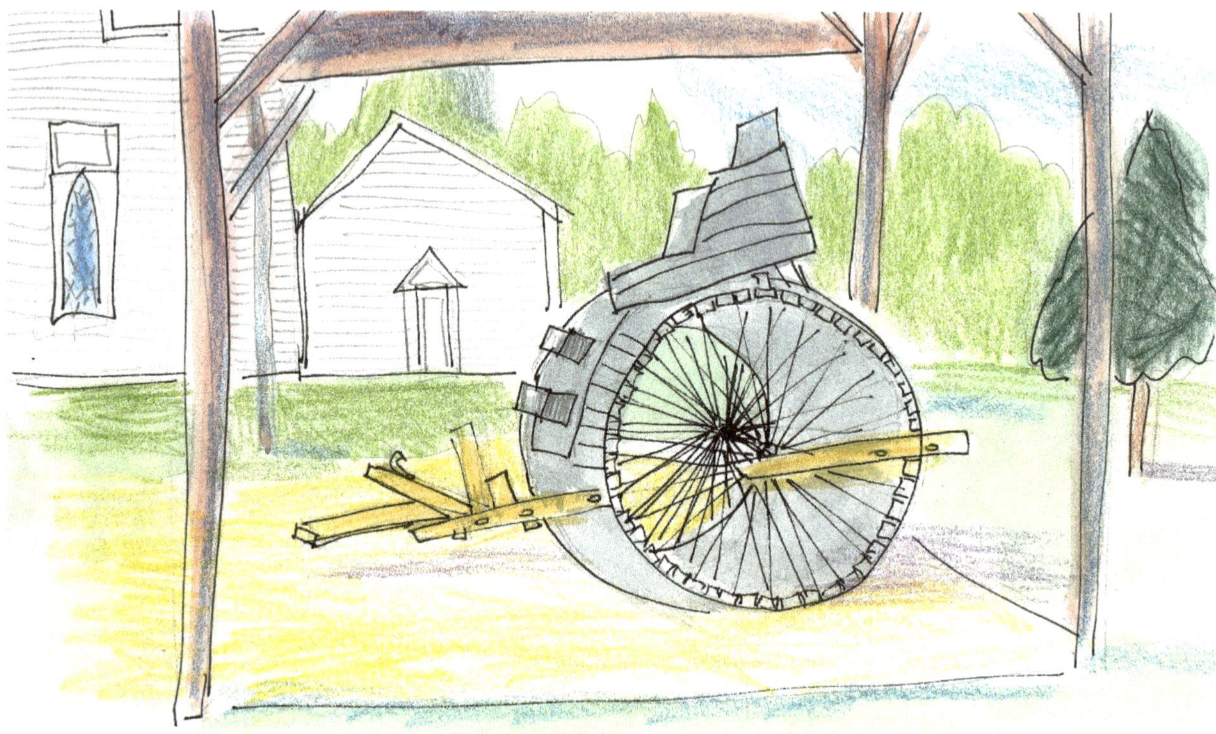

This town, named for the British Prime Minister William Pitt, is small in population (under 1000 people) but large in area (291 square miles).

On the border with Canada, Pittsburg was known as the Republic of Indian Stream for a few decades in the 19th century. The governments of both the United States and Great Britain claimed it as their own. The confusion seemed to do with disagreements over the location of the head waters of the Connecticut River. The townspeople objected to being taxed twice, so they formed their own country with a government and a constitution.

A huge snow roller, protected by a roof, sits on the town green.

STARK

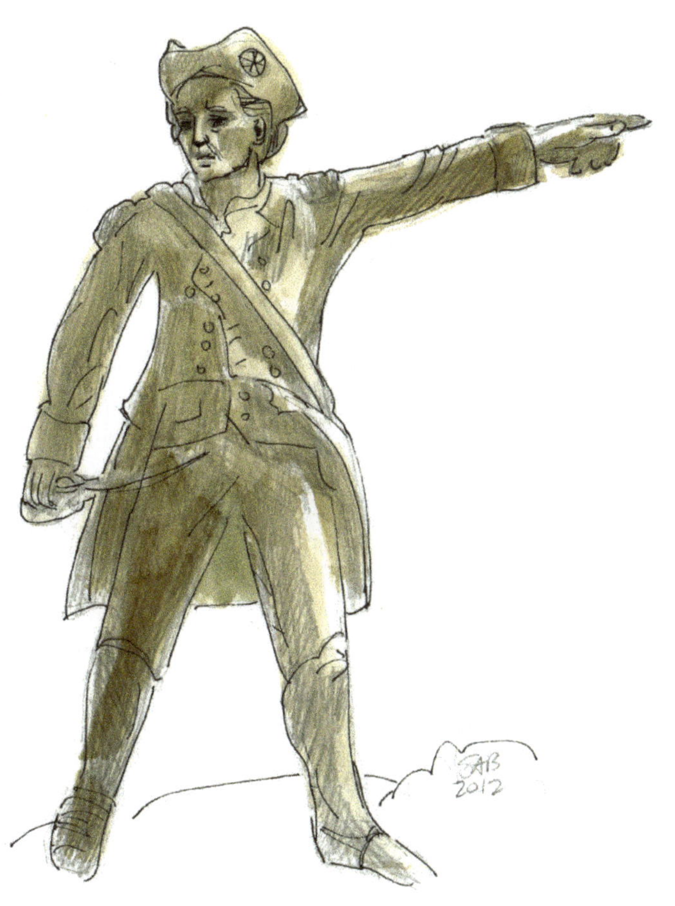

Stark is a quaint place with a few white buildings, a covered bridge, inn, church, library, and town hall. The large, bronze statue of General John Stark (1728–1822) stands on the green. He and his troops were the victors at the pivotal Battle of Bennington, 1777. He spoke the words "Live Free or Die", now the motto of New Hampshire.

Skipping ahead to 1944–1946, Stark was the location of a World War II Prisoner of War camp. Two hundred German prisoners worked in the woods as lumberjacks, preparing logs to send down river to the paper mills of Berlin. Berlin, New Hampshire, that is!

Several of the former POWs from Camp Stark returned to visit and live in the United States after the war. They had been treated well and had positive memories of the people of New Hampshire.

STEWARTSTOWN

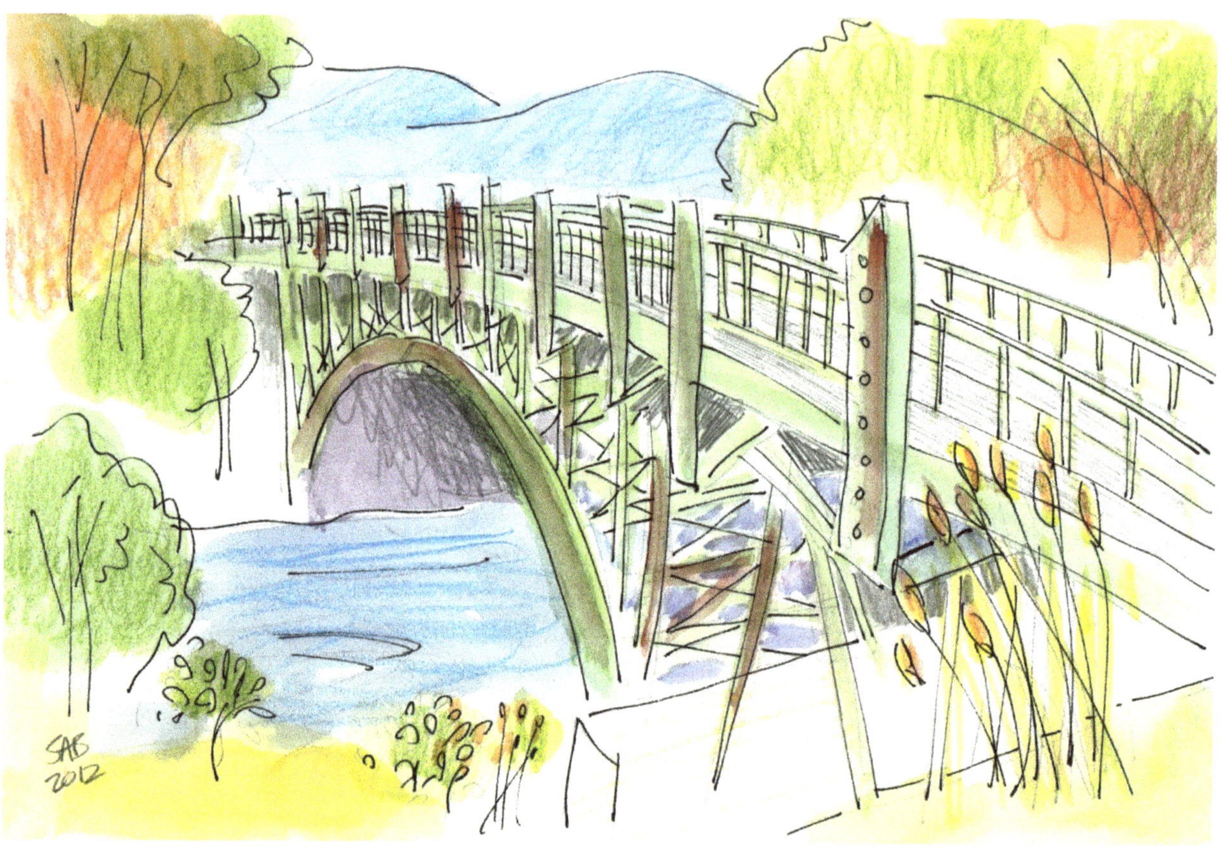

The Connecticut River flows under this bridge in Stewartstown. The Vermont towns of Canaan and Beecher Falls are on the other side of the river.

I stood at the corner of Church Street and Bridge Street to draw this view, carefully watching my footing. There's a very thin slice of Vermont on the other side, and after that comes the Canadian border. We could see the border station a short way down the road. But we didn't have our passports with us. The border requirements are much more formalized now than they once were.

The town land includes most of Coleman State Park.

STRATFORD

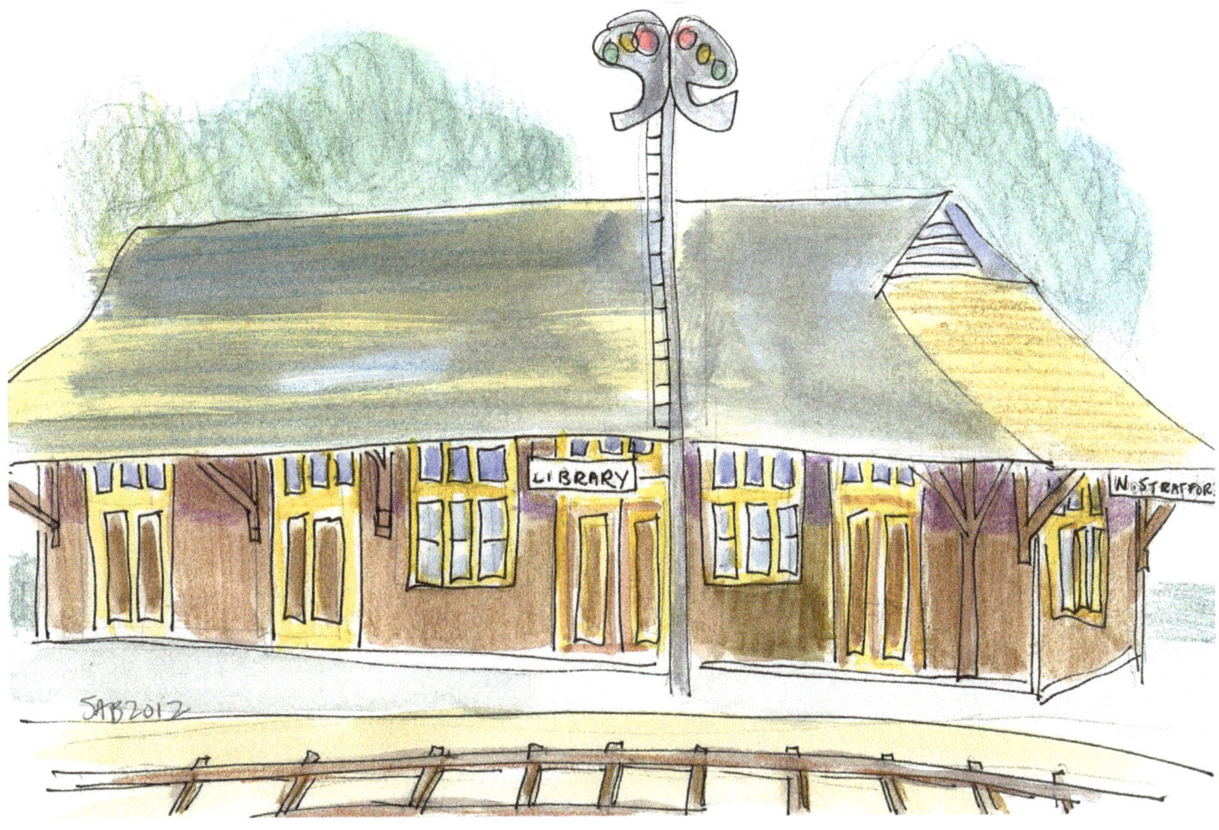

While I was drawing this building, a farmer's market was setting up on the green. It included a band.

The town was first named Woodbury, and then regranted in 1773 as Stratford.

With the villages of North Stratford and Stratford Hollow, it is indeed named for the slightly more well-known town of Stratford-upon-Avon, in England.

This one is on a river too, the Connecticut River. During the early days, logging was a big industry, and logs were sent down the river, as well as loaded onto railroad cars. Now, the railroad station has been repurposed as the town library.

WHITEFIELD

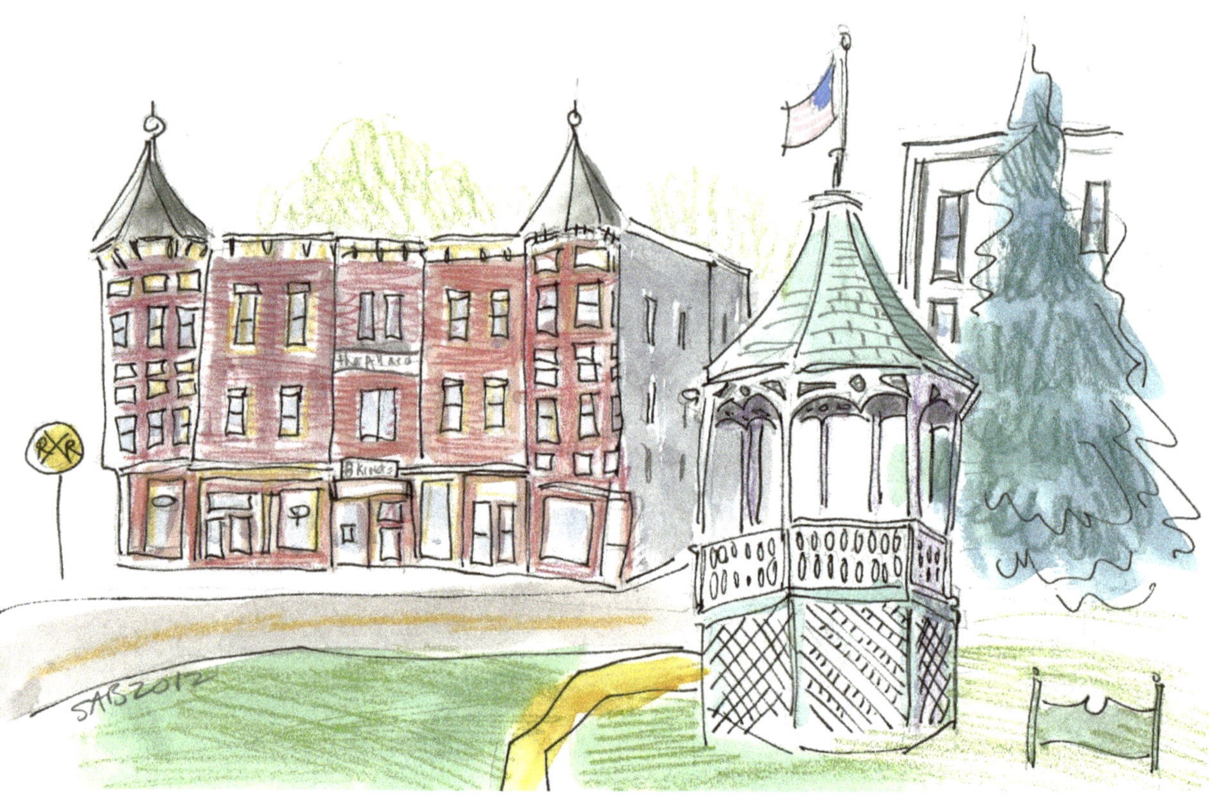

I found plenty more turrets and peaked roofs to pique my interest in Whitefield. As I drew this from the town green, a few people were keeping an eye on me. They wondered about my unusual interest in the old commercial block of shops, called The Allare, and the ornate bandstand.

A few miles from the square, a grand old hotel from the heyday of the area, the Mountain View Grand Resort and Spa, still greets its guests with a panorama of the Presidential Range of the White Mountains. The sprawling hotel has recently been renovated.

Weathervane is a repertory company theater in town.

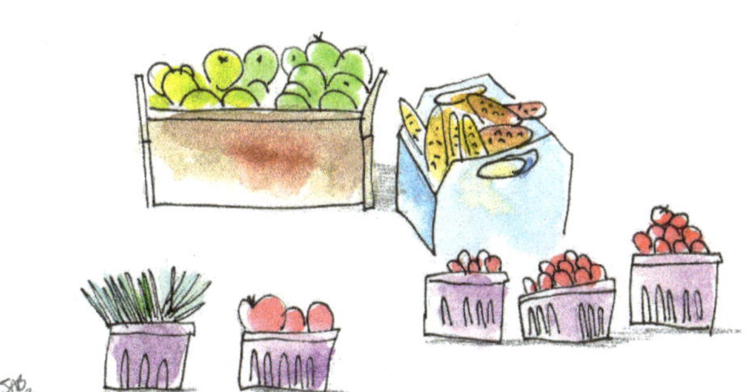

Seacoast

ATKINSON

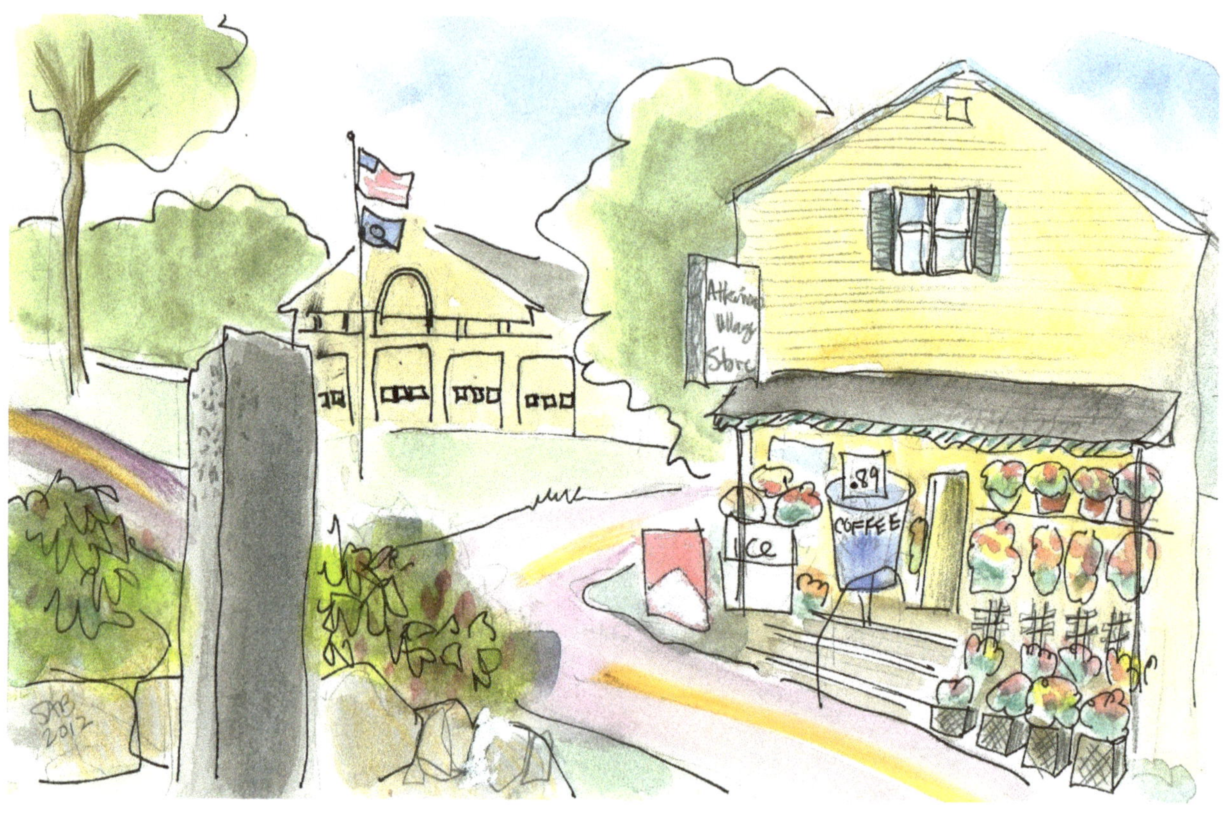

This small roadside store in Atkinson was filled to bursting with beautiful flowers and plants. Mother's Day was just around the corner, so the owners were preparing their springtime inventory.

Standing across the road, I made sure to include the granite post. The nickname for New Hampshire is the Granite State, which refers to the ubiquitous hard stone and the toughness and resiliency of its inhabitants. Some stone posts have metal rings on them, leftovers from the days of tying one's horse up at curbside.

Established in 1787, Atkinson Academy is the oldest co-educational school in the country, and is now a public grade school.

BRENTWOOD

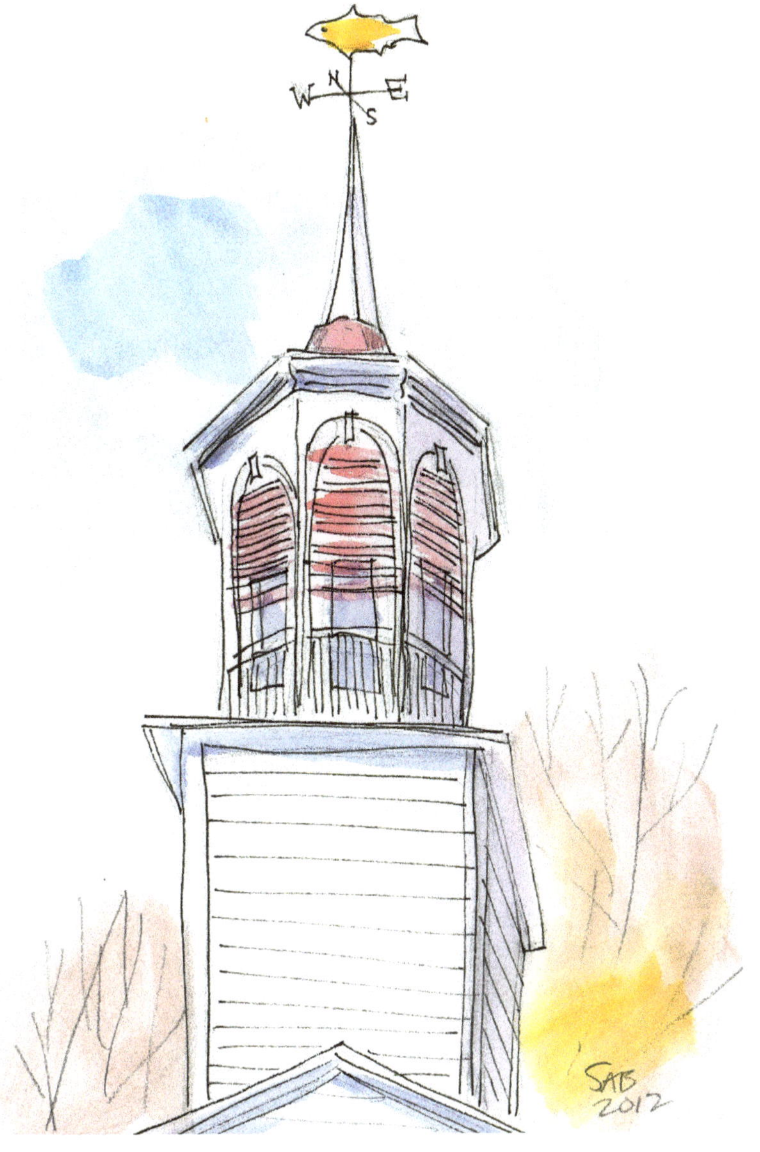

The steeple of the Pilgrim United Church of Christ in Brentwood is trimmed with red paint instead of the standard green.

I was taken by the golden fish weather vane. The old churches of New Hampshire always seem to have a weather vane on the top.

An historical marker to the side of this church told of a peace rally here in 1812. Two thousand people gathered to hear Daniel Webster speak against Americans entering into the War of 1812 against the British. I shut my eyes to try to imagine the crowds in that quiet place.

A lot of Native American artifacts have been found in the area.

DANVILLE

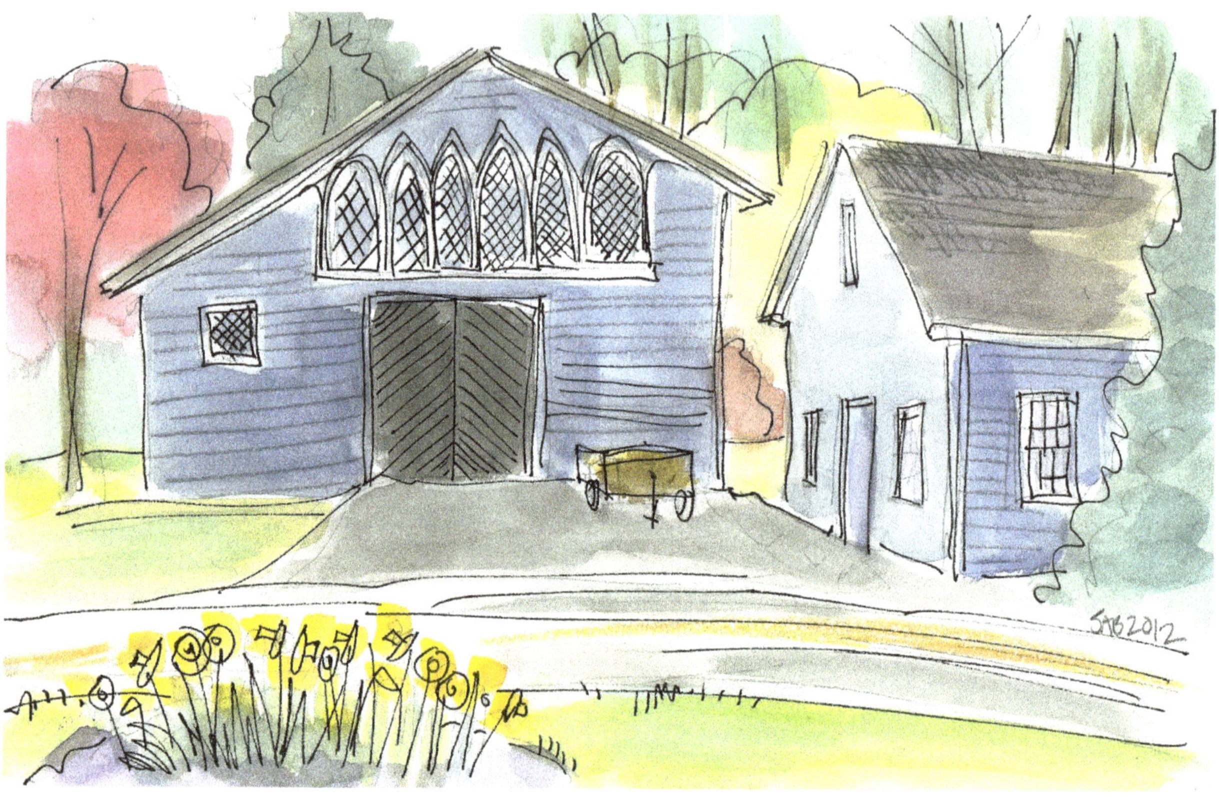

The town is sort of tucked away, just off the busy Route 125. While a part of Kingston, the locals called it Hawke.

When incorporation took place in 1836, the town became Danville, some say because many residents were named Daniel. The town land contains Long Pond and part of Rock Rimmon State Forest. On a spring day, with daffodils in bloom, I sat on the ground to draw this house and garage, with its extremely unusual arrangement of windows. The town hall was directly behind me. Nearby is Danville's old meetinghouse, built in 1759 and largely unchanged since then.

While I was sketching, the happy sounds of a softball game floated across the nearby field.

DOVER

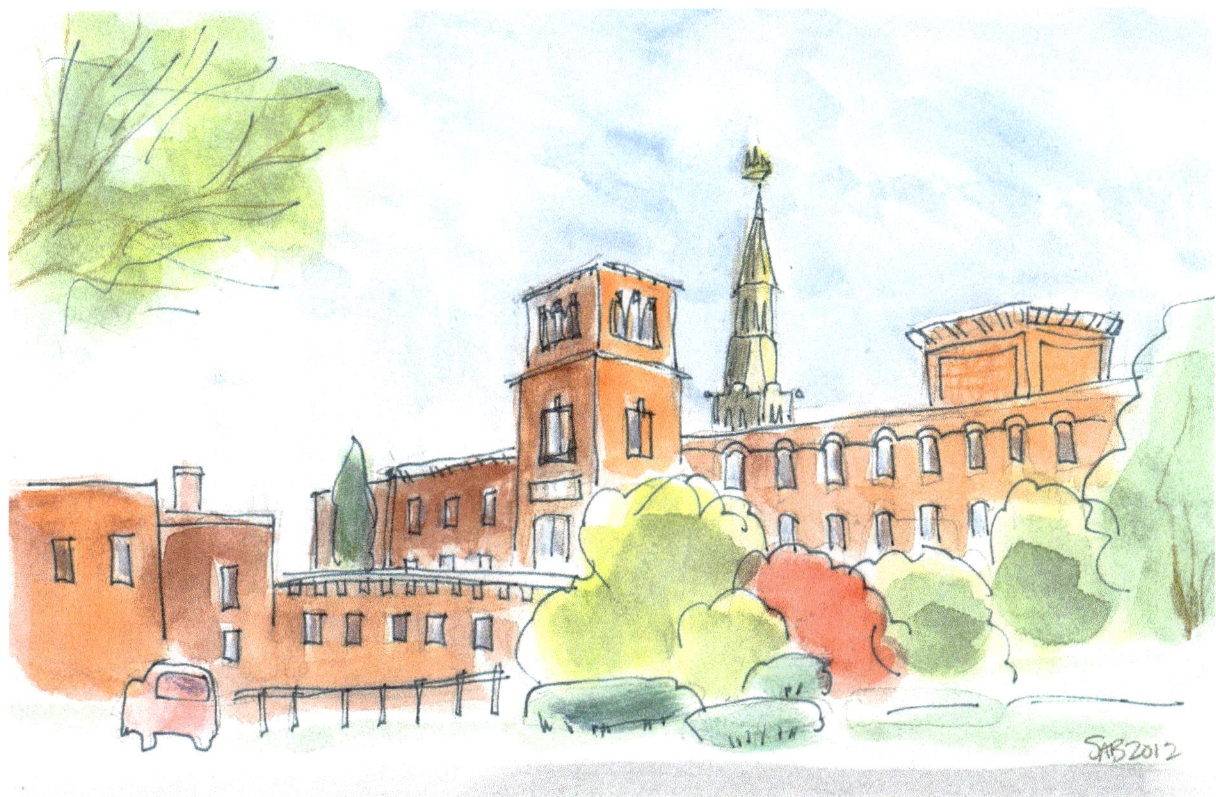

Dover, first called Bristol, is New Hampshire's oldest permanent settlement.

The Cocheco Mills were built in 1815 to make printed cotton fabric. In 1828, the workers, mostly young females, went on strike for better working conditions.

The strike was remarkable and memorable, as it was organized by women. The mills lasted until 1937. Today the solidly built structures are used for housing and small businesses. The spire of the church in the background, St. John's Methodist Episcopal, is topped by a weather-vane in the design of a three-masted sailing ship. Yes, I had to walk over to the church to more closely study the weathervane.

DURHAM

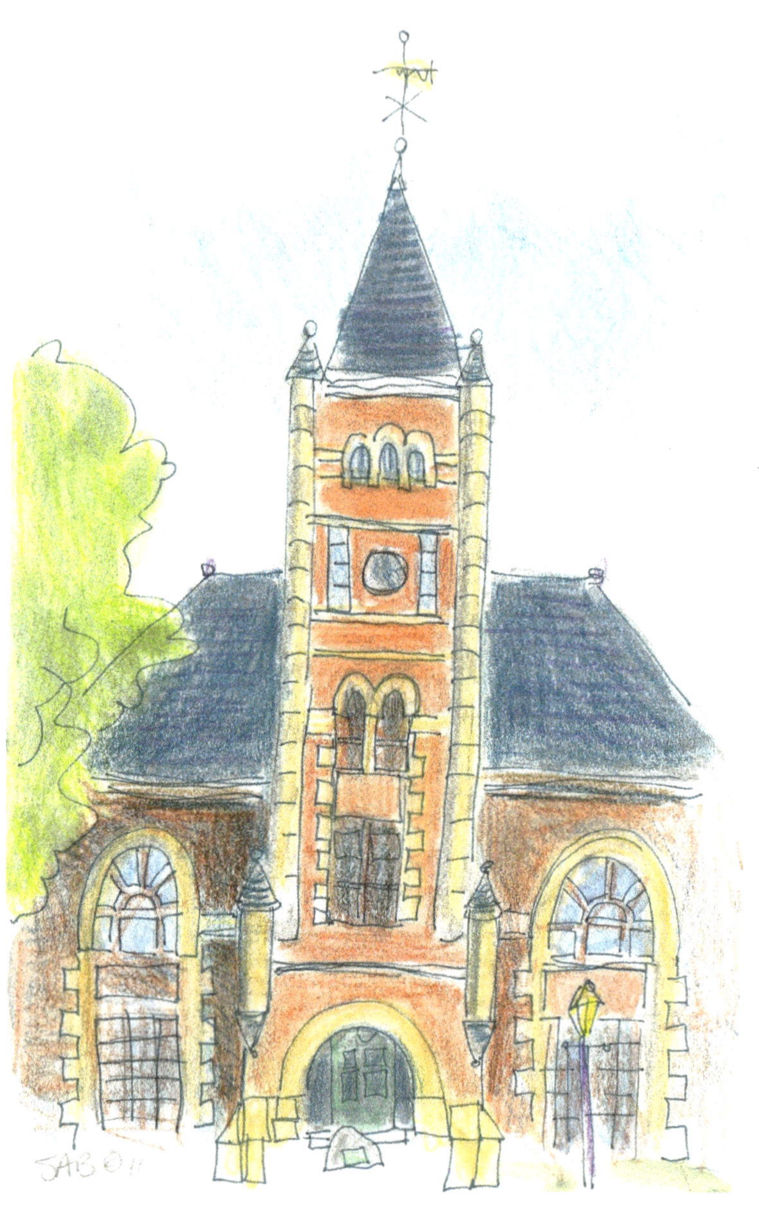

Durham has a population of 15,000, and that number doubles with the inclusion of students at the University of New Hampshire.

The college campus straddles Main Street and flows into the commercial area of town. Dimond Library on the UNH campus serves both the town and the university.

The Thompson Hall tower looks over the campus. This Romanesque Revival style building, nicknamed T-Hall, is across the street from the dormitory where I lived during my time on campus. The bells and carillon in the tower can be heard everywhere. And are plenty loud enough to wake you up.

Durham, first settled in 1635, was once named Oyster River Plantation. It was a part of Dover.

EAST KINGSTON

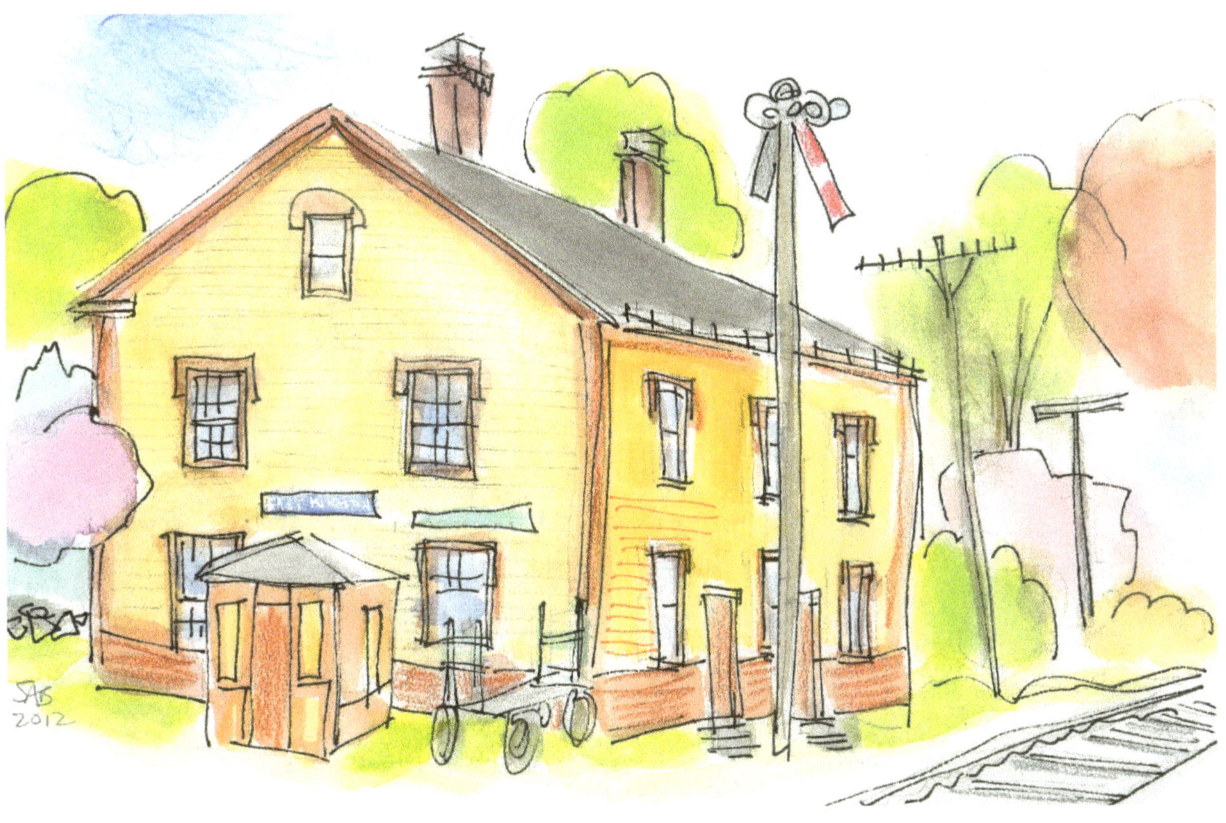

Yellow and brown were the colors of the Boston and Maine Railroad. For more color, note the spring blooming lilacs.

The town was originally called Kingston East Parish until 1738 when the current name was chosen. East Kingston is indeed a separate town, though many places whose names feature compass points are just informally designated areas of towns.

The early industries at the Trickling Falls on Powwow Pond were mills – a saw mill and a grist mill. Locals cut ice on the pond in winter, before the age of refrigeration. Much New England ice was shipped to faraway places in the warmer parts of the world, and a lot of money was made in the frozen water trade. The New England Brick Company was a well known industry in town.

EPPING

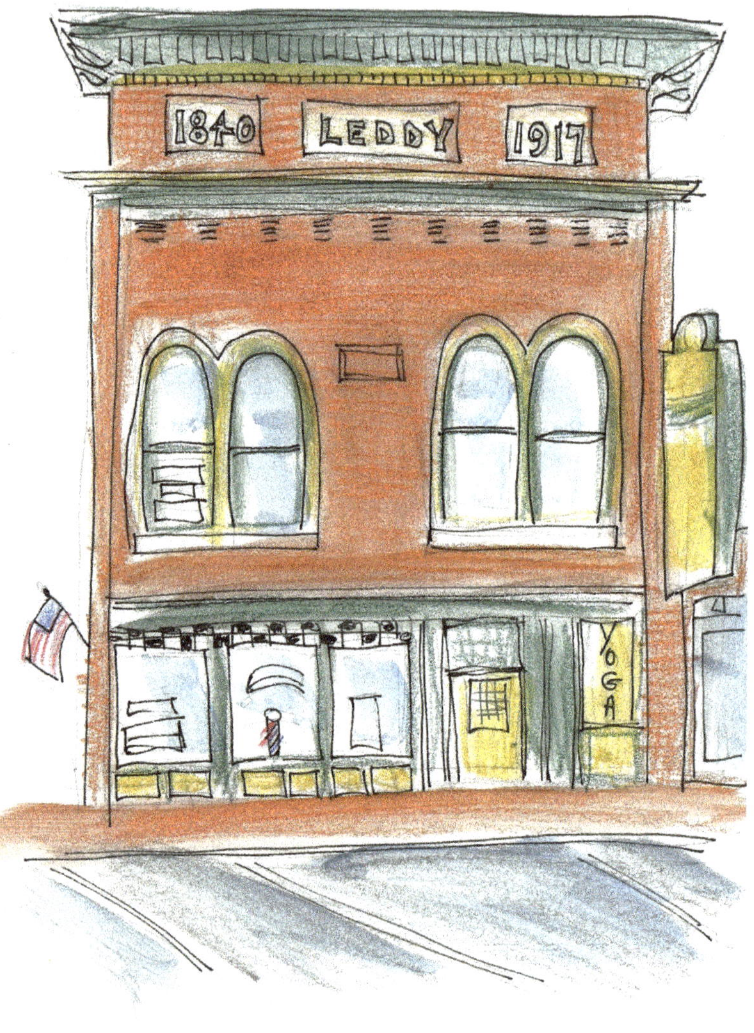

Once a part of Exeter, a charter was granted in 1741 and the settlement took the name from Epping Forest, England.

Local clay from the town was used to produce bricks. The building I drew surely must be made from Epping Bricks.

The Leddy Building on Main Street in the old downtown area houses a barber shop and a yoga studio. From 1975 to 2008, the Leddy Center for the Performing Arts used a second story space in this building. Now the Leddy Center has a modern space about a mile away on Ladd's Lane.

The quiet, quaint, Epping old town is just two blocks north of busy Route 101.

EXETER

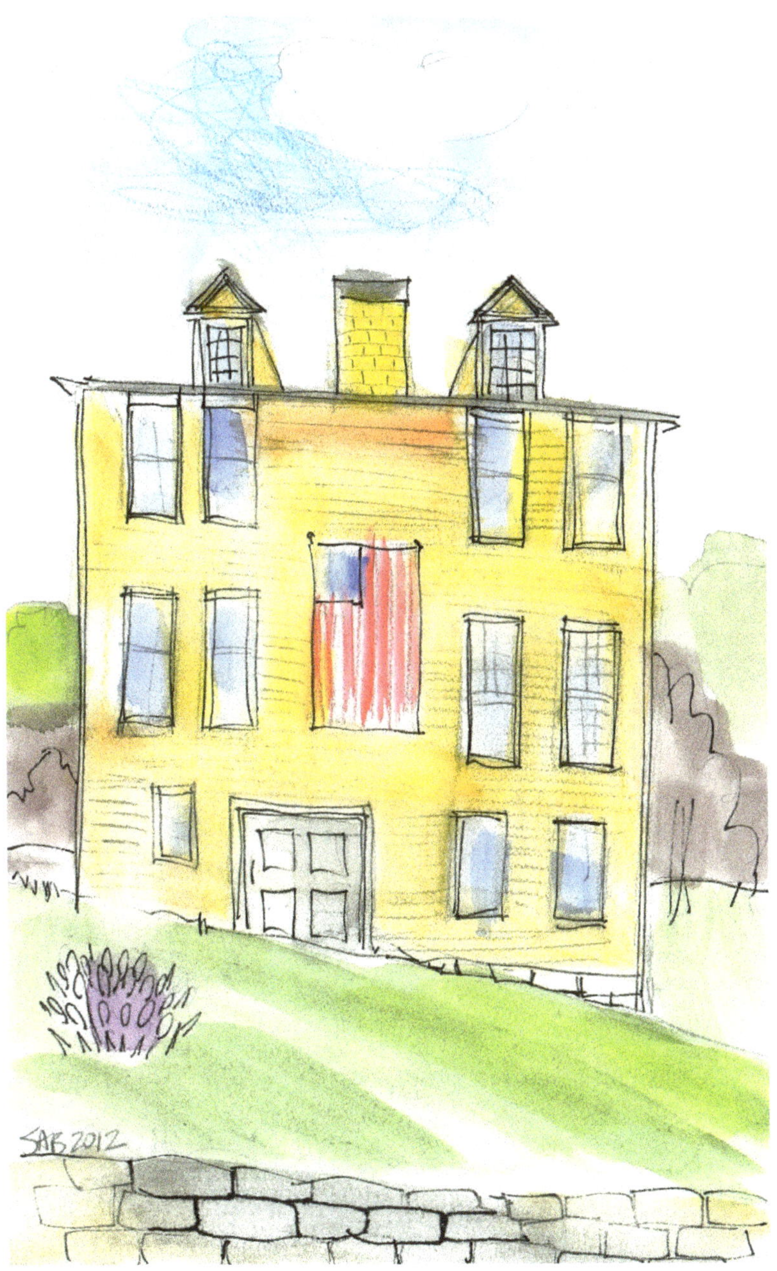

Exeter, settled in 1638, at one time included the present day towns of Newmarket, Newfields, Brentwood, Epping, and Fremont.

The falls on the Exeter River provided water power for mills. Manufacturing thrived and so did politics. Exeter was the *de facto* capital of New Hampshire, until Concord was chosen in the early 1800s.

The Ladd-Gilman house, seen here from the side, boasts an enormous flag. The viewpoint is from a street, way below the brick and clapboarded structure. The building is a part of Exeter's American Independence Museum. Nearby, the famed and well regarded Phillips Exeter Academy has an enrollment of about 1,000 students.

Exeter, it seems to me, has a larger number of Colonial-era yellow houses than the typical New Hampshire town. I once counted 13 close to downtown, and there may be more.

FREMONT

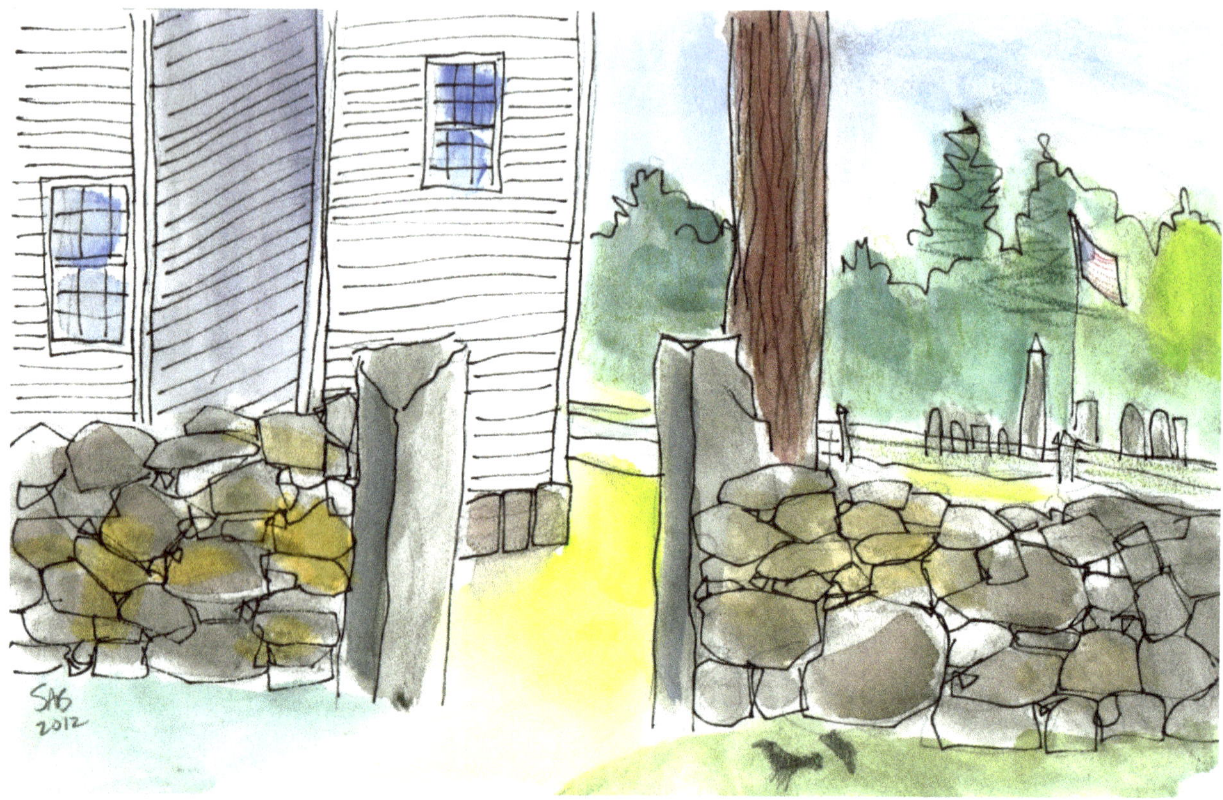

In past times, wandering livestock would be corralled into this enclosed space, the town pound, until the owner could come claim them for a fee.

On the left is the Poplin Meetinghouse, 1800, with its twin porch design. This architectural term describes the two stairwells, built off the opposing sides of the square structure.

In 1734, the Fremont Mast Riot occurred between local land owners and the English Crown. The British government reserved the tallest and straightest white pines as masts for the king's ships. Many settlers who owned the forests objected to this requirement.

Fremont is part of the Rockingham Recreation (bike) Trail.

GREENLAND

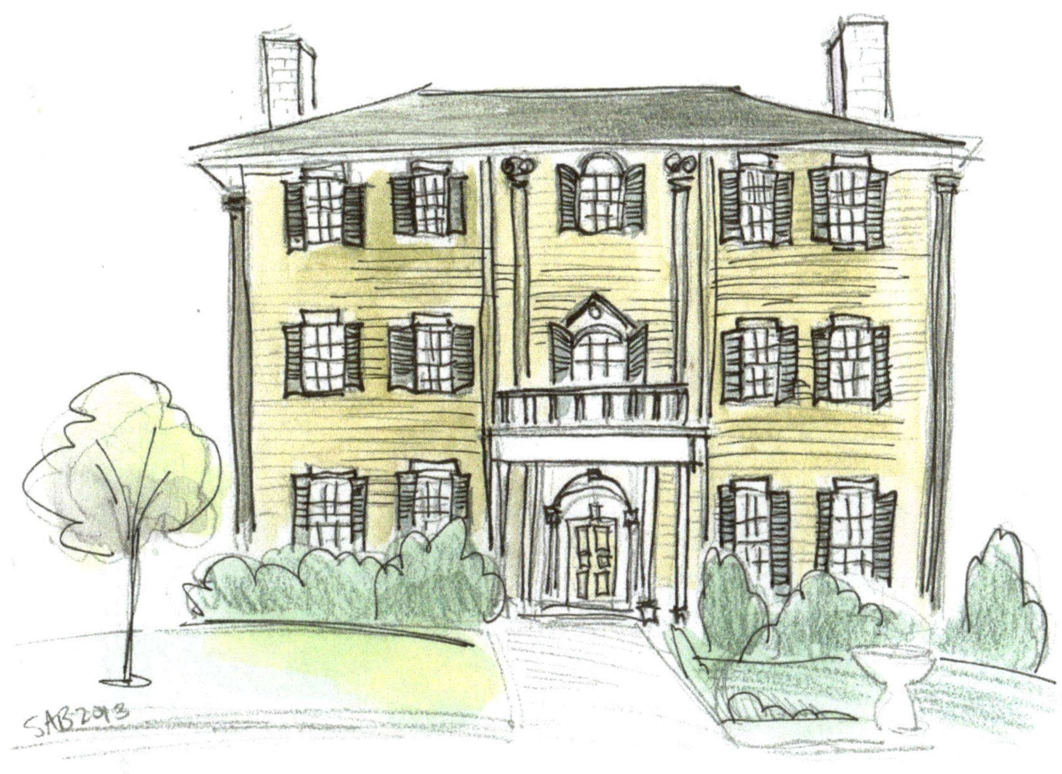

Read the life of Oney Judge, an escaped slave of George Washington who lived in this town.

Much of the town land borders beautiful Great Bay. An early settler, Captain Francis Champernowne, moved here from Portsmouth and named his farm Greenland.

After lunch with friends in the early spring, I roamed around the oldest parts of the village. This private residence sits at the intersection of three roads. The wooden clapboarded house dates from maybe 1800-1830, judging from the size and style. Six flat columns, green wooden shutters, and white brick chimneys make a handsome façade.

HAMPSTEAD

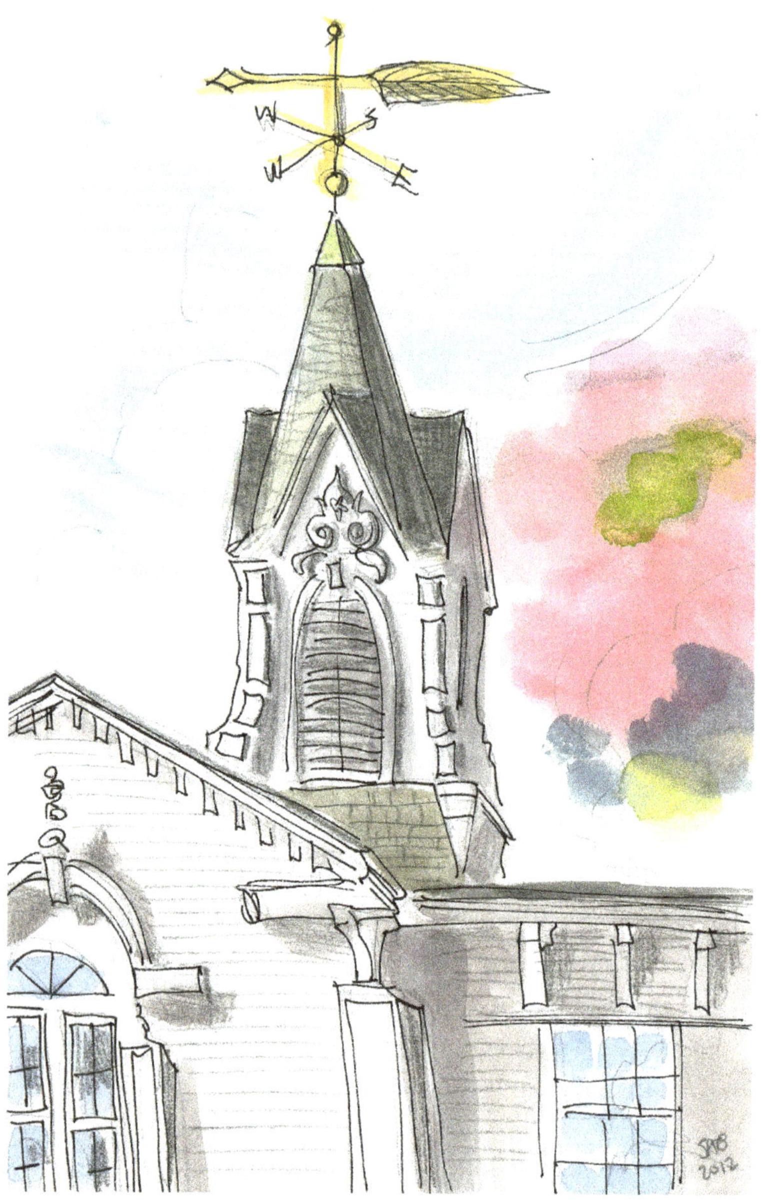

The town, just east of Derry, once was a part of Amesbury and Haverhill, Massachusetts. When the Massachusetts/New Hampshire border was finally established, it was incorporated as a separate town with a new name.

The winding Main Street, lined with old maple trees, has a pleasant grouping of municipal buildings, churches, and residences. The town office building, and especially its tower, is highly ornamented with wooden sculptural details. The afternoon sunlight highlighted them beautifully, and the shadows helped me to see these details. The pink cherry blossoms on the tree and that yellowish green of the brand new leaves shout out spring!

The weathervane is modeled after an old fashioned feather pen.

HAMPTON

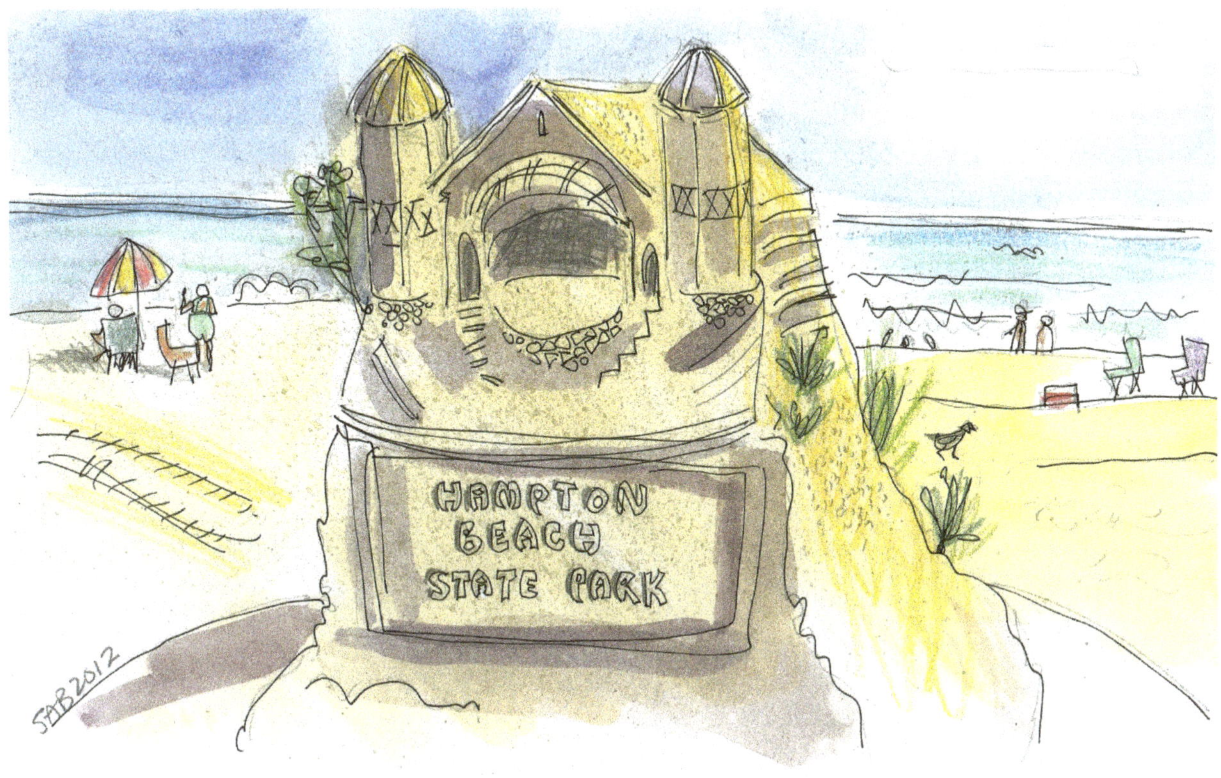

A large part of the town is the Hampton Salt Marsh Conservation Area.

The town was incorporated in 1639 and was large enough to encompass eight neighboring towns that we know today.

When the railroad came in the 1850s and a trolley line followed, the resort era of Hampton Beach began. We never seem to get to the annual Hampton Beach Sand Sculpture competition at the correct time. Either we are too early before its completion, or we are very late and the sand sculptures are already sprouting weeds. This sand castle depicts the Hampton Beach band stand. The beach facilities, including the band stand, were recently remodeled.

HAMPTON FALLS

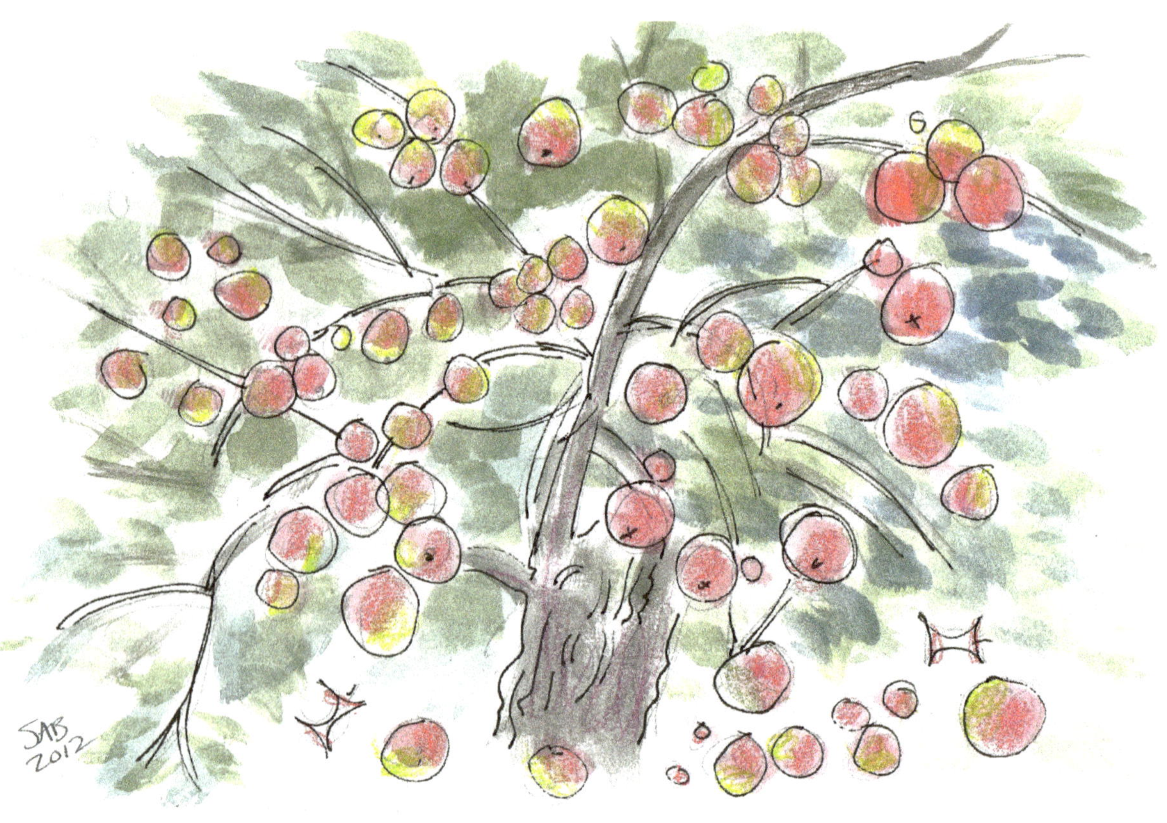

The town was settled by Europeans in 1638. Its borders have shifted, become larger or smaller, through political and social changes.

The eastern border is the bay of Hampton Harbor. The water power generated by the Taylor River allowed mills to form and thrive. Today, Hampton Falls is known for antique shops along Route 1 and for the Applecrest Farm Orchards, a family business which began in 1913. Fall Festivals are very popular in New Hampshire, and Applecrest has an enormous one that features cider, pumpkins, and doughnuts. Everyone wants to enjoy the blue sky days and crisp air of the season.

The ripe, sweet apples were plentiful on the gnarled old tree.

KENSINGTON

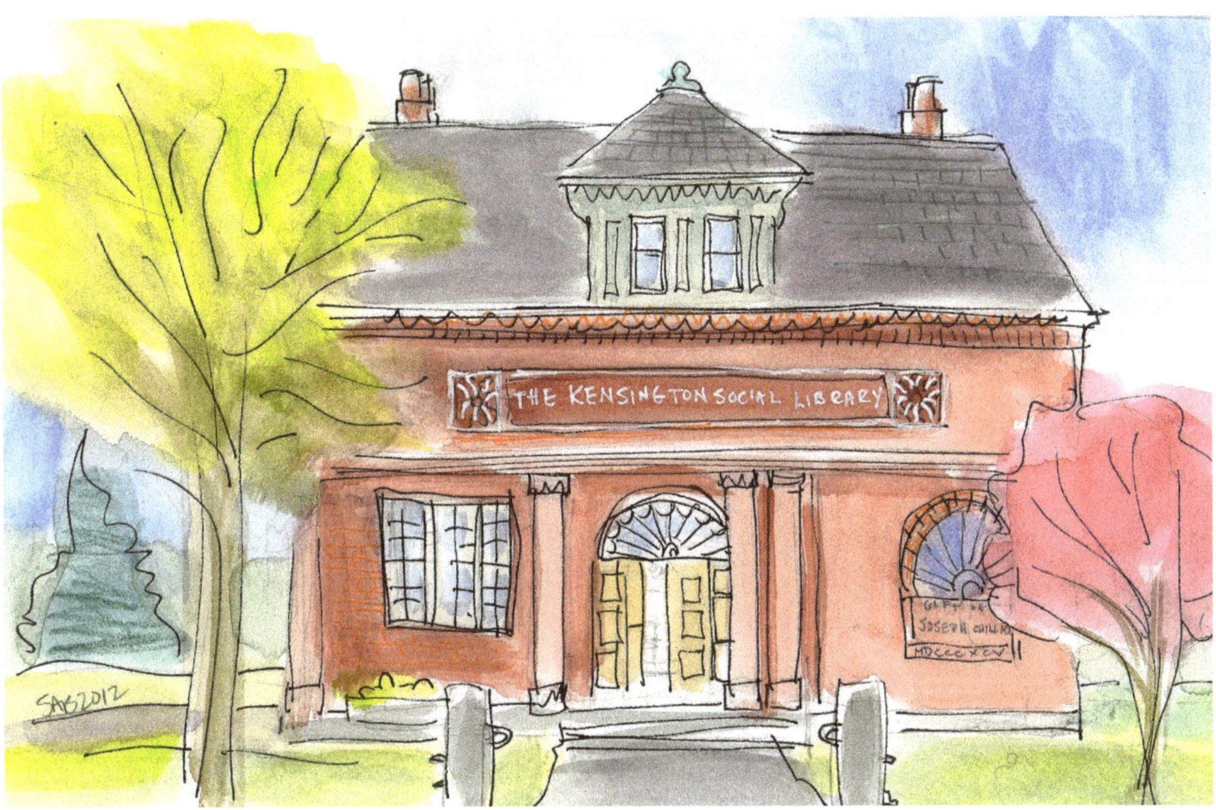

The Kensington Elementary School is very conveniently located next door to this beautiful library.

The small rural community was incorporated in 1737 and named for Baron Kensington, owner of Kensington Palace in London.

The handsome brick library was a gift of Joseph C. Hilliard in 1895. The architectural style of this era features both symmetrical and asymmetrical design elements. The sign above the door says in white letters, The Kensington Social Library, although its modern name is the Kensington Public Library. The term 'social library' is a holdover from the 1800s. At that time, private collections were opened to members, for a fee.

KINGSTON

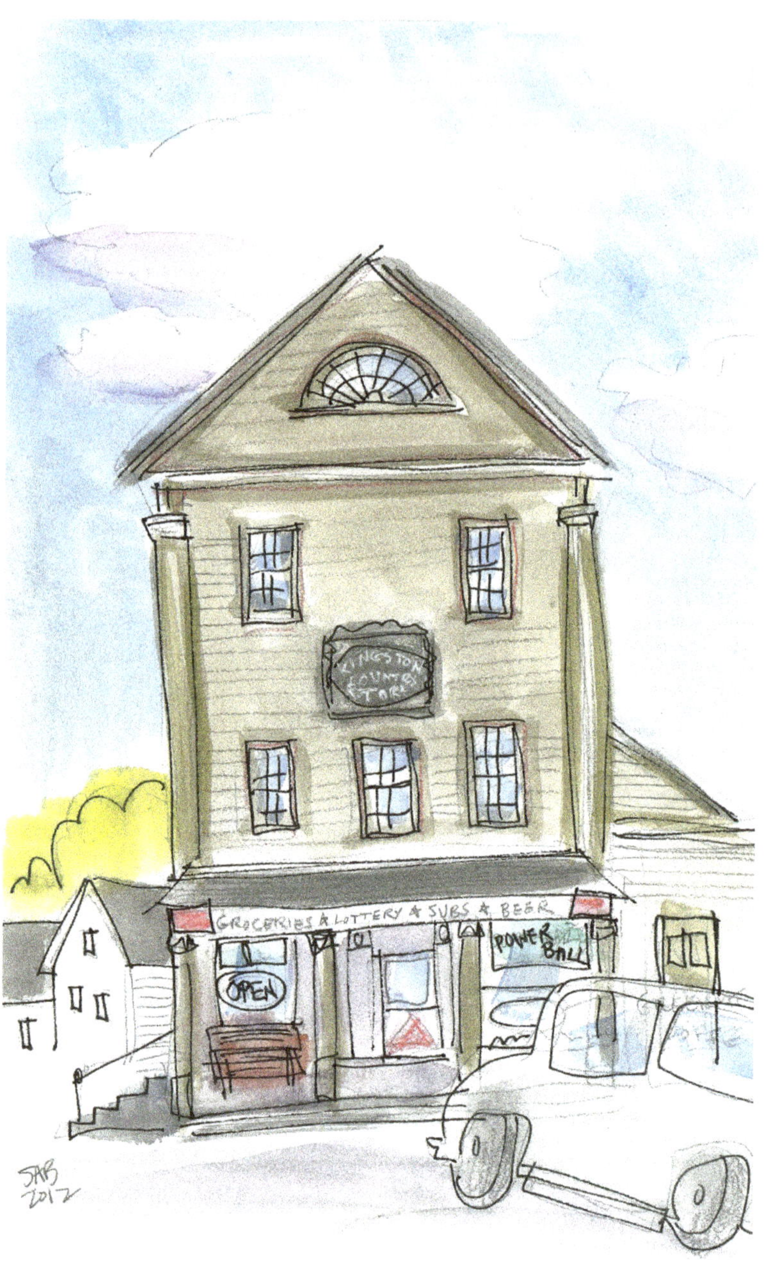

The town, population 6,000, was originally a part of Hampton. In 1694 it was granted status as a new town called Kingstown, named by King William of England.

Early industries included shoe making in one-room shops and homes, and silversmithing. The town's extensive charcoal manufacturing industry supplied many of the growing industrial cities of northeast Massachusetts. The Kingston Country Store, on the very long town green, has a touch of grandeur with the columns and fan light window.

Kingston's town land includes six ponds and the 44-acre Kingston State Park.

LEE

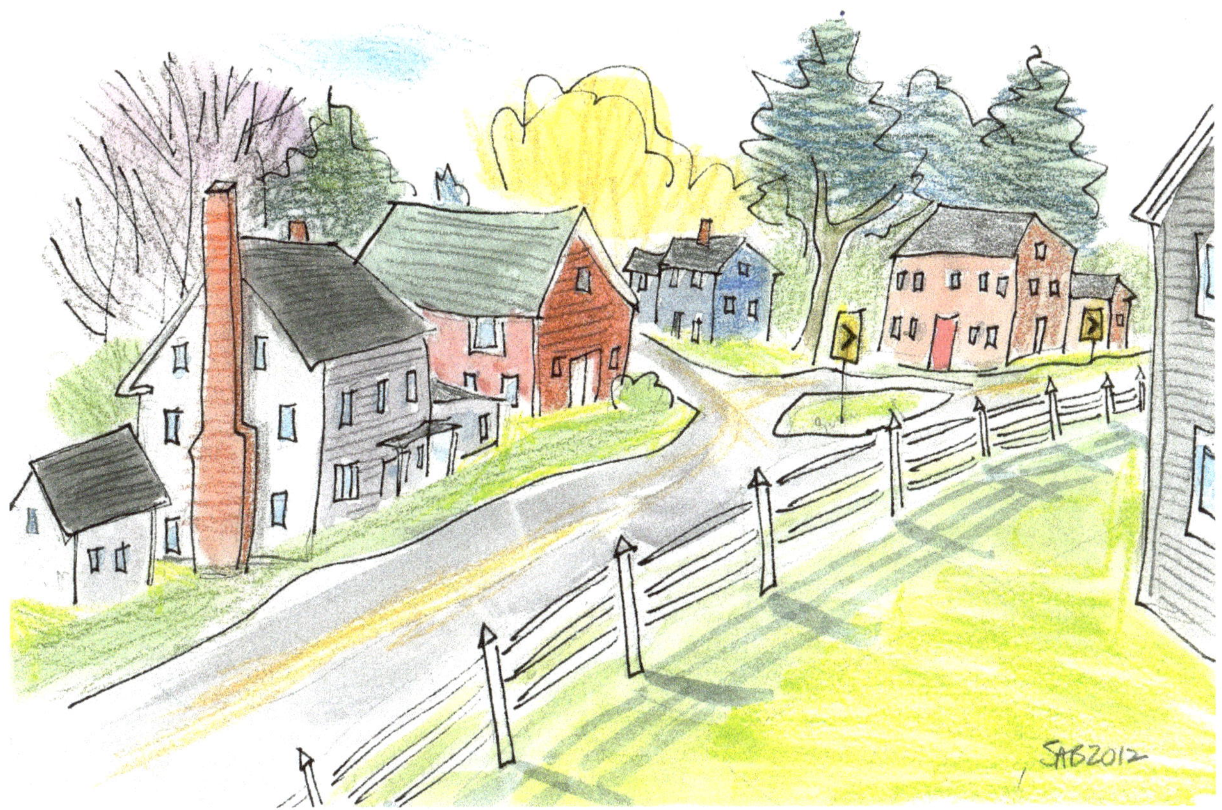

Lee is home to many students, professors, and staff of the nearby University of New Hampshire.

The town was settled early, and separated from Dover to be named Lee in 1766. The boxy style of architecture in this intersection dates from approximately mid 1770s to early 1800s.

The red painted building is a barn. Red was an inexpensive color, made from iron oxide. Many houses were originally left unpainted. Others were white, yellow, or other bright colors. Pigments could be ordered from England.

MADBURY

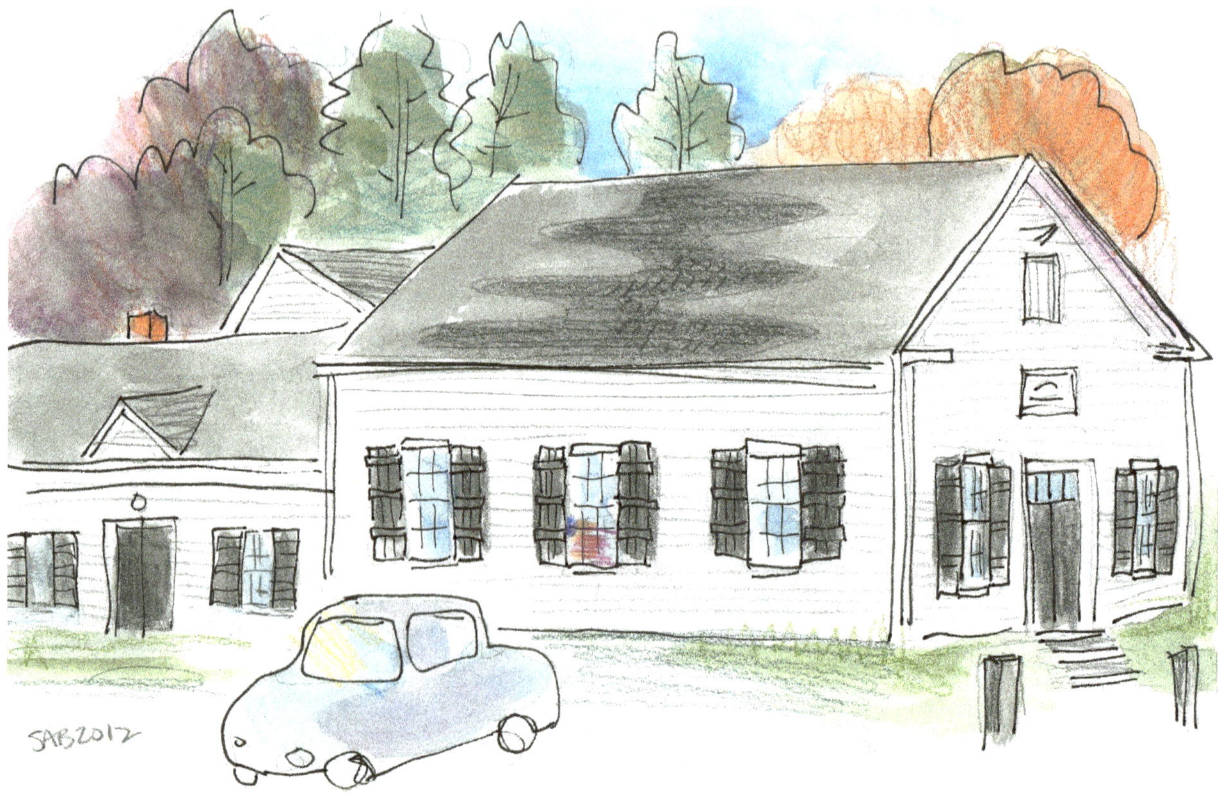

Madbury is 12 miles square and shaped like a wedge. The narrow end of the wedge ends at Cedar Point on Little Bay.

Madbury's original village settlement was called Barbadoes (really spelled that way), after the town's West Indies trading partner. Lumber was shipped to the Caribbean island in return for molasses, a key ingredient in rum. As I was drawing, I could see volunteers setting up voting booths in the Madbury Town Hall for the upcoming Presidential election.

The name Madbury is said to come from Modbury, in Devon, England, the home of local land owner Sir Francis Champernowne.

NEW CASTLE

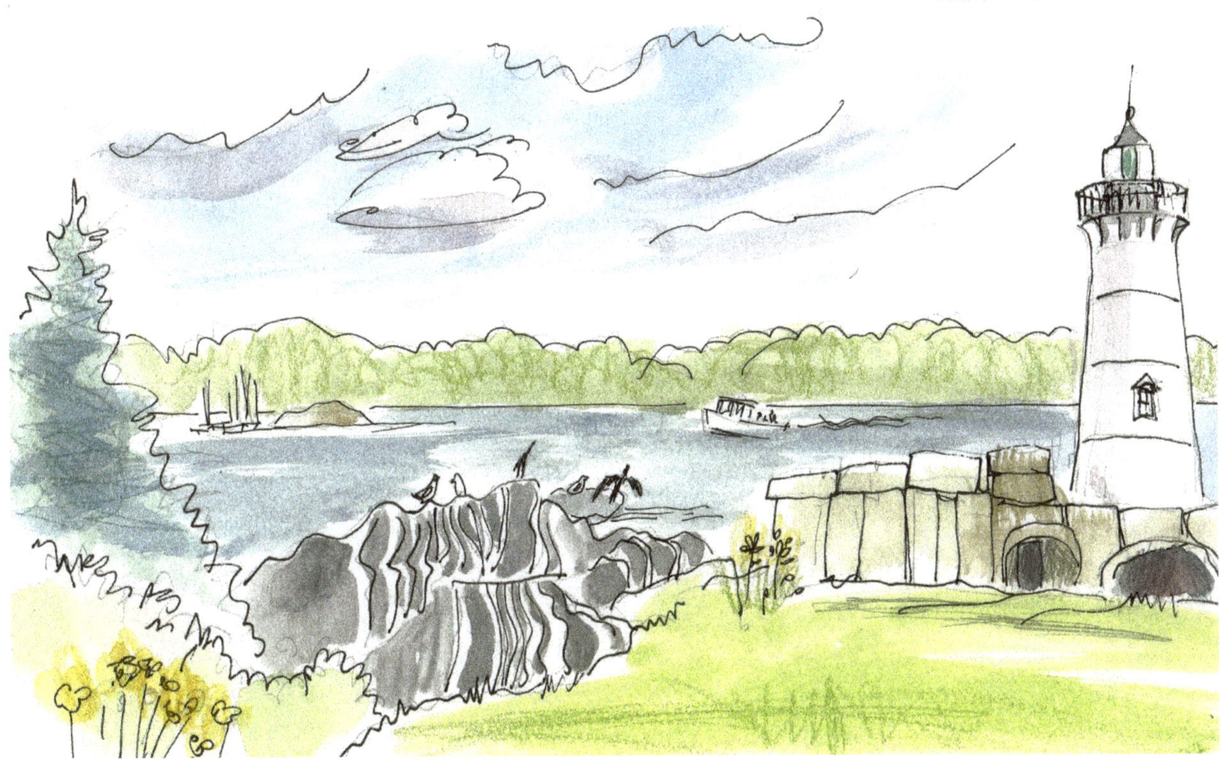

The lighthouse is the entrance to the Piscataqua River and the Portsmouth Harbor.

New Castle is located entirely on islands. Fort Constitution has been there since Colonial times, protecting the harbor and its long established Naval facilities.

Originally a British installation named Fort William and Mary, the fort was the scene of what could have been the true start of the American Revolution. Paul Revere rode up from Boston four months before the famous battle of Lexington and Concord to warn the locals that the British were on their way to reinforce the fort. A battle ensued and the colonists stormed the fort, capturing five tons of gunpowder and a number of cannons.

NEWFIELDS

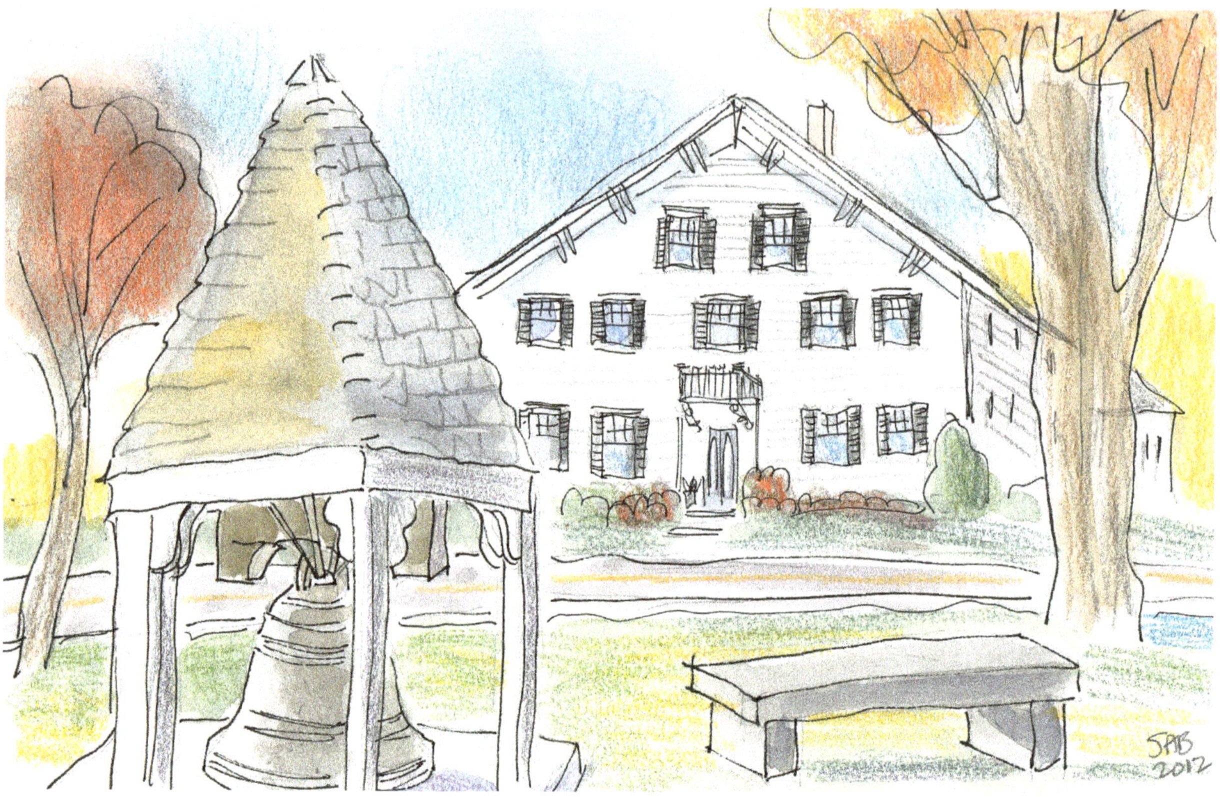

On quiet Main Street, a Revere Bell sits at eye level in the Newfields Memorial Park. A roof protects it from rain and snow.

The bell hung in the Methodist Episcopal Church from 1836–1923 and was given to the town in 1975. A crack in the bell probably resulted from a fire in the church. In New England, Revere Bells are revered. They truly were manufactured by the metal worker and patriot Paul Revere and his employees in his foundry in Boston. Between the years 1792 and 1828, a total of 398 bells were cast. They varied in size, but they all had an excellent tone.

The town land includes the west bank of the Squamscott River, which leads to Great Bay.

NEWINGTON

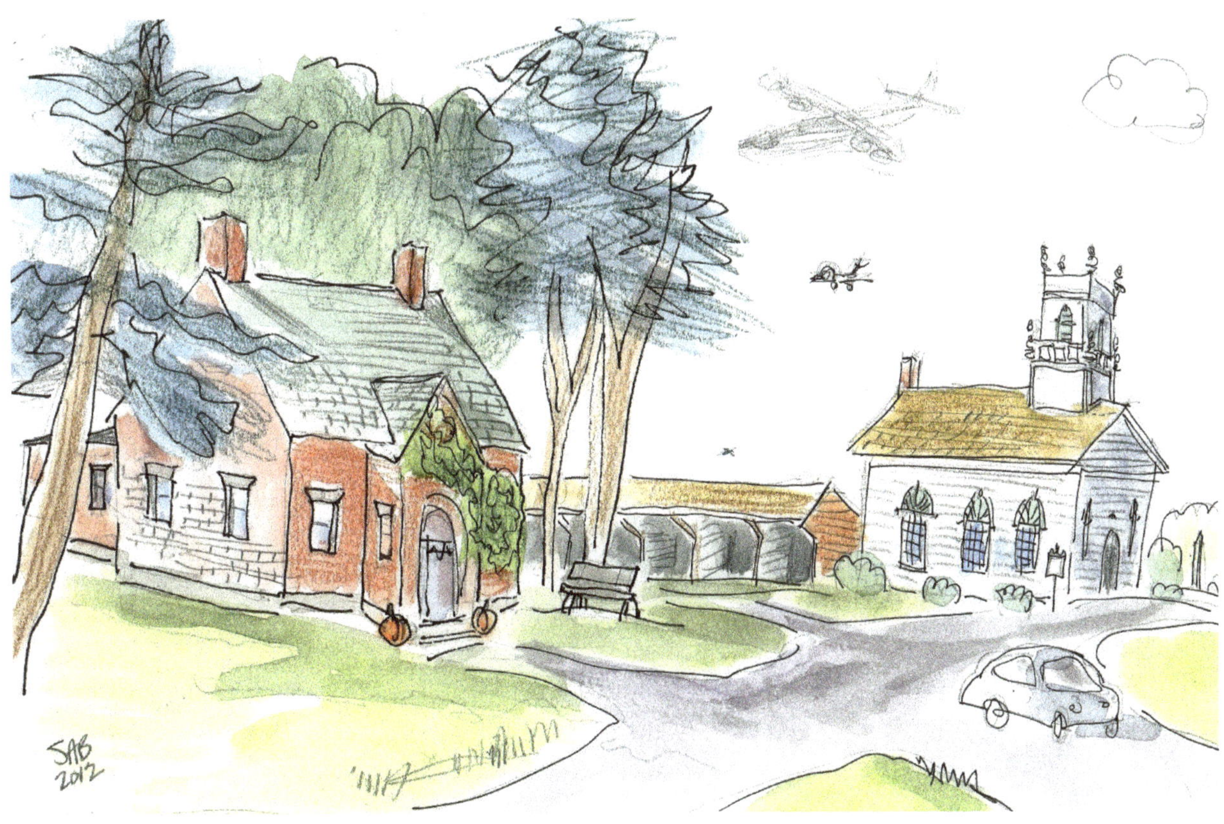

The 1000-acre Great Bay National Wildlife Refuge was established in 1992.

Newington, with a population of 800, has an old village center as well as big box stores along Woodbury Avenue. The residents of Newington, England sent over the bell for this meetinghouse, built in 1712.

In 1956 Pease Air Force Base opened after the land was acquired by eminent domain. The Cold War base was officially closed in 1991, but the facilities have been reused, and planes are constantly arriving at what is now the Pease International Tradeport. Three airplanes got included in my sketch. The Langdon Public Library has recently doubled in size with the completion of its new addition. I'll be back to sketch an updated version.

NEWMARKET

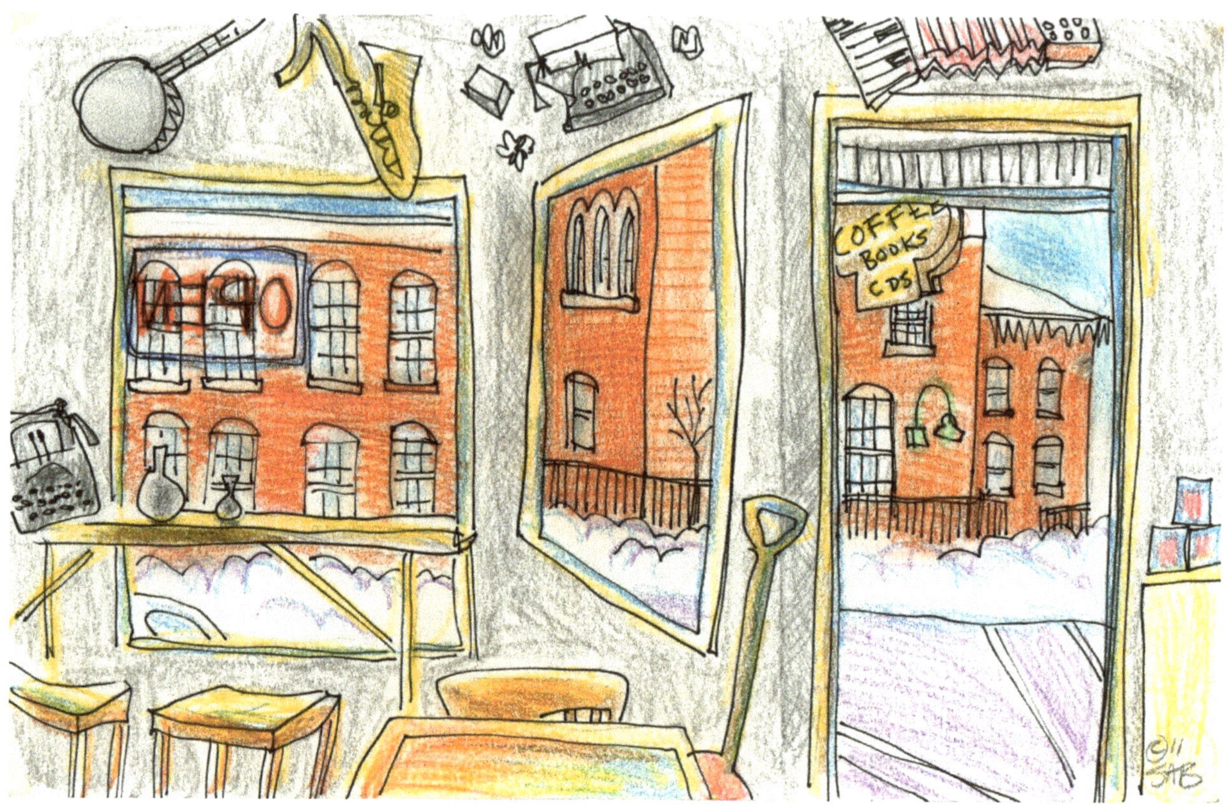

New Hampshire has a long history of mills and manufacturing, based on water power. The cotton mills in Newmarket produced textiles from 1823 to 1929.

The mills closed, lay empty for years, and are now coming back to life, housing small businesses and private residences. Crackskull Coffee and Books has an amazing array of items adorning their walls: old typewriters and musical instruments, for example. The selection of second-hand books is fine too. On a cold February day, it provided me with hot coffee, warm shelter, and a view of the mill.

The town seal shows local landmarks and includes a gundalow, a local style of boat, on Great Bay.

NEWTON

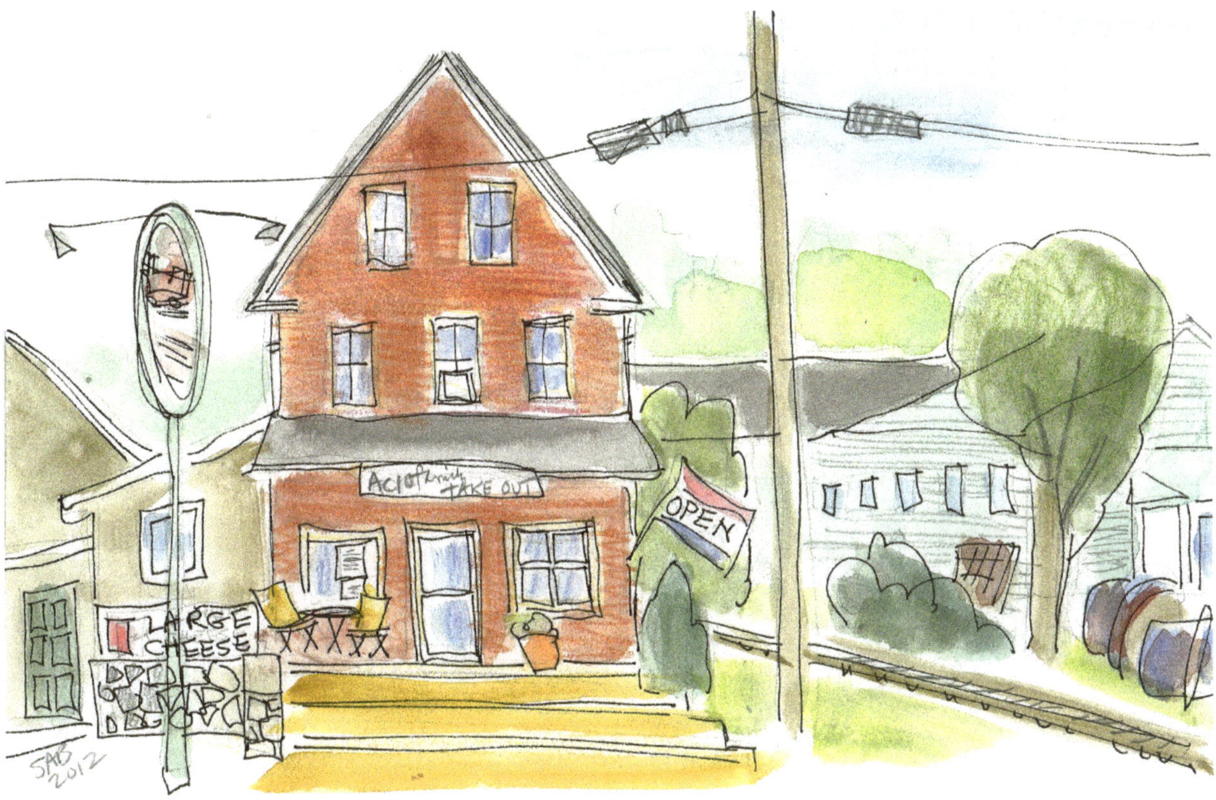

The nearby Gale Public Library occupies a former elementary school.

Governor Benning Wentworth incorporated the town in 1749 as Newtown. It wasn't until 1846 that the name was officially changed to Newton, a subtle difference for sure.

Like all the towns on the southern border, it was a part of several towns in Massachusetts at different times. This building is in the part of town called Newton Junction. The oval sign identifies the red structure as the Trackside Professional Building. On the ground floor is Acio's Family Takeout, serving up pizza and sandwiches. The shape of the building indicates to me that it was originally a general store.

NORTH HAMPTON

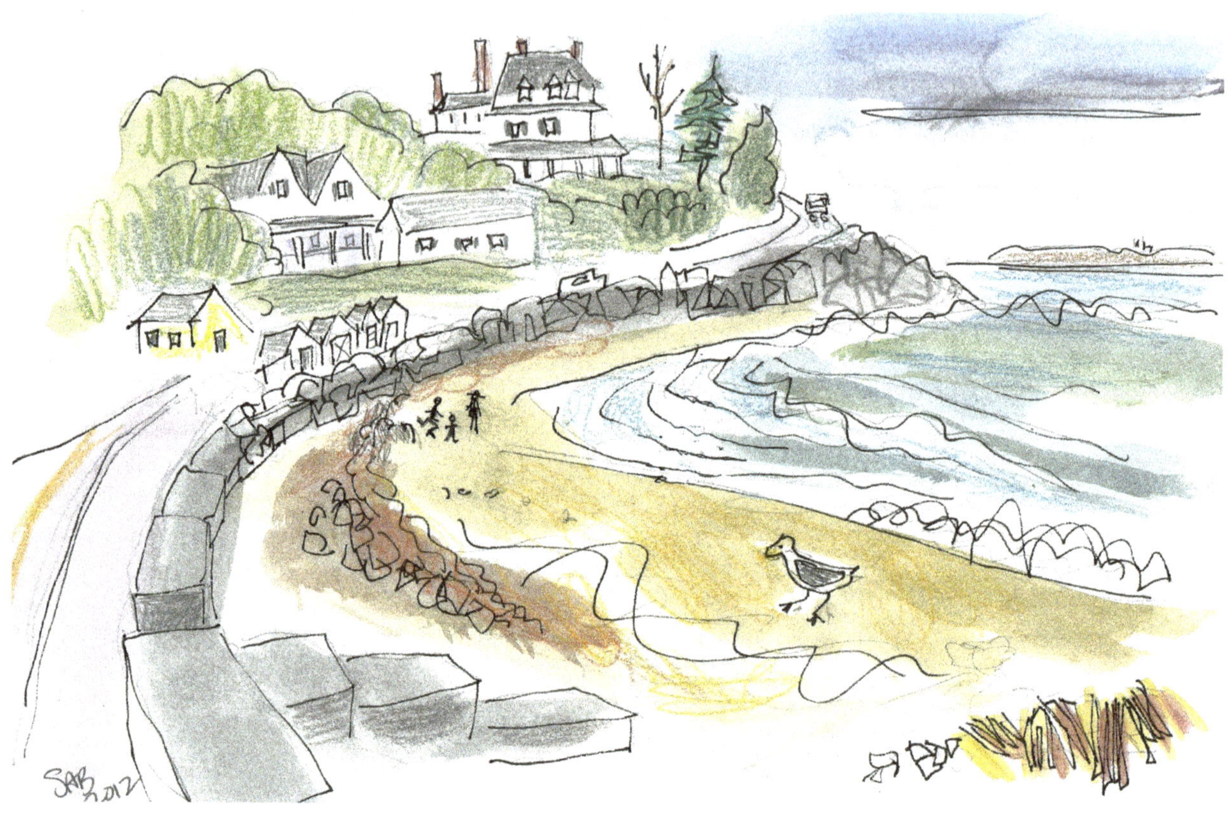

The first colonists arrived here in 1639. The settlement, a part of Hampton, was called North Parish. In 1742, the town was granted as North Hampton.

The view is looking north, up the sheltered beach. The houses on the hill are part of Little Boar's Head, a fashionable resort in the 19th century. The pathway in front of those little fishing huts, now vacation rental properties, is called King's Way. We strolled along the path, next to the crashing waves. The strong surf was rolling the rocks up and down the beach and creating quite a roar. The Isles of Shoals, 6 miles out, were easily seen on this clear day.

Huge mounds of sweet smelling beach roses lined the path going up the hill. The blooms were a delicate pink.

NOTTINGHAM

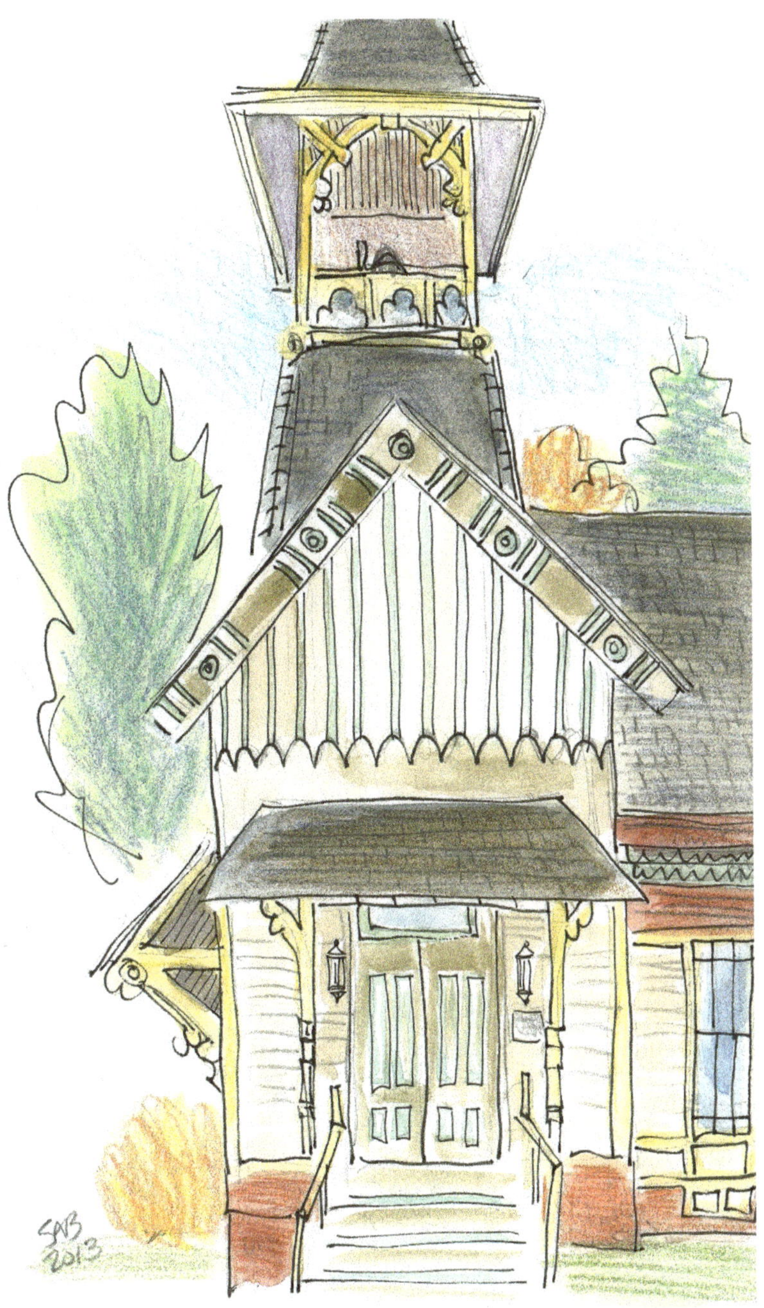

The town was incorporated in 1722 and named for Daniel Finch, the 2nd Earl of Nottingham, England.

Present day towns of Deerfield and Northfield were once included in the town land. Pawtuckaway State Park is entirely within the town borders.

The Nottingham Community Church was constructed in 1875, probably by a local carpenter with a handful of pattern books. The wooden building features a number of Victorian architectural flourishes and gingerbread charm. The decorative shingles, the elaborate millwork, and the exposed wooden roof braces were the height of fashion at the time.

I did my best to record the scene on a cold day when I had forgotten my gloves.

PLAISTOW

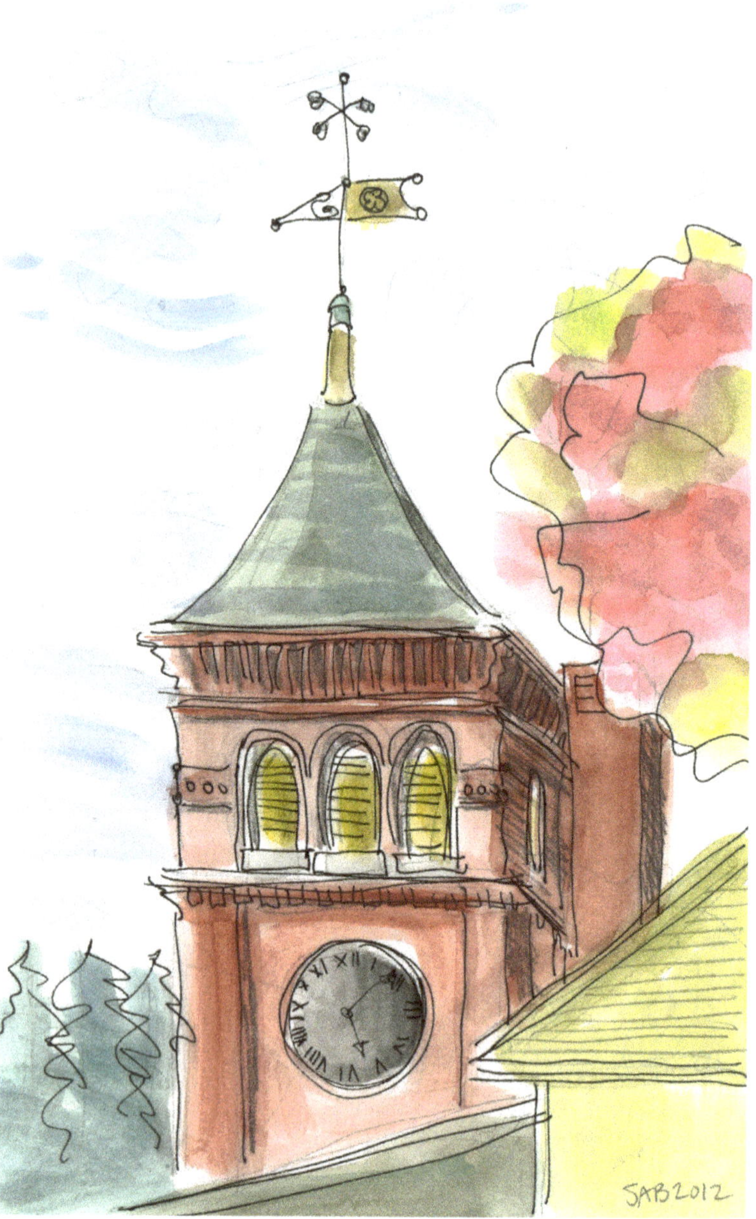

The town lines were firmly established in 1749, after the disputes with the Massachusetts colony were settled.

The brick and slate Plaistow Town Hall, circa 1895, sits in the middle of Pollard Square. An intriguing weathervane spins atop the tower. In the park are memorials to war veterans and to a local victim of terrorism on 9/11. An annual Old Home Day fills the park with activities for all. This holiday, created as a full week's event in 1897, was a yearly effort throughout New Hampshire to persuade people who had moved elsewhere to return to their home towns for a summer visit.

Nearby, a beautiful modern library serves the town's 8,000 residents.

PORTSMOUTH

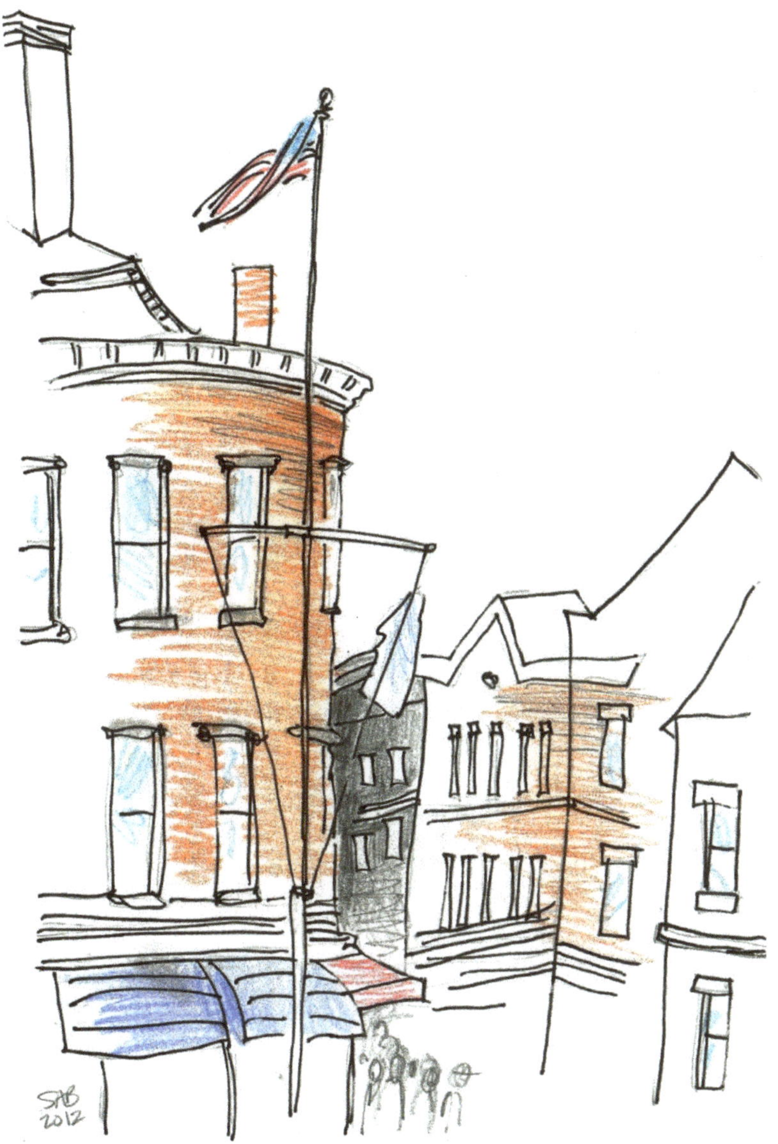

Portsmouth is a city of about 22,000 residents at the mouth of the Piscataqua River. The first known European settlement, 1630, was at Puddle Dock, near the current Strawbery Banke Museum.

The city grew prosperous with the trades of shipping, lumber, fishing, and shipbuilding. A disastrous fire in 1813 destroyed 244 buildings. All rebuilt structures were required to be of brick and slate.

Strolling around the city is a delight due to its compact size and lively street scene. The 1878 Music Hall, still very much in operation, is well worth a visit too. The Market Square makes a fine sketching spot.

The Portsmouth Black Heritage Trail has 24 sites that call attention to the labor of African-Americans and their contributions to the growth and prosperity of the city.

ROCHESTER

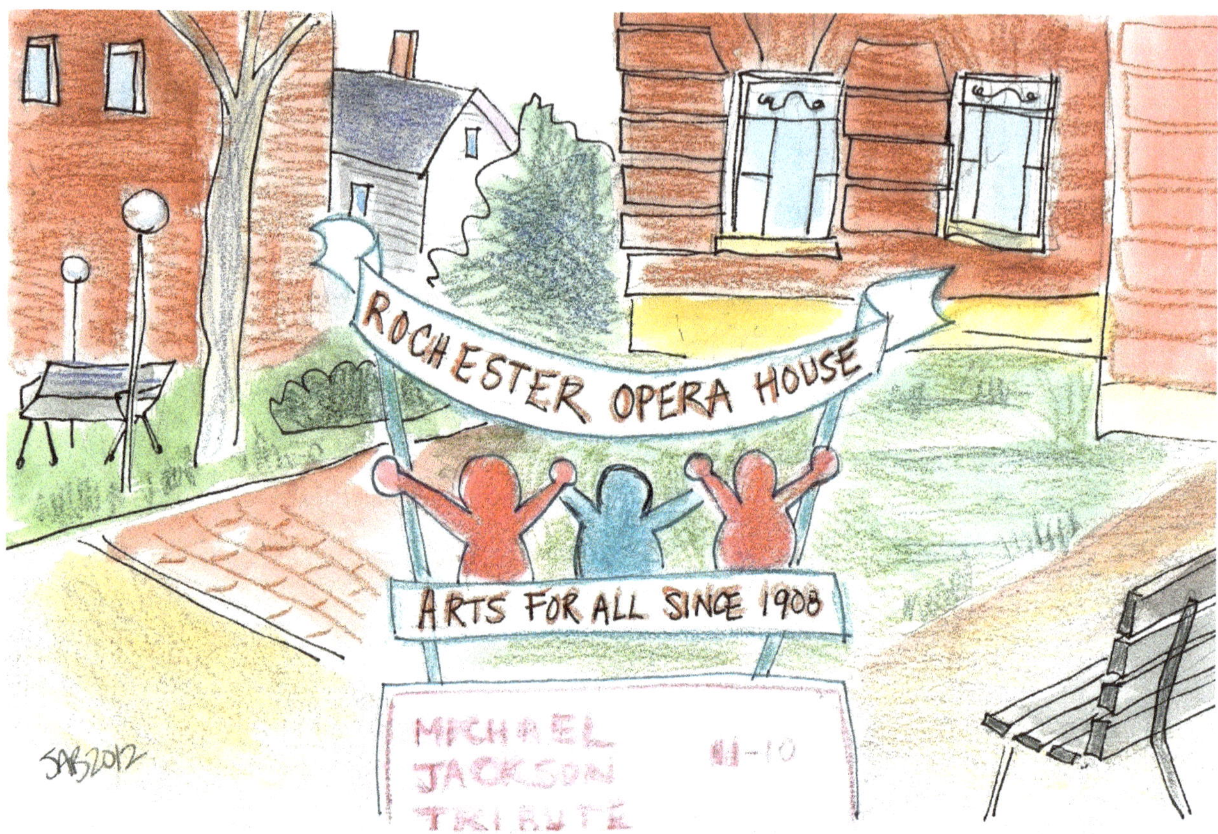

Rochester, with 30,000 residents, is a city on the Cocheco River. The water provided the power for the mills.

For about 70 years, textile mills produced fine woolen blankets. Bricks from Rochester were used to construct the buildings of Harvard College. The Rochester Opera House, built in 1908, was designed by George Gilman Adams. He specialized in dual purpose town hall/opera concepts. An audience floor was designed to be raised or lowered by a complicated mechanism of cranks, levers, pulleys, and leather belts. The city recently restored the opera house floor system to full working order.

The Rochester Public Library received building funds from philanthropist Andrew Carnegie.

ROLLINSFORD

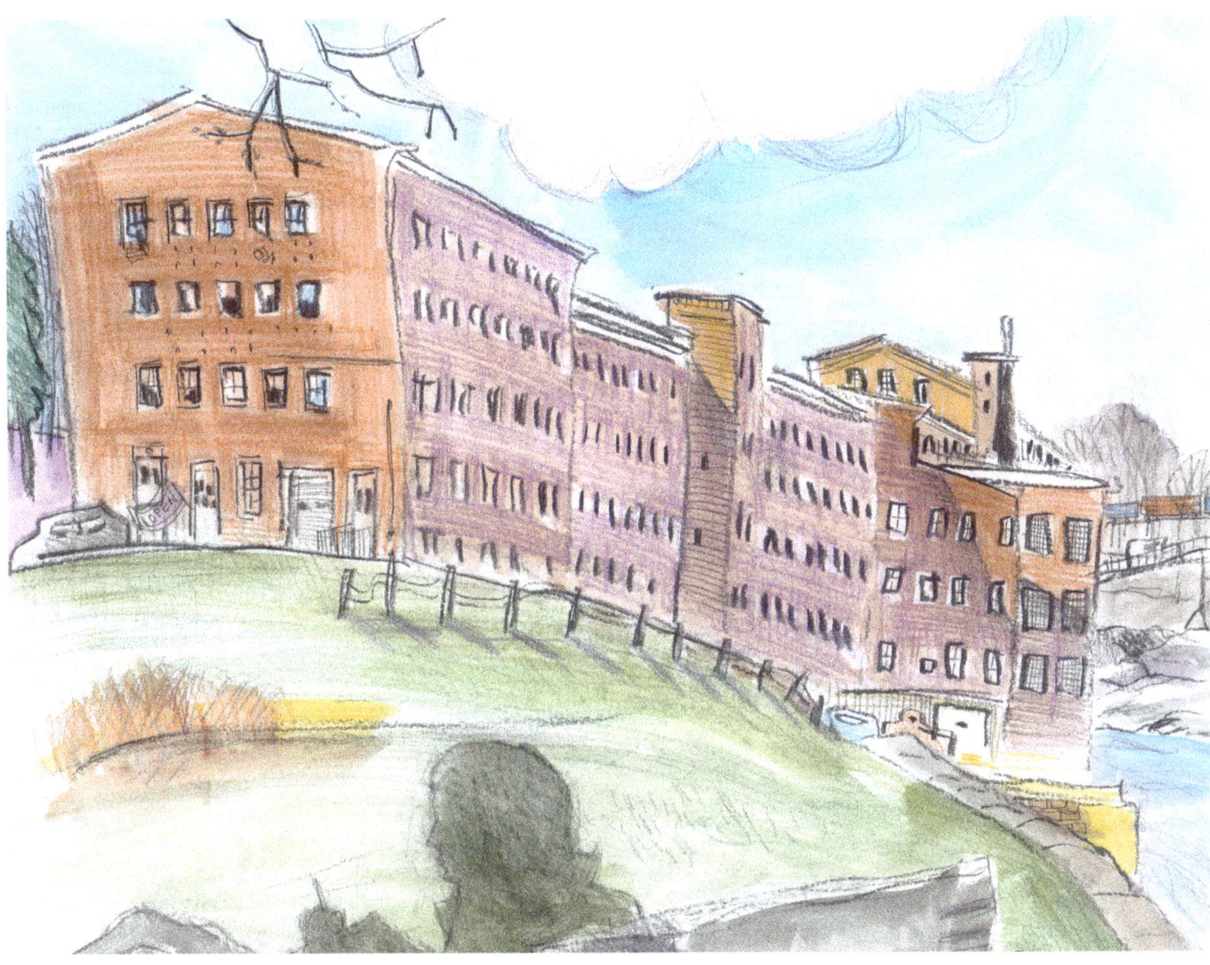

On a crisp, blue sky, November day, I finished my DRAW-NH project here. Rollinsford was town #234 in my quest.

The first European settlement began in 1630, when the area was a part of Dover. Rollinsford was incorporated in 1849.

The Salmon Falls Mills perch on the west bank of the Salmon Falls River, with Maine on the other side. Investors from Boston built them to produce woolen textiles, then changed to cotton products. The industry moved to the southern states in the early-mid 1900s. The long brick building has a new life as artists' studios. In the former weaving rooms, over 80 artists find spaces to create, exhibit, and sell their work. The town library has found a wonderful home here, too.

RYE

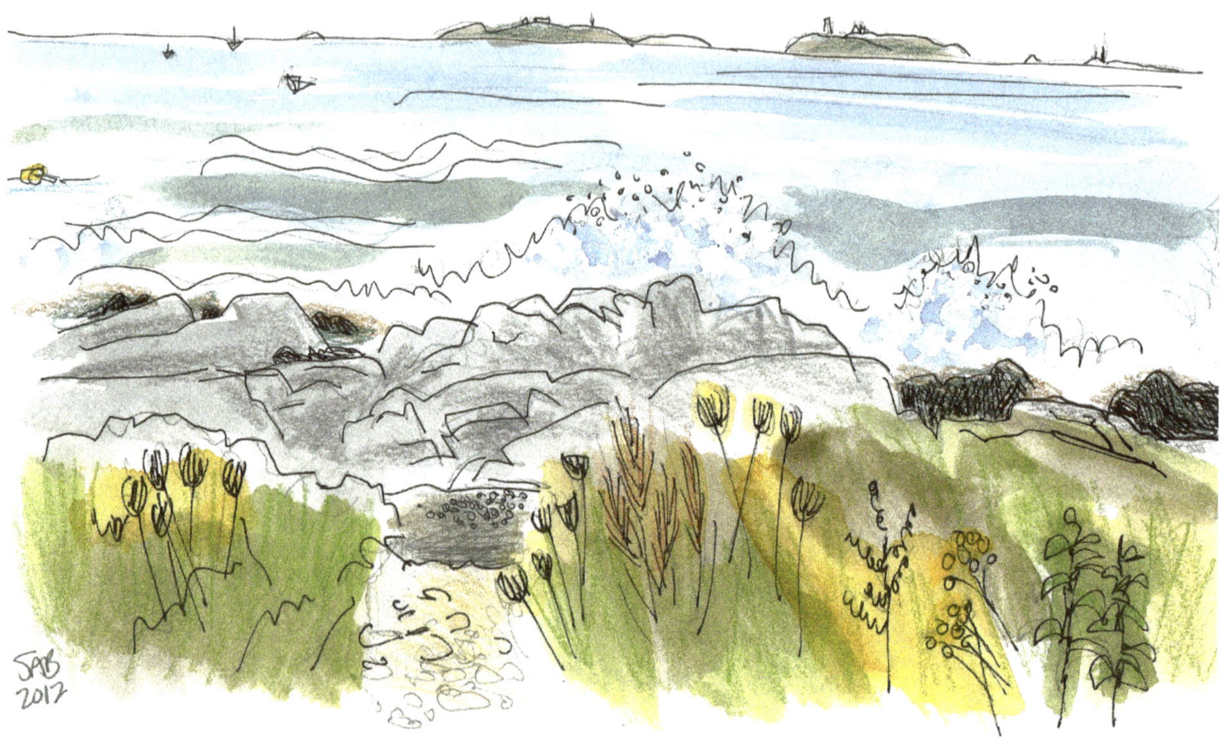

Pannaway Plantation was Rye's original name, when it was a part of Dover. The town has 12 square miles of land and 24 square miles of water. Rye also encompasses four of the nine islands of the famed Isles of Shoals, six miles out to sea.

Odiorne Point was the first settlement, originally a farming area and then a summer resort. During World War II, much of the land was bought by the federal government, and defenses were constructed to protect Portsmouth Harbor. A few concrete structures remain.

The 330-acre Odiorne State Park is home to the Seacoast Science Center.

SANDOWN

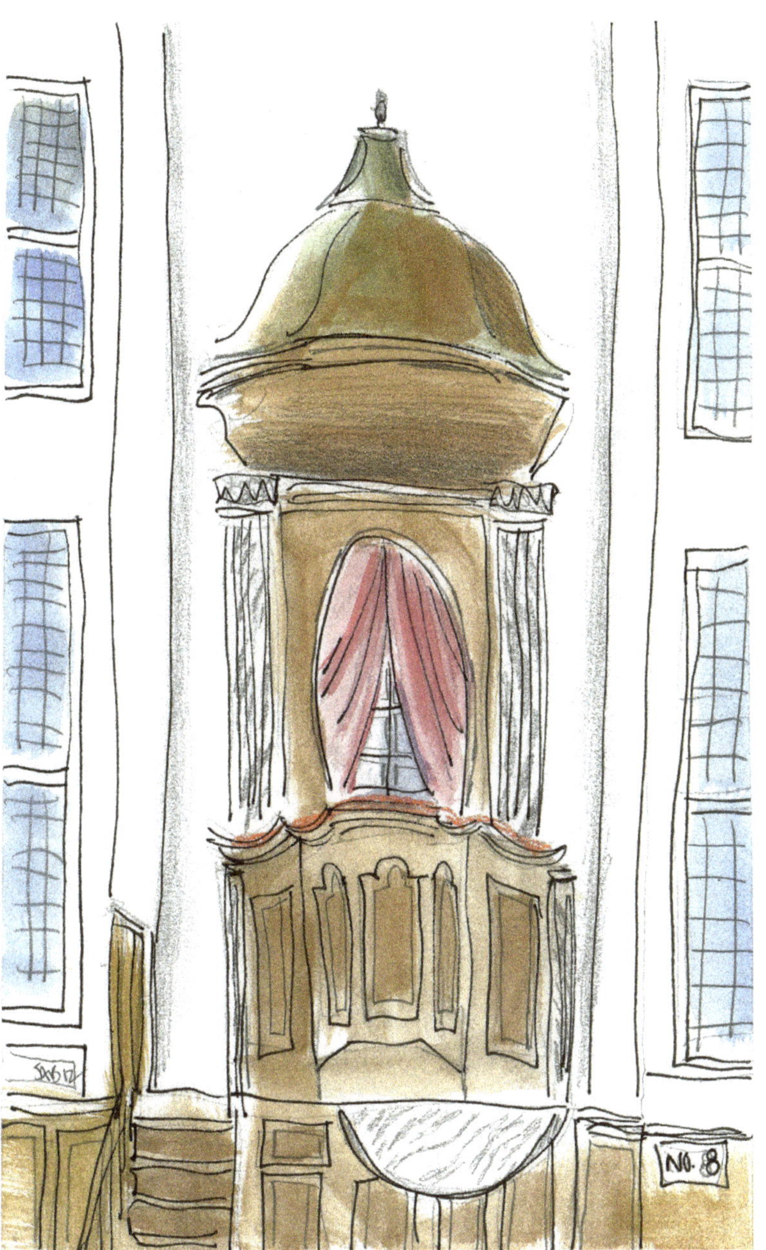

The Sandown meetinghouse, with its old closed pews, was built in 1774. Large clear glass windows flood the space with light.

The raised pulpit is 11 feet above the floor. The sounding board directly above the pulpit will amplify a speaker's voice. The columns on the sides of the pulpit and the folding half table below it are of wood, painted in a marble pattern.

The white clapboarded building with three green door entrances was used for over two centuries as a place of church services, but also for social gatherings, town meetings, and voting. Ballots were filed here for presidents from George Washington to Herbert Hoover.

A film company had rented time to be in the meetinghouse just when I arrived, so I really had to focus.

SEABROOK

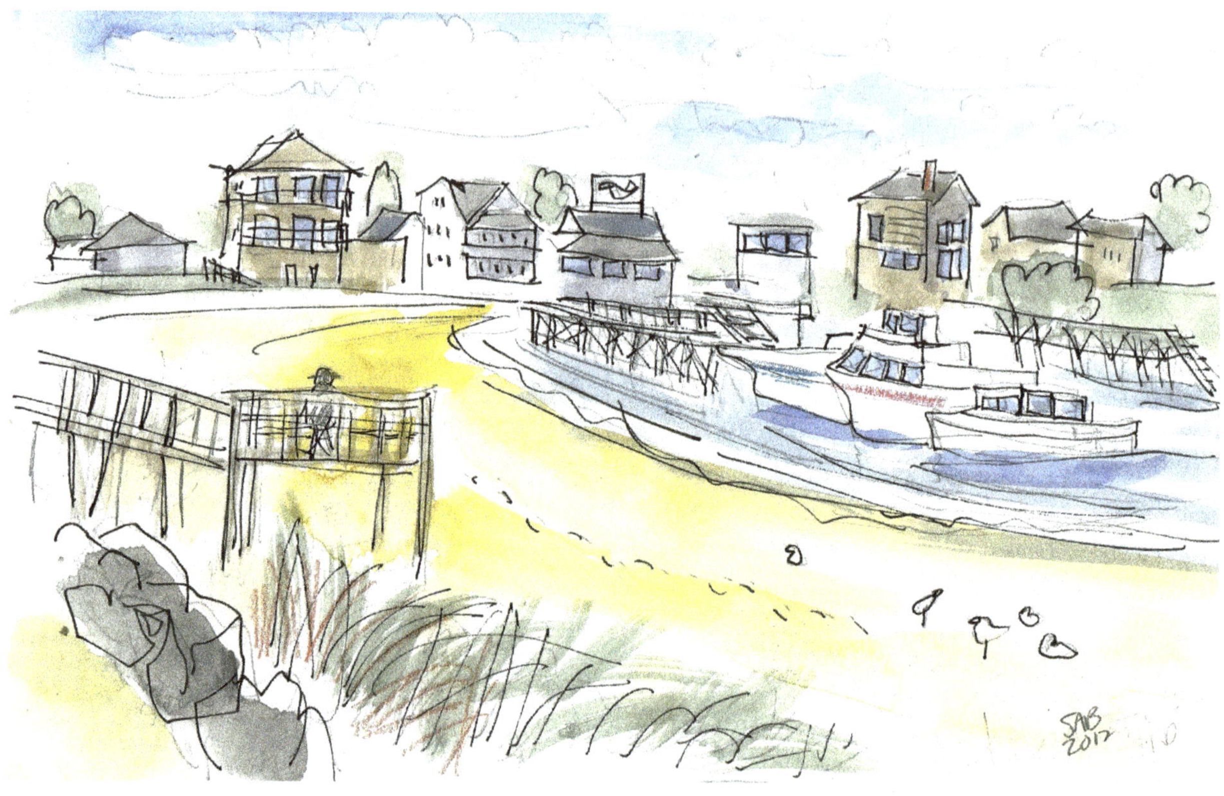

Seabrook is the most southern of the five towns that make up the New Hampshire seacoast, all 16 miles of it. Massachusetts lies just to the south. Settled by colonists in 1638, Seabrook was incorporated in 1768.

The town of 8,700 residents has it all: major roadways, industry, shopping, salt marshes, a fishing cooperative, and beach homes for year-rounders and summer folk. Boats for whale watches, deep sea fishing, and trips out to the Isles of Shoals are resting here at their docks.

This inland-facing beach is protected from the open sea.

SOMERSWORTH

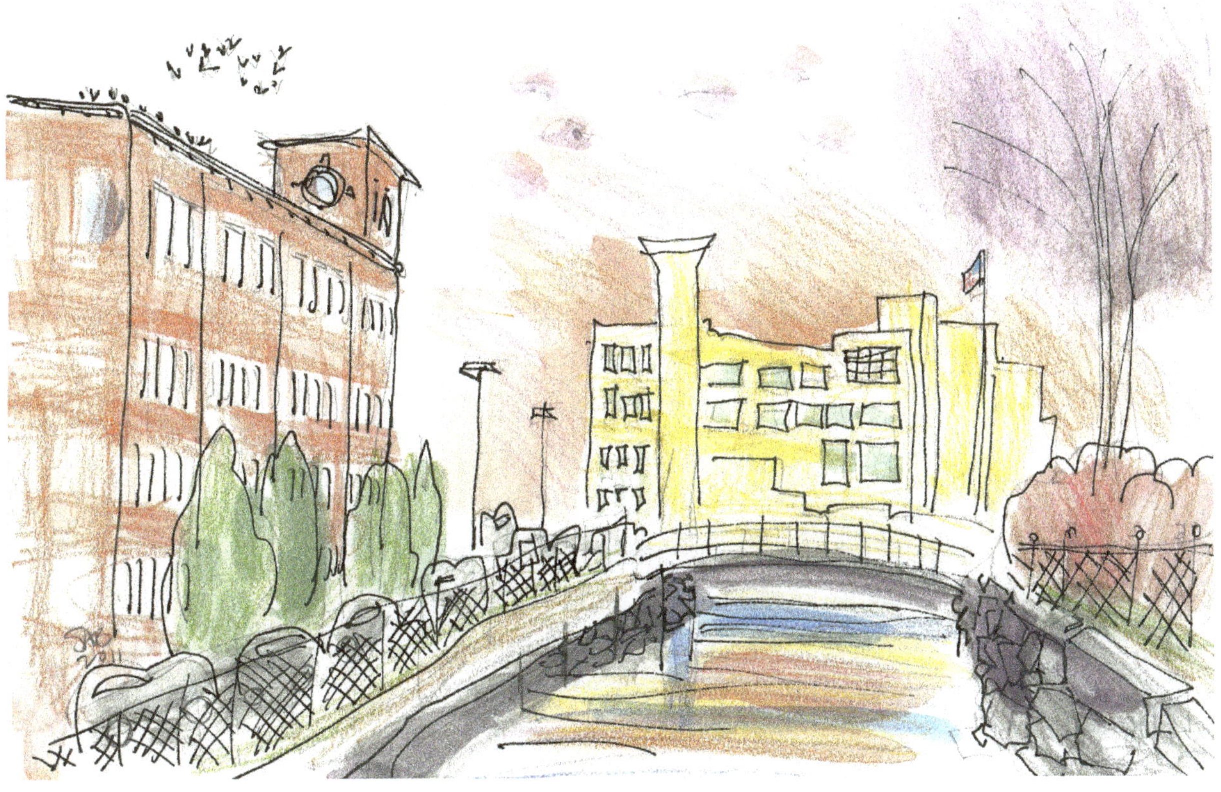

The birds swooped above a salmon colored sunset on the Salmon Falls River.

Somersworth, a city of 12,000 residents, is built along the banks of the Salmon Falls River.

The canal was constructed to harness the water power. When the mills were first built in the 1820s, workers walked over the bridge from Maine. Later, they were hired from Ireland and from Quebec Province. An opera house was built for the enjoyment of the mill workers. Trolley cars once ran over to York Beach, Maine, for Sunday outings. The yellow mill in the background is still going strong and is operated by the General Electric Company for manufacture of electrical meters.

SOUTH HAMPTON

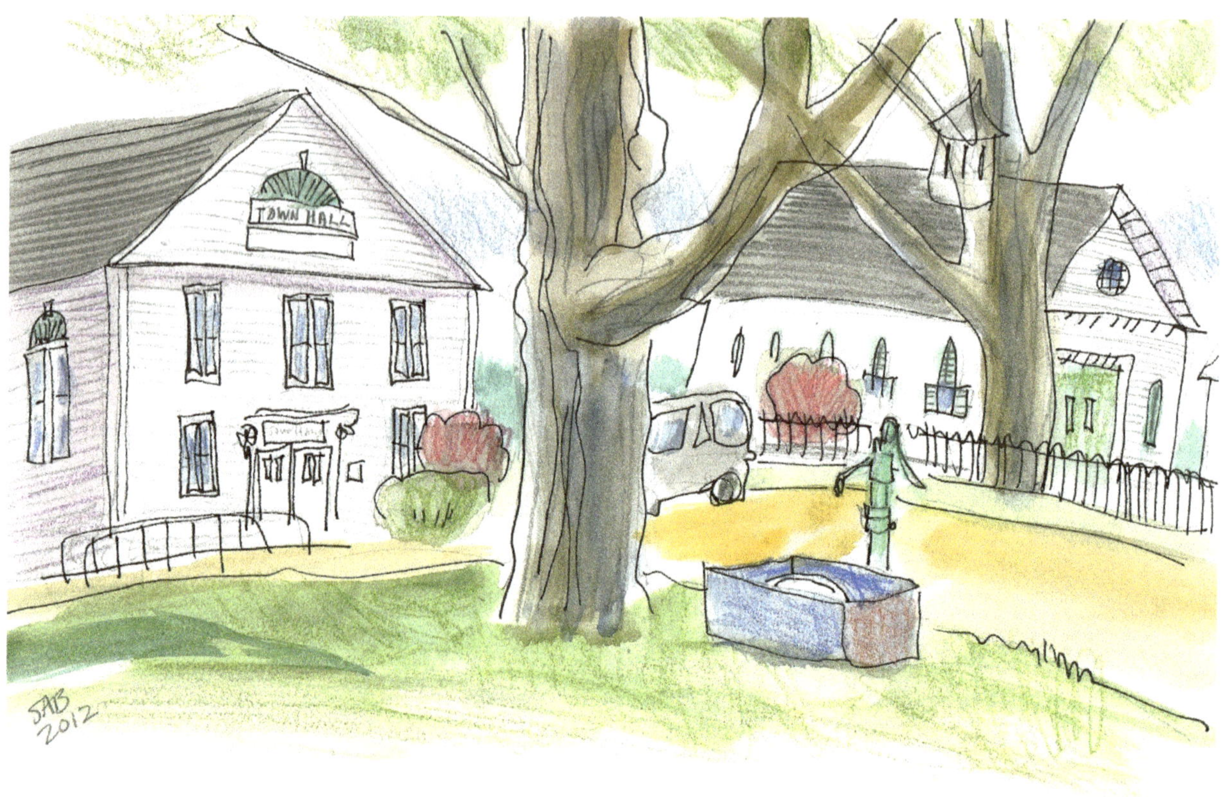

South Hampton has a land area of eight square miles and under 1,000 inhabitants. It was once a part of Amesbury, Massachusetts.

On the left stands the combination town hall and grange. The town library attaches to the side on the right, tucked away out of vision. The barn on the right is large and more ornate than usual, with its shuttered windows and a fancy cupola on the roof. A man near the barn was watching me very carefully. I focus so intently on drawing that I usually forget to toss off a friendly wave.

The hand pump and the water trough hark back to another era.

STRATHAM

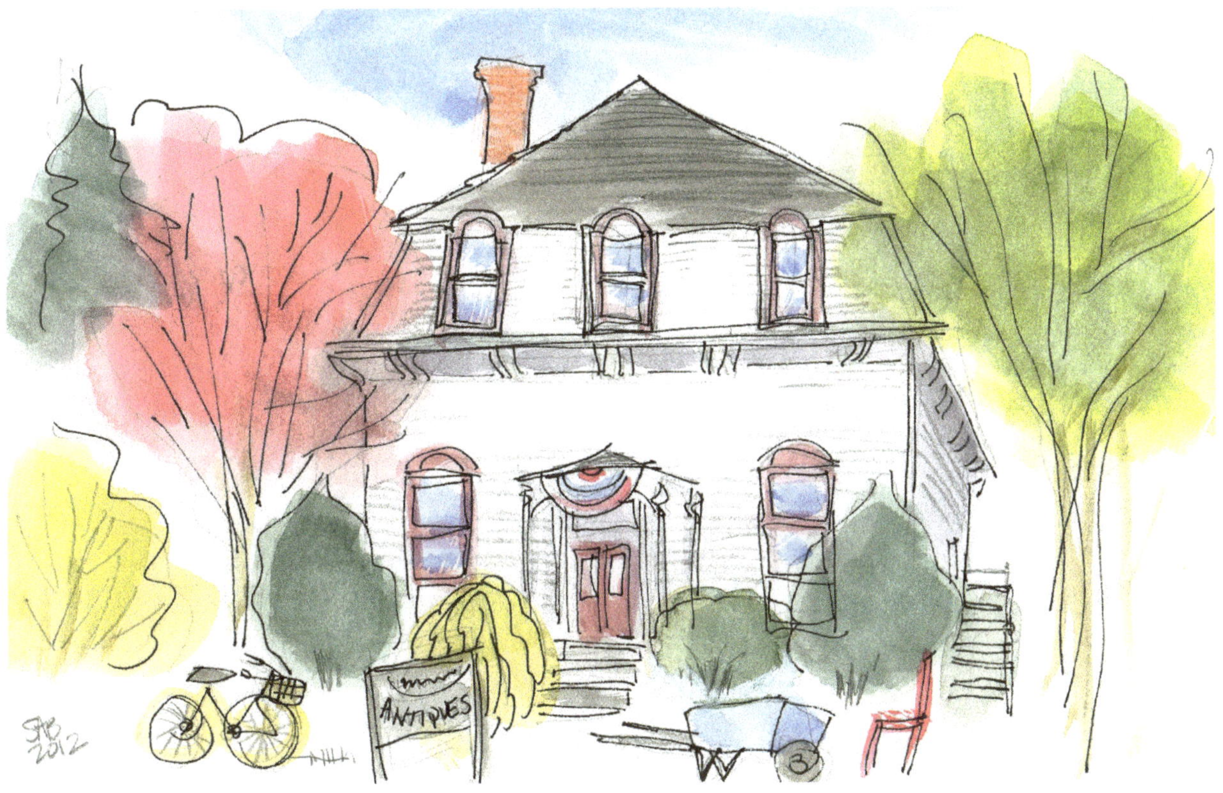

Stratham, Winniconic, and Winnicut Mills are the town's three villages.

Stratham, on Great Bay, was settled early, circa 1631, and incorporated in 1716. Today the town is a combination of quiet residential and busy commercial areas, with a part of town called Antique Row.

The former town hall is now this antique shop. It is a late Victorian style, maybe 1890, with a French Mansard roof. And it is chock-a-block full of antiques and oddities. The new town library is the Wiggin Memorial Library, while the older library building now houses the town's historical society. This sort of repurposing is common in New Hampshire, as are local historical societies. One list I've seen shows over a hundred of them.

White Mountains

ALBANY

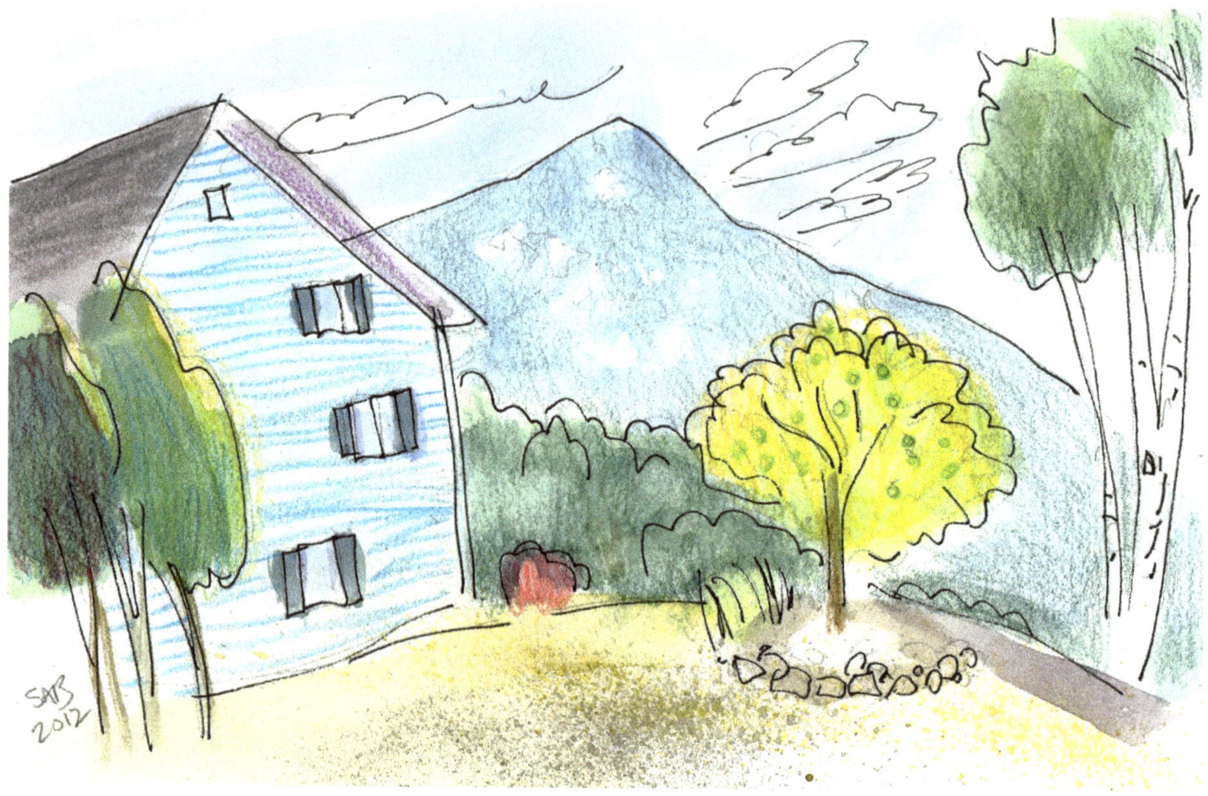

When I was drawing the view of South Moat Mountain from the Darby Field Inn, I wondered about the name.

Darby Field ran a ferry service across Great Bay from Durham to Newington. In 1642 when he was 32, he decided to climb Mount Washington. He left journals describing the walk of many days to the mountain, the ascent, and precise details of the topography all the way to the top.

85% of the land within the town borders is part of the White Mountain National Forest.

BARTLETT

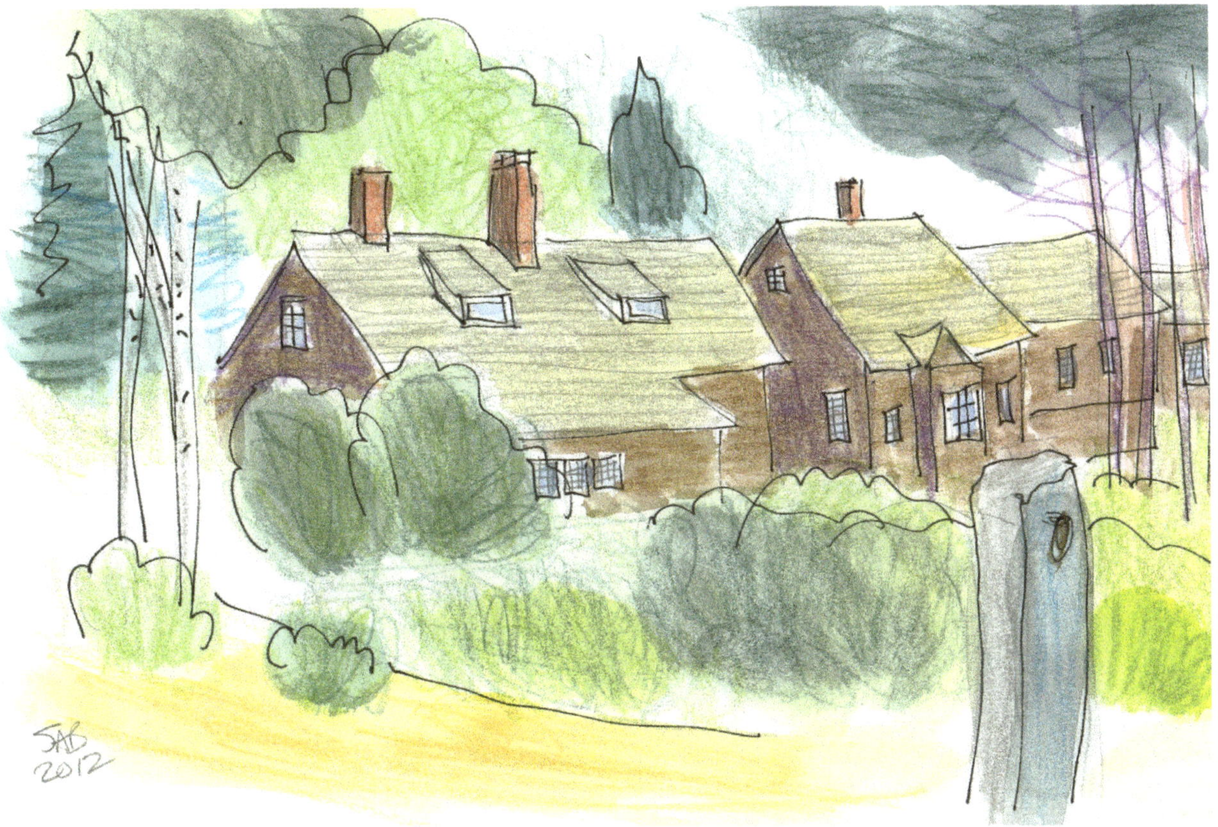

Storyland and Attitash Ski Resort are in the town's village of Glen.

New Hampshire historic marker #109 in front of this small cottage tells the story of the occupant of the house, an Englishwoman by birth named Lady Blanche.

She was the daughter of an earl, and is said to have been the godchild of Queen Victoria. The story goes that she fell in love with a commoner whose name was Thomas Murphy. They eloped, set sail, and lived here in Bartlett. She became a writer, and some say an artist as well. She wrote for *Harper's*, *The Atlantic Monthly*, and *Catholic World*.

BATH

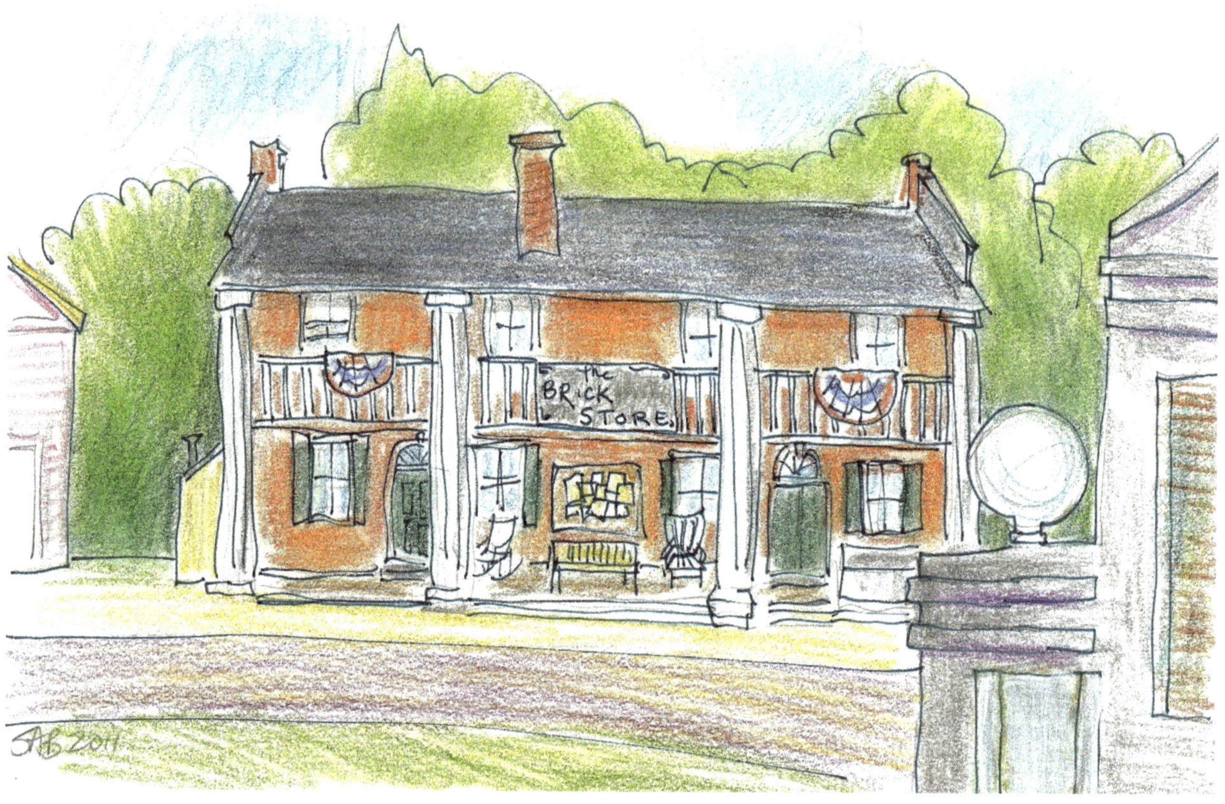

Bath is at the head of navigation on the Connecticut River. The valley is fertile soil, and the river gave the farmers a way to transport their products to markets.

The major industries in the 1800s were sheep, copper, lumber, and potatoes. The town center boasts The Brick Store, the oldest continuously operated general store in the United States. Built in 1824, a general store in brick was unusual and denoted prosperity. The columns were a touch of grandeur in the wilderness. I included the small yellow smoke house attached to the left of the store.

The smoked cheddar cheese that I bought here was wonderfully flavorful.

BENTON

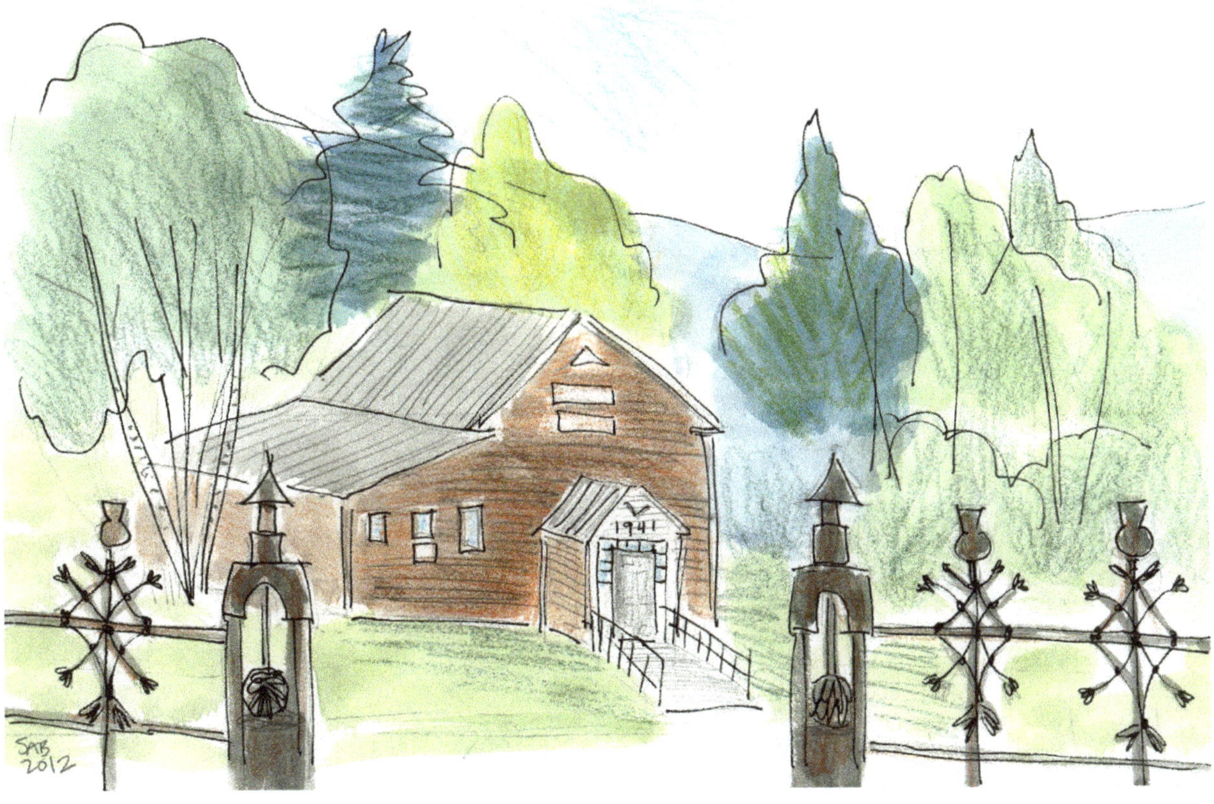

The 2,200 mile-long Appalachian Trail passes through the town.

Benton, a small town with a population of fewer than 400 residents, is almost entirely surrounded by the White Mountain National Forest.

Senator Thomas Hart Benton is the namesake of this small community, and his great nephew of the same name was a prominent painter. Senator Benton is one of eight senators featured in John F. Kennedy's book *Profiles In Courage*. He led a fascinating life. Benton's town hall and offices were built in the 1940s. The very ornate wrought iron fence across the street and up the steep hill is from a very different era, perhaps Victorian.

BETHLEHEM

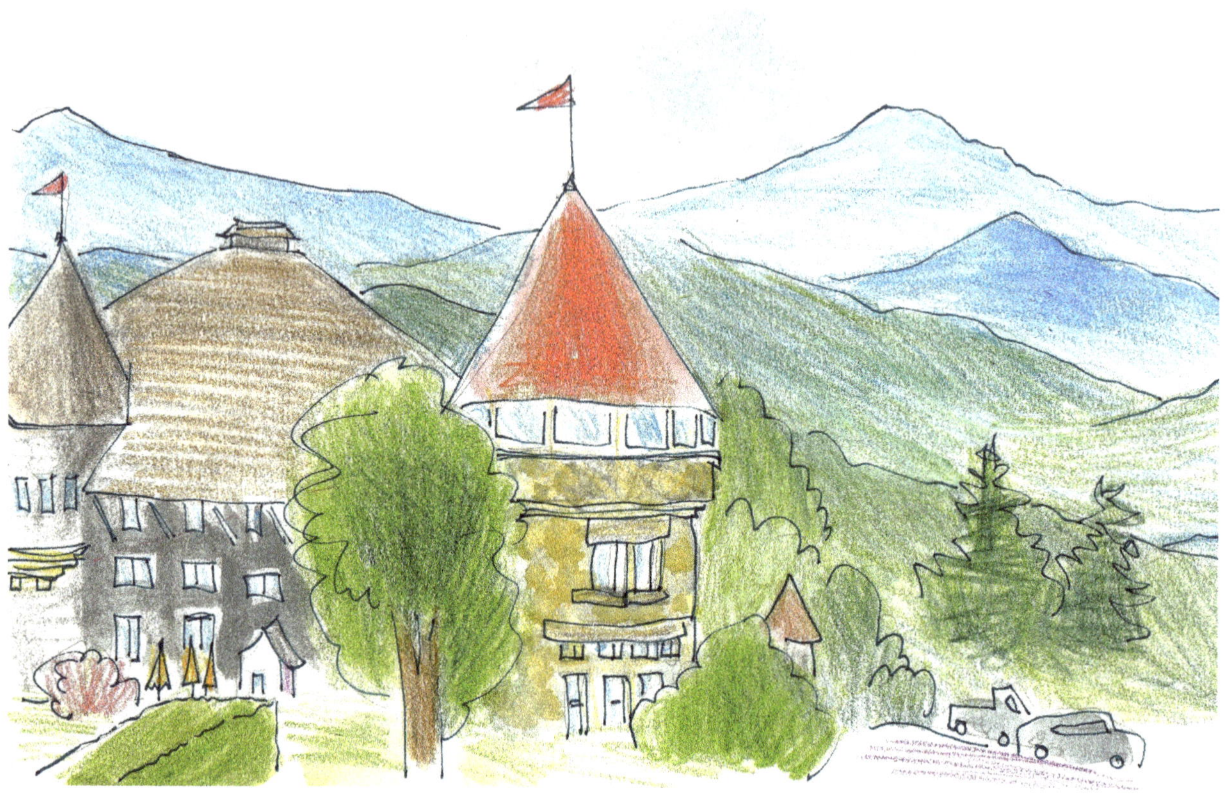

In 1867, the railroad arrived in this town high in the mountains. Families traveled by train to spend the summer in the cool, clean, alpine air.

They came from Boston, New York City, and beyond. The town was advertised as pollen free, and many businesses were formed here to serve the needs of hay fever sufferers.

With the invention of the automobile, an end came to most of the large hotels. Smaller inns and hotels survive, as well as the 1919 Maplewood Golf Course shown here. Skiing and other winter sports are very important to the economy of the mountain area too.

People around the world send Christmas cards to be postmarked in this town.

CAMPTON

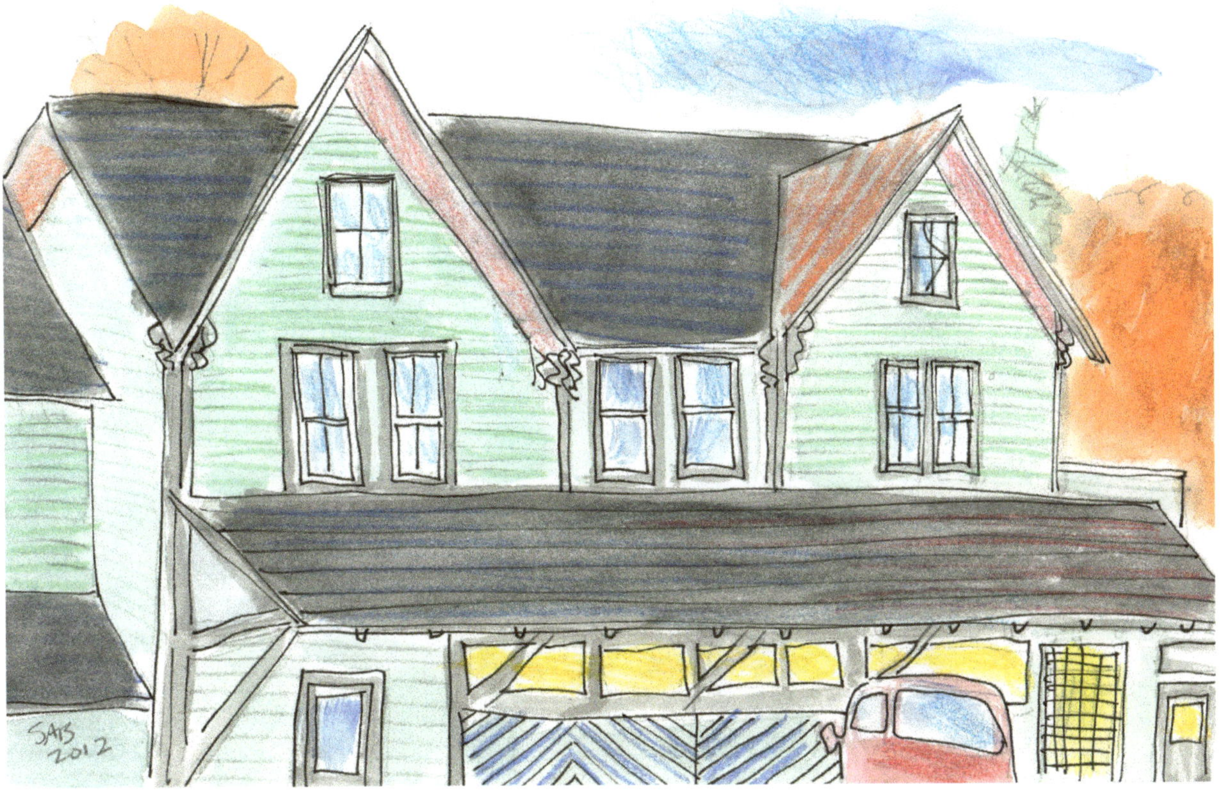

The orange autumn leaves make a nice contrast with the green-blue of the building.

Campton, a town of 3,400 people lies in the foothills of the White Mountain National Forest and is the location of Livermore Falls State Forest.

Campton has four covered bridges. The longest one at 292 feet, Blair Bridge, crosses the Pemigewasset River. It was built in 1829, rebuilt in 1870, and damaged by Tropical Storm Irene in 2011.

This sturdy and impressive wooden building appealed to me when I was focusing on drawing the general stores of New Hampshire. It looks a bit like a railroad station because of the bracing of the overhang.

CARROLL

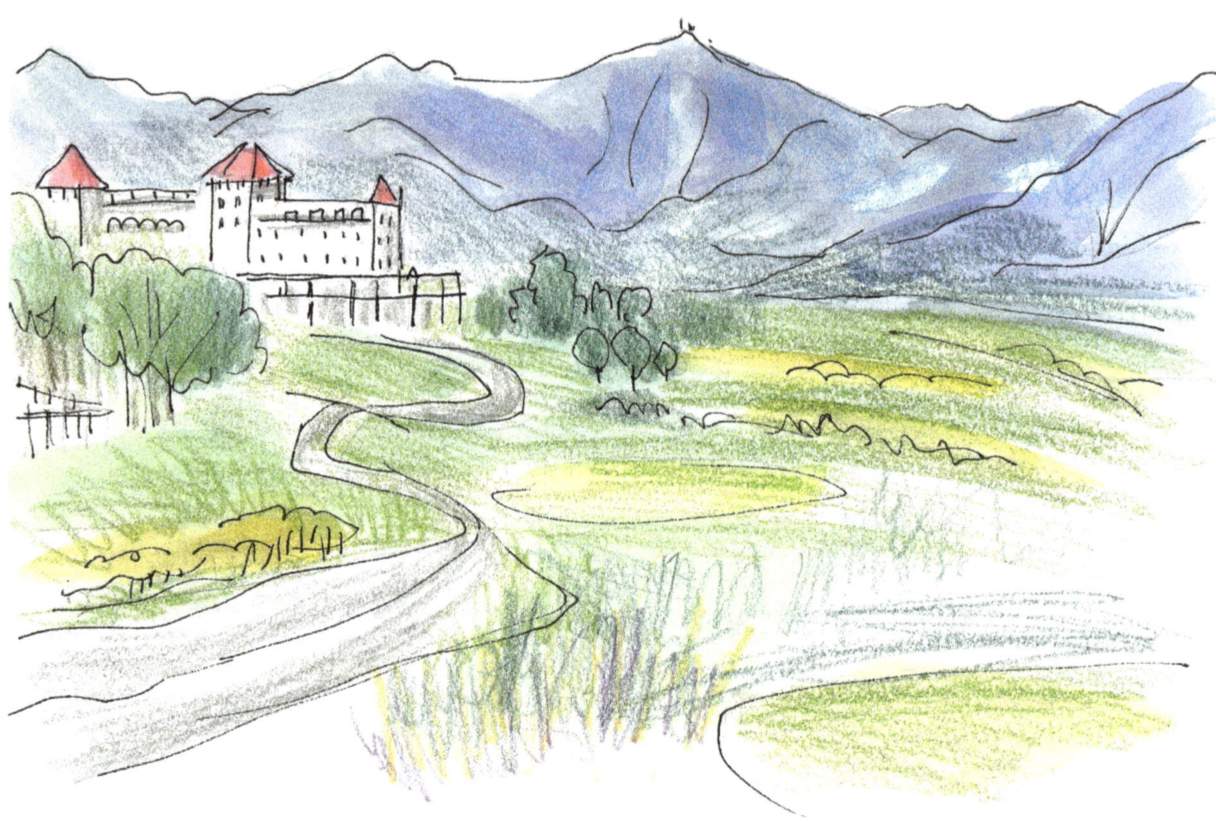

Bretton Woods and Twin Mountain lie within the town of Carroll. The large, rambling hotel is the Mount Washington Resort, built in 1902.

The attractions include the golf course seen here, as well as 101 ski trails. Mount Washington is the center peak. At 6,288 feet, or 1,917 meters, it is the highest peak in the northeastern United States, and is in an alpine climate zone. Foot trails and bridle trails surround it. A paved road leads to the summit. The structures atop the mountain are designed to withstand winds up to 300 mph. For many years Mount Washington held the world record for highest recorded wind speed.

A cog railroad, built in 1869, takes visitors to the top of Mount Washington.

CHATHAM

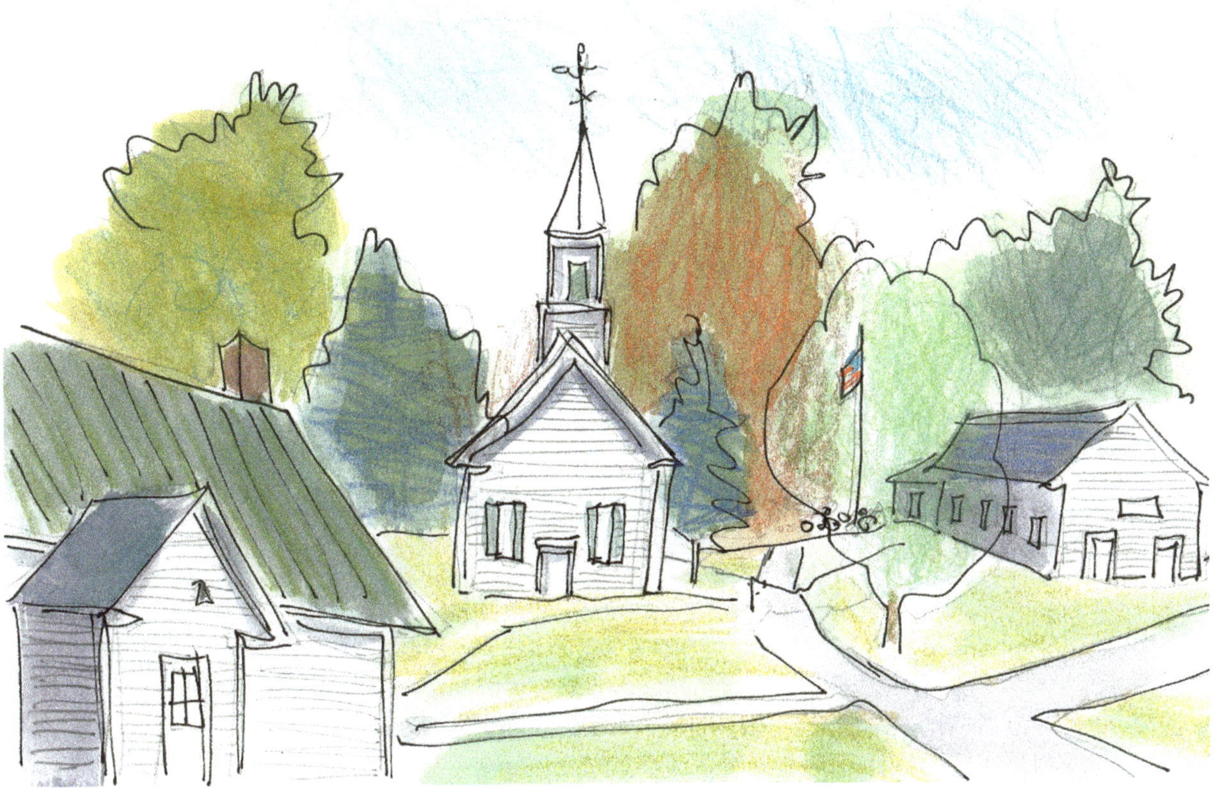

There's lots of room to breathe here at a density of six people per square mile.

The town was incorporated in 1767, and named in honor of William Pitt, Earl of Chatham and Prime Minister of Great Britain.

Not far from Conway, the town is almost completely within the White Mountain National Forest. The easiest way to get to Chatham is to drive from New Hampshire into Maine and then back again into New Hampshire. From left to right are the library, the Congregational Church, and the town house.

CONWAY

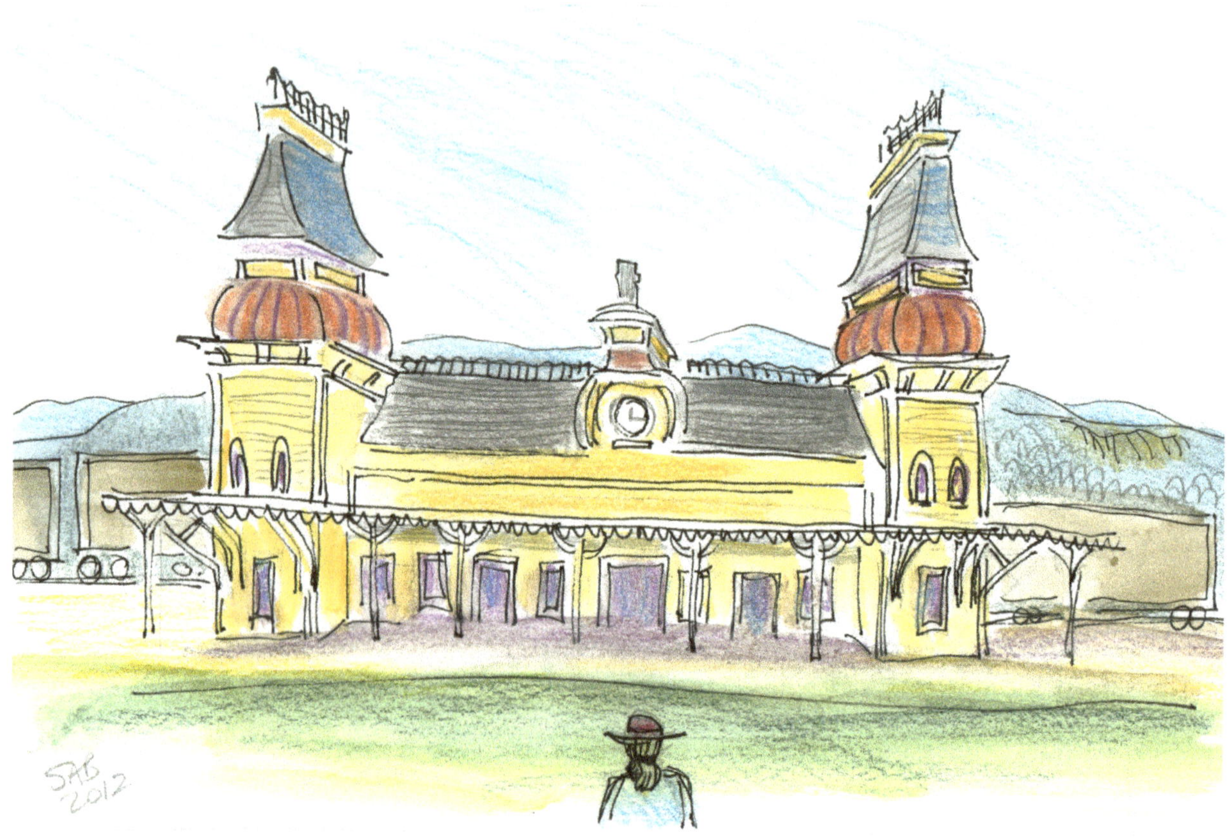

I sat directly in front of the Conway railroad station, built in 1874. The White Mountains, blue in the summer, peek behind it.

This station was the destination for families from Boston, New York City, and Philadelphia, arriving to spend the summer at one of the many Grand Hotels of the era. So the railroad station too had to be grand. Today the Conway Scenic Railroad operates on two historic rail lines during the summer season. Conway, the gateway to the White Mountain region, is still a very bustling resort area.

Artists discovered the beauties of the area in the mid 1800s, and captured the scenes in panoramic oil paintings.

EASTON

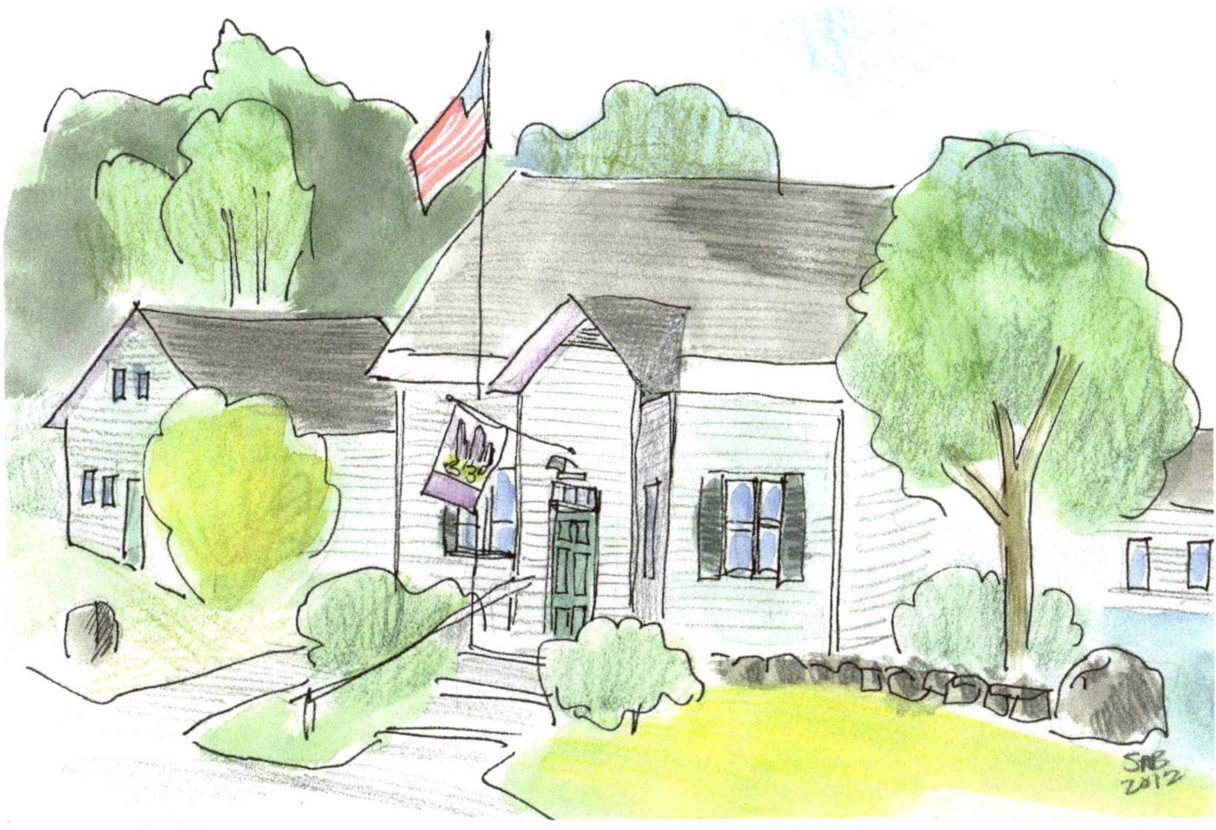

The town of Easton was incorporated in 1876 when it separated from Landaff.

The Kinsman families were early settlers in the town.

Easton's Kinsman Ridge includes the peaks of North Kinsman, South Kinsman, and Cannon Mountain, all over 4,000 feet. Cannon Mountain is well known for its aerial tramway cable car. Serious hikers make a point of climbing all forty-eight mountains in New Hampshire that are over the magic 4,000 number.

The town hall is flying the flag of the spring Lupine Festival, in conjunction with the festival events of nearby Sugar Hill. Near the town hall grew a beautiful grouping of the tall spiky blue flowers.

ELLSWORTH

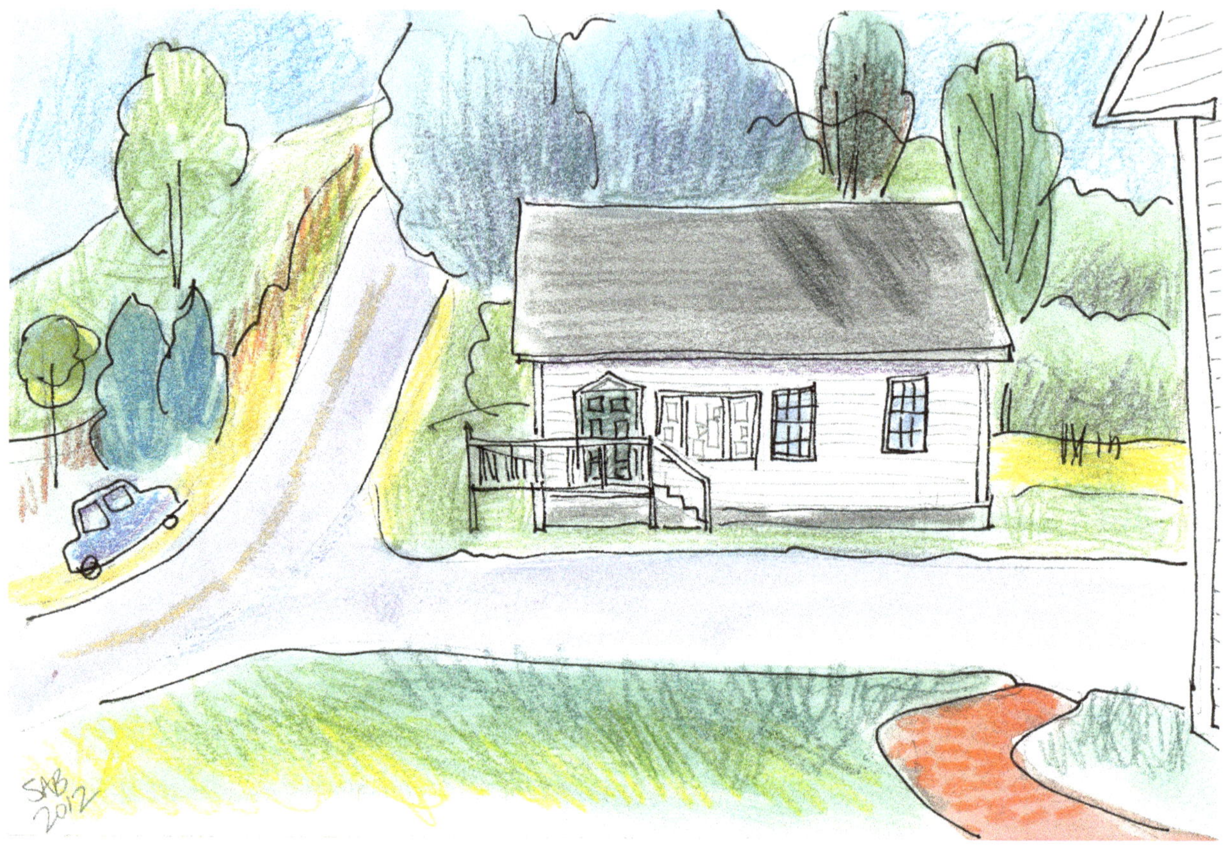

Ellsworth, with a population of 83 people at the 2010 census, is not too easy to find, but the residents probably like it that way.

The combination town hall and school house was built in 1814. The bulletin board on the outside of the building gives a voter list for the town. There were 7 Democrats, 7 Republicans, and 57 undeclared voters. Undeclared voters are usually called independents. New Hampshire has a lot of independents, and independence. The bench on the front lawn of the St. John of the Mountains Interdenominational Church provided the perfect place to sit as I sketched.

The road next to the town hall is as steep as a ski slope. Our little car is parked at the edge.

FRANCONIA

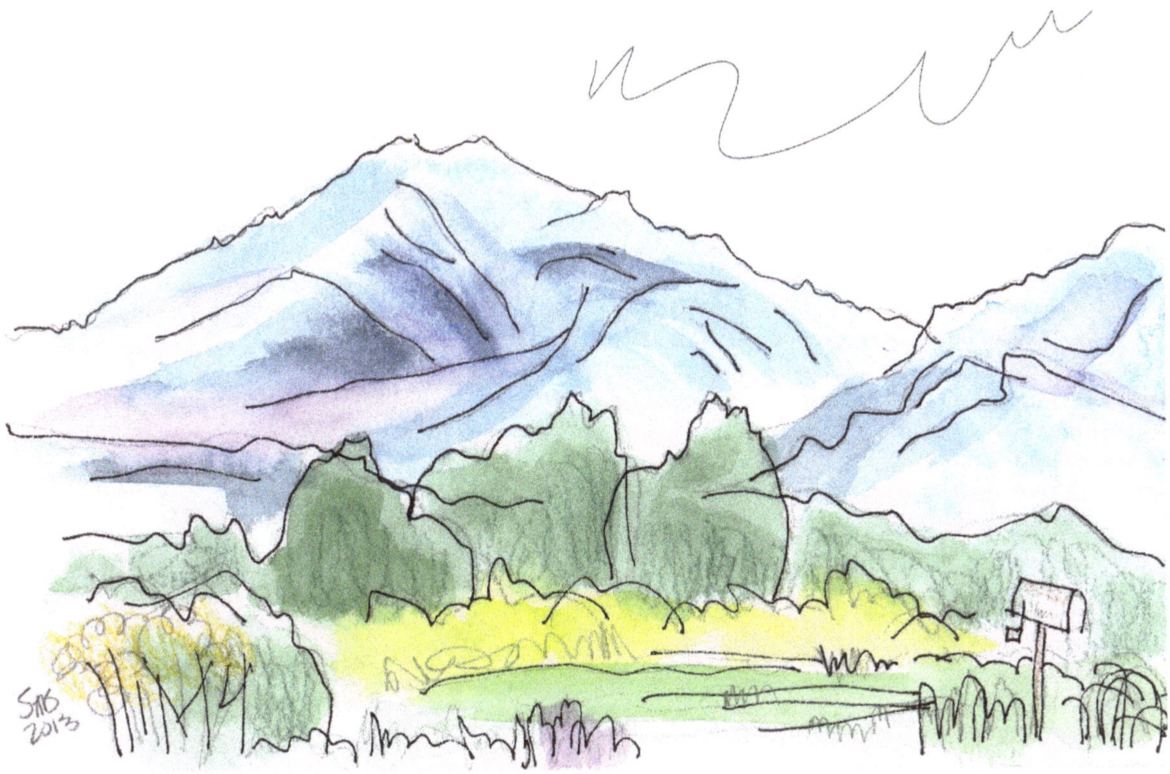

I drew the view of the mountains from poet Robert Frost's home, now a center for poetry.

Franconia Notch is formed by the towering Cannon Mountain on the west side, and Mount Lafayette on the east. The town's name is derived from a region of Germany.

On the side of Cannon Mountain, the famous Old Man of the Mountain looked out across the area. The natural stone profile was 1,200 feet above Profile Lake. It became the state's emblem in 1945 and was featured on the state quarter. The five cliffs that made up the face were 40 feet high. Sadly, it collapsed in 2003. A cleverly designed sculpture park now optically recreates the landmark for each visitor.

GORHAM

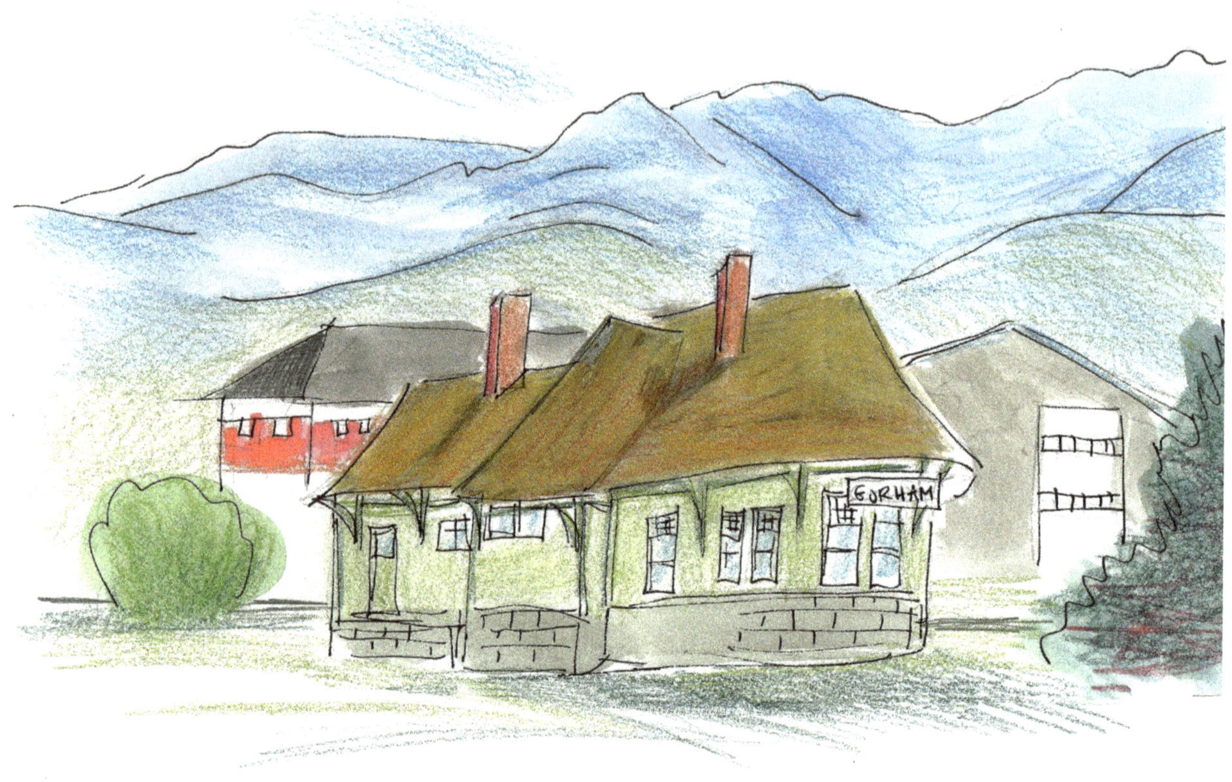

Gorham, population 2,900, was chartered in 1770 as Shelburne Addition. When it was incorporated in 1836, a resident formerly from Gorham, Maine, suggested the new name.

The railroad came to town in the mid 1800s, bringing summer visitors from Boston and farther south. Gorham, half way between Montreal and the seacoast, became a busy resort town with its breathtaking views of the White Mountains. Residents saved this 1907 railroad station from demolition in 1973. Now the Historical Society of Gorham manages it as a museum.

On this day the White Mountains were quite blue with the haze of the summer heat.

HART'S LOCATION

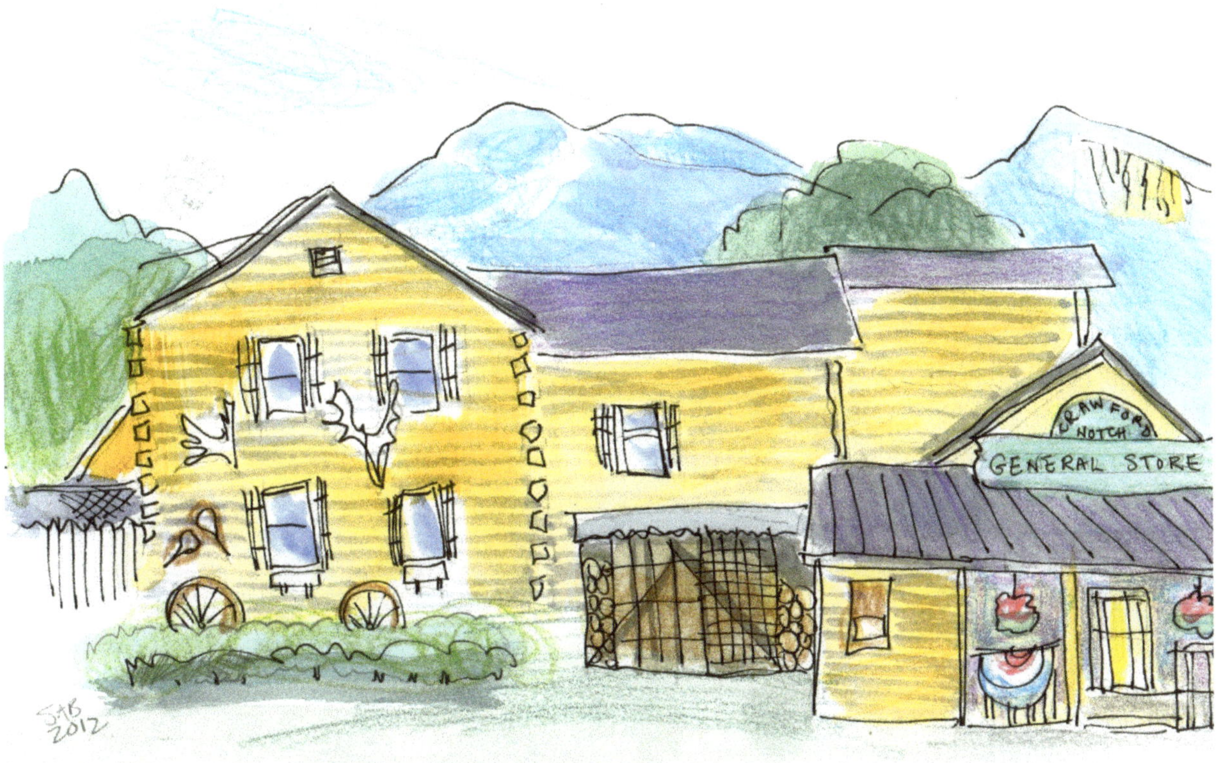

The rock outcropping is called the Frankenstein Cliffs, named after a German artist and not the more famous, fictional, Dr. Frankenstein.

The Crawford Notch General Store is a landmark in Hart's Location, with its population of 41 people. It is a ribbon shaped town, 11 miles long and 1.5 miles wide and running along the Saco River in the White Mountains.

New Hampshire state law allows a town of fewer than 100 residents (not just registered voters) to open its polls at midnight and close when all have cast their votes. Therefore this small community, along with the neighboring Dixville Notch, gets a lot of attention during New Hampshire's first-in-the-nation presidential primaries for their early results.

HAVERHILL

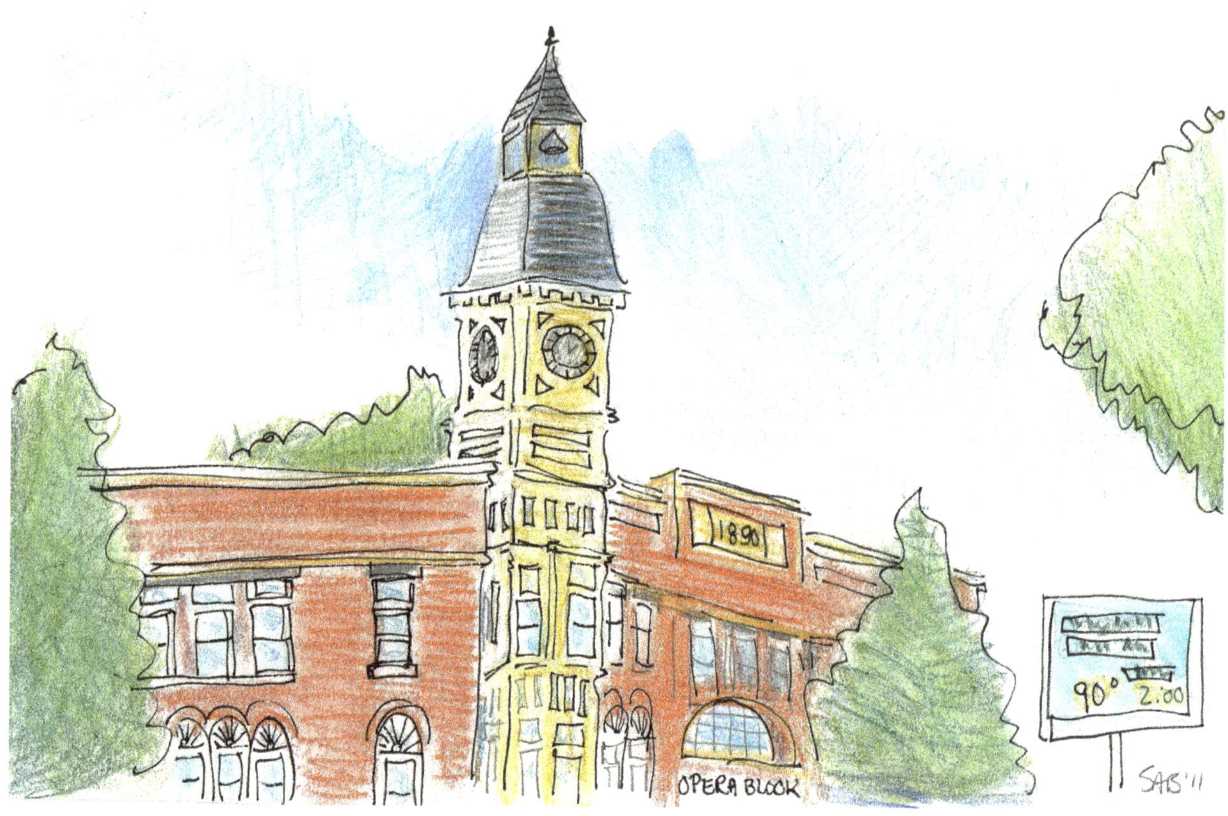

In 1763, settlers arrived to this northern area from Haverhill, Massachusetts. They named their village Lower Coos (pronounced 'co-os').

Today's villages are called Woodsville, Pike, North Haverhill, Haverhill Corner, and Mountain Lakes.

The Woodsville Opera House dates from 1890. In contrast to some of the other opera houses in the state that are still used as performance spaces, Haverhill's is now used as housing. The digital sign of the local bank, giving the time and the very high temperature was included as a modern counterpoint to the old structure.

The stage curtain and a chandelier from the Opera House are now part of the Alumni Cultural Center.

JACKSON

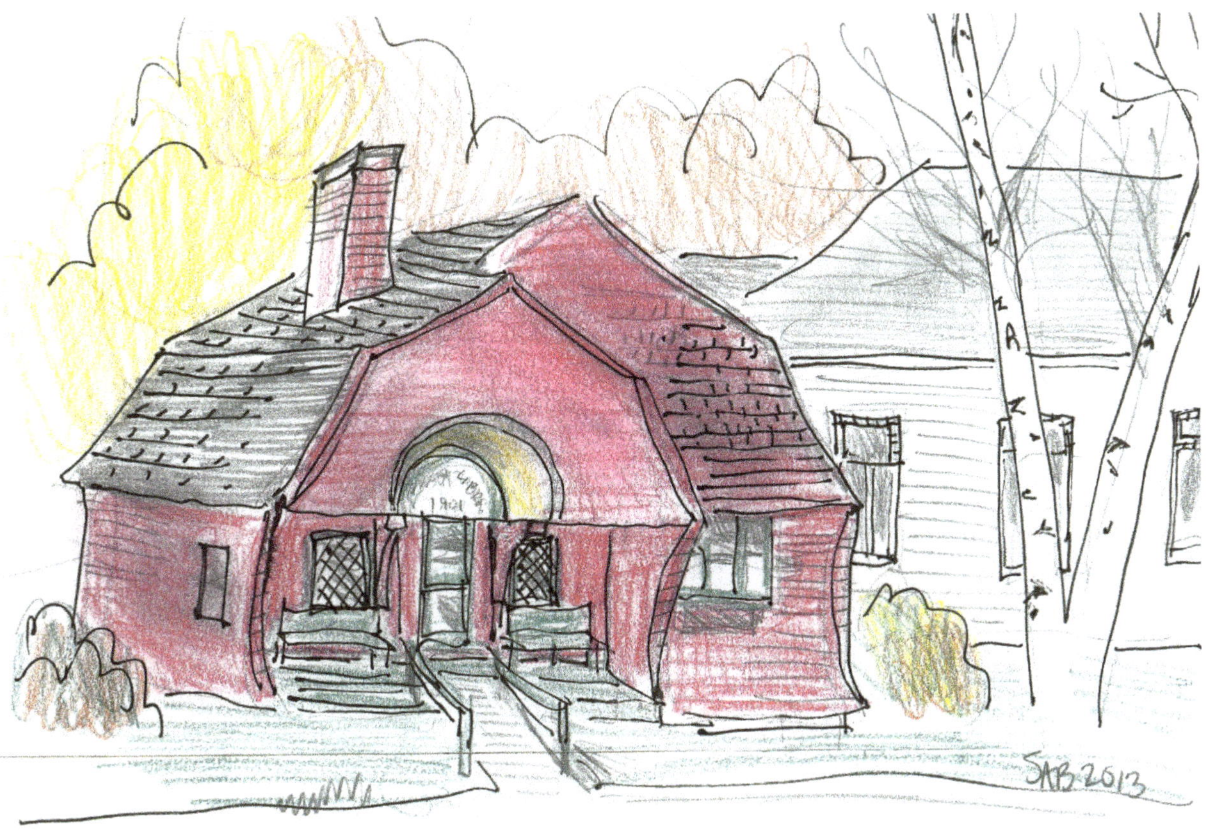

The red building is the former library, still used for community events, and the new library is an old barn, moved, redesigned, and rebuilt.

Jackson is a lovely resort town in the White Mountains. Once named Adams, in honor of President John Adams, it was renamed Jackson to honor President Andrew Jackson.

In 1847, artists of the White Mountain School in nearby North Conway began arriving in Jackson to paint. Over four hundred artists were known to have come here in the early 1800s, prompting tourists to arrive to see the beauty for themselves. In the latter half of the century, some artists had studios in the hotels. By 1900, many of the artists had moved west to paint the Rocky Mountains. Panoramic paintings by White Mountain School artists are on display at the Jackson Historical Society.

JEFFERSON

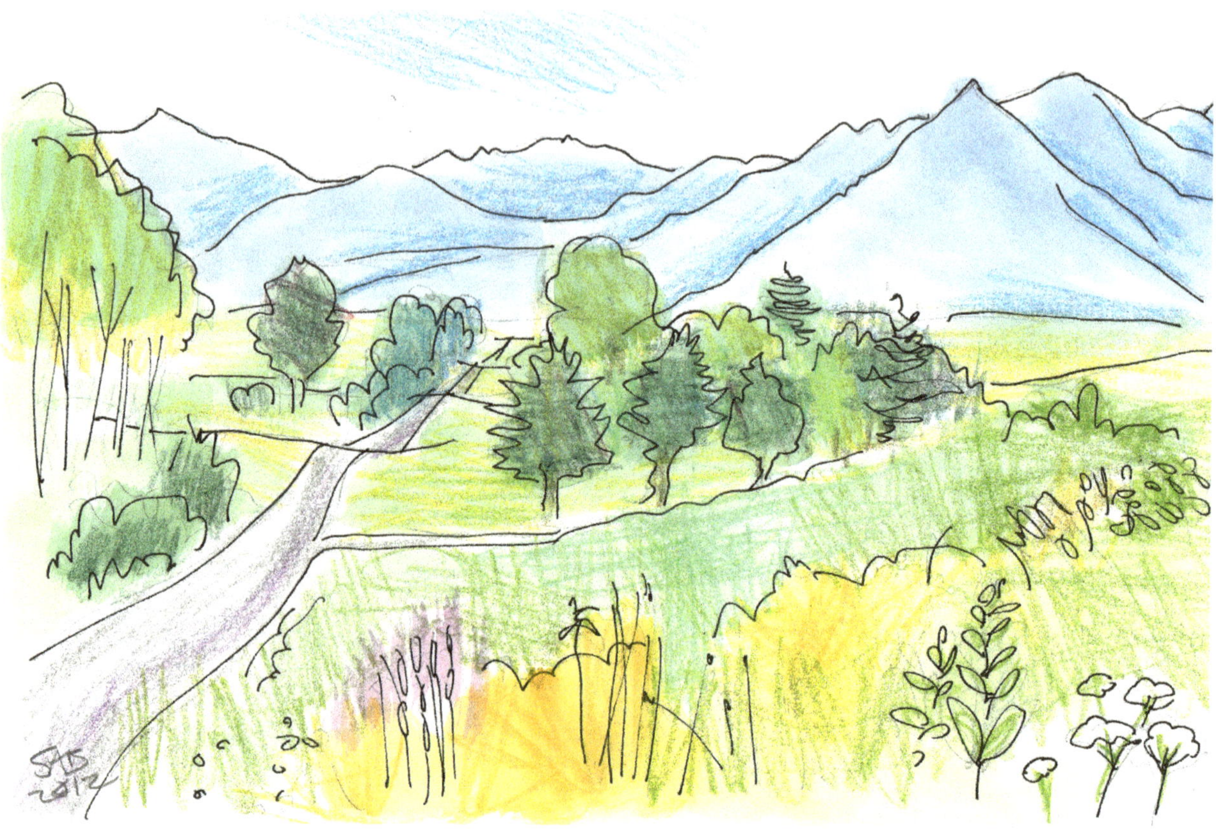

An early settler, Joseph Whipple, named the town for Thomas Jefferson, four years before the Virginian became president.

Colonel Whipple's brother, William Whipple, was a signer of the Declaration of Independence, so he must have admired Jefferson from the start. This section of town is called Jefferson Meadows, and behind is the Presidential Range of the White Mountain National Forest. The names in the range are Mt. Washington, Mt. Adams, Mt. Jefferson, Mt. Madison, Mt. Monroe, and Mt. Eisenhower. One of the largest summer hotels of the Victorian era, The Grand Hotel Waumbeck, had its own railroad spur.

Hilly and curvy roads
disappearing into the distance
just call out my name.

LANDAFF

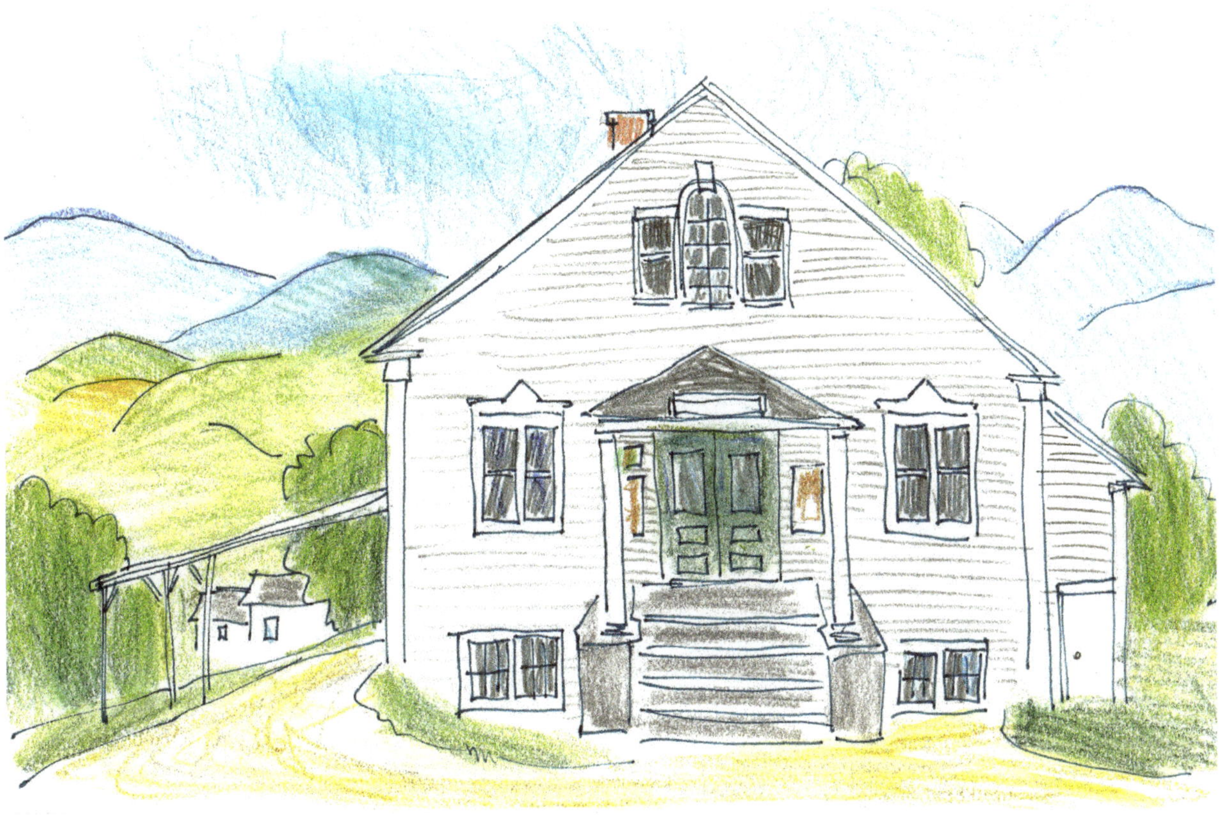

Llandaff, with a double L (pronounced 'thl'), is a cathedral city within Wales, a part of Great Britain.

Landaff, a small town of 415 residents, is just south of Lisbon. The town was originally called Whitcherville in 1764. It was incorporated with its current name in 1774.

As we drove the narrow winding roads, we admired the rolling open fields. At the village center, a splendid 360-degree panorama of hazy blue hills lay around us. I drew the dignified Landaff Town Hall and Mount Hope Grange. A sign stated that this building, built in 1923, is named the Morse Memorial Hall in honor and memory of Ellen Chandler Morse.

LINCOLN

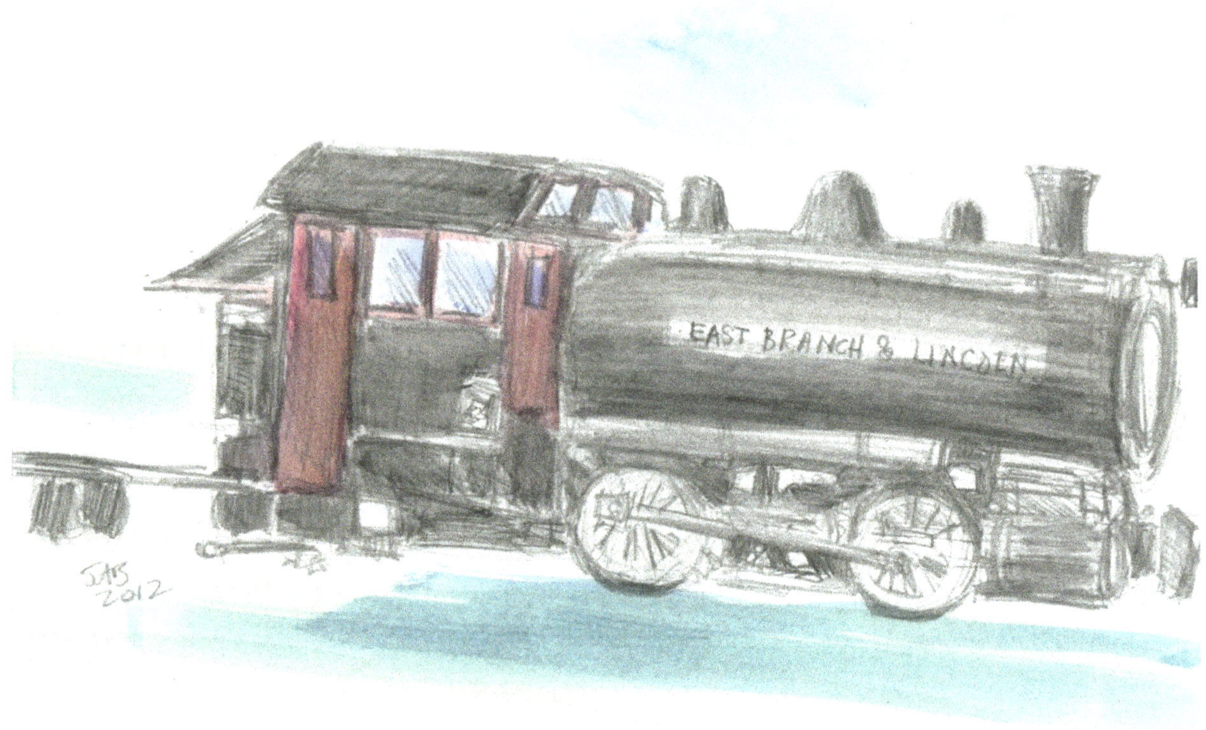

Lincoln, named for an earl in England and not for the president, is the second largest town in the state by area at 130 square miles.

Settled in 1782, the logging and papermaking industries were the town's economies until the paper mill closed in 1971. The vehicle I drew is the engine of a lumber train. Engines like this one used to pull train cars loaded with logs, three trains per day. Logging practices of the time included destructive clearcuts. Environmental concerns and restrictions on the industry led to the creation of the White Mountain National Forest.

Loon Mountain Resorts hosts the New Hampshire Scottish Games each September.

LISBON

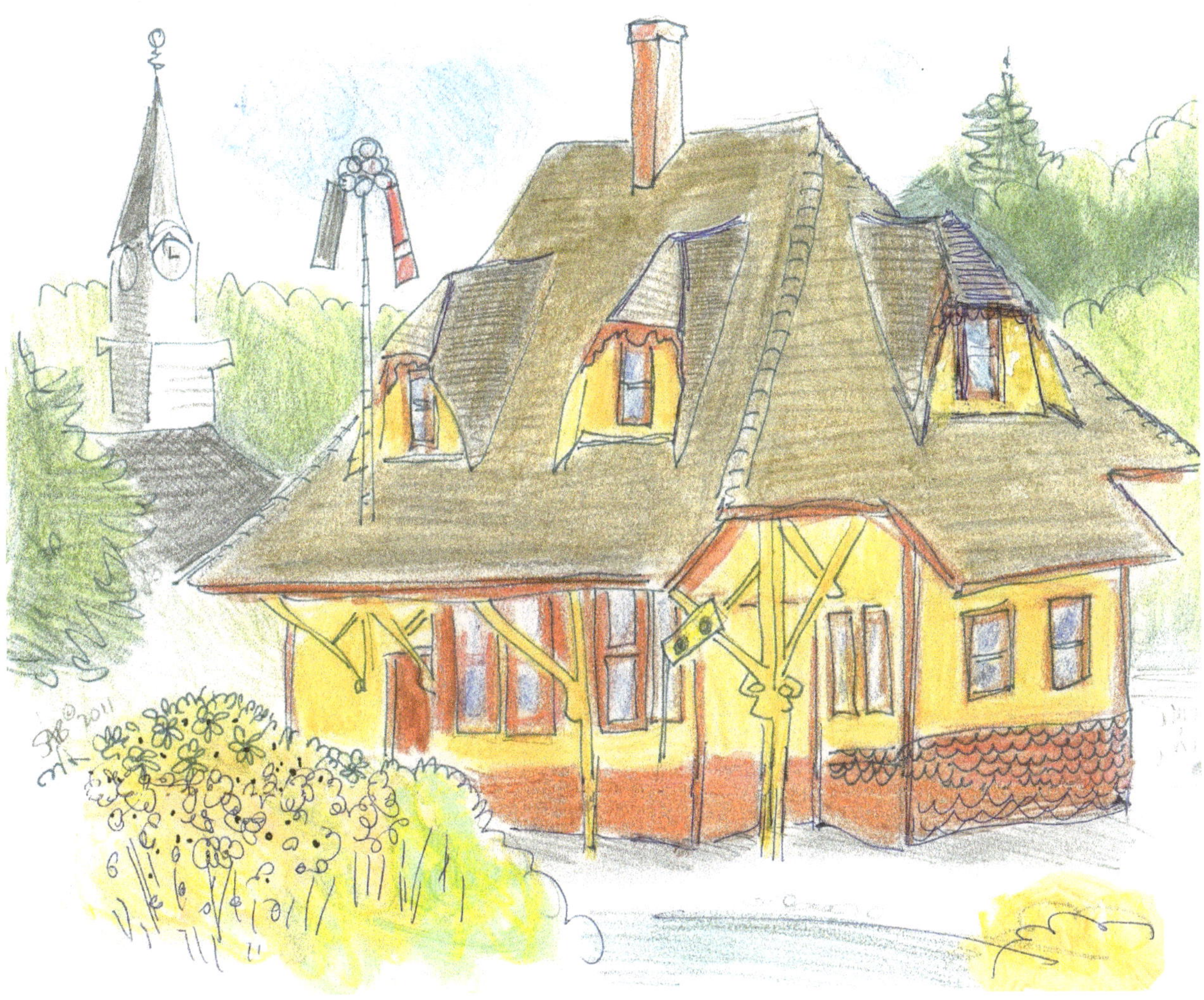

Whereas other nearby towns have Lupine Festivals, Lisbon has a Lilac Festival.

The town was first settled in 1763, and went through many names before becoming Lisbon in 1824.

Early industries included charcoal manufacture, and mining for iron and other minerals. One factory along the Ammonoosuc River even produced piano sounding boards for the world. This railroad station has an unusual roof line and charming windows and trim. Built in 1868 by the Boston, Concord, and Montreal Railroad, it has recently been wonderfully restored and now serves as a museum and visitors center.

LITTLETON

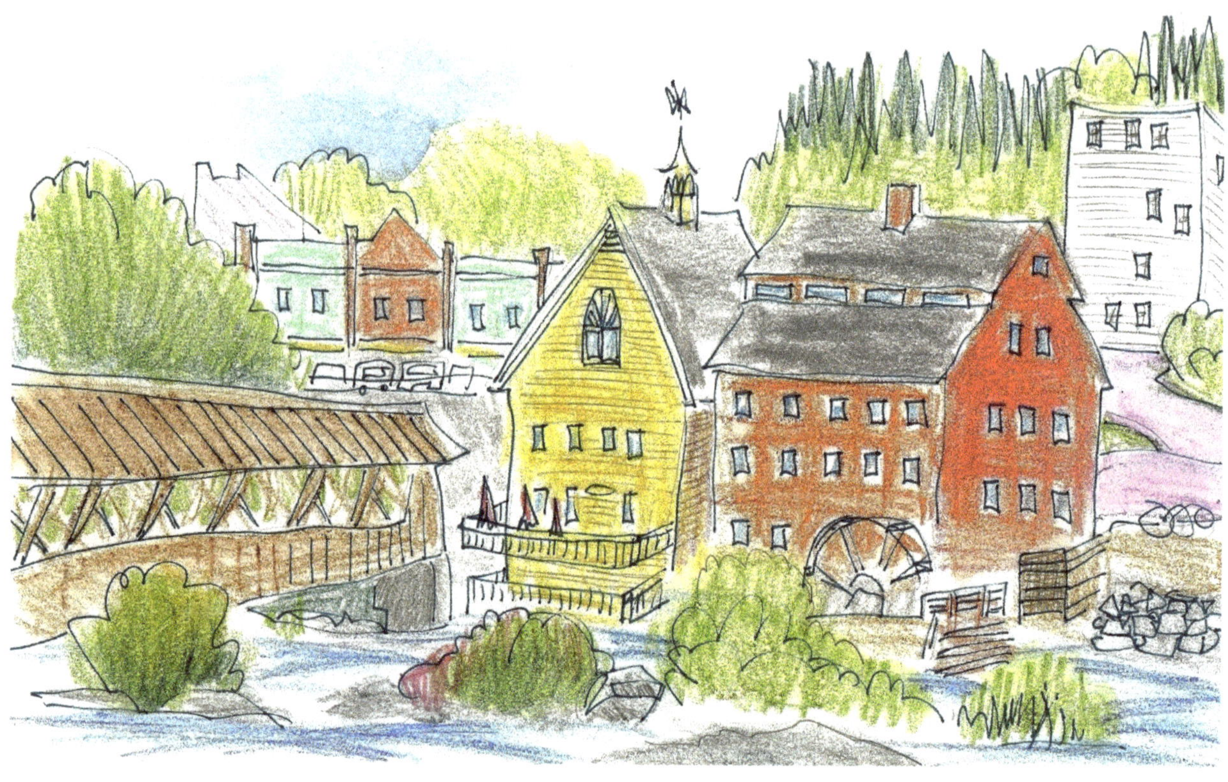

The Riverwalk gives a pleasing view of the town. The Ammonoosuc River once powered the old grist mill, and the yellow building is now home to a gift shop and café.

The grist mill has been recently converted into a brewpub.

The row of buildings behind the riverfront is Main Street. A stroll along Main Street takes you past the restored opera house, the court house, an enormous candy store, a 3-D movie theater, and a library with a statue of Pollyanna next to the front door. Her arms stretch out to greet you as you climb the stairs.

LYMAN

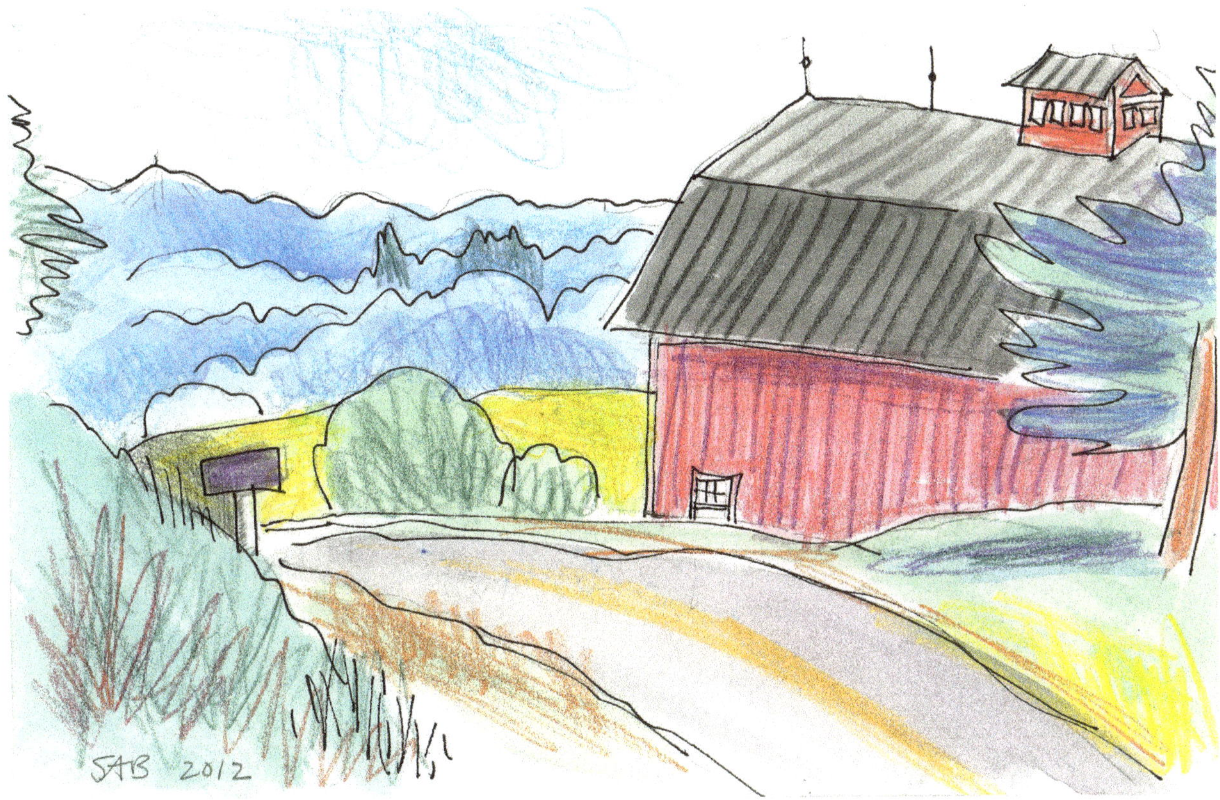

I am fond of curves in a road, barns, and blue mountains. I yelled 'Stop' when we got to the crest of this hill.

Lyman was granted in 1761 to 65 settlers, eleven of them named Lyman. In 1854, the families who lived near the Connecticut River part of town voted to separate to form the town of Monroe.

First we went to Monroe to draw their library. Then we decided to take a short cut to Lyman. A sign did warn that it is an unmaintained road. For a few extra miles, we could have stayed on Route 135, but we chose to take the most direct way, over the hills. It was the bumpiest road ever.

MONROE

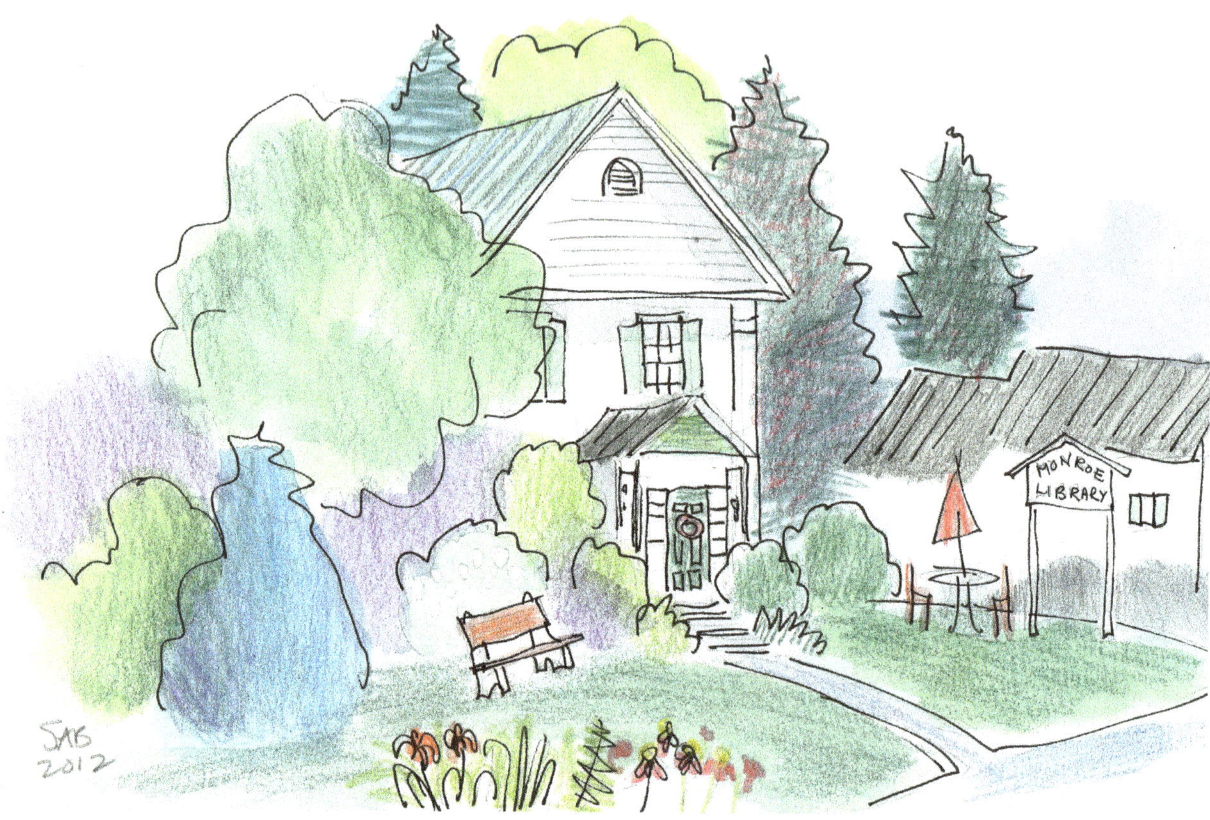

Monroe, with a population of 800 residents, used to be part of Lyman, a town to the east. The ridge of Gardner's Mountain presented too great an obstacle for travel.

So the settlers of West Lyman, along the Connecticut River, separated and formed the town of Monroe in 1854. President James Monroe got the honor. The town library is in an old dignified home. The library sign out front is even more charming than I've been able to show here. It has two profiles of little children reading. The silhouettes just didn't fit into my small scale drawing.

The hills of Monroe are known to contain copper and gold.

PIERMONT

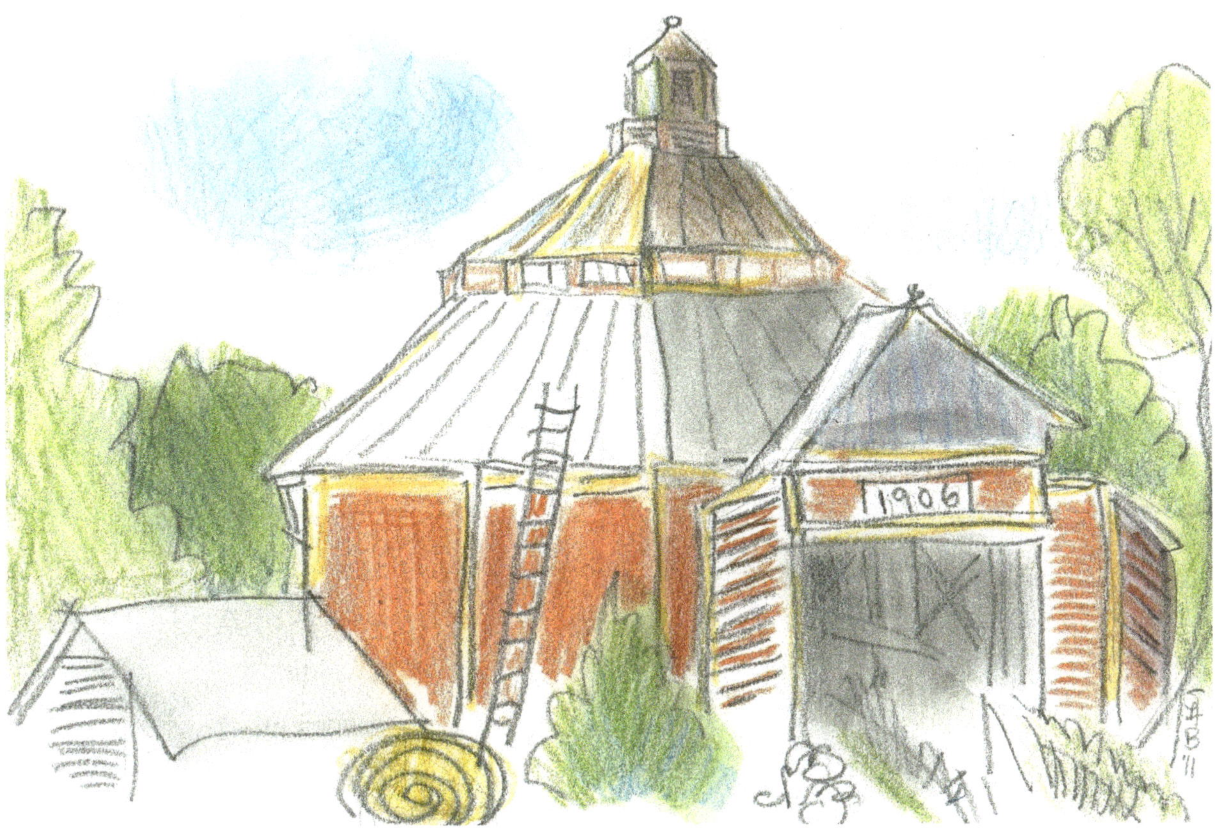

As I had never seen a barn that looked like this, I had to reach for my pencil.

The town of Piermont is on the Connecticut River, the border with Vermont. Town historians state that the name Piermont comes from the Italian word for foothill, *piemonte*.

The famed Piermont Round Barn is right next to Route 25. It is actually octagonal as you can see. Round and octagonal barns were considered to be a more efficient use of the farmer's time. The configuration called for less walking between cows. The newer mechanization improvements soon eliminated this efficiency and the design popularity faded.

PLYMOUTH

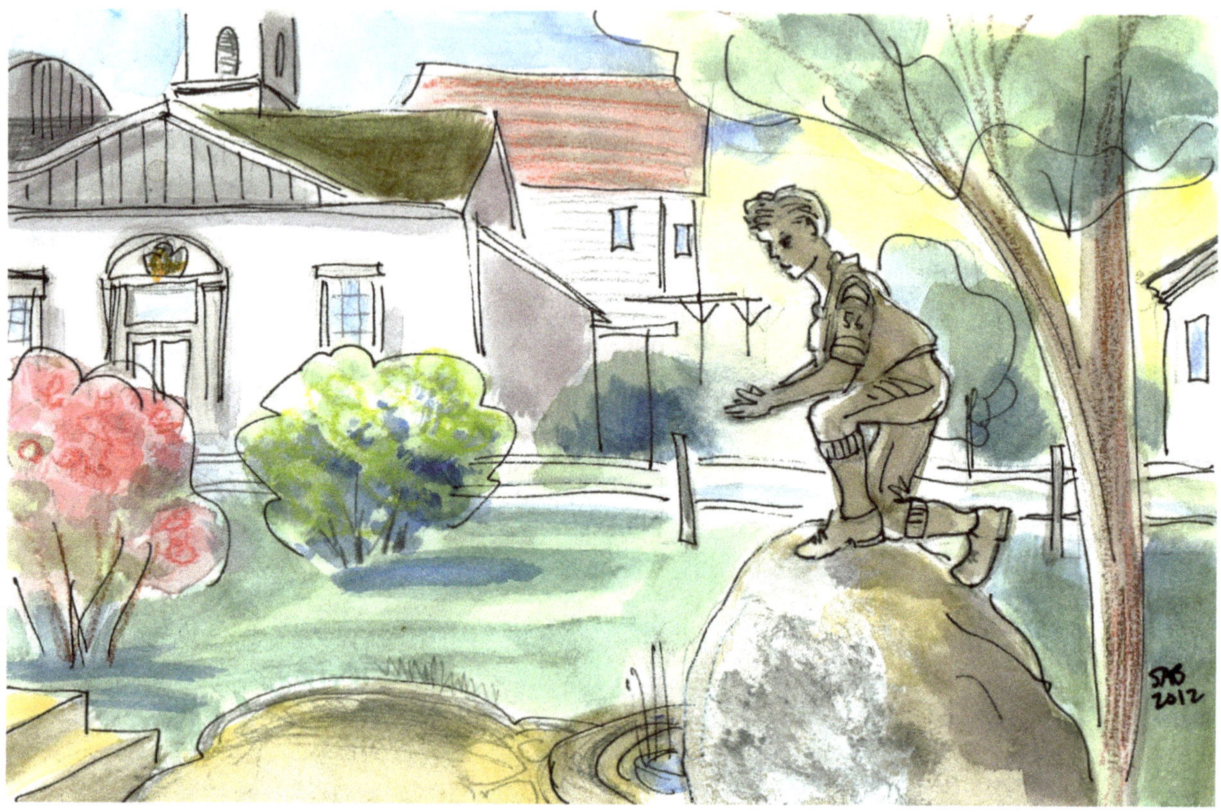

Plymouth, a small city at the southern edge of the White Mountains, has an oval shaped town common. Sculptures in parks always draw my attention. The figure represents a Boy Scout from Plymouth and was sculpted in 1932 by G. H. Borst.

The Plymouth State University campus is up on the hill behind the white post office. The wonderful Museum of the White Mountains opened on campus in 2013. A few steps from the museum, a small white building used for offices today was once a home of poet Robert Frost, his wife Elinor, and their several young children.

Plymouth is well known for the Flying Monkey Movie House and Performance Center.

RANDOLPH

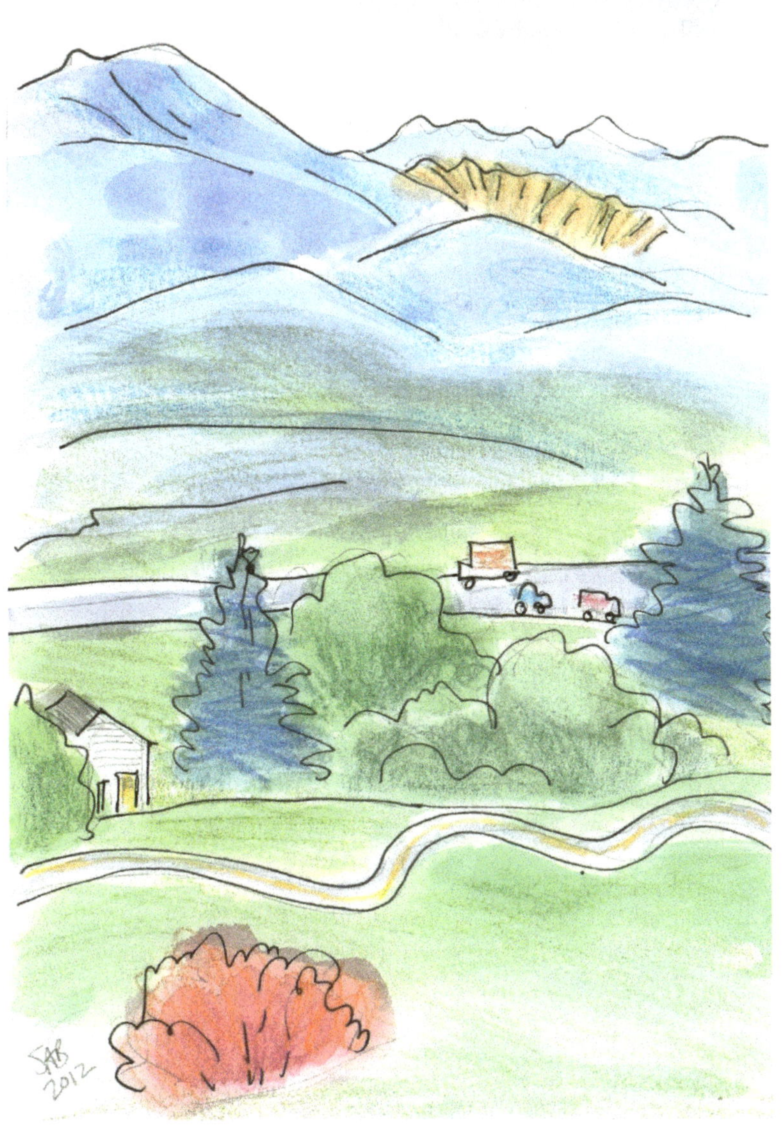

Randolph has a very small population, under 300 residents, who all have a wonderful view.

The town was named for the senator John Randolph of Virginia, who was a descendant of the Indian woman Pocahontas. The mountains to the north of town are Mount Crescent, Black Crescent Mountain, Mount Randolph, and Pond Hill, while the Presidential Range is to the south of town.

My drawing includes the cross-continental US Route 2 highway and the narrower and winding Durand Road. It is a bird's eye view of the two roads from my imagination, but the land forms themselves are drawn accurately.

The Randolph Mountain Club was founded in 1910. Its hundreds of members maintain the local trails.

SHELBURNE

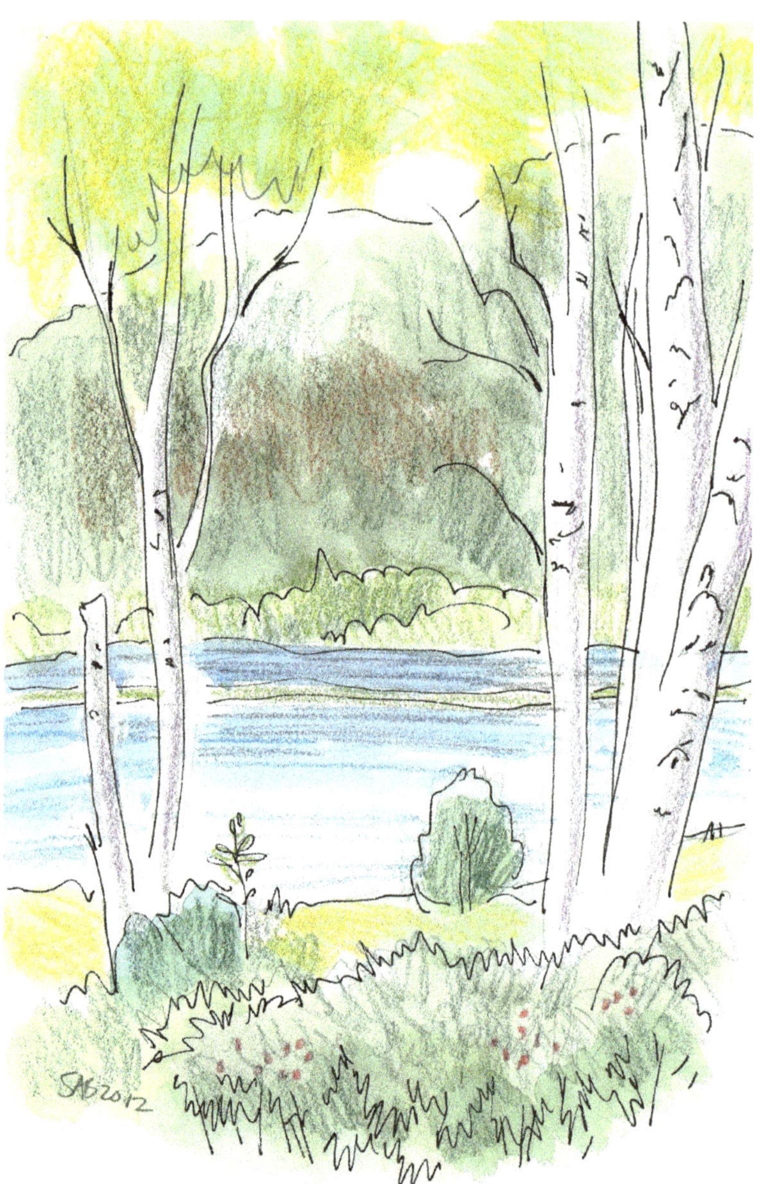

Shelburne, on the border with Maine, is bisected by Route 2, which goes right across the entire United States. The town's population of less than 400 residents is smaller than it was 100 years ago, a pattern common throughout rural New England.

Shelburne was named for William Petty Fitzmaurice, Earl of Shelburne. He is remembered for advising King George III to recognize the new country of the United States of America. The town is located at the southern end of the Mount Washington Valley.

An amazingly lovely grove of paper white birch trees lines the banks of the Androscoggin River.

SUGAR HILL

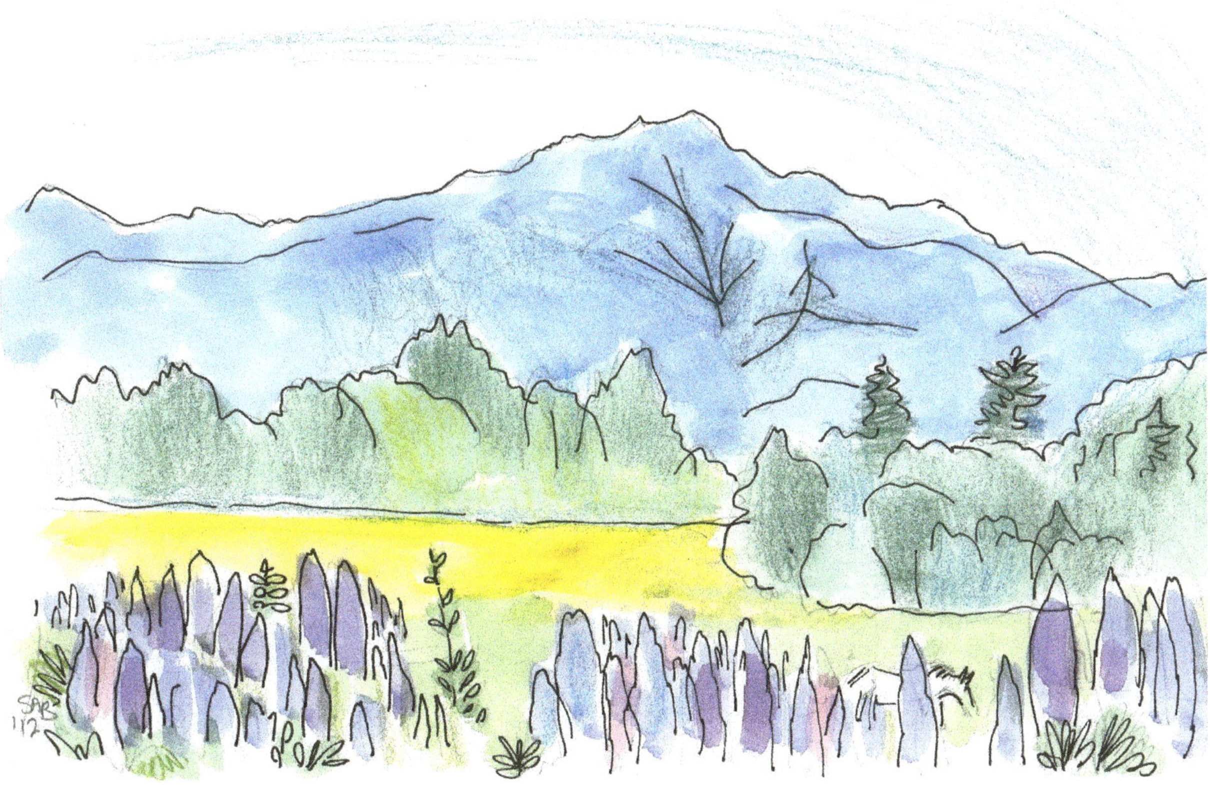

Lupine plants grow around the world. In some regions, they are called bluebonnets.

Sugar Hill was incorporated in 1962 from a part of Lisbon, perhaps the final time that a new town will appear in the state. This scenic area has long been a four-season resort. A ski school opened in 1929, and ski trains from Boston came the next year.

The peak is Mount Lafayette. With lupines in the foreground, a yellow field of buttercups and a white horse complete the pleasant scene. After this drawing was finished, we drove to a larger field of lupines, with a mown path inviting a stroll. We were able to enjoy this private land because the owner wished to share it with the public during the spectacular lupine season.

THORNTON

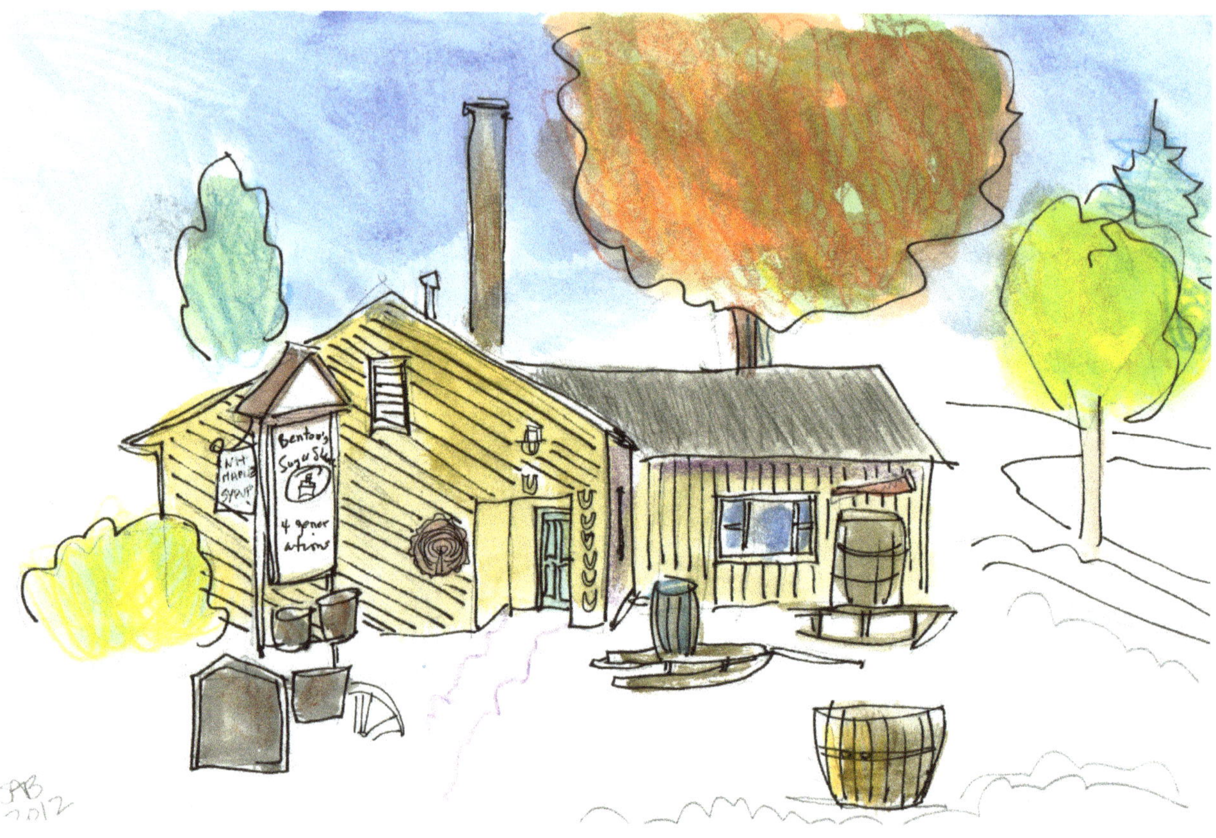

The town of Thornton is named for Matthew Thornton, a signer of the Declaration of Independence. On a summer day, I sketched Benton's Sugar Shack.

Scattered around the ground was old, wooden, syrup making equipment. In March, the sap in the sugar maple trees begins to flow. After puncturing a hole in the bark of the tree, the running sap is captured in buckets or plastic hoses. Then it is boiled down to make maple syrup. Forty liters of sap produce one liter of syrup. It is a health food containing all sorts of minerals and good things.
I combined several seasons within this one sketch.

Open houses at the sugar shacks are a big attraction of New Hampshire's annual Maple Weekend.

WARREN

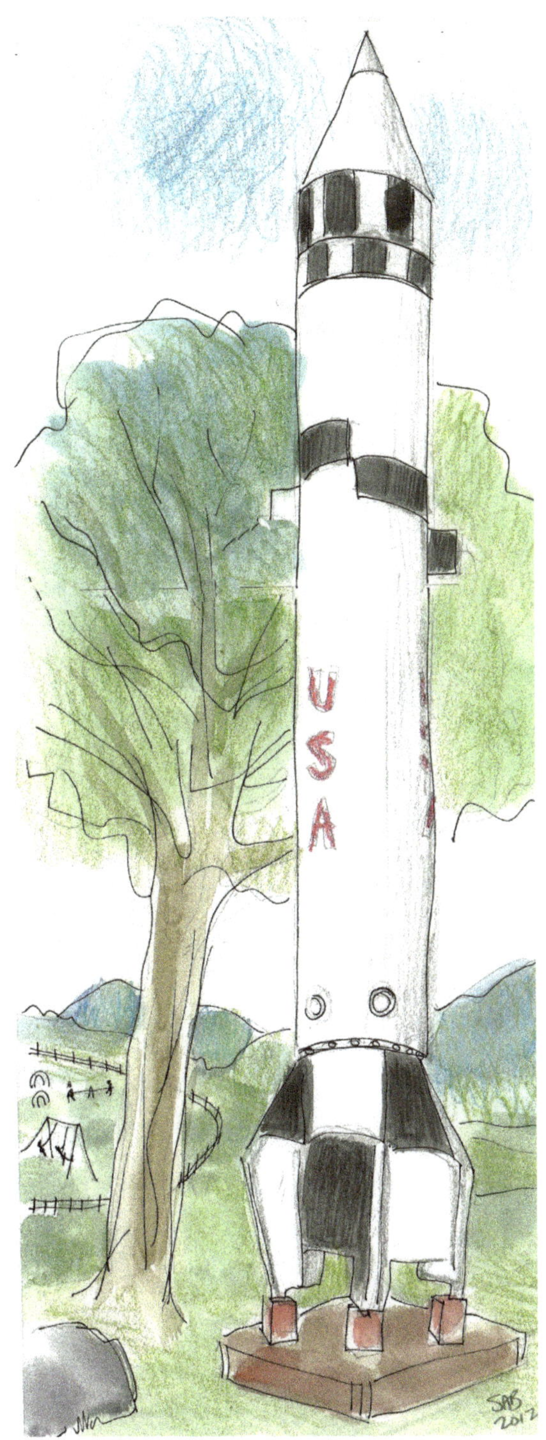

Warren was settled in 1767 and incorporated in 1770. The town center includes the customary town hall, library, church, school, and a play-ground off in the background. This black and white missile sits in a nearby park. It is a most unusual addition to a small town in New Hampshire.

The Redstone ballistic missile was given to the town in 1971. Missiles like this, and perhaps this very one, were positioned in NATO bases in Germany during the Cold War (1947-1991). The Western Allies and the USSR faced off in Eastern Europe after World War II. The fall of the Berlin Wall in 1989 was the beginning of the end of this period.

Warren is known for its fish hatchery. I have memories of visiting it with my father, grandfather, and uncle as a child.

WATERVILLE VALLEY

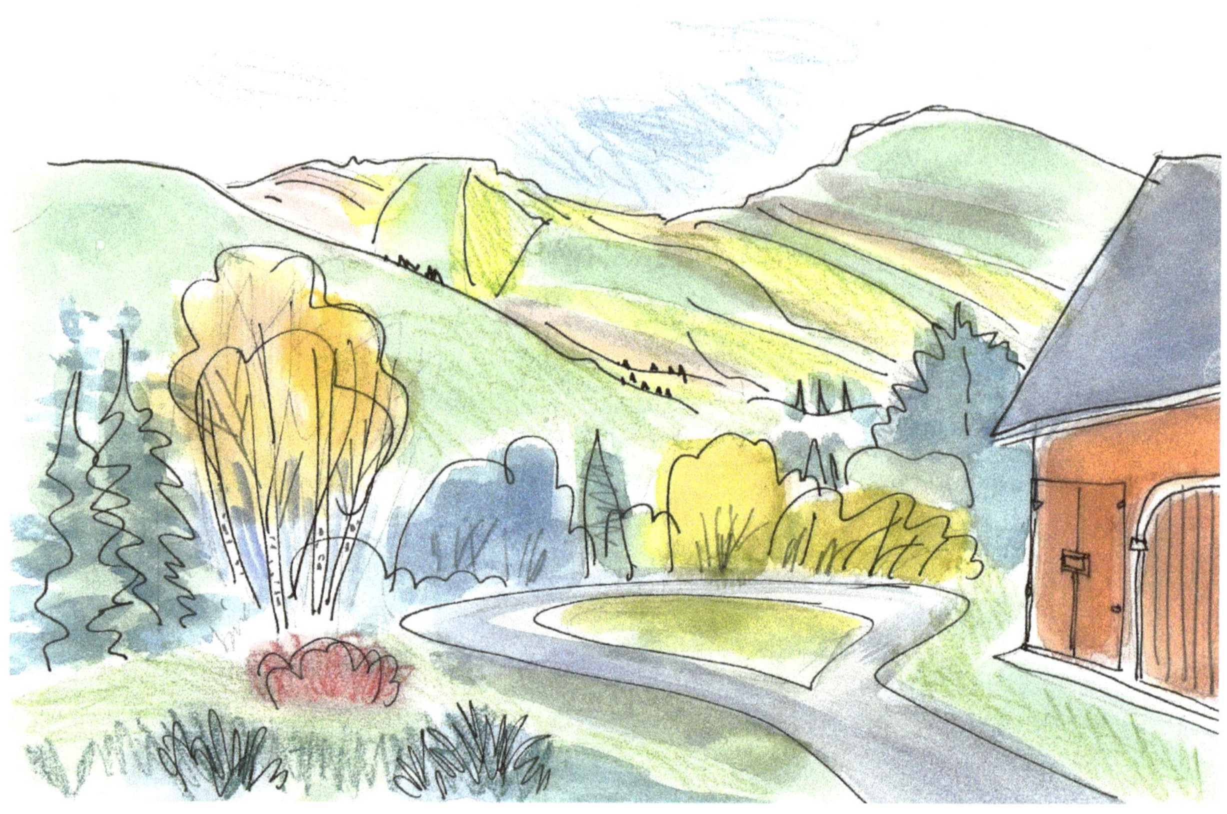

Waterville was incorporated in 1829, and the word 'Valley' was added in 1967. The settled area with the Little Red School and the town's Osceola Library is at the end of Route 49.

The White Mountain National Forest surrounds the village. Commercial skiing began in the 1930s on trails built by the Civilian Conservation Corps, a Depression era undertaking whose positive impact is still with us today. National ski champion and Olympian Tom Corcoran established the Waterville Valley Resort in 1966. The hillside, sketched in late May, shows the colors of the new spring foliage.

The creators of the book series *Curious George*, H. A. Rey and his wife Margret, lived in town for many years.

WOODSTOCK

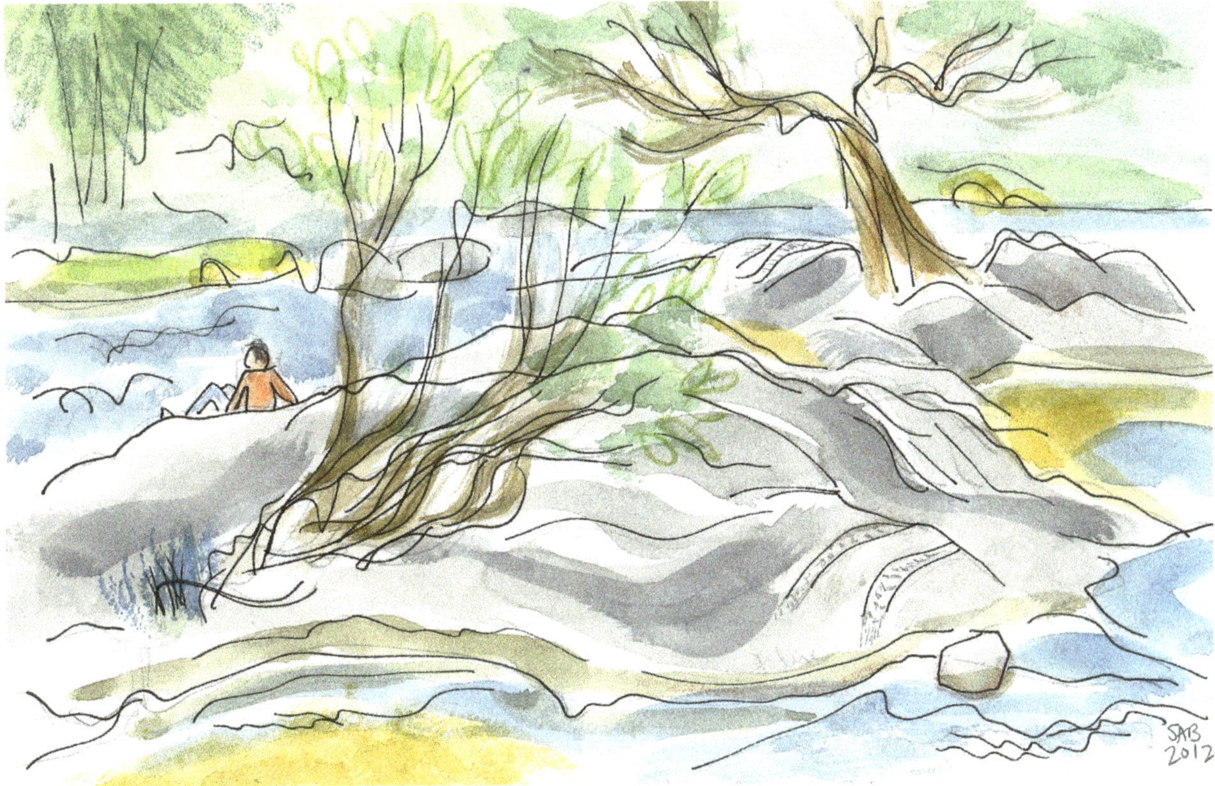

The Lost River Gorge and Boulder Caves are local attractions.

The town was first named Peeling, then Fairfield, finally becoming Woodstock in 1840.

The commercial part of town is North Woodstock, with stores, boutiques, restaurants, bars, and a brewery. I walked through Cascade Park, a small urban space, to the banks of the Pemigewasset River.

The ledges have been shaped by the water over eons of time. The river must flow up over the trees in spring runoff to curve the trunks in such a way. Tiny beaches of sand have formed here and there. One person was relaxing with his feet in the cool water.

Index of Towns

ACWORTH 126
ALBANY 224
ALEXANDRIA 44
ALLENSTOWN 82
ALSTEAD 127
ALTON 45
AMHERST 83
ANDOVER 6
ANTRIM 128
ASHLAND 46
ATKINSON 188
AUBURN 84
BARNSTEAD 47
BARRINGTON 48
BARTLETT 225
BATH 226
BEDFORD 85
BELMONT 49
BENNINGTON 129
BENTON 227
BERLIN 170
BETHLEHEM 228
BOSCAWEN 86
BOW 87
BRADFORD 7
BRENTWOOD 189
BRIDGEWATER 50
BRISTOL 51
BROOKFIELD 52
BROOKLINE 88
CAMPTON 229
CANAAN 8
CANDIA 89
CANTERBURY 90
CARROLL 230
CENTER HARBOR 53
CHARLESTOWN 130
CHATHAM 231
CHESTER 91
CHESTERFIELD 131
CHICHESTER 92
CLAREMONT 9
CLARKSVILLE 171
COLEBROOK 172
COLUMBIA 173
CONCORD 93
CONWAY 232
CORNISH 10
CROYDON 11
DALTON 174
DANBURY 12
DANVILLE 190
DEERFIELD 94
DEERING 132
DERRY 95
DORCHESTER 13
DOVER 191
DUBLIN 133
DUMMER 175
DUNBARTON 96
DURHAM 192
EAST KINGSTON 193
EASTON 233
EATON 54
EFFINGHAM 55
ELLSWORTH 234
ENFIELD 14
EPPING 194
EPSOM 97
ERROL 176
EXETER 195
FARMINGTON 56
FITZWILLIAM 134
FRANCESTOWN 135
FRANCONIA 235
FRANKLIN 98
FREEDOM 57
FREMONT 196
GILFORD 58
GILMANTON 59
GILSUM 136
GOFFSTOWN 99
GORHAM 236
GOSHEN 15
GRAFTON 16
GRANTHAM 17
GREENFIELD 137
GREENLAND 197
GREENVILLE 138
GROTON 18
HAMPSTEAD 198
HAMPTON 199
HAMPTON FALLS 200
HANCOCK 139
HANOVER 19
HARRISVILLE 140
HART'S LOCATION 237
HAVERHILL 238
HEBRON 60
HENNIKER 20
HILL 21
HILLSBOROUGH 22
HINSDALE 141
HOLDERNESS 61
HOLLIS 100
HOOKSETT 101
HOPKINTON 102
HUDSON 103
JACKSON 239
JAFFREY 142
JEFFERSON 240
KEENE 143
KENSINGTON 201
KINGSTON 202
LACONIA 62
LANCASTER 177
LANDAFF 241
LANGDON 144
LEBANON 23
LEE 203
LEMPSTER 145
LINCOLN 242
LISBON 243

LITCHFIELD 104
LITTLETON 244
LONDONDERRY 105
LOUDON 106
LYMAN 245
LYME 24
LYNDEBOROUGH 146
MADBURY 204
MADISON 63
MANCHESTER 107
MARLBOROUGH 147
MARLOW 148
MASON 149
MEREDITH 64
MERRIMACK 108
MIDDLETON 65
MILAN 178
MILFORD 109
MILTON 66
MONROE 246
MONT VERNON 110
MOULTONBORO 67
NASHUA 111
NELSON 150
NEW BOSTON 112
NEWBURY 26
NEW CASTLE 205
NEW DURHAM 68
NEWFIELDS 206
NEW HAMPTON 69
NEWINGTON 207
NEW IPSWICH 151
NEW LONDON 25
NEWMARKET 208
NEWPORT 27
NEWTON 209
NORTHFIELD 113
NORTH HAMPTON 210
NORTHUMBERLAND 179
NORTHWOOD 114
NOTTINGHAM 211
ORANGE 28
ORFORD 29
OSSIPEE 70
PELHAM 115
PEMBROKE 116
PETERBOROUGH 152
PIERMONT 247
PITTSBURG 180
PITTSFIELD 117
PLAINFIELD 30
PLAISTOW 212
PLYMOUTH 248
PORTSMOUTH 213
RANDOLPH 249
RAYMOND 118
RICHMOND 153
RINDGE 154
ROCHESTER 214
ROLLINSFORD 215
ROXBURY 155
RUMNEY 71
RYE 216
SALEM 119
SALISBURY 31
SANBORNTON 72
SANDOWN 217
SANDWICH 73
SEABROOK 218
SHARON 156
SHELBURNE 250
SOMERSWORTH 219
SOUTH HAMPTON 220
SPRINGFIELD 32
STARK 181
STEWARTSTOWN 182
STODDARD 157
STRAFFORD 74
STRATFORD 183
STRATHAM 221
SUGAR HILL 251
SULLIVAN 158
SUNAPEE 33
SURRY 159
SUTTON 34
SWANZEY 160
TAMWORTH 75
TEMPLE 161
THORNTON 252
TILTON 120
TROY 162
TUFTONBORO 76
UNITY 35
WAKEFIELD 77
WALPOLE 163
WARNER 36
WARREN 253
WASHINGTON 37
WATERVILLE VALLEY 254
WEARE 121
WEBSTER 38
WENTWORTH 39
WESTMORELAND 164
WHITEFIELD 184
WILMOT 40
WILTON 165
WINCHESTER 166
WINDHAM 122
WINDSOR 167
WOLFEBORO 78
WOODSTOCK 255

www.ingramcontent.com/pod-product-compliance
Lightning Source LLC
LaVergne TN
LVHW060615110826
845154LV00003B/89

9781939739544